Scenes From
Provincial Life

AND

Scenes From
Metropolitan Life

Scenes From Provincial Life

AND

Scenes From Metropolitan Life

WILLIAM COOPER

E. P. DUTTON, INC.   NEW YORK

Published in the United States by E. P. Dutton, Inc.,
2 Park Avenue, New York, N.Y. 10016

Library of Congress Catalog Card Number: 83-71498

ISBN: 0-525-24198-1

OBE
10 9 8 7 6 5 4 3 2 1

First Edition

Scenes From
Provincial Life

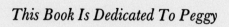

This Book Is Dedicated To Peggy

CONTENTS

Contents

PART FOUR

INTRODUCTION

Scenes from Provincial Life came out in 1950, apparently the first
novel of a writer who in fact proved to have published fiction
before under his own name, H. S. Hoff. It won good reviews
and then increasingly it began to exert an influence on a number
of writers rather younger than its author, who was born in 1910.
'Seminal is not a word I am fond of,' wrote one of them, John
Braine, 'Nevertheless I am forced to use it. This book was for
me—and I suspect many others—a seminal influence.' Now,
looked at from today's standpoint, it seems to belong to the
fifties as exactly as a certain kind of tweed sports-jacket. In saying that, I have no intention of belittling or limiting it, of sug-
gesting that it counted then but not now or that its only importance was as an influence; anyone who reads it for the first time
in this new edition will find it in all things fresh, alive and very
perfectly done. But this other importance of the novel has
grown rather clearer; *Scenes from Provincial Life* has a lot to do
with a stylistic turn that happened about the time the book came
out, and perhaps even *because* the book came out, a turn which
affected the fortunes of the postwar English novel and made
them rather different from those of contemporary American or
French fiction. It was a modest revolution (like all the revolu-
tions of the 1950s in England), but it was quietly considerable
and significant. The novel's qualities are not perhaps what one
would ordinarily expect in a radical book. It is a fairly simple
(but artfully simple) lyrical novel set in the English provinces,
self-conscious about the ordinariness of the life it deals with and
the particular limitations and innocence of the main characters,
caught in their twenties and their teens and in that sharp state of
emotional intensity that belongs to the hunt for partners. The

book doesn't even have the 1950s as its subject—it is set, of course, on the other, 1930s side of that considerable cultural divide that was formed by the war. And the writers you might be led to think of as you read it are possibly H. G. Wells or, going further back and in a rather different direction, Turgenev. All this hardly sounds like a testament to modernity; and those critics who have seen the modern novel as marching resolutely forward from the ground cleared by Joyce and Proust, to greater technical complexity, greater crises of fictiveness, greater manifestations of modernist style, have been ready to cry *retreat!* at the book and its influence. But if it is true that a good part of the literary styles and temper of the 1950s was set by this book, and then by this *sort* of book, there may be good grounds for supposing that what it stands for was a movement towards fictional expansion and survival.

To show that, one needs to look at the particular value and interest of the novel itself; but a little more needs saying first about the fact that the novel did obviously count as the representative of a particular force at work in postwar fiction. For the progress of the novel has usually depended on an oscillation between two parts of its powers and its nature. Novels tend to lie, as Iris Murdoch once observed, somewhere between the 'journalistic' and the 'crystalline'; which is to say that they can participate in the contingent and particular realities of the world as they are known and shared *as* realities, or they can explore art as a specialised knowledge, being concerned with the mode of existence of words, languages, structures, fictions. *Scenes from Provincial Life* is not of course an artless novel, but it is the novel in its empirical form. It could and did stand for an important swing away from the stylistic backlog of modernism, or what William Cooper calls the 'Art Novel': a swing towards an art of reason, an art of lived-out and recognisable values and predicaments, an art, even, of the social places we associate with ordinariness—the provinces, the lower middle classes, the world of growing up and getting on. Virginia Woolf once suggested that modernism had set the writer free, led him from the kingdom of necessity to the kingdom of light, by allowing him to dispense with traditional plot and character, traditional detailing and chronology, the need to tell a story or report material reality. But such freedom, as we can see from the deep sense of predicament that marks the great works of modernism, was of course itself conditioned. In any case, the revolt against the Victorian 'reality' and the Victorian conception of the artist produced a new convention, and a new socially specialised locale for art in the cosmopolitan and avant garde intelligentsia. By the postwar period the root-conditions of modernism were more or less exhausted in English society, and the cultural dominance of Bloomsbury was certainly coming to an end; it was hard for the new generation of English writers to take up the modernist mode for the exploration of their culture. Cooper later placed himself in the context of an explicit revolt against the 'Thirties' novel in its mannerist and experimental guise, and against the French *anti-roman*. Art, he said in an essay of 1959, depended not on a series of attacks on the powers and place of the human mind, but an assertion of mind. It needed not a *reductio ad absurdam* of experience, but experience itself as it is given. It needed not the intense specialisation of the artist in his own universe, but the sharing of the extant universe with others. Or that, at least, is what I read him as saying, since it is an argument that influenced me very considerably, just as his novel influenced me: not only in what I wrote, but in my very belief that I could, on the basis simply of intelligently being, become a writer.

So what came out of the novel and its climate—it is a simple truth that criticism has a way of forgetting—is that we do not need to abide by the climate of modernism, since it is not historically inevitable. I would not say, as William Cooper sometimes seems to say, that modernism does not count; and I would certainly deplore an evident slackening of scale that became part of the climate brought about by feelings of this sort. But we should also remember that this sort of statement is a statement on behalf of the humanist powers of art and their connection with life. It is an assertion that we live life above all in the realm of the given; that to find ourselves alienated from society or absurdly placed among things is an intellectual or technical abstraction as much as a recognisable truth, and it can be a limitation on our way of knowing ourselves or our world. It looks now as if we are moving into another phase of ideology and alienation theory, of grand resentment about the given realities and their meanness;

and no doubt, if the novel still counts at all, it will seek to show that. But *Scenes from Provincial Life* has no such resentment about the given world, and it believes too in the active powers of the living mind and the consonance between that and the making of art. There is no assumption that the truth about man is that he is alienated, that realities are an enormous deceit, that the artist has no words left that are uncorrupted. Rather it is a book about how dense, substantial and complex life is, taken on its ordinary terms; and about how a writer can take fictional life from such things; and how even if the provinces are not cosmopolis and the place of high and abstract art they still have a culture which can itself lead to art. It is not all a writer today might say, but it is enough.

II

What is this provincial life from which the scenes of the novel are thrown up? It is the life of a largish provincial town left deliberately unnamed ('I will not describe our clock-tower in detail, because I feel that if you were able to identify our town my novel would lose some of its universal air'). If Cooper says that with mild self-irony, he also says it to make his town a representative instance of the familiar social web in which men live, amid composed institutions (pubs and the grammar school, parks and cafés, the market-place and the clock-tower) and equally composed if sometimes strange customs (like the Sunday afternoon visits of Mr Chinnock, 'regular as clockwork,' to the landlady's niece). The story is firmly set in its place, or one ought to say its culture; and amid a particular strata of its life, its intelligent if not quite intellectual young people. If they do not quite belong, in the sense that they are somewhat shockingly advanced, if they seem to have yearnings that take them outside and beyond, if their roles don't always quite fit ('What *can* I behave like?' wonders Joe Lunn, the narrator, when told he doesn't behave like a schoolmaster), then that is provincial life too. They are schoolmasters and accountants and commercial artists who are also writers and poets and painters, but although they may be more ambitious in their aims and their feelings than others this does not separate them dreadfully off from their

Introduction

world. Joe is cautious about the proprieties and the bohemianism of all the group is of the most modest kind; even Myrtle's
gramophone-record-playing sessions and her late nights are, by
his sense of fitness, going a little too far. But of course the point
is that they feel their place as well as their detachment from their
place. And because of that, even though the action really concentrates on four figures only, it gives us a full sense of the
community that surrounds and feeds them. Throughout the
novel they talk of leaving it, to go to America under the fear that
Hitler's aggression in Europe will end with a totalitarian state in
England: 'Though we were three very different men, we had in
common a strong element of the rootless and the unconforming,
especially the unconforming. We had not the slightest doubt
that were some form of authoritarian regime to come to our
country we should sooner or later end up in a concentration
camp.' But one senses, of course, that they won't leave, for it is
the web of relationships, these meeting-places and events and
the things that go with them, that stay real in the novel. The
impending dislocation is an unreality. The dangers of 1939
count, of course, and they do finally *become* real; but that is
beyond the end of the story.

But that isn't to say that the characters are passive, unintelli-
gent or unaware of what is happening. The narrator and his
friends are all lively-minded people who are seeking to make
sense of their passions, their ambitions, their environment. They
have a strong sense of their slightly excessive pretensions; that is
particularly true of Joe Lunn, and is part of his tone as the
recollecting narrator. They enjoy bold emotional manoeuvres
but they usually end up with an unwonted feeling of tenderness,
responsibility or concern. They are not grand masters or moral-
ists of personal relations, but they do know how to give them
their due, to care sufficiently about others while caring
sufficiently about themselves. The relationship between Joe and
his mistress Myrtle, with Myrtle shifting beyond passion to
marital ambitions and Joe wriggling to be free for ends not clear
even to him, is conducted with a certain moral toughness on
Joe's part but also with a precise moral delicacy. That, indeed, is
one element that keeps it alive for so long; another is the human
inconsistency by which feeling in any case countermands logical

decisions, and which sets up those contrary pulls for permanence and impermanence which are central to the lyrical mood of the novel. Joe is half the ironist about these matters, and half the man of feeling:

> It was a light evening, and I could see from a long way off that she was in a state of abysmal depression. She had begun to look sadder and sadder during the last days. I suppose I was unfeeling and detached; I thought of it as her 'I'll-never-smile-again' expression. Really, she overdid it. I felt genuinely upset and, such was the weakness of my nature, faintly irritated by remorse. I kissed her warmly on the cheek.

If this sort of alternation of emotion is so very recognisable, it is because Joe is comically independent of the situation and also inevitably drawn, by 'something like instinct,' as he says, to the power of the person, the place, and the feeling. The tone is a mixture of lyricism and comedy, which means that we are not asked very explicitly to judge matters of moral quality and characteristic; in any case, Joe can claim the privileges of the narrator to be independent from that sort of judgment. But we do recognise, in what Joe does and feels and the way he tells the story, the presence of a real intelligence which includes, among other virtues, the capacity to know oneself as absurd or ridiculous or obstinate and yet forced to act according to certain decencies. As Joe says, that becomes the more important if one believes one *isn't* a good man. All the characters show this kind of inconsistency, and it is very much what makes for that ebb and flow of life and feeling out of which the book is made. But my point is that it is the sense of living in a society and in the context of the values of a culture that has an existence in place and time that makes this so much alive.

We can see, of course, what this culture is; its roots are basically domestic and practical, and it thrives through a kind of middle-class and unromantic good sense. It supposes that people are relatively comprehensible and relatively rational, and you can know sufficient about them to share feelings and values and make relationships. But then there are elements of the un-

Introduction

knowable and the strange, which are personal and are as much there in oneself as in others. So relationships have a kind of mysterious rhythm to them; and one acts in the middle of them with a certain intelligent degree of comprehension of one's lovers and friends, and another element of incomprehension, a sense of the 'unknowable' that is 'something like instinct'. One catches in Cooper's style a certain conventionalised quality about the conversations, something tangental in them as each character follows out his own expression of the self's needs; but of course this is not the Pinter-esque convention that really nobody can communicate with anyone else, that they live in totally subjective systems of reality. It is really only in a fictional world that is both public and private that you can have a genuine sense of the moralities of actions and relationships; and that Cooper gives us, the moral life of the ordinary world. For though Joe is an artist, and expresses his obstinacy sometimes as a matter of artistic need, it is out of that ordinary stuff that he makes his choices and finds his feelings. His strains, and those of the other characters, come from life and not from art; and art comes later, as the act of recollection, the turning of experiences offered and created as thoroughly authentic into 'material', 'delightful and disastrous, warm, painful and farcical. I reach for a clean new notebook. I pick up my pen.'

The book is made of this sort of illuminated and worked life. It is indeed *scenes* from provincial life—moments of meeting and parting, episodes of friendly conversation, love-making, love-talking—but a sequence of scenes distilled into an emotional whole. The action consists basically of a succession of episodes in the lives of the four central characters, caught up with many surrounding ones, and it covers the spring and summer of 1939. A good deal is kept out of the telling to make the distillation exact. Before the action begins, the two essential relationships—the affair between Joe, the schoolmaster narrator, and Myrtle, the commercial artist; and that between his friend Tom and *his* boyfriend and protegé Steve—have already begun. After it ends, in the coda of the last chapter, comes the roll-call of marriages and the record of war-experiences. The threats of Hitler and marriage hang over the basic sequence—that phase of human life before marriage which does work out as a pattern of scenes and crises, imperfect understandings and regrets, strong feelings and cautious fears—and help us to see that the phase of life must be the very nature of love and history come to an end. The ebb and flow of feelings comes to contain—as Joe says of Myrtle's feelings—'too much ebb and not enough flow', and it moves, through its small world of constant meetings and a few basic locales, gradually toward final dissolution:

> The end. And I knew with certainty she was there at last. I did not know the reason. I supposed that something I had said or done during the last few days must have been the last straw. I do not even know now what it was, and if I did I should not believe in it as she did. To most of us the movements of the soul are so mysterious that we seize upon events to make them explicable.

The theme *could* have led to a tragic mood of betrayed hope in passion that affects many nineteenth century novels, but of course that is not the tone. For the novel is very much a comic novel, a comedy of authenticity; Joe's late and not entirely final discovery about Myrtle—'. . . . I can only say that to the very depths of my soul I was fed up with her'—has that touch of truth that fiction only catches in rare moments. This is the authenticity of its culture *and* of its modernness, and it is what helps us to feel that the book is a book of its time.

Many critics lately seem to have suggested that what characterises this kind of fiction is its sociological realism; I have been trying to suggest that if this means anything it means a much fuller use of the languages and tones of its culture than that phrase usually suggests. For the novel is much more than a report; it is a lyrical and comic evocation that is very carefully made and worked. We can see this in the position and character of the narrator, Joe, himself; and the kind of comedies and ironies he plays over his story. He stands in a positon beyond it, a position more advanced in time and in a bigger world. And so he can see the elements of innocence and absurdity in the story he tells: 'We were completely serious about it [the state of the world], and we became even more serious even as our actions became more absurd.' The provinces and the past intertwine as a recollected place and let him, too, be a little ridiculous; but his absurdity, and that of Tom, with his dubious insights into human conduct, Myrtle, with her red setter and her gun, and Steve, with his contradictory responses to the role of protegé, is part of the common fortune. For Joe as narrator does finally belong to this world, and so he is neither emotionally nor technically patronising. His own lack of feeling, his absolute refusal to marry Myrtle—these things which are the spring of most of the events—are his own foible and also his human right, part of his intelligent ridiculousness. The irony is therefore not complex and the tone is comically generous, the tone of a human openness that condemns very little, observes a great deal, and carries a wide range of feelings. Joe is the lyricist of the novel and the man who also sees life-history as a stuff to write about; his independent obstinacy is a convincing part of his total psychology as a man who also happens by nature to be a writer. The art he makes, the book he writes, is as much a product of this sort of life and place as the experience he feels. Life is a sequence of scenes and felt moments, something that derives from what exists in the given world to experience, to know, and feel; and novels are the products of one's own life-history, the product of all one's delights and disasters ('I think of all the novels I can make out of them—ah, novels, novels, Art, Art, pounds sterling!'). Joe's are not the modernist ironies of artistic distance, but they are those of character which somehow become those of an artistic position. So Joe not only makes a world as a writer must (as when he chooses not to emphasise politics for reasons of literary necessity: 'For some reason or other political sentiment does not seem to be a suitable subject for literary art'), and he does not only judge that world as a writer must; he also finds one in life. You can be an artist because you have intelligently seen, known and can shape the experiences of the ordinary world.

III

It was no new discovery, of course. The book's newness lay in the particular kind of ordinary life, the particular culture, it found; and in the way it brought that alive as a vision, a pattern

Introduction

of motives, meanings and significance, a way of living in the present. This has a lot to do with the way many writers in the 1950s did find means of bringing a sense of cultural observation and moral analysis of their changing society into relation with a new, an idiosyncratic, and very often a comic viewpoint upon it. If, over that period, the viewpoints and judgments of a provincially 'irreverent' (to use a favourite reviewer's word of the period) fictional attitude became vigorous enough to constitute a rich literary perspective, then clearly a great deal of credit is due to William Cooper. One has, perhaps, to remember how little this particular class and viewpoint has been presented in the fiction of the previous two decades to feel how important this opening out was; but it would not have been important had there not been writers who could manage the task with the kind of perfect lucidity William Cooper brought to it. But I must also stress that *Scenes from Provincial Life* is in fact much more accomplished than many of its successors. It brings its language (usually) and its perspective (always) so thoroughly alive that it has a survival-value profoundly in excess of any sociological interest in it that might also hold us. If, too, it helped to keep alive the social and moral tradition of the English novel vigorous, in a phase where the direction of the form itself seemed uncertain, that was good fortune; its real and final interest is the pleasure we can still take in it, here, as it stands.

MALCOLM BRADBURY

PART I

CHAPTER I

TEA IN A CAFÉ

The school at which I was science-master was desirably situated, right in the centre of the town. By walking only a few yards the masters and boys could find themselves in a café or a public-house.

I used to frequent a café in the market-place. It was on the first floor, and underneath was a shop where coffee was roasted. A delicious aroma drifted through the maze of market-stalls, mingling with the smell of celery, apples and chrysanthemums: you could pick it up in the middle of the place and follow it to the source, where, in the shop-window, a magnificent roasting-machine turned with a flash of red enamel and chromium plate—persistently reminding you that coffee smelt nicer than it tasted.

Two or three times a week I had tea in the café with a friend of mine named Tom. He was a chartered accountant, and the offices of his firm were in a building between the school and the market-place. By specialising on income-tax claims, Tom made a comfortable living: it could have been luxurious, had he accepted the invitation of certain townspeople to visit their business premises after hours and falsify their returns. Tom had other things to do in his spare time.

We had been friends for several years. Both Tom and I had literary ambitions. During my six years spent teaching in the town I had published three novels. Tom had published one. I secretly thought I was three times as good a writer as Tom. At this time, February 1939, I was aged twenty-eight and Tom twenty-seven.

For reasons of delicacy I will not disclose Tom's surname. Other things about him it will be impossible to conceal. With the best will in the world you could not help noticing immediately that Tom was red-haired and Jewish—it fairly knocked you down. He had rich, thick, carroty curls and a remarkable nose. He was nearly a stone heavier than me; and he gave the impression that he would be a good deal heavier than that, were he not always engaged in bustling physical activity. He had a rounded head, with greenish eyes and a rather pouting mouth. He was intelligent and high-spirited, and I was very devoted to him. It was not apparent that he had a formidable personality.

Sometimes what a man thinks he is can be just as interesting as what he really is. In Tom's case it was just as interesting and decidedly more wonderful; it had an endearing romantic grandeur. Tom saw himself as a great understander of human nature, a great writer, a great connoisseur of the good things in life, and a great lover. He did not see himself as a great chartered accountant. Nor did he see himself as a great clown—in that respect not differing substantially from the rest of us.

Tom possessed a formidable capacity for psychological bustling. In an easy agreeable way he bustled other people into doing things they did not want to do. He was always trying to bustle me, especially for instance over our country cottage. Tom and I shared the tenancy of a cottage ten miles outside the town, and the arrangement was that we should spend alternate weekends there. Now I had two very strong reasons for wanting to stick to the arrangement: one was my legal right, and the other was because I was visited there by a young woman, a very pretty young woman called Myrtle.

My desire to preserve my legal right was therefore unusually strong. Tom, made in a different mould, did not see it that way. In a style more heroic, more passionate, more expansive, more wonderful than mine, he systematically tried to bustle me out of my turn.

There was some basis for Tom's picture of himself. He was courageous and he had a great fund of emotion: he had a shrewd down-to-earth insight into human nature and tireless curiosity about people. He was the ideal listener to one's life-story—the only trouble was that in order to encourage the next person to tell his life-story Tom was liable to repeat under the seal of secrecy one's own.

I usually arrived in the café first. It was superior, and chosen by me because there were no cruets and bottles of tomato ketchup on the tables at tea-time. Tom thought this showed I was finicky. 'You wouldn't notice the cruet if you were interested in the human heart,' he said, with great authority.

As the café was superior Tom could never resist ordering his tea and cream cakes with a superior manner. He waved his hand, which was small and comely, in an aristocratic gesture. The waitress appreciated it.

Perhaps I might go so far as to disclose that Tom's name was definitely not Waley-Cohen or Sebag-Montefiore—alas! very far from it. He would dearly have loved to be an aristocrat. He might have carried it off with his hands, but his face was against him. There was nothing coarse about his features, but unfortunately there was nothing even faintly aristocratic. His red hair gave him no help at all, and he was sensitive about it. When he first read *A la Recherche du Temps Perdu,* and discovered that Swann's hair was red, he was overjoyed.

For Tom it was then but the smallest step to identify himself completely with Swann—red hair, aristocratic birth, peculiar sexual temperament and all. 'Ah,' he would say, sighing: 'How I know the torments of jealousy!' And his voice, though low, carried such tremendous emotional weight that I listened with my deepest sympathy.

As Tom came into the café I thought he had an unusually preoccupied expression, but it disappeared as he sat down. When he had concluded the artistic performance of ordering his tea, he said:

'Any news of the book?'

'Not a word.'

Tom was referring to the manuscript of my latest novel. Most young novelists decide somewhere in the early stages of their careers that they have written something a class better than anything they have written before. I had reached this point with my fourth book. My publisher had naturally, but not promptly, turned it down. It seemed to me in my inexperience that my publisher asked one of two things from me: either to write my previous novel all over again just as it was, or to write it again with a stronger story, sharper characterization, deeper revelations of truth and much, much funnier jokes.

For the benefit of anyone who does not already know, I can say that the recognised thing to do, when a young novelist has written the first novel that he thinks good and it is turned down by his publisher, is to send the manuscript to a writer of distinguished reputation. This is what I did. An earlier novel had produced an unsolicited letter of praise from Miss X.Y: she had consented to read the manuscript of my latest. Her secretary had acknowledged receiving it three weeks ago.

'Not a word?'

'I suppose she's busy,' I said, for some reason or other trying to excuse her. I think I felt I had to excuse my ally.

Tom raised his eyebrows.

'How's Myrtle?' he asked tactfully.

'All right.' As might be expected I was continually haunted by the possibility of Myrtle's not being all right.

I said diffidently: 'We had a very enjoyable Sunday together.'

Tom's eyes appeared to bulge a little with disapproval.

'Why don't you let her come out on Saturday night? You know perfectly well she wants to.'

I felt badgered, and tried to sound confident. 'Propriety, my dear Tom. I don't want to risk village gossip and so on.'

It was natural for Tom not to let pass an opportunity for getting the better of me.

'How completely unrealistic of you.' He shrugged his shoulders in the manner of a great understander of human nature. 'You introverts.'

Tom and I had recently been studying the works of Jung. We were agreed that by Jungian definitions he was an extravert and I an introvert. Consequently he saw fit to use the word 'introvert' as a term of abuse.

I knew perfectly well that it was unrealistic. The real point was that I had said 'propriety' because I was too ashamed to say 'caution.' I did not let Myrtle live with me in the cottage for the same reason that I did not call regularly upon her family—in fact I never went near them. Caution.

I did not reply to Tom.

'It would not do for me,' he said. He smiled reminiscently, like a great lover. 'I like my Saturday nights.'

6

'So you may!' I said, and laughed aloud. 'You don't live in the shadow of a girl wanting you to marry her!'

Tom replied amiably: 'My dear man, I live in the shadow of something else.'

I saw the truth of this remark. The reason Tom did not live in the shadow of a girl wanting him to marry her was that when it was his week-end to occupy the cottage he took out a boy.

I nodded sagely.

'Ah,' said Tom, with a sigh. 'The shadows one has lived under! It makes one feel very, very old.'

One of Tom's women loves had been absurd enough to tell him that she thought he was an 'old soul'. Tom had taken it very seriously, and for months afterwards had gone about feeling older in soul than anyone we knew. It was only quite gradually that his oldness of soul had worn off, and it still cropped up on occasion.

I did not take him up because he had previously proved conclusively that I was a young soul.

I poured out some tea, while Tom began eating a chocolate éclair. We were sitting beside the window, looking out on to the tops of the market-stalls. The ridges of those at right angles to the last rays of sun gleamed with a golden light. In the air hung faint blue fumes from the coffee-roaster below. There seemed to be a lot of people wandering about, carrying baskets and bunches of bright yellow daffodils.

'You probably ought to have Myrtle out on Saturday nights, anyway,' Tom said.

'Why?'

'You know where she spends them when you won't have her.'

'Yes.' I did know. Often it was with a young man named Haxby.

'Well, if you know . . .' Tom's voice trailed off doubtfully. I could see that he was thinking again 'You introverts'.

I considered the matter. Tom was not the only person who thought my behavior towards Myrtle was strange. To me it seemed perfectly understandable. I loved Myrtle but I did not want to marry her—because I did not want to marry anybody. That was the point, and I was puzzled that everybody else found it so difficult to comprehend. Having had to put up with so much opprobrium, I was rather on the defensive about it. Many a man before me had not wanted to be married, I argued. It might be called abnormal, but nobody could pretend it was unusual. My argument made not the slightest impression. Nor did other people's arguments make any impression on me. I did not want to be married, and that is all there is to it.

And yet I have to admit there was something more—such is the contradictory nature of the heart. I hated the idea of Myrtle marrying anyone else.

'Now,' said Tom, 'I want to talk to you seriously.'

Our main conversation was to be about his week-end in Oxford. The friend of ours with whom Tom had been staying was Dean of the small college at which I had been educated. His name was Robert, and he was a few years older than us. He was clever, gifted and wise; and he had a great personal influence on us. We had appointed him arbiter on all our actions, and anything he cared to say we really accepted as the word of God. We spent most of the time talking about the state of the world.

I listened. Tom and I talked a good deal about politics—so did we all, Myrtle and her friends, the masters in the staff-room, even the boys. Unfortunately it is very difficult to write about politics in a novel. For some reason or other political sentiment does not seem to be a suitable subject for literary art. If you doubt it you have only to read a few pages of any novel by a high-minded Marxist.

However I am writing a novel about events in the year 1939, and the political state of the world cannot very well be left out. The only thing I can think of is to put it in now and get it over.

Robert, Tom and I could be called radicals: we were made for a period thirty years earlier, when we could happily have voted liberal. The essence was that we thought life for us would be insupportable in a totalitarian state. We did not argue very much: it went without saying. It may have been because we thought of ourselves as artists: it may not—we might have been just the same if we had not been artists. Though we were three very different men, we had in common a strong element of the

8

rootless and the unconforming, especially the unconforming. We had not the slightest doubt that were some form of authoritarian regime to come to our country we should sooner or later end up in a concentration camp.

So much for our political sentiments, if that is what they should be called. They led us to be deeply pessimistic about the state of the world. We were completely serious about it, and we became more serious even as our actions became more absurd.

When Tom said he was going to tell me what conclusions Robert had drawn, my spirits sank. Our spirits had been low ever since we came to the conclusion that the government of our country was not disposed to challenge National Socialism, though never so low as on the night the Prime Minister returned from Munich. I always recalled buying an evening newspaper: Tom was with me and we spread it out between us to read it together. And a great wave of despair overwhelmed us, the deeper and the blacker because in some inexplicable way we felt caught up in responsibility. We had still not recovered from it in the spring of 1939. Our sense of shame had induced a mood in which we became certain that the same thing would happen again. And the second time would be the last.

'The old boy says that if there isn't a war by August we shall be refugees by October.'

I stared at Tom, thinking 'March, April, May . . .'

'We ought to be thinking about moving,' said Tom, 'while there's a reasonable amount of time at our disposal.'

The idea had made fleeting appearances in our talk during the last few months. Tom's big, greenish eyes bulged unblinkingly.

'He's beginning to bestir himself.'

I felt there was nothing for me to say. I glanced through the window. The sun had disappeared from the market-place and naphthalene flares were flickering out brightly from the stalls.

Tom went on: 'He's decided America's the best place. He proposes I should go first.'

This proposal was obvious because Tom was Jewish while Robert and I were not. I thought it was hard luck on Tom; because his attitude would have been just the same if he were not

Jewish, and because of the three of us he probably had the greatest share of physical courage—certainly he was the most rash.

Tom began to outline his plans. We thought we were men of more than average intelligence and gifts and we were not particularly alarmed at the prospect of having to make our way in another country—certainly we were not alarmed at all so long as the project remained in the air.

My spirits rose a little. I could not help seeing our gesture in a romantic light. We were proposing to leave our country for the sake of Freedom. I have to confess that I sometimes saw us as Pilgrim Fathers, though admittedly of a rather different type from the originals. And in moments of honesty I realised that there was a distinct attraction in the idea of leaving everything, and—more detestable still and never to be admitted to Tom— even in the idea of leaving everybody.

I thoughtfully inscribed a pattern on the tablecloth with the haft of my knife.

'I advise you to start considering what you're going to do about Myrtle,' said Tom.

I blushed. 'What do you mean?' I said, as if I had not the slightest idea what he was talking about.

'You presumably aren't thinking of taking her with you to America, are you?'

'I hadn't thought about it,' I said.

'Really!' said Tom, with a mixture of incredulity and indignation. It was clearly, 'You introverts' again.

'There's no hurry, is there?' I said amiably. 'I shall finish the year out at the school.' I was thinking of the delight with which I should hand in my notice in July.

'I should have thought it was hardly fair to Myrtle,' said Tom. 'You do intend to tell her, of course, don't you?'

'Of course,' I said, with the mental reservation that it was to be in gentler terms. 'Actually we've discussed it already. She knows that it's a possibility.' I knew that Myrtle, though I truly had discussed it with her, did not think for a moment that it would ever happen.

'If it were me,' said Tom, 'I should probably begin breaking it off now.'

Immediately my memory took me back to a previous occasion. I had been in love with a married woman whose husband earned £5000 a year against my £350. 'If it were me,' Tom had counselled, 'I should break up the marriage.' Happily it was not Tom.

Tom said: 'You don't consider her feelings as I should. It could be done understandingly and subtly.'

I thought there was a contradiction somewhere, as there was in most of Tom's counsels, but I could not put my finger on it before he went on.

'I think I should lead her to feel that it was'—he waved his hand elegantly—'best for both of us.'

'In that case you don't know Myrtle!'

Tom shrugged his shoulders.

We abandoned the topic, and went on planning how to earn a living in America. I was troubled all the same. Tom was capable of infecting me with doubts. I was in a vulnerable position, because I knew I was behaving like a cad. I intended to go to America. I did not want to marry Myrtle.

But was it essential that Myrtle should be left behind? I wondered. I did not want to make up my mind. Tom was probably right on psychological grounds. The point that Tom, with his penchant for violent ridiculous upsets, did not see but which occurred to me only too readily was this: outside psychological grounds, breaking it off with Myrtle had for me a very obvious drawback. I drew the generalisation that one's friends find nothing easier than advising a course of action which involves ceasing to go to bed with one's young woman.

I did not tell Tom what I intended to do.

CHAPTER II

A DAY IN THE COUNTRY

After Sunday lunch at the Dog and Duck, Myrtle and I strolled back over the fields to my cottage. It was a regular thing—I saw to that.

On Sunday mornings she came out on her bicycle, looking fresh and elegant and lively. Sometimes she found me washing-up my breakfast pots in the scullery, where I had been keeping an eye open for the flash of her handlebars coming up the lane; sometimes she found me having a bath under the pump, which provoked a blushing, sidelong glance and the remark: 'Darling, I don't know how you can stand that cold water'; and sometimes she found me just ready for a bit of high-toned conversation about reviews in the Sunday newspapers.

'Darling, I've brought you this.'

It might be anything that had caught her fancy, a tin of liver *pâté,* or a book of poems by T. S. Eliot. This time it was a bunch of freesias. I should have received a tin of liver *pâté* much more warmly, a book of poems by T. S. Eliot much less.

Then we set out for the Dog and Duck. The cottage was two miles from the nearest public-house; but over the fields, choosing gaps in the hedges and jumping narrow brooks, we could get to the Dog and Duck in twenty minutes. Neither of us had any inclination to exhaust ourselves in the labour of cooking lunch.

The stroll back was singularly pleasurable. It did not take too long. Also it gave our lunches time to digest, and brought to our notice the beauties of nature.

As we had been his regular customers for over a year, the pub-keeper shared his lunch with us; and his wife, to please either him or us, cooked it superbly. Myrtle and I drank two or three pints of beer apiece while waiting for it: Myrtle would have drunk more, but I thought it would not be good for her. Then we sat down to slices of roast beef, red and succulent in the middle and faintly charred at the edges; apple pie with fresh cream liquid enough to pour all over it; and cheese, the unequalled, solid, homely cheese of the county.

We walked very slowly at first, for we both took a pleasure in digestion. We patted our stomachs and sighed at the prospect of the first hill. The country rolled gently, and there was a second hill to climb before we came in sight of the cottage. If I happened to belch, Myrtle gave me a ladylike look of reproach and I begged her pardon. I took her by the hand.

At the top of the first hill we looked around. It was a heavenly afternoon. The sun was shining. It was only the end of February and we could feel its warmth. The rime on the naked hedgerows had melted, and drops of water glittered like the purest glass on twigs and thorns. The sky was covered in a single haze of milky whiteness; and the tussocks of grass, wilted and brown and borne down with water, caught heavily at our feet.

'How I long for the spring,' said Myrtle in a faraway tone. Her voice was lightly modulated and given to melancholy.

It was on the tip of my tongue to say: 'Yes, and when it's spring you'll be pining for summer.' It was true: she had a passion for hot weather. But had I said it she would have looked hurt. Instead of speaking, I glanced at her. What I saw was entirely pleasing. The sooner we reached the cottage the better.

Myrtle was modestly tall and very slender. She was wearing grey slacks and a cerise woollen sweater. Her breasts and buttocks were quite small, though her hips were not narrow. She was light-boned, smooth and soft. There was nothing energetic or muscular about her. She walked with a languid, easy grace—I walked with a vigorous, over-long stride and perpetually had the impression that she was trailing along behind me.

Myrtle felt me looking at her, and turned her face to me. It was oval and bright with colour. She had round hazel eyes, a long nose, and a wide mouth with full red lips: her hair was dark, her cheeks glowed. She smiled. Then she turned her head away again. I had no idea what she was thinking. I was thinking of one thing only, but Myrtle might easily have been thinking about El Greco—equally she might have been thinking about the same thing as me.

Whatever she was thinking about, whatever she was doing, Myrtle preserved a demeanour that was meek and innocent—especially meek. Sometimes I could have shaken her for it, but on the whole I was fascinated by it.

With a demeanour that was meek and innocent, Myrtle had two characteristic facial expressions. The first was of resigned reproachful sadness; the other was quite different, and only to be described as of sly smirking lubricity. As her face was both mobile and relaxed, she could slip like a flash from one expression to the other, naturally, spontaneously and without the slightest awareness of what she was doing.

We walked down the first hill, and this seemed to me an opportunity for moving a little faster. I was not as relaxed as Myrtle. However, she comfortably took her time, making a detour to cross the brook by a plank. Two horses, their coats shaggy with moisture, raised their heads to look at us. The brook was high with spring water, and the weeds waved in it sinuously. I put my hand on Myrtle's waist.

As we climbed the opposite hill Myrtle called to the horses, but they sided with me and paid no attention.

At the top of the hill we always paused and sat on a gate for a few minutes. It was a sort of ritual, and to me it seemed a thoroughly silly sort of ritual. Below us we could see the cottage. No sooner had I settled on the top bar than I was ready to leap off again. But Myrtle always took her time, and as she went by atmosphere I could never tell how long it was going to be. It was at such moments that I sensed the great gulf between our temperaments: Myrtle went by atmosphere and I went by plan.

My plan was lucid and short. There, shining in its cream-coloured wash, small, intimate, isolated from everything, was the cottage. I felt as if my skin were tightening. No doubt I had a hot fixed look on my face.

Suddenly Myrtle slid down from the gate and quietly made off beside the hedgerow.

'What on earth?' I began, jumping down.

She stooped, and I saw that she was plucking some celandines she had spied on the brink of a ditch. She held them up, glistening in the sunshine.

'What are you going to do with those?'

Myrtle's face promptly took on a distant unconcerned look, as if she were going to start whistling. I laughed aloud at her, and grasped her to me.

'Darling!' I cried. I kissed her cheeks: they had a soft bloomy feel.

I slipped my hands down from her waist. She struggled away from me.

'We're in the middle of a field, darling,' she said.

It was my turn now. I am too direct to look lubricious. I took her firmly by the hand. 'Come on, then,' I said. And down the hill we went, in the plainest of plain sailing.

Whatever she was doing, Myrtle preserved a demeanour that was meek and innocent. She preserved it to perfection as I finally turned back the sheets for her. Yet, meek and innocent though her demeanour was, virginal and ladylike, anything else you may be pleased to call a nice girl, it was more than Myrtle could do, not to take a furtive sideways glance at me. I caught her.

I have said that Myrtle had two characteristic facial expressions. As a result of her furtive glance she managed to wear both of them, resigned, reproachful, sad, sly, smirking and lubricious, all at once.

Some time later we were just finishing a short rest. Idle thoughts floated vaguely through my mind. A spider was spinning down slowly from the corner of the room. Nameless odours stirred under my nose. A crow's wings flapped past the window. I was sweating profusely, because Myrtle insisted on having a lot of bedclothes. It occurred to me that there is a great division of human bodies, into those which feel the cold and those which do not. Myrtle and I belonged one to each class. How many marriages, I meditated, had been ruined by such incompatibility? Marriage—my thoughts floated hastily on to some other topic.

Myrtle was wide awake. I thought she was probably thinking how a cup of tea would refresh her. Suddenly I heard the sound of a car coming up the lane. We never expected to hear any traffic go by the cottage. It was approaching at a moderate speed, and I thought I recognised the sound of the engine. I jumped out of bed and ran to the window.

I was just too late to see it pass, so I flung down the sash and put my head out. Again I was just too late.

'Who was it?' said Myrtle.

'It sounded like Tom's car.'

'What was he doing here?'

I shrugged my shoulders. I had my idea. There was a pause.

'Don't you think you ought to come away from the window, darling?'

'Why?'

'You've got nothing on.'

'All the better . . .' Out of respect for her delicacy I closed the window with a bang that drowned the end of my remark.

She was smiling at me. I went over and stood beside her. She looked appealing, resting on one elbow, with her dark hair sweeping over her smooth naked shoulder. I looked down on the top of her head.

Suddenly she blew.

'Wonderful Albert,' she said.

I may say that my name is not Albert. It is Joe. Joe Lunn. Myrtle looked up at me in sly inquiry.

I suppose I grinned.

After a while she paused.

'Men *are* lucky,' she said, in a deep thoughtful tone.

I said nothing: I thought it was no time for philosophical observations. I stared at the wall opposite.

Finally she stopped.

'Well?' I looked down just in time to catch her subsiding with a shocked expression on her face.

'Now,' I said, 'you'll have to wait again for your tea.'

'Ah . . .' Myrtle gave a heavy, complacent sigh. Her eyes were closed.

In due course we had our tea. Myrtle felt the cold too much to get out of bed, so I made it. She sat up and put on a little woollen jacket: it was a pretty shell pink to match the colour of her cheeks. Her eyes seemed to have changed from hazel to golden. We held an interesting conversation about literature.

I felt a slight check on me when I held literary conversations with Myrtle, because her taste was greatly superior to mine. I wrote novels, and when she brought to light the fact that I had no use for long dramas in blank verse, I felt coarse and caddish, as if lust had led me to violate a creature of sensibilities more delicate than I could comprehend. Secretly I thought she was invariably taken in by the spurious and the pretentious, but this I put down to her youth. She was only twenty-two.

It grew dusky outside whilst we finished our tea. As we settled down again, the firelight began to glow on the ceiling. A wind was rising in the branches of the elm trees across the road, furiously rattling the bare twigs against each other. 'If only we could stay here,' was what we were both thinking from time to time; and at first sight it was not obvious what prevented us. Certainly it was not obvious to Myrtle at all. It was with difficulty that in the end I persuaded her to get up.

'Come along, darling,' I said. I was thinking how necessary it was for us to get back to the town, she to her parents' home, I to my lodgings. Atmosphere did not indicate to Myrtle that this was the case.

'It's so cold outside, I shall die,' she said, hopelessly.

I bent down and kissed her: she put her arms round my neck. I could not resist it.

At last we were dressed and ready to go. I drank the remainder of the milk.

'I know you need it, darling,' Myrtle said in a subtle tone that I could not quite place.

A final glance round the living-room, at the dying fire and the empty flower-vases, and we went out into the darkness. There was a moment of nostalgia, as I turned the key in the door. We felt impelled to say something foolishly sentimental, like 'Goodbye, little home'.

On the journey back our spirits rose again. We pedalled cheerfully against the wind, our lamps flashing a wavering patch on the road ahead. We had good bicycles, with dynamos to light the lamps. Myrtle said she was tired, and sometimes I tried to tow her, but it was too difficult an operation mechanically.

The lights of the town came into view, looking particularly bright in the cold, wintry air. In the distance lighted trams passed each other slowly. The roads on the outskirts were lined with trees, and there were big houses far back from the road: this was the way into the town which did not lead through slums. Big lamps swayed over the tram-lines: in their light I could see Myrtle's eyes glowing. I put my hand on her shoulder.

At a cross-roads we parted. It was our convention that it would be indiscreet to go to each other's house. With our bicycles leaning against the small of our backs we embraced fervently. At this time on Sunday night there were few people about, especially when the wind was icy.

'When shall I see you again, darling?'

Myrtle shivered, and looked woebegone.

This was always an apprehensive moment for me. It sometimes happened that I already had an evening booked in advance: Myrtle was certain to light upon it. There was nothing wrong about it, but she made it only too plain that she was wounded. I could never think how to explain and reassure. She had all my love: I wanted no one else: she had no cause to feel a moment's jealousy. Yet she was wounded if I disclosed that there was one evening when I was not free. And somehow I wanted that evening to myself, that evening and possibly one or two more. It was the moment when I sensed another great gulf between our temperaments.

On this particular occasion, I had arranged to go out for supper on Tuesday evening—Myrtle and I lived in the social stratum where the midday meal is often called lunch instead of dinner, but where the evening meal cannot properly be called dinner and so goes by the name of supper.

'When shall I see you again, darling?' I waited with my fingers crossed.

'Not tomorrow, of course.' Then in a melancholy tone: 'And I've promised to go to the dressmaker's on Tuesday . . .' Her voice trailed off, and returned with surprising briskness. 'Wednesday.'

I kissed her. Relief multiplied my fervour by about fifty per

18

cent. Myrtle looked sad. We arranged to telephone each other, and parted.

As I cycled fast down my own road, I felt as if I were borne on a stream of the purest, most powerful emotion. It almost seemed to lift the bicycle off the ground. Everything seemed entrancing, permeated by the atmosphere of joy—the prospect of a hearty supper that my landlady would have waiting for me, of a hot bath that I needed, and of the blessed sheets of my own bed. Myrtle, Myrtle. The sting of cold air on my forehead, the strange brilliance of the streetlamps, the bare trees waving in the shadows.

I put away my bicycle and slammed the garage door. I was thinking of Myrtle, and I looked up at the sky. There were stars, sparkling. I was feeling happy and I had left Myrtle looking sad. Why, oh why? I am an honest man: one of my genuine troubles with Myrtle was that I could never tell whether she was looking unhappy because I would not marry her or because she was feeling cold.

CHAPTER III
A MORNING AT SCHOOL

Next morning I had to get up and go to school. It was going to be a bright day. The balls of my feet felt springy as I ran downstairs, and as I jumped on to my bicycle the saddle felt springy. Hoorah! for Myrtle, I thought; there is nothing makes a man feel so wonderful as a wonderful girl. Flying downhill past the cemetery I skidded violently in the tram-lines and gave myself a fright: a wonderful girl does not fill a man with courage to face death—quite the reverse.

The school was a big grammar school for boys, in the centre of the town. The building was Victorian, dark, ugly, ill-planned, dirty and smelly.

Instead of going to morning prayers I went down to the laboratory. My task in the school was to teach physics, and for the whole of the morning I was due to take the senior sixth form in practical work. I felt more inclined to prepare the apparatus for their experiments than to take part in communal devotions.

Every so often the headmaster sent round a chit, asking all masters to attend morning prayers, but it produced not the slightest effect. One half of the masters claimed more important matters of preparation, and the other just did not go: I fluctuated between the two. The headmaster was zealous and high-minded, but he had not a scrap of natural authority. He ought to have been a local preacher, on a circuit with very small congregations.

This school was the first at which I had ever taught, so I had no other to compare it with. And I found that like many other men I had no objective recollections of my own school, or of half the things I did there—this appears to be nature's way of avoiding embarrassment all round.

I could not help feeling this school was something out of the ordinary. On my very first day there I overheard a small boy, apparently also on his very first day, say to another small boy in the crowded corridor: 'It's like Bedlam, isn't it?' After six years I still could not improve on this innocent description.

The small room used as a laboratory by the sixth form was on the ground floor at the end of the building; I could only get to it by going through the main laboratory, which was empty. Though both rooms were empty neither was quiet. Traffic roared past a few feet from the windows, while upstairs the school was singing its head off with 'Awake, my soul'!

There were four boys aged eighteen or nineteen, in the senior sixth form, and they did experiments in pairs. I was at work, with all the cupboard-doors open, when one of them came in. He was mature in appearance, and greeted me in a friendly fashion.

''Ello, Joe,' he said. 'I'n't it a luvly day!'

The local dialect was characterized by a snarling, whining intonation: Fred spoke it in the soppy, drawling, baby-talk of the slum areas.

The school did not have number one social standing in the town, and the pupils all came from the lower middle class and upper proletariat. Fred came from the proletariat. He was strong and stocky, with a sallow, greyish skin. His hair was covered with brilliantine and his hands were always dirty—I thought it was the grease off his head which made his hands pick up the dirt so readily.

Like Fred, most of the older boys called me by my Christian name, outside the lessons if not inside. I had wanted to get on free-and-easy terms with the boys—how else could I find out all about them?—and I had achieved the feat with little trouble, chiefly through letting them say anything they liked.

To an outsider the manners of my pupils must have been surprising. It happened that I was not given to being surprised; which very soon made the manners of my pupils more surprising still. The boys, when they discovered there was nothing they could say that would shock me, relapsed into the happy state they appeared to be in when I was not there.

At one period the upper forms had devoted a few days of

their attention to choosing theme-songs for members of the staff. I was told that mine was 'Anything Goes': it seemed to me fair. Unfortunately my free-and-easy attitude was strongly disapproved by my senior master. He wanted to have me sacked, and frequently expressed his point of view to the headmaster.

It was absolutely necessary, if I wanted to become a novelist— and that was the only thing I wanted to do—that I should keep my job. Nevertheless I found it unbearably tedious to pretend to be surprised when I was not, to be shocked when I was not, to be ignorant when I knew all about it, and to be morally censorious when I did not care a damn. To be frank, I found it impossible.

Fred was mooning about, so I told him to get out the travelling-microscope. At this point a boy called Frank came in.

Frank was the eldest and the cleverest of the four. He was captain of the school rugby football team, more because he had an eager, pleasing personality than because he carried a lot of weight. He had wavy hair, high cheek-bones, and a rather long nose that, to his secret sorrow, turned up at the end. Had it not been for his nose he would have been very handsome. He was an old friend of Tom's.

'Have a good week-end?' he said.

'Very.'

He glanced at me briefly. I suspected he had found out from Tom where I had spent it, though the cottage was supposed to be a secret. All the boys showed powerful curiosity and imagination about the private lives of the masters.

'It's time you and Trevor tried to find Newton's rings,' I said. It was a difficult experiment, appropriate as Frank had won a scholarship to Oxford.

It may not have occurred to everybody that most schoolmasters are preoccupied not with pedagogy but with keeping the pupils quiet. There are numerous methods of achieving this, ranging from giving them high-class instruction to knocking them unconscious.

Frank began to search for his experiment in the index of a text-book. Fred interrupted him.

'Fred,' I said, 'you and Benny can do Kater's pendulum.'

This was where my guile came in. The experiment necessitated one of them counting the oscillations of a pendulum and the other watching a clock, so precluding all foolish conversation.

Suddenly there was a distant roar as the school came out of prayers. They thundered down the staircases out of the hall, stamping their feet and raising their voices. It was no longer possible to hear the traffic outside the windows.

The last two boys, Trevor and Benny, came into the laboratory. Benny was big and ugly and heavy, with the comic-pathetic expression of a film-comedian. He generated a superabundance of emotion and physical energy, and he was not clever.

Trevor was quite different, unusually small, fair, pale and delicately formed. He had beautiful silky golden hair that he was always combing. He was languid, petulant, sarcastic, quick-tempered and horrid to anyone who gave him an opening. I was quite fond of him because he was intelligent and inclined to be original. He wanted to be an artist, and he had failed badly in the Oxford scholarship examination. I was worried about his future, and afraid that we might have trouble with him one day.

'What are we going to do, sir?' said Benny, standing too close to me and hopping about from one big foot to the other. Trevor went and combed his hair in front of a glass cupboard-door.

I paused for a moment. A form was assembling in the main laboratory next door and the wooden wall between was resounding like a huge baffle. There was a loud hallooing shout from a master, and the noise subsided. I explained to my pupils what they had to do. Then I sat down in my chair to meditate.

One of the boys asked a question. 'Do as you like,' I said. I addressed the form as a whole. 'It's important that you should all learn to be resourceful.'

Trevor turned his small sharp face and laughed nastily.

'It saves you a lot of trouble.'

I did not speak to any of them.

'Come on, Trev,' said Frank, and ran his fingers through Trevor's hair.

Benny dropped a couple of metre sticks on the floor. On picking them up he discovered he could make a clacking noise by shaking them together. In a few moments this pleasure palled and they were all settling down to work.

I began to think about Myrtle.

The brightness of the day was beginning to be manifest. A pale ray of sunlight cut across the little room and glimmered on the green-painted wall. Trevor was trying out a piece of asbestos soaked in brine over a bunsen flame, and it made spluttering yellow flashes. Sounds of all kinds kept the room echoing. It was another day in which you could feel the air cleared and sharpened by dormant spring. My thoughts drifted into fantasies as they do when I listen to music.

There was another hallooing shout in the room next door. Then silence.

'It's Roley,' said Frank. Roley was the boys' name for my senior master, Roland Bolshaw.

There was a crash against the wall: it was the unmistakable sound of a boy being knocked down.

'The sod!' said Trevor, in a superior accent.

'Oo-ya bugger!' said Fred, in the language of the town.

We listened, but nothing else happened.

Frank went on polishing a lens with his handkerchief.

'You haven't got anything to do,' he said. 'Haven't you brought a novel to read?'

I shook my head. He had reminded me of the fact that I did not read much nowadays. I was faced with an inescapable truth: you cannot have a mistress and read. Sometimes my illiteracy made me ashamed: at other times I thought, 'Bah! Who wants to *read*?'

From his pile of text-books Trevor produced a copy of *Eyeless in Gaza*. I had read it once and found it too unpleasant to read again.

'If I go to my locker I shall have to stop and talk to Bolshaw on the way,' I said thoughtfully.

Immediately Benny was standing beside me. 'Let me go and fetch you something, sir!'

I refused, and that committed me to going through Bolshaw's room.

The headmaster of the school was regarded by staff and pupils alike as ineffective. The result of this diagnosis, right or wrong, was that there was little discipline among the boys, and a high degree of eccentricity, laziness and insubordination among the staff. The manners of the staff were no less surprising than those of the boys. By my simple standards of common sense, about one-third of them not only qualified for dismissal from this school but would never hold a job in any other. To say they habitually cut lessons, or spent lunch-time in a public-house, or held hilarious sessions of beating, was putting it mildly.

There were of course a number of masters, another third, who were ordinary decent men. The sort of men we all remember as the schoolmasters of our youth—a little less clever, shrewd, ambitious and successful than ourselves, but firm, honest and hard-working. Unfortunately these were not the men who made much impression at the time upon any of the boys I had a chance of observing.

My senior master fell into a third category. He was immediately recognisable as a schoolmaster, while at the same time he was impressive. I think he was most impressive because in the staff-room, the class-room, or any other gathering, he had the power of confidently assuming he was the most important person there.

Bolshaw was built on a big scale. He had a large heavy body, with thinnish arms and legs, and a slight stoop. He was fair-haired and blue-eyed, but that is not to say he was an example of nordic beauty. He was in his fifties, and his hair was thinning everywhere except on his upper lip, where it grew in a tough, straggling, fair moustache. He had to blow the whiskers of his moustache away from his mouth in order to speak. His eyes were sharp and clever, and he wore steel-framed spectacles. And he had one of the loudest booming voices I have ever heard.

It was the way his head came up out of his collar, and the way his moustache fell back from his greenish, ill-fitting, false teeth, that gave him the vigorous tusky look of a sea-lion. I could imagine such a head emerging from the surface of icy waters to blow and boom at other sea-lions.

By temperament Bolshaw looked solid and conventional. He was arrogant, lazy, more or less good-natured, statesman-like, and given to confident disapproval of others. Bolshaw disapproved of me, with enormous confidence: he disapproved of the headmaster with equal confidence. The headmaster was conventional but possessed not a scrap of natural authority. I was solid enough but wilfully showed no signs of decorum.

On the whole, Bolshaw and I did not dislike each other. Had we not been members of the same profession I doubt if we should have quarrelled at all. Bolshaw merely wanted me to behave like a schoolmaster. He wanted me to conform. You may ask, who was he to demand conformity? The answer is, Bolshaw.

Bolshaw had natural authority and he exerted it. He entered the class-room in a solemn, dignified, lordly manner. He was, I repeat, a solid and conventional schoolmaster. On the other hand I am forced to record that he never taught the boys anything.

I bore Bolshaw very little ill-will. I was always interested in his devices for avoiding work, and enthralled by the tone of high moral confidence in which he referred to them. Also I appreciated his sense of humour: he made harsh, booming jokes. It was a pity he was trying to have me sacked.

As I passed through Bolshaw's room I tried to evade him, though nothing pleased him more, when he was supposed to be teaching a form, than to gossip with me. On this occasion I failed. He had adopted the schoolmaster's legal standby for keeping the pupils occupied—a test. He looked up at me as I passed, with his steel spectacles gleaming and his yellow moustache revealing a tusky grin.

I glanced at his list of questions on the blackboard, and then at the form, which was composed of louts. Bolshaw strolled across my path.

'I always think,' he began—it was one of his favourite beginnings, especially for a statement of egregious arrogance—in a loud confident undertone that carried to the other end of the laboratory, 'that I'm the only person who knows the answers to my own questions.'

There was a pause.

'Have you heard this morning's news?' Bolshaw said.

I was a little surprised. At first I thought he must mean Hitler's latest move, but as we disagreed over politics we did not pretend to discuss such things. Bolshaw approved of Hitler in so much as he approved the principle of the Führer's function while feeling that he could fulfil it better himself.

'Simms is away again.'

I looked at him with interest. Simms was the senior master of all the departments, physics, chemistry, mathematics and biology: as such he was paid more money. Bolshaw, though he spoke as if he were headmaster of the school, was only senior physics master. Simms was a kindly, sensitive, unaggressive old man who suffered from asthma. Bolshaw was waiting for him to retire.

'I told the headmaster only last week,' said Bolshaw, 'that Simms is a sick man.'

I smiled to myself at the phrase. If your friend is ill, you say, 'So-and-so's down with asthma.' 'So-and-so's a sick man' is the phrase reserved for someone you hope will be eliminated to the material improvement of your own prospects: it has a lofty, disinterested sound.

Bolshaw was a power-loving man. Getting Simms's job meant a great deal to him. It meant something to me too; since I argued that if he got Simms's it would be difficult to prevent me getting his, Bolshaw's, job—which also carried more pay. This was only the beginning of my argument. Bolshaw was not only strong: he was wily and circuitous. And he was in a position to make the running. Up to date I had held my own, by at least keeping my job—but this, I reflected, might not be due as much to my own moral strength and manœuvring power as to the headmaster's utter supineness.

'My wife and I went out to see him yesterday. I thought he was a very sick man.' He spoke with the solemn grandeur of his knowledge. 'I'm afraid he doesn't believe in his own recovery.'

I said I thought Simms would recover. 'Asthma's really a defensive complaint. The poor old man's asthma keeps him out of the hurly-burly for a while. It may be . . .'

'I always think,' interrupted Bolshaw, raising his voice by several decibels, 'the most important thing is that a man should believe in himself. It encourages the others.'

I had heard enough. 'Do you believe in that boy over there?' I said, pointing to a boy who was blatantly copying from his textbook.

The form heard what I said, and there was a sudden stillness.

As Bolshaw turned to look, I made for the door.

In a few minutes I returned, and to my surprise Bolshaw did not attempt to waylay me again. I was suspicious.

I sat down in my own room and said:

'What's Bolshaw been up to?'

Frank said: 'He came in to see if he could catch us playing the fool. He threatened Benny.'

'What was Benny doing?' Benny was always playing the fool.

'Nothing, sir!' Benny put on a look of ludicrous innocence.

'Benny wasn't,' said Frank. 'Roley only said he was so as to criticise you.'

'Nonsense,' said Trevor malevolently. 'Roley enjoys threatening.' He giggled.

I began to read.

After an hour or so I noticed that the sun was shining quite brightly. I stood up and stretched my limbs. I thought how much less cramped I should feel if I were sauntering over the fields with Myrtle. I threw my book down on the bench and leaned against the wall. Fred and Benny were counting with concentration; Frank was looking down the travelling-microscope; Trevor was filing his nails. A neighbouring church clock began to chime. Something inside me was chafing, and I said aloud:

'Que je m'ennuie!'

There was a pause.

'Why don't you go out?' said Trevor.

'Go and have a cup of coffee,' said Frank. 'We shall be all right.'

''E can telephone somebody,' said Fred suggestively.

I shook my head. 'It means another encounter with Bolshaw.'

'Go through the window,' said Benny. 'Roley won't know you've gone.'

One of the panes of the window at the end of the room could be opened. If I climbed over the bench I could just squeeze through and drop into the street. I had tried it before.

Benny had already climbed on to the bench and was eagerly holding the window for me.

'We'll promise to help you in again,' he said.

A Morning at School

I did not trust him not to play tricks that would bring in Bolshaw and reveal my absence. It was tempting fate; but I decided to risk it.

A moment later I was walking outside in the cold sparkling sunshine. It made a pleasant relief to a morning in school.

CHAPTER IV

TWO PROVINCIAL MÉNAGES

Tom's boy was named Steve, and he was aged seventeen. I suggest that anyone who is in the act of picking up a stone to cast at Tom, should change his target and cast at Steve instead. Many a man, were the truth but known, would find himself in as weak a moral position as Tom: on the other hand any man whatsoever might count on being in a stronger moral position than Steve. Steve had practically no moral position at all.

Steve was tall and gauche and precocious. He was pleasant-looking, with a shock of soft dark hair that kept falling over his eyes, and a wide red-lipped mouth. There was nothing particularly effeminate about him. He hunched his shoulders shrinkingly and wore a faintly rueful smile, as indications of his delicate nature: there was not the slightest need for either, since physically he was well-formed and temperamentally as self-centred as anyone I have ever known.

As with Tom, it was Steve's idea of himself that guided his actions. He saw himself as hyper-sensitive and artistic, in need of protection, help and support. Much happiness and satisfaction was created by Tom's seeing him in the same way. It was Tom's role to give Steve protection, help and support. Their relationship was that of patron and protégé.

I liked Steve. He wrote some poems that showed talent. As I felt that writing poems was a very proper occupation for the young I encouraged him. I subscribed to Somerset Maugham's theory, that creating variegated minor works of art is part of juvenile play: it seemed to me that the young might play at much worse things, such as rugby football which left them tired out with nothing to show for their pains.

30

Most of all I enjoyed Steve's company. Like most people of weak moral fibre he was thoroughly engaging. It is a sad reflection that everybody admires persons of strong moral fibre but nobody shows any inclination to stay with them for more than five minutes. We all agreed that it was fun to be with Steve for any length of time.

Though the relation between Tom and Steve was that of patron and protégé, I thought their behaviour was more like that of corporal and private. Tom was energetic and bustling: Steve was incorrigibly lazy. Much of their time together was spent in Tom's giving loud commands: 'Now Steve, do this!' and 'Now Steve, do that!' and Steve's putting up, as befitted his station, a token show of obedience.

Steve appreciated readily the advisability of a protégé's retaining his patron; but where his token show of obedience required physical action he was usually careless and inept to say the least of it. This promptly led Tom to give him suitable instruction, to which Steve submitted uncomplainingly—far too uncomplainingly, in my opinion, as much of the information Tom saw fit to impart was grossly inaccurate. Fortunately Tom was satisfied by the act of imparting, and Steve neither knew nor cared about inaccuracy.

Tom was very serious about his devotion to Steve. It was Myrtle and I who had conceived the idea of renting a country cottage, and Myrtle who had found it: it did not take Tom long to see that Steve's devotion to him would be increased if he were able to entertain him over the week-ends in the country.

Furthermore Steve sighed with relief when Tom bought a car. Steve did not own a bicycle, and when Tom offered to lend him one there was some doubt about whether Steve could ride it without falling off every few yards. In the end Steve got more than he bargained for, because Tom was a wild and impulsive driver—he had excellent eyesight but he did not appear to use it. Steve, like all the rest of us, was terrified. 'It does him good to be thoroughly frightened now and then,' Tom confided to me, with a meaningful smile. Tom's devotion was very great, but it did not entirely eclipse his shrewdness.

When Tom was arranging to entertain Steve for a week-end at the cottage, it was his habit to indicate that he, like Myrtle and

unlike me, went by atmosphere. There is a very simple difference between going by atmosphere and going by plan. If you go
by atmosphere you spend week-ends at a cottage when you feel
like it—which is every week-end. When I insisted on taking my
turn Tom denounced me as cold, methodical and machine-like.

There were additional complications. Tom did not mind my
being present when he was entertaining Steve; the last thing I
wanted was his presence when I was entertaining Myrtle. And
more troublesome still was the fact that I was supposed to conceal Steve's visits from Myrtle—looking back on it, I cannot for
the life of me see why. Myrtle would certainly not have been
shocked or disapproving. Women take such matters much less
seriously than men: they sometimes express passing displeasure
at the thought of two men being out of commission as far as they
are concerned, but that is all there is to it. I did not think: I acted
with cold, methodical, machine-like loyalty to Tom. The result
was farce.

The existences of Tom and Steve were enlivened by frequent
scenes of passion and high emotion. Mostly it was beyond my
powers to fathom what they were about. I really thought Tom
invented them. He reproached me with not having scenes with
Myrtle.

'I must say I find it slightly . . .' he paused, 'surprising.'

'Indeed,' I said, crossly.

Tom gave a distant, knowing smile, as truths about passion
crossed his mind that were beyond my comprehension. I could
see that he thought scenes were absent from my life with Myrtle
because of serious deficiencies in my temperament, if not actually in my powers as a lover.

Anyway, scenes were constantly present between Tom and
Steve, and since Steve was too lazy and conceited to initiate anything they must have originated with Tom. There was one in
progress, goodness knows why, over Steve's career.

Steve had left school the previous summer and had been articled to Tom's firm of accountants. It was in the office that they
first met. By the spring Steve's helpless and sensitive nature had
found its fulfilment in Tom's masterful capacity for support.

Steve decided he was not cut out to be an accountant. Trouble promptly broke forth.

Steve's parents had very modest resources, and had been forced to to borrow money to pay his premium. Tom, partly because he wanted Steve to be kept in his office, and partly out of sheer common sense, told Steve he would have to stay where he was. Steve began to suffer.

'Think of it, Joe,' Steve said to me. 'Five years as an articled clerk!' His pleasant face contorted with an expression of agony. 'It will be like prison.' He paused, as a worse thought struck him. 'Only *duller*.'

I could not help smiling.

Steve's expression of agony deepened. 'You don't understand, Joe. I can't do *arithmetic*.'

I shook my head.

'I never could,' he said. 'Think of becoming an accountant if you can't do arithmetic.' He glanced at me sharply, to enjoy my amusement. Suddenly the agonised look disappeared, his narrow grey eyes sparkled with hard realism and his tone altered completely. 'I can tell you it's terribly hard work, too.'

When Steve dropped his nonsense and came out with the truth he was at his most engaging.

I thought it was time to bait him a little. I said: 'Tom will teach you arithmetic. He likes teaching.'

'I don't want to learn arithmetic.'

'What do you want to learn, Steve?'

'I want to learn about love, Joe. Everybody does.'

'I should have thought you were doing quite nicely.'

'I'm not, Joe,' Steve said with force. 'I'm not!'

I shrugged my shoulders. 'You'll be a poet some day.'

'I'll never be an accountant. I never wanted to be. It's my parents' fault.' Steve looked at me. 'They chose accountancy because it's *respectable*.'

'In that case they made a singular choice,' I observed.

Steve grinned with satisfaction.

I surmised that Tom's conversations with Steve on the same theme had a different tone and went on much longer. Tom took Steve seriously, for one thing, and was easily roused to rage, for another. They had passionate quarrels over whether Steve could do arithmetic.

The upsurge of a quarrel led to an atmosphere of emergency in which previous arrangements about who should go to the cottage were swept aside, that is, if it were my turn. Tom rang me up early on Saturday morning, just as I was about to leave my lodgings.

'Are you having Myrtle out tomorrow?'

I said I was.

'In that case I think we'll come out today. Naturally we'll leave before Myrtle arrives tomorrow.' Tom paused diffidently. 'Steve wants us to come.'

I was annoyed. The only thing Steve wanted was physical comfort and unlimited admiration. On the other hand Tom had special claims because it was only a matter of months before he went to America.

A few minutes later Myrtle rang up.

'Darling, can I come out to see you this afternoon?'

Nothing would have pleased me more, but it was too late to stop Tom. I could not let Myrtle come, because I had told her I was going to be alone, writing.

'I was going to come into town to see you, darling,' I said, resourcefully. 'I thought we might go to a cinema.'

'But darling! . . .' Myrtle's voice broke off in surprise—as well it might, since the day was exquisitely sunny, I was in excellent health, and none of the cinemas sported a film that anybody in his right mind could want to see. I decided to banish Tom and Steve from the cottage immediately after lunch.

At lunch Tom displayed irritation that I had not put Myrtle off.

'What time will she be leaving tonight?'

'About ten o'clock.'

We ate our lunch in a state of tension, which increased on my part as Tom showed no signs of hurrying when the time approached for Myrtle to appear. Tom and Steve were quarrelling because Steve had surreptitiously eaten an apple before lunch and would not admit it.

'There were eight in the bowl before lunch and now there are only seven!' Tom was saying furiously. 'Neither Joe nor I ate it.'

Steve looked sulky and tortured. He was still growing quite fast and he was always hungry. Nobody objected to his eating anything, but he did it secretly and denied it afterwards. Food was always disappearing mysteriously when Steve was about.

'Myrtle will be here any moment,' I said, on tenterhooks.

I should like to point out that I thought none of this scene was in the least funny.

Tom looked at me, disgusted with my incapacity for understanding the overwhelming importance of conflict.

A bicycle bell rang joyously in the lane, and in came Myrtle.

Tom swept forward and greeted her effusively. He presented Steve to her. And then he said:

'How nice you're looking, Myrtle.'

She did look nice. She gave Tom a bright-eyed, smirking look. The smell of her scent caught in my nostrils. I could readily have taken a carving-knife to both Tom and Steve.

'Now what Myrtle would like,' said Tom, 'is a nice cup of tea.'

'I'm dying for one,' said Myrtle, in an expiring voice.

'Of course you are, my dear.' He paused. 'I understand these things.'

Myrtle played up to him shamelessly. 'I know, Tom.'

Tom's face wreathed itself in a silky smile.

Tom's stock method of making an impression on anyone was to indicate that he understood them perfectly. In this strain he was setting to work on Myrtle.

'Now Steve,' he said, 'put the kettle on!'

Steve shambled into the scullery, and reappeared in a moment looking tragic.

'The primus is broken.'

I pushed him out of the way. The primus was not broken: he had never tried. When I returned with the tea Tom and Myrtle were in full flood of the most inane conversation I could imagine.

'I love dogs,' Myrtle was saying, in a soulful tone.

'So do I,' said Tom, copying it ridiculously.

'I wish I had three.'

'One can't have too many.'

'Red setters,' said Myrtle. 'Don't you love red setters?'

'Wonderful,' said Tom.

'And their eyes!' said Myrtle.

'So sad!' said Tom.

'I know.'

'Just like us, Myrtle.' He gave her a long look.

Myrtle sighed.

Steve and I caught each other's eye, and I signalled him to help me hand round the cups. There was no place for us in the conversation.

At last Tom decided to take himself off. He made signs at me behind Myrtle's back. 'Ten o'clock!'

Myrtle and I stood in the doorway and watched his car disappear round the bend in the lane. Big white clouds went floating across the sun. The hedgerows were leafless and glistening—I watched a twittering troop of little birds which every so often took it into their heads to move on a few yards. I did not speak to Myrtle.

'What's the matter, darling?' Myrtle said, innocently.

'Nothing.'

'Is anything wrong?'

'Nothing at all.'

She put her arm round me, but I would not speak. Her body leaned softly against mine. She began to caress me: I decided to sulk a bit longer. I tried harder and harder to go on sulking. Suddenly I turned to her. She looked beautiful.

'I love you,' I whispered into her ear, and bit the lobe of it.

'Darling!' She struggled away from me.

We looked into each other's eyes.

'You didn't mean this afternoon as well, did you, darling?' she said, in a shocked reproachful tone.

'You know perfectly well, I did,' I said, and bit her again.

Instantly Myrtle looked away, and I knew that I had made a mistake. I was being found lacking in romance. I held her close to me. 'Poor Myrtle,' I thought; 'and poor me, as well'. I went on holding her close to me till I ceased to be found lacking in romance.

Saturday afternoon passed like a dream—in fact, much more satisfactorily than any dream I have ever had. Men can say what they like about dreams. Better awake, is my motto.

We were happy, we were harmonious, we were ravenously

hungry. The dusk fell and we cooked a meal. By daylight you could see that the cottage was filled with everybody's cast-off pieces of furniture. At night, by the light of candles and the fire, it was transformed. We lingered over our eating: we lingered over each other. And the clock moved round to ten.

Myrtle showed no signs of going. I ceased to linger over her: she did not cease to linger over me. I had promised to get her away by ten, and it was useless to pretend I had not. Myrtle began to look at me reproachfully. I now suspected her of planning to stay the night; and realised that in a simple way she had broken me down to the idea. She put her arms round my neck. We were one: I would have given anything for her to stay the night with me, sleeping peacefully together. Like husband and wife.

Tom's car drove up, and Tom came in. He saw Myrtle. His face was distorted with anger and passion.

'What, Myrtle!' he said. 'Are you still here?'

Myrtle, not unnaturally, looked surprised and hurt. His tone was very different from that in which he had unctuously explored their identity of tastes earlier on.

'We were just going,' I said.

'That's right.' Tom relaxed a little, and smiled at Myrtle. 'And take Joe with you!'

I stood on my dignity. 'I always take her as far as the main road.'

Myrtle and I stepped out into the night, and picked up our bicycles. There was no sign of Steve in the car. Tom must have left him under a hedge.

We cycled down the lane. It was calm and starless.

'What was the matter with Tom?' She sounded miserable.

'I don't know.'

'He seemed strange.'

I did not speak. This was unfortunate as it enabled Myrtle to hear Tom start up his car and drive away in the opposite direction.

'Where's Tom gone?' she asked.

'Goodness knows,' I said.

I felt furious. Suddenly I felt cold as well. I had forgotten to put on a top coat. There was nothing to do but go back for it. I told Myrtle to wait where she was and pedalled hastily away.

I returned to meet Myrtle wheeling her bicycle towards me, with no light showing.

'The dynamo's broken,' she said, with deep pathos.

I think she thought she was going back for the night now that Tom had gone.

'You must take my spare lamp,' I said. 'You must!' We were nearly at the cottage again.

We heard Tom's car coming back.

'Tom's car's coming back,' said Myrtle, in a voice that had reached its peak of astonishment and could go no further.

I waved my lamp wildly to warn Tom.

The car drew up. Only Tom got out. I presumed that Steve must now be under the seat.

Tom rudely persuaded Myrtle to take my lamp, and we set off again.

We did not speak very much until we came to the main road. There we paused and embraced. Myrtle leaned against me passively, and I tried to revive her.

'Darling,' I said.

There was a long silence.

'You want to get rid of me.'

It was too much for me. I wished Tom were in America and I was not far from wishing he were removed from this world altogether. We stood in the middle of the road, our bicycles ledged in the small of our backs, weeping on each other's cheeks.

'Darling, I do love you,' I said, wondering why on earth we were not married to each other.

I held her face between my hands: it was so dark that I could barely see it.

'Please come to me tomorrow afternoon.'

Myrtle did not speak. A tear rolled on to my thumb.

'Promise, promise!'

Myrtle nodded her head.

I resolved that Tom should be got rid of next morning, if it meant dissolving our friendship for ever. When she came in the afternoon everything should be as if this night had never happened.

I took out my handkerchief and dried her face. In a little while we parted. Then I rode slowly through the empty lanes.

You may wonder why I put up with all this nonsense, why I did not break my word to Tom and tell Myrtle what was going on. There were two reasons. The first I am so ashamed of that I can barely bring myself to write it, but I shall have to write it in order to explain some of the later events: it is this—realizing that I was not a good man, I was trying to behave like one; and to me that meant being patient, forbearing and trustworthy to the last degree.

The second reason is this—frankly, I had no sense.

CHAPTER V

A PARTY OF REFUGEES

I advised Tom to emigrate to America as soon as possible. International events gave me a strong explicit foundation for my advice. From time to time we met for tea in the café and counted the growing roll of disasters.

'A fortnight since Hitler took Memel, and the British Government has done *nothing*!' said Tom.

'Nothing,' I echoed.

Alternately we received gloomy letters from Robert, which we read to each other. 'If there isn't a war by September we shall be refugees by November.' I noticed the date had slipped on a month, but did not point it out to Tom. I thought there was every reason why he should move without delay.

As the afternoons lengthened, we were leaving the window before the lights came on in the market-place. Easter was approaching: blue fumes of coffee mingled with the spring dust that circulated in the wind. The twilight glimmered on hosts of flowers, on waxen Dutch tulips in exquisite shades. Some of the shoppers had discarded their top coats. The weeks were passing: we could feel it, with nostalgia for the summer and apprehension for our fate.

Tom had a newspaper spread before him.

'Chamberlain Pledges Defence of Poland,' he read aloud. 'Balderdash! Poppycock!' Excepting the glare of his greenish eyes, his head began to look red all over. 'We shall give Poland away just like the rest. We shall see Chamberlain fly to Berlin in a golden aeroplane, accompanied by Peace in the shape of a dove.'

I smiled faintly and Tom blinked.

'Why is it always a dove?' he asked me. 'The *horse* of peace would be better. Doves are stupid, back-biting creatures, but horses are noble and intelligent.' He thumped his fist on the table. 'I can't stomach doves!'

The atmosphere lightened momentarily. Tom had the power of being able to hearten me. There was a good robust sense of life in him that made one's troubles seem smaller—one's own troubles, that is: it made his seem larger, absurdly larger.

We began to talk about writing. Tom was not working on a new novel, because of the prospect of his being uprooted. He declared that he was too busy, making preparations, to write: I agreed from observation that he was too busy—he was too busy pursuing Steve. I, on the other hand, had been brought to a standstill by Miss X.Y. She had still not written to me.

'I think you ought to write to her,' said Tom, always counselling action.

I shook my head. I already had some experience of reading unpublished manuscripts, and knew how maddening it was to be prodded by an impatient potential novelist.

Tom shrugged his shoulders, and then began to console me.

'She's bound to like it,' he said. 'She liked your first, and this is so very much better.' He spoke with great authority. His tone reminded me of Robert, whom we both copied when we spoke with authority. 'You're one of the most gifted writers of our generation.'

I did not reply. I was making a feeble effort to discount some of Tom's exaggeration—about five per cent of it.

'She may have sent it to her own publisher,' Tom said. 'I would, in her place.'

I believed him. When he was not in the grip of one of his passions, Tom could be most sympathetic. He was capable of unconsidered acts of kindness. He could be momentarily free from envy and jealousy. It was for this that I valued his friendship. It is characteristic of our own egoism, that we value others for their selflessness.

'It's a remarkable novel.'

I did not speak. I found myself contrasting Tom's attitude with Myrtle's. Whenever we met, Tom asked me first of all if I had heard from Miss X.Y. Whenever I met Myrtle she failed to speak of it unless I raised the subject myself. I had given her the manuscript to read, and I strongly suspected that she had not read it all—my fourth novel, a class better than the other three, forty thousand words longer and nowhere near as funny. For Myrtle not to have read it all seemed to me next door to perfidy.

'How,' I asked myself, 'can Myrtle love me and not want to read my books? How can a woman separate the artist from the man?'

The answer came pat. Women not only can: they do. And they have a simple old-fashioned way of selecting the bit they prefer. At the same time I have to admit that if Myrtle had made the other choice I should have accused her of not loving me for myself. Men want it both ways and I am surprised that women do not make a little more pretence of giving it—especially when they want to marry the men in question.

'What are you thinking about?' said Tom.

'Meditating on incompatibility. On the utter incompatibility of two people who want different things and can't accept compromise.'

Tom's mouth curved knowingly. 'Have you made up your mind if you want Myrtle to go with you to America or not?'

I stared at him. I had not, of course. And I did not like the question.

Tom began to smile. He made a smooth gesture with his hands. He said: 'My dear Joe, there's no need . . .'

'If she likes to go under her own steam,' I said, 'I see no reason why she shouldn't.' I paused. 'She can support herself.'

I made the latter remark with emphasis. Tom had been getting at me: this was my way of getting at him. I meant that our party should not include Steve.

Tom said equably: 'It sounds perfectly sensible.'

'I'm a sensible man,' said I.

'Have you told her definitely that you're going?'

'Not in so many words.' I liked this question even less than the earlier one.

Tom shrugged his shoulders. He began to read the newspaper.

I began to think what I was going to do about Myrtle, which brings me to the point where I must complete my description of her.

Myrtle was very feminine, and I have described up to date those of her traits which everyone recognizes as essentially feminine. She was modest, she was submissive, she was sly; she was earthy in its most beautiful sense.

In addition to all this, Myrtle was shrewd, she was persistent, and she was determined. At the time I thought she was too young to know what she wanted. Looking back on it I can only reel at the thought of my own absence of insight and capacity for self-deception. She knew what she wanted all right: it is just possible that she was too young to know exactly how to get it.

Myrtle was a commercial artist, employed by a prosperous advertising agency in the town. In my opinion, based on her salary, she was doing well. This much at least I could see. At a hint of the intellectual Myrtle's eyes opened in wonderment, at a hint of the salacious she blushed; and at a hint of business she was thoroughly on the alert.

Myrtle had been trained at the local School of Art. She had talent of a modest order—that is, it was greater than she pretended. Her drawings were quick, lively, observant without being reflective, pretty and quite perceptibly original. I, with her talent, would have been trying to paint like Dufy or somebody: not so, Myrtle. There was no masculine aspiring about her. Trying to paint like Dufy with her talent I should have been a masculine failure. Myrtle with feminine modesty and innocence took to commercial art.

Myrtle's talent was not of the primary creative order that sometimes alarms the public: it was the secondary talent for giving a piquant twist to what is already accepted. She was made for the world of advertising. And she accepted her station in life as an artist as readily as she accepted her salary. My efforts to encourage her to rise above this station, which would have brought her little but misery, fortunately made no impression upon her whatsoever.

In her business dealings Myrtle showed the same flair. It was one of her gifts to accept quite readily men's weaknesses. She was tolerant and down-to-earth about them: she fought against them much less than many a man does.

Myrtle's employer was a middle-aged man who had introduced his mistress into a comparatively important position in

the firm—to the envy and disapprobation of everyone but Myrtle. Myrtle accepted that such things were likely to happen,
made the best of it, and showed good-natured interest in the
other girl. In due course Myrtle found, to her genuine surprise,
that the boss began to show much greater appreciation of her
work.

So you see that Myrtle was by no means a poor, helpless girl
who had fallen into the clutches of an unscrupulous, lust-ridden
man. I may say that I saw it, plainly, while I sat in the café with
Tom reading his doom-struck newspaper. I was behaving like a
cad—admitted. But anyone who thinks behaving like a cad was
easy is wrong.

As a result of Tom's pressing me I made a definite plan. It was
to include Myrtle in our party of refugees without marrying her.

I was convinced that Myrtle could earn a living in America. If
only I could convince *her!* If only I could persuade her to *act* on
the conviction! Then there was no reason why our relationship
should not go on just as it was.

That was how I came to my plan. It was only too easy for Tom
to say afterwards that I never intended to carry it out, that if
Myrtle had agreed I should have been something between
alarmed and appalled. I at least half-believed it. As a love affair
declines one can still go on making plans for a future that does
not exist. And that is what I was doing. For, alas! make no
mistake, our relationship really was declining.

There is a kind of inevitability about the course of growing
love: so there is about its decay. It comes from time flowing
along. You can shut your eyes and pretend that you are staying
still—and all the while you are just being carried along with your
eyes shut. You can make plans—but if they do not fit in with the
flow of time, you might just as well save yourself the trouble. So
with Myrtle and me. Wanting something different and being
unable in our hearts to compromise we were being carried along
towards final separation. We appeared to be doing things of our
own volition: we had our breaks and our reconciliations. Round
and round we went, spinning together like planets round the
sun. May I remind you that even the solar system is running
down?

To begin with I thought I had had a stroke of luck. Myrtle rang me up to tell me that she had been promoted to a better job in the firm. In the evening she came round to my lodgings for us to drink a bottle of beer to her success. 'Now,' I said to myself, 'now is the time!'

My landlady was clearing away the remains of my supper, when Myrtle sauntered into the room with an alluring whiff of cosmetics. The landlady retired promptly. Myrtle stared at me with a meek smirk of triumph. I kissed her. I wanted to know exactly what difference promotion made to her salary.

When questioned on matters of money, Myrtle always became quite unusually vague and elusive. I asked my questions, and somehow found myself listening to an elaborate account of intrigues in the firm, and adventures of Myrtle's employer and his mistress.

When the turn ended I quietly returned to my aim. Myrtle's face was still lit up with the pleasure of entertaining me. Instead of asking my questions all over again crudely, I led up to them by another spell of enthusiastic congratulation.

Something happened. Myrtle looked at me suddenly with a different expression.

Insensitively I forged ahead.

'It really is wonderful!' I said.

After remaining silent, Myrtle spoke in a hollow voice. Into her words she put sadness and reproach.

'It isn't *really*.'

'But it is!' I insisted. 'It proves you'll be able to get a job anywhere.'

Myrtle said nothing. She stood up and walked slowly across to the window. She stared out.

I was disturbed, but determination had got the better of me. I followed her, and stood beside her. I lived in the back room of a small semi-detached house. We were looking through a french window at a narrow strip of garden that sloped down to the garden of another semi-detached house in the next road. It was dusk.

I patted her. 'The more money you earn, my girl, the better.'

'Why?'

'Because you're an artist,' I said encouragingly. 'And Art must pay.' I kissed her cheek. 'We're two artists,' I said.

Myrtle did not speak. Being two artists is one thing; being husband and wife another, quite different. Then suddenly she turned on me and said with force:

'You *know* that I don't care.'

I looked down. Sad words, they were, falling upon my ear. When a woman tells a man she does not care about her career he ought to make for the door. It means one thing—the end of liberty for him.

I did not make for the door. I was overwhelmed by tenderness and I embraced her. It was no use making for the door because I still had to broach the subject of her taking a job in America.

I broached it. And it was a failure.

I suppose I was being singularly insensitive and obtuse, but I do not know what else I was to do. I thought: 'How strange—she doesn't realize that if she sticks to her career she can follow me to America.' And I will not swear that I did not think: 'And in America she might even succeed in marrying me.'

Alas! the flow of time asserted itself. I made matters worse.

'The world's going to be in a chaotic state,' I said. 'We shall all do best if we can fend for ourselves.'

Myrtle showed no sign of following me. The last thing she wanted to do was to think of fending for herself in a chaotic world. She was powerless to stand outside her personal affairs of the moment.

'I'm sure you could get a job in America.'

'Whatever for?'

'If we all decide to go.'

'Oh, that!' Myrtle moved away from me, as if the idea were tedious and repugnant and unreal.

I realized that I had not the courage to tell her that we were definitely going to America. I thought: 'I must tell her. I must!' And I said:

'I'm sure you'd be a great success in America.'

Myrtle tilted her head back to look at me. Her eyes were round and golden and unbearably appealing. I took her into my arms. You can see that I am both obtuse and a failure as a man.

The conversation went on a little further. I could hardly have been more inept, so I will not record it. I was direct, and for anyone as evasive and suggestible as Myrtle, directness was positively painful. My efforts to discover whether Myrtle's firm had American customers led us nowhere. She replied to my questions in an abstracted tone. I was tormenting her, and that was literally all. We were both completely trapped in our own worlds, quite separate, quite cut off.

At last the conversation dwindled into nothing. I thought Myrtle suffered from a low vitality of interest. I suggested that we should go to the cinema.

Immediately Myrtle perked up. Low vitality of interest, laziness, instinctive self-preservation—which was it? I do not know. We went to the cinema.

That was what became of part one in my plan. I moved to part two. Robert was coming to visit his friends in the town. I asked him to lunch at the cottage on Sunday and invited Myrtle. Tom was out of the way: he was supposed to be taking Steve up to London to see *The Seagull.* I hoped that when Robert saw Myrtle without any distraction, he would deem her worthy to join our party of refugees.

I was anxious. Up to the present Robert had deemed Myrtle distinctly unworthy. On having her presented to him he had commented that his remarks appeared to bounce off her forehead. I was willing to admit that Myrtle had an uncogitating, unreflective air; but Robert's comment seemed to me both unkind and untrue. Being Robert's comment, it had to be accepted all the same. I was hurt. Myrtle and I may have been quite separate, quite cut off, and all the rest of it: but when Robert said his remarks bounced off her forehead, she was my mistress, my love, my choice and part of me.

I had difficulty in persuading Myrtle to come to the cottage at all while Robert was there.

'You won't want me,' she said. I think she would rather I assumed she was jealous of my friendship for Robert than that she was frightened of him.

Myrtle was abashed by the idea of Robert's being an Oxford don, which she associated, wrongly, not with intellectual but with social superiority. In the society of people she considered her social superiors, Myrtle was thoroughly ill at ease: she was only really completely free with her social inferiors. Robert saw her at her worst.

'Of course I want you, darling,' I said. And encouragingly: 'Robert will want to see you.'

Myrtle stared at me in disbelief. And I thought fate had been hard on me in sending a woman who could not meet my friends.

Nevertheless Myrtle arrived at the cottage bright and smiling on Sunday morning.

'I passed Robert. He's walking.' She glanced at me slyly. 'I told him I couldn't stop because you were waiting for me.'

I felt more cheerful. Robert came. We walked over to the Dog and Duck and had a most enjoyable lunch. Robert and I talked about literature. Myrtle was impressed. She drank an unduly large quantity of beer. Robert was impressed.

We walked home in good spirits, to find Tom in the cottage. He had driven back from London that morning. Robert greeted him affectionately, and so did Myrtle. I did not.

'I have a letter I wanted you and Joe to see.' Tom pulled the document out of his pocket and passed it round.

The letter was from one of the American professional associations of chartered accountants. Tom had been writing about jobs. I did not look at Myrtle. I had warned Robert not to tell Myrtle that our plans were already far advanced, but I had never dreamed that Tom would appear. He and Robert sat down and began openly to discuss our project.

If it had been possible for Myrtle to doubt our intention in the beginning, the possibility must have entirely disappeared in five minutes. I was too alarmed to say anything.

Tom had completed his five years of professional practice as an associate of the Institute of Chartered Accountants, and attached importance to being elected to fellowship. There had been a hitch because he had seen fit to quarrel with the senior partner of his firm; but he computed that the formalities would be complete by June. He proposed to leave England immediately afterwards.

The plan for me was to follow as soon as the summer school term ended. Robert had ordered himself to come last. Tom argued with Robert about cutting it fine. I watched Myrtle. I was more than surprised that Tom and Robert did not see the effect they were having on her. She was taking no part in the conversation, and it was plain that she was too wretched even to follow it properly.

They went on to argue about how Robert and I should earn our living, by writing or by teaching. Neither of us wanted to teach. Tom was slightly huffed and pointed out a paragraph in the *Sunday Times*, which we had already seen, about a slump in the book trade. 'One bookseller this week reports no sales whatever.'

Robert suggested that he and I might have to live on Tom to begin with: the whole talk had been high-spirited instead of grave, and now Robert induced an air of mischief and nonchalance. Myrtle looked as if she was going to burst into tears. She got up and went into the scullery.

I followed her, expecting to find her weeping. She was taking down cups and saucers.

'I thought I should like some tea,' she said, in a flat voice.

I stroked her hair. Suddenly she looked at me and I was accused of heartlessness and treachery. I turned away without speaking and went back to the others.

After tea Tom drove Robert away. Myrtle and I were left alone. I did not know how to look her in the face. There was nothing I could say. The damage was done. We cycled back into town without discussing it.

This was our last meeting before the Easter holidays. I arranged to ring up Myrtle as soon as I returned to the town. I told myself she might have got over the damage in the meantime. I was apprehensive.

PART II

CHAPTER I

UP AT THE GAMES FIELD

During the holiday I received no letter from Myrtle. And when I returned to the town she had gone away. I telephoned each day till she came back: it was a Friday, and she agreed to meet me on the following afternoon. I was down for duty at the school games field, so she said she would join me there. It did not seem a good arrangement to me, but before I could persuade her to do something else, she rang off. Whatever had gone wrong was not repaired.

Saturday afternoon came; and with it, for the opening of the school cricket season, a spell of cold drizzly weather. Usually I enjoyed my tour of duty. The boys played cricket in a comparatively orderly fashion, and those who were watching the match came and talked to me in a tone designed to shock less than usual. The field was attractive. At the gates there was a nicely planned tram-terminus and modern public lavatory, but neither was visible from inside. On the left of the pitch there was a line of poplars and on the right of sycamores and oaks; and straight ahead the ground fell away to a view of the town, with gasometers shimmering through the smoky haze of middle distance.

I stood in my overcoat pitying the boys in their blazers and white flannels. In a feeble effort to compensate for deficiency of social *cachet*, the headmaster insisted on the boys wearing white flannels whenever they went to the field in the summer term. It was about the only rule they kept, and they looked surprisingly presentable as a consequence.

On a summer evening, with golden light slanting through the trees on active little white-clad figures, it was easy to catch again the romantic air of boyhood—that air which every man delights to remember, whether he has ever breathed it or not. There was everything present: the heart-touching mixture of repose and vigour, the small sounds of the game, the occasional voice, the clapping of a few hands, the calm and movement, the green glow of the ground. On a cold drizzly Saturday afternoon they were present, but, it seemed, to a lesser degree.

Keeping my eye open for Myrtle, I shook off boys who were inclined to come and converse, and stood alone near the sightboards.

''Ello, Joe!' My interest in the match was cut short by Fred who had sidled up without my noticing.

Fred's white flannels were spotless. The green of his blazer was echoed in the greyish colour of his skin. His hair was dripping with brilliantine.

'You're looking very spruce, Fred.'

Fred grinned foolishly. 'Mr Chamberlain's got me!'

For a moment I could not think what he meant. He was referring to the prospect of conscription. The crisis had reached the boys. It came as a shock.

'He's got us all,' said Fred.

'He's welcome to you,' said I.

Fred stood still. It seemed as if my remark made its impression gradually. In the end he sighed and drifted away.

I sat down on the sub-structure of the sightboards. For me the match might not have been going on: Myrtle was late.

The sky began to cloud over a little more, but the drizzle ceased. The first innings ended unexpectedly, and I noticed Frank coming round the boundary towards me.

'Do you mind if I come and talk to you?'

I glanced up at him without enthusiasm.

'I'm sorry to bother you.' He paused: there was something the matter.

As he had seen me often enough with Myrtle, I told him I was waiting for her.

Frank sat down beside me. 'I'll go away as soon as she comes.'

We were both silent.

Frank said: 'It's about Trevor.' He was apparently watching the match.

'Oh?'

'I wish you could use your influence over him a bit.'

'What for?'

'To make him pull himself together.'

'What's the matter with him?'

'He isn't doing any work, for one thing.'

'He never did do much.'

'He's doing none, now.'

'I suppose he'll go in for art.' I glanced at Frank, slightly amused.

'He's not doing any work at that, either.'

My interest began to stir. 'What *is* he doing?' I stopped looking across the pitch and looked steadily at Frank.

'He's going to stupid parties, night after night, and getting drunk.' Frank's voice grew louder. 'He's doing himself no good.'

I did not care very much whether Trevor was doing himself good or ill; nor was I seriously troubled by Frank's alarm. I do not know why I persisted with the conversation. Somehow I was drawn on.

'What parties?' I said.

Frank muttered something about the School of Art. Immediately I knew why I had been drawn on.

'Who goes to them?'

Frank suddenly glanced at me. 'I've only been to one . . .'

'But you must know. Hasn't Trevor told you?'

'I don't think you'd know them. They're not the sort of people you'd know.'

'Not any of them?' I could not make my voice sound unconcerned.

'I think Myrtle goes, as a matter of fact.'

Frank looked at me, diffidently. I said nothing. I remembered Tom's solemn warnings about what Myrtle did when I would not have her.

'Does Tom go to these parties?' I said.

'No. But I think that friend of his called Steve does.'

I have to admit that I felt a gleam of satisfaction.

'They're very bohemian parties,' said Frank.

'What does that mean?'

'They drink a lot of beer and lie on the floor.'

I said nothing.

55

Frank said: 'I hope you don't think I'm a prude. I suppose it's all rather silly.'

I said: 'Who invites Myrtle?'

'A journalist on one of the evening papers. Called Haxby, or something. They say he's in love with her.' Frank's voice warmed to me. 'I know he doesn't stand a chance.'

I turned a little. 'Look, Frank,' I said. 'I'll have a word with Trevor.' I felt that everyone was the worse for going to such parties. I would have liked to stop them all, forthwith.

'It won't be easy. He's very flattered at being invited.'

'I'm surprised he's so popular. I thought you and I were the only people who liked him.'

'He's allowed to take the family car and drive people home afterwards.'

'Don't worry, Frank.' I tried to make the remark sound conclusive. I wanted to get rid of him. I felt uneasy and alarmed. Bohemian parties. Haxby. Vistas opened before me, thoroughly unpleasing vistas. I was not thinking for a moment about Trevor.

Neither of us spoke. There was a cry from the field as the bowler and his mates appealed for l.b.w. It was disallowed. Frank glanced at his watch, and then gave his collar a stylish look by pulling the points against his chin.

I was too proud to look at my own watch. I glanced at the sky, which was brightening.

'I think this is the cue for my exit,' said Frank.

Myrtle had just come through the gates at the far end of the field. I went to meet her.

'What a dreadful day!' Myrtle's first remark seemed to set the tone for us completely. Her voice sounded hollow and distant. I kissed her on the cheek.

'Not as bad as all that. I'm glad to see you, darling.'

Myrtle glanced at me, and then looked away. Some woe appeared to be weighing her down, though she was clearly making a gallant effort to bear up. I noticed that she was wearing a new coat. It was made of black persian lamb and suited her well. I commented upon it, and she drew it closely round her.

'I'm so cold.'

I suggested that we should stroll a little. After all, what better way is there of getting warm than exercise? Myrtle gave me a look to indicate that my imagination was inconceivably earth-bound. We strolled, all the same.

I was disturbed. A month of separation had elapsed, but we were just in the same state as before. Our first meeting for a month—how I had been looking forward to it! Myrtle was displeased with me. Absence had not lived up to its reputation.

Myrtle's presence beside me raised my spirits a little. In spite of her displeasure, her cheeks glowed prettily and her eyes were bright. I began to try and raise her spirits, too. I began to think about plans for the evening.

Myrtle gave me a sudden flickering look. This time I sensed not so much reproach as will. She intended to do something.

'What's the matter?' I asked.

'Nothing.' Myrtle turned away.

I suppose I might have pressed her. Instead I glanced idly across the field. I saw Bolshaw coming towards us.

I was surprised. Bolshaw rarely showed any sign of being interested in doing games duty when it was his own turn, let alone mine.

'Do you want to meet Bolshaw?' I asked Myrtle.

'If you like.'

She was looking so elegant and attractive that I would have liked. It would have given me innocent pleasure to show her to Bolshaw. His wife was bossy rather than pretty.

Myrtle was undecided, I wavered, and Bolshaw went past us. Myrtle in spite of herself, glanced at him with furtive interest.

'You'd be amused by him,' I said.

'Would I?' She now glanced at me with furtive interest.

Encouraged, I began to tell her about Bolshaw's most recent activities in the staff-room. I do not profess to be a mimic, but I did my best, saving my greatest efforts for a remark that had caught my fancy.

'When I look round me at my colleagues,' Bolshaw had said, 'I can always tell the married men.' Pause, while he looked round at his colleagues, most of whom actually were married. 'They have that *tamed* look!'

I can only repeat that the remark had caught my fancy. It did not catch Myrtle's. She did not say anything: she did not need to.

In common language, the fat was in the fire.

I tried feebly to carry it off. I doubt if I should have redeemed myself if I had managed to achieve levitation. I did not achieve levitation.

Myrtle looked at her watch. She paused; and then she broke the news to me that she was not going to spend the evening with me.

I was astonished. I had sensed that she intended to do something, but not this.

'You didn't give me a chance to tell you,' she said.

'What are you going to do?'

'I've been invited to a party.'

I did not go on. I stared at Myrtle. Suddenly tears came into her eyes and disappeared again. I looked away, embarrassed and touched. I should have liked to put my arms round her. It was the moment to do it. But we were standing in the middle of the field with scores of boys watching.

Having broken the news to me, Myrtle seemed as if she could not bring herself to leave. I was certain that she did not really want to go to the party.

'Oh dear!' I sighed.

'What's the matter?' Myrtle was genuinely concerned.

'You've got to go.'

'Yes.' She drooped her head, and pulled her coat closely round her again.

Quietly I walked her to the gates. She hesitated.

'There's your tram,' I said.

Myrtle held out her hand and I took her fingers in mine. And then she went towards the tram. I watched it move clatteringly away. 'There goes sweetness and sadness,' I thought.

I speculated about the people, other than Haxby, who would be at the party. Saturday night—I did not doubt that it was one of the parties Trevor and Steve had started to go to. Frank had observed that they were not given by the sort of people I knew. That was true. Unhappily for me, the people who went to them got to know each other. Yet although I was jealous, I intended not to follow suit. I had several circles of friends in the town.

This was a circle that I meant to keep out of. It was not in my style.

Perhaps I ought to remind you that I had several circles of friends that were not necessarily shared by Myrtle and Tom. I had a circle of artistic friends made through my interest in writing: I had a circle of bourgeois friends made by letters of introduction from Robert: I had a couple of friends on the staff of the school: and in another town I had my family circle to which I was devoted. For the sake of describing myself completely, I should have to explore the lot. Let me give prompt assurance that I do not intend to do so.

Trollope discourses somewhere upon the difficulty that arises in novel-writing of disentangling men and women from their surroundings in order to isolate them as literary characters. A novel cannot contain everything. This novel is the story of Tom, Steve, Myrtle and me. In between us and the circles of friends I propose to leave out altogether, there are two people who played a part in our story whom I propose to leave half-in and half-out. Robert and Haxby.

Robert was a man of remarkable stature; to do him justice I should be inclined to give him the novel to himself, and that would make you feel he played a more important part than he actually did. On the other hand I never knew Haxby, so I cannot write about him: not being the kind of man who is impelled to establish intimate relations with his rival, I never tried to meet him. If you want to know more about Robert, ask me to write another novel: if you want to know more about Haxby, ask someone else.

Pondering on how little we can share of the sum of someone else's life, through not being present at the parties she goes to, for instance, I returned to my duty. I found Bolshaw walking in front of me again. This time he beckoned to me.

'Come and have a chat with me,' he said.

We walked back to the pavilion. Bolshaw dislodged a row of small boys who were sitting on a bench in front of it. He ordered one of them to bring his attaché case out of the pavilion. I waited: I did not know what we were to talk about.

The afternoon had brightened a little. The cold breeze had dropped: the clouds had thinned and there was a glowing patch where the sun was. Many of the boys had gone home, and those who still played on moved in a tired, desolate fashion. Yet the growing light brought the green of the grass and trees to life again. The air was warmer.

Bolshaw opened his attaché case and pulled out a notebook and a sheaf of papers. He handed them to me.

'It's my research,' he said.

I was astonished. I had heard him mention his research, but I did not really believe in its existence. I had imagined him much too lazy.

I recovered from my astonishment while Bolshaw was explaining to me his problem. It was a piece of theoretical research in astrophysics. I can tell you that it was of practical importance to anyone interested in certain of the spiral nebulae.

'Of course, I don't expect you to understand it,' Bolshaw said.

I suppressed the desire to say: 'Then why are you showing it me?' Bolshaw was making a friendly gesture. I thought of his job. Even if I was leaving the school at the end of the term I wanted to be offered his job. Since the headmaster was likely to do what Bolshaw recommended, Bolshaw's friendly gesture had extraordinary, almost spiritual significance for me. 'What's the next move?' I asked myself.

'I can simplify it for you,' he went on.

I listened. He did simplify it. Whatever his failings, he had considerable intellectual power and acuity. He drew the skeleton of his work beautifully.

'And now,' he said, 'this is how I'm attacking it.'

I listened again. I did not understand it, of course. It was not in my line—a long way from it. Yet the principle of his attack was ingenious, and I grasped it just well enough to see that if it came off he could make an elegant coup. I admired. But listening and admiring were all very well—I did not know what he was leading up to.

'Now,' said Bolshaw, pointing with his pencil at the sheet of paper on which he had been writing down headings as he went along: 'Now, I may run into a bit of trouble here.'

'Trouble?' I looked closely at the paper, though I do not know how that could have helped me. 'A bit of trouble?' I said rashly. 'You mean a bit of hard work!'

Bolshaw's expression did not change by a flicker. 'Do you think so? Do you think you could see your way through it?'

I had been neatly trapped. I had meant what I said. He needed somebody to try out a number of tedious calculations. I could do nothing but nod my head.

'That's interesting.' Bolshaw spoke with weight, and then looked at me suddenly. 'Would you like to join me in this work?'

I could have kicked myself. 'I'd be delighted,' I said, and mumbled, 'Honoured.'

Bolshaw then said: 'Would you care to take the papers with you now?'

'Oh!' I stared at him with a pained expression, largely at the thought of having to do the work. 'I'm afraid I'm not free at the moment.' I saw what seemed a clever way of getting out of it. 'I'm just completing the manuscript of a book.'

Bolshaw looked at me.

'I've just received some extremely interesting suggestions from a distinguished critic,' I said, lying for the sake of verisimilitude. Of course Miss X.Y. had not returned the manuscript.

Bolshaw nodded his head understandingly. I wondered if I had done right.

Bolshaw put his papers away with equanimity. I felt a slight exhilaration.

I changed the subject. 'By the way,' I said, 'what's the news of Simms?'

'He's very sensibly taking my advice,' said Bolshaw. 'He's putting in his resignation.'

Instead of saying, 'You'll be getting his job; what about me?' I kept my glance firmly fixed on the case containing the work he wanted me to do, and said in a solemn tone:

'I think it's the wisest course. For everyone.'

Bolshaw suddenly said:

'I intend to think about your position.'

It sounded like a remark from one of God's first conversations with Adam. I looked forward to the consequences just as hopefully. I went home, pondering them.

And then I rang up Myrtle again. I was told that she had gone out to a party. I felt gloomy and spent the evening alone.

CHAPTER II

NOT AS GOOD AS A PLAY

I bore Myrtle's new tactics with patience. The next time we spent an evening together there was no quarrel. To avoid it I took Myrtle to a cinema. We did not mention Haxby. On the other hand it was impossible to pretend that either of us was lighthearted. Myrtle's expression of unhappiness was deepening. Day by day I watched her sink into a bout of despair, and I concluded that it was my fault—had I not concluded that it was my fault, the looks Myrtle gave me would have rapidly concluded it for me.

The topic of conversation we avoided above all others was the project of going to America. Even a casual reference to Robert made Myrtle shy desperately. I cursed the tactlessness of Robert and Tom. I felt aggrieved, as one does after doing wrong and being discovered. I did not know what to do.

When you go to the theatre you see a number of characters caught in a dramatic situation. What happens next? They have a scene. From the scene springs action, such as somebody pooping off a revolver. And then everything is changed.

My life is different. Sometimes observant friends point out to me that I am actually in a dramatic situation. What happens next? I do not have a scene; or if I do, it is small and discouragingly undramatic. Practically no action arises. And nothing whatsoever is changed. My life is not as good as a play. Nothing like it.

All I did with my present situation was try and tide it over. I quail at the thought of tiding-over as a dramatic activity. Anybody could have done better than me. You, no doubt, could have offered me a dozen suggestions, all of them, as they were designed for someone else to follow, setting a high moral standard.

When Myrtle emerged from the deepest blackness of despair—after all, nobody could remain there indefinitely—I tried to comfort her. I gradually unfolded all my plans, including those for her. It produced no effect. She began to drink more. She began to go to parties very frequently. It was very soon clear that she had decided to see less of me.

I did not blame Myrtle. Had I been in her place I would have tried to do the same thing. Being in my own place I tried to prevent her. I knew what sort of parties she was going to: they were parties at which Haxby was present.

We now began to wrangle over going out with each other. She was never free at the times I suggested. Sometimes, usually on a Saturday night, she first arranged to meet me and then changed her mind: I called that rubbing it in a little too far. Here is a specimen of our conversation upon such an occasion, beginning with an irascible contribution by me.

'Where *are* you going?'

'Nowhere, darling.'

'Then why can't you meet me?'

'Because I've got to stay at home.'

'What *for?*'

'Some people are coming round to listen to gramophone records.'

'Gramophone records!' I knew what that meant. Haxby and his friends listened to gramophone records for hours on end.

'It was the only night they could. I'm sorry, darling.' Myrtle paused, and then said in half-hearted reassurance: 'I *am* going to see you tomorrow.'

'But what am I going to do tonight?' Saturday night.

Myrtle reminded me that my circle of bourgeois friends had invited me to a dance. She advised me to go.

'I said I wouldn't go because you wouldn't go with me.' Myrtle did not dance.

'They don't like me.' Myrtle's voice came over the telephone like that of a soul in purgatory.

'You don't try with them,' I said, thinking, 'Why on earth can't she get on with my friends?'

There was a pause.

'You can come round to my place if you like.' Her voice trailed off.

'To listen to gramophone records!'

We had reached an impasse.

I decided to follow Myrtle's advice. As a matter of fact I greatly enjoyed dancing. I also enjoyed listening to gramophone records.

Myrtle's behaviour, I repeat, was perfectly sensible. By seeing less of me she stood a chance of finding somebody else, or of making me jealous, or of both. Either way she could not lose.

The impasse being reached, my behaviour became perfecty odious.

Myrtle said: 'I've just bought some records of the Emperor.'

'Good heavens! Where did you get the money from?'

'I earned it, darling.'

'I shouldn't have thought you could afford it.'

'I shall be broke for weeks.'

'What a prospect!' Some vestigial restraint prevented me from saying that I should have to pay for all her entertainments, which would have been quite false.

'Hadn't you got a record of the Emperor?'

'Yes, but this is a better one. I shall sell the old one.'

'Who to?'

'Somebody will buy it. A girl at the office.'

'Oh.'

I paused, seeking new fields for odiousness.

'What else are you going to play in the cause of culture?'

'I haven't thought.'

'Beethoven followed by Duke Ellington?' This was a hit at Haxby's friends who followed the high-brow cult of respectfully admiring jazz. Myrtle had told me.

'What's wrong with that, darling? I thought you liked the Duke?'

I said with rage: 'The Duke, indeed!'

Myrtle did not say anything. I had started off feeling righteous. Now my righteousness took control of me.

'I suppose,' I said, 'you've had to buy lashings of drink?'

'What makes you think that?'

'You don't appear to be able to take your culture without it.'

Myrtle actually laughed, or at least it sounded like it on the telephone. And it could only have been me she was laughing at.

'If you want to make yourself ill, I suppose you can,' I went on.

'I shan't drink it all, darling.'

'Other people will!'

'But if they drink it, I can't, darling.'

'I meant they'll make themselves ill.' My voice rose. 'At your expense!' I cannot think which appalled me more, the drunkenness or the cost of it.

'You're wrong,' said Myrtle.

'I'm not. After the last of these parties you looked like death, yourself.'

There was a long pause. Out of the silence I heard Myrtle simply say:

'I feel like death now.'

My righteousness was removed in a single twitch. I saw myself without it. I had nothing to say. The fact of the matter is that my righteousness and my odiousness were the same thing, and they were both something else. Plain jealousy.

On the following afternoon the weather had changed to something more nearly like what is expected of April. The sun was shining. I lay on the sofa in my lodgings, reading the *Observer* and wishing I were at the cottage. From where I was lying I could see some lilacs in the next-door garden: the buds were unopened, and they rocked gently in the breeze. I closed my eyes—it was after lunch and I was waiting for Myrtle.

I forgot that Sir Nevile Henderson had been to Berlin to explain British plans before Parliament heard them: I forgot that Myrtle had probably been drinking herself silly with Haxby and others till two in the morning. I imagined piles of chestnut flowers, some of them tinged with pinky-brown now the leaves were unfolded; and ash trees in the lane, rustling with handsful of silver-green feathers. Red campions in the ditches: white and yellow stars all over the meadows: the hedges and the animals and the birds.

I was awakened by the landlady's niece showing in Myrtle. I

rolled back lazily. Myrtle looked ravishing. Her cheeks were lightly coloured and her eyes bright golden brown: from where I lay her long nose looked shorter. Over the back of the sofa I took hold of her hand, and drew her down to look into her face. She smiled at me with gaiety and innocence. Her despair had vanished. There was no sign round her eyes of a drunken debauch. Her breath was clean and fresh. I could hardly believe it. I rose to the occasion like a shot.

'Kiss me, sweet,' I said, and she did.

'You lazy old thing, you were asleep!'

'I was dreaming about being at the cottage, darling.'

'You would!' Her look indicated what she thought I had been dreaming about—thus showing that a girl who is earthy in its most beautiful sense can be totally wrong about a man.

'I was dreaming about flowers,' I said.

Myrtle shook her head, smirking at the thought of how I could lie. She came and sat beside me on the sofa.

I caressed her. In this mood I did not intend to mention Haxby. As I touched the bloom of her skin and felt the warmth of her flesh, my jealousy disappeared. She smiled at me encouragingly. I knew and she knew—she was almost telling me—that Haxby was nowhere.

'Darling,' I whispered into her ear.

This went on for a little while. There were sounds outside the door and Myrtle sat up attentively.

Anyone who has ever lived in lodgings, especially respectable lodgings in a semi-detached house on the outskirts of a provincial town, will know the obstacles to enjoying illicit love therein.

We both listened.

'It's all right,' I said.

Myrtle was much too indirect to nod, but somehow I knew she concurred. We had heard sounds that we recognised.

By a stroke of good fortune the obstacles in our case removed themselves on Sunday afternoon. It was good and rather peculiar fortune, such as is not commonly associated with a semi-detached house in a provincial town. I can only describe it truthfully. Every Sunday afternoon, at precisely two-thirty, the landlady's niece was visited by a very respectable-looking middle-aged man, who lived higher up the street. The landlady was sent out for a two-hour walk with the dog, no matter what the weather; whereupon the niece and the respectable-looking middle-aged man promptly went upstairs.

'He's as regular as clockwork,' Myrtle whispered.

She was right. It was a singular performance and it fascinated us constantly. The explanation that had come first to our minds was that he was a married man. Not at all. I had drawn the landlady into conversation about him, and had discovered that he was a bachelor living quietly with his mother and father.

'Why doesn't he marry her?' Myrtle would ask.

'*I* don't know.' I felt that Myrtle was insensitive, putting such a question to me. Nevertheless I felt exactly as she did. One can always have the conventional response about somebody else. Why on earth did not he marry her?

The man was never referred to, by the landlady or her niece, as anything but Mr Chinnock. He was well built and rather handsome, in a solid, meaty way. The suit he wore on Sundays was made of hairy tweed: across the waistcoat was stretched a heavy gold chain with a framed golden sovereign dangling from the middle. In manner he was slow, gentle and more than a little stately.

I suppose Myrtle and I ought to have assumed that the niece and Mr Chinnock went upstairs for a Sunday nap. Going by the sounds, we should have thought them restless sleepers. I am afraid we judged their conduct by our own—in fact, we used to speculate on how far their conduct differed from ours. Myrtle imagined the niece called him Mr Chinnock in all circumstances. 'Now *then*, Mr Chinnock!' Or '*That's* it, Mr Chinnock!' I was beguiled by such invention, though Myrtle pretended to have no idea what it was about. She smirked at the ceiling. The thought of somebody else, in the room above, on a Sunday afternoon— the mystery of it! What man can honestly say he does not know what I mean?

The Sunday afternoon I began describing passed rapidly and delightfully. Myrtle and I stood beside the french window, arms round each other's waist, looking down the garden at the grass and budding plants and the smoke rising from chimneys of little houses like our own.

At exactly four-thirty we heard the niece and Mr Chinnock

come downstairs. They went into the scullery.

'*I'll be loving you, always,*' sang the niece in a quavering soprano.

'*With a love that's true, always,*' sang Mr Chinnock in a full baritone.

'Phon and antiphon,' said I to Myrtle.

'Mr Chinnock's putting on the kettle,' said Myrtle to me.

All was right with the world.

It may seem strange that Myrtle and I could feel that all was right with our particular world. We ought not to have done. There was a dramatic situation; but nothing had happened. Myrtle had introduced Haxby into the situation. I was jealous of him. Still nothing had happened. Instead we were mysteriously enjoying an interlude in the same old way.

Only by strenuously searching my memory can I recall a novel incident. That night I broke my custom and visited Myrtle's home.

There was no one in the house and she took me up to her room. It was a pretty room, decorated by herself. With humility she had hung no drawings of her own on the walls. The colour scheme was warm and rosy. There were leopard-skin rugs, deep red curtains and looped muslin over the windows. A little vulgar? I suppose it was. Myrtle was a little vulgar, and I must say that I liked it. The room was evidence that she could let herself go, and that was what I liked. People who cannot let themselves go on occasion will not do for me.

I sat down on the bed. Myrtle sat beside me. I put my arm round her. The minutes passed.

Suddenly it felt as if she softly collapsed against me. I was utterly seduced. It felt as if she had melted into the marrow of my bones—my woman, my wife, my squaw. And then—

'That *tamed* look!'

'By Heaven!' I thought. 'What am I doing with a woman, a wife, a squaw?' I sprang off the bed. Tamed!

Myrtle looked up at me, startled. Our eyes met. There was a fleeting moment of clairvoyance. She read my thoughts.

'My foot's gone to sleep,' I said, and stamped it on the ground. Myrtle did not say anything. She knew, I was certain she knew, that I had in some way recoiled from her. I sensed the shock to her as clearly as I sensed the other shock to myself.

I stretched out my hand and stroked her hair. Myrtle remained still, with her head bent. She began making small pleats in the bed-cover.

'Is it getting better?' she said, lightly.

'Yes, I think so.'

I looked down at her. I wondered what had happened. She was apparently paying no attention to me. The air was warm and scented; the light glowed on her hair; she was breathing softly, all on her own. Suddenly I felt in touch with something inexplicable, far beyond the place where our thoughts revolved and our wills told us what to do. I felt in touch with something like instinct. And I knew how little, how hopelessly little our thoughts and wills affected us. At the root of everything we did was . . . the unknowable.

'No wonder,' I thought, as I remembered to give my foot a last shake, 'we go on doing such damned unknowable things.'

CHAPTER III

TWO DRAMATIC TURNS

The mysterious interlude with Myrtle lasted. There were no more incidents of recoil, no more intimations of anguish to come. Three weeks later I was spending Saturday at the cottage, happily looking forward to Myrtle's visit next day. From time to time I wondered where she was spending the night. I was not seriously worried: Haxby was nowhere, I thought.

It was a beautiful May afternoon. Our private lives were drifting inexorably towards dissolution, like the whole of Europe towards catastrophe: the weather was perfect. The sun was shining; cloud shadows passed slowly over the grass, dousing the glow of daisies and buttercups. I roamed over the meadows, half intending to pick some flowers to decorate the house, but really passing the time in aimless thought. I was wondering what to do about Miss X.Y. and my manuscript.

It was the time of year when the whole countryside seemed to be bursting into bloom. The hawthorn was not yet fully out, but the air was strong with the sweet light perfume of wild flowers. Under the hedges were campions and dead-nettles and bird's-eye, turning their petals to the sun: beside the brook there were some big late mayflowers: sprinkled over the slopes were a few cowslips, looking dusty and etiolated beside the brilliant buttercups. I plucked a bunch of wild forget-me-nots and greeny-gold wild mignonette. I thought it really was time Miss X.Y. did something about it. I was going to America.

I sat on top of a gate, filled with the poignance of leaving such a lovely country. Where could America show anything to compare with this for delicate, sweet-smelling lushness? Where else could the sky be so luminous and yet so gentle, the flowers so bright and yet so freshly perfumed? Where else could I feel was

70

home? The beauty of it shone over everything, like a shimmering haze—one could stretch out one's hand and seem to touch it with one's finger-tips. Where else, except over English meadows, does beauty leap so nearly to the verge of being palpable? Do not ask me. I do not know.

Idly I watched some lambs cropping the grass. They had grown to look more like sheep; but every now and then one of them reverted to earlier lambhood, tried to take a pull of mother's-milk, and got buffeted in the ribs for its pains. I wondered where their fathers were—over the hills and far away. Only the human male is tied to its female and its young, tied and tamed. Oh! to be a ram, I thought, and then be over the hills and far away: till it occurred to me that rams cannot write books or get drunk with their friends—and in fact only feel rammish for deplorably limited periods.

I climbed down from the gate. I had decided to write to Miss X.Y. If it irritated her, so much the worse. If she did not want to read my book the lapse of more weeks would not bring her round to it. I walked down to the cottage and wrote her a polite letter immediately: the letter could not be posted for another twenty-four hours, but I felt much better for having written it. I made myself some tea and lay in my armchair dreaming of Myrtle.

The door of the cottage was open, and a bluebottle buzzed in. Suddenly I realized that summer had come. The end of summer is signalised by the last rose: the beginning by the first bluebottle. My last summer in England, and here it was. I was roused from my dream. The beginning of the summer: the end of an epoch. The bluebottle buzzed round the room, and I felt very solitary. Restlessly I went and stood in the doorway.

To my surprise I saw Steve coming up the road, alone and on foot. He appeared to be swinging along steadily, judging by the way his dark head bobbed up and down above the hedgerows. When he came into the last stretch, and saw me watching, he began to drag his feet.

'I hope you don't mind me coming to see you, Joe.' He looked diffident and awkward. 'I came on a bus to the village. I won't stay long.'

'You're just in time for tea.'

'Good.' The diffident expression changed immediately to one of simple anticipation. Steve came into the cottage. 'I'll get the cup and saucer myself,' he mumbled. 'Please don't bother about me, Joe.'

I sat down. I did not intend to bother about him. 'Look after yourself,' I said in a tough, hearty tone.

Steve glanced at me, and then poured himself some tea. Then he helped himself to a single chocolate biscuit—a very unusual performance. I waited to see what he had come for. I felt sure from his manner that he was eluding Tom for the afternoon.

Steve drew a deep breath, and then said:

'Joe, I've just done something terrible.'

'Oh, what?'

'I suppose everybody will say it's terrible . . .' He glanced down.

'Come on—out with it, Steve.'

Steve looked at me with a solemn tragic expression. He said: 'I've volunteered for the Merchant Navy.'

'Good Lord!'

Though I did not exactly burst into laughter, I was not far from it. I said: 'Say it again!'

The reason I asked him to repeat it was that I did not for a moment believe him. By nature I am a credulous man, but with Steve I had been forced to see that credulity, admirable though it may be, rarely offers the best means of arriving at the truth.

'I've volunteered for the Merchant Navy.'

Steve's tone deferentially indicated that he thought it was rather captious of me to make him repeat a remark I must have already heard.

'You can't have,' I said. I suppose it was a cold, unfeeling way of receiving such a dramatic piece of news, such a solemn, tragic, false, dramatic piece of news.

'But I really have, Joe.' Steve put down his cup and saucer, and looked at me with an anxious, imploring expression. Although Steve was given to egregious lying, he never took umbrage at being accused of it.

I knew nothing about the normal age of entry to the Merchant Navy, but I recollected reading parliamentary discussions about the age at which young men might be called up for compulsory military training.

'You're too young,' I said, on the off chance of defeating him.

'I'm not, Joe. Not for the Merchant Navy.' Steve was too tactful to make any such remark as 'You don't seem to believe me'.

'Have you actually signed on?' I said.

'Of course.'

'When?'

'This morning.'

'Is the office open on Saturdays?'

'Yes. How could I have signed on if it weren't?'

Steve sometimes broke down if you asked him enough questions. This time I saw that he was patiently going to prove that he had done it. I paused. During the pause Steve helped himself to another chocolate biscuit. He munched it. Then he poured out another cup of tea. Naturally I had not varied a hair's breadth from my original disbelief. I was inclined to think he had *thought of* volunteering: there were some handsome recruiting posters plastered about the town. In fact I thought he might have visited the recruiting office and made some inquiries. I took another biscuit myself. I said:

'What made you decide on this powerful step?'

'I've got to do something.'

'Going to sea is a bit drastic, isn't it?'

'It's the only way of escaping, Joe.'

'Escaping from what?'

'Tom, I suppose.'

'Good Lord!'

Steve glanced at me seriously. I turned to face him.

'Do you really want to escape from Tom?' I said, in the shrewd, penetrating manner of a psychologist.

'I don't want to be an accountant!'

'Is the Merchant Navy the only alternative to accountancy?'

'You don't understand, Joe.'

'What?'

Steve looked at me. 'Imagine what it's like to be in my place.'

'For once, Steve, my imagination boggles.'

Steve had been on the point of assuming his suffering look, but a smile supervened.

'I've always wondered,' I said, 'exactly what caused technical boggling of the imagination. Now I know.'

'It's nothing to laugh about. It's terrible.' Steve stood up. He walked across to the doorway, picking up another biscuit as he went.

'I'm sorry, Steve.' I followed him, pushing the plate of biscuits out of my sight as I passed.

'Anyway, I've taken the step now, haven't I?'

'*You* know that, Steve.'

'You don't blame me, do you?'

'Blame you, Steve? Of course not.'

'Other people will.'

'Blaming is one of the favourite human occupations. People blame you whatever you do.'

'You are the first person I've told. I daren't tell my mother and father.'

'I think,' I said, 'you can expect Tom to do that.'

'Joe!'

We strolled across the road and leaned against a gate, looking idly at the cottage.

'I had to do it, Joe. I can't go on being an accountant.' Steve looked at me. 'It's the arithmetic. It's torment. And Tom wants me to go round to his house for a lesson three evenings a week.' His voice rose. 'Three evenings a week!'

'That certainly is torment,' I agreed, disloyally to Tom.

Steve paused. 'Anyway, it will be over now.' He pondered. 'I won't have to do any arithmetic in the Merchant Navy, will I?'

'Not much.' I grinned. 'I guess you've already received enough training for the Merchant Navy in arithmetic. As in certain other basic subjects, too.'

An amused flicker appeared in Steve's eye, in spite of his agonised expression: it was merely momentary. He said:

'You don't understand, Joe.'

'What?'

Steve suddenly spoke with force. 'I want to sleep with women.'

'You get that as well in the Merchant Navy. While you're in port.'

'I mean it seriously.'

I looked away. 'I did realise that.' There was a long silence

74

broken only by the occasional chirping and flutter of birds in the hedge. Steve stirred—I imagined he must be turning to look at me more closely as he spoke.

'Do you think it's silly of me? I mean, I'm only seventeen.'

'I don't think it's silly at all, Steve. No more than the things we all do are silly.'

'I want to get to know some girls.'

I nodded my head.

'I suppose you think I'm being stupid and conventional, Joe.'

I could not help smiling. 'No, Steve.'

'Sometimes I want to be just ordinary, Joe. Terribly ordinary.'

'I think you'll find it terribly tame.'

'I suppose I would. That's the trouble.'

'Don't let that put you off, Steve!'

'It doesn't. I want to start going out with girls, even if it is tame.'

This was not what I meant, but I did not propose to argue.

'I wish Tom would realise this,' Steve said.

It seemed to me that if Tom was trying to make Steve go round to his house three evenings a week he must have a pretty shrewd idea.

'I don't seem to be able to talk to him about it, Joe.'

I foresaw the day when he would, but held my tongue.

Steve turned and leaned his chest against the gate, looking up the field. The movement attracted the attention of some bullocks, who began to advance under the impression that we were going to feed them. Steve picked up a boulder and rolled it towards them.

'It's a relief to have told someone about it.'

I did not know whether he meant the relief of having told me about his signing-on for the Merchant Navy, which was fantasy, or of having told me about his adolescent woes, which were real. It is possible to get a deep relief from confessing something that is untrue: Steve got it frequently.

I said: 'These things work themselves out, you know.' I did not know what it meant, but I had learnt that meaningless remarks of this kind give a bit of comfort.

Steve said: 'I suppose I ought to be going back. Is there a bus?' He gave me a helpless look.

'There's a timetable on the desk. You know where it is.'

Steve slouched across the road and disappeared into the cottage. I began to meditate, on Steve and Tom, on Myrtle and me; and on the difficulty, the transience, the poignance of all human relationships.

I was roused from my meditation by the arrival of Tom's car. As an arrival it was sudden, noisy, unexpected and menacing.

'Have you seen Steve?'

'Yes. He's here.'

'Where?'

'In the cottage.'

Tom got out of the car. I did not move from where I was leaning against the gate. There were signs of passion in his face, a slight goggling of the eyes.

'I thought I'd find him here.'

I was puzzled. The cottage seemed an odd place for Tom to look for Steve—I began to wonder if it might have been pre-arranged.

Tom came and stood beside me, making an effort to look unconcerned. He straightened his tie, which was wine-coloured—a mistake, in my opinion, since it enhanced the contrast between the gingery redness of his hair and the purplish redness of his face.

'It's been a beautiful day.' Tom glanced at the sky, which was melting into the tender shades of twilight; at the hedgerows, leafily stirring in the evening breeze. Glanced is the word for it: before I could expatiate on the charms of the flora, Tom said:

'Shall we go indoors?'

As if to convince me that he was not making a beeline for indoors to discover what Steve was doing, Tom said in a weighty, pompous tone:

'I have an announcement to make.'

We went into the cottage. Tom stared at Steve. Steve fluttered the pages of the bus timetable furtively.

Tom sat down. We all sat down.

'I have some news for both of you,' said Tom. 'I've had a most satisfactory talk with our senior partner this lunch-time, about my fellowship of the I.C.A. That's all settled—'

'Good,' I interrupted, thinking this was the announcement.

'Consequently,' Tom went on, 'I've decided my date of departure for the U.S.A. I've just ordered my tickets. I leave this country on June 15th.'

Steve and I were completely silent, I with surprise and Steve with shock. Tom had his eyes fixed on Steve.

It was useless to pretend the news had not induced a high state of tension, but I said, 'Well, well,' in a light easy tone, hoping to reduce it thereby.

Steve had his eyes fixed on the ground. Tom looked strong and determined.

'It means a break,' Tom said, 'but it's got to be done. Thank God we shall do it in time!' He looked at me. 'Robert says we must decide when you're to go.'

I nodded. I must say that I felt a pang. I thought Tom's tone was bullying. It is all very well to agree on the analysis of a situation; but to act upon it does not follow so readily for every man. Tom sensed my failing enthusiasm.

'It would be most unwise to delay it any longer.'

'I agree.'

My failing enthusiasm sprang from reluctance to leave England, not from lack of faith in our historical prophecy. I had great faith in our historical prophecy, based as it was on the word of Robert.

Tom and I exchanged our interpretations of the latest European events. I will not record them because they will make you think us feebler prophets than we really were—this may be called omission of true facts in the cause of art. Anyway, I think our motives were far from contemptible. Sympathy, I beg, for those who were wrong before the event instead of right after it.

The exchange of interpretations was brief, because Tom's interest was focused entirely on Steve's reaction. I felt embarrassed. It seemed to me the odds were now at least ten to one on Steve's producing his story about the Merchant Navy. There was a peculiar silence. I said:

'Would you like some sherry?'

Tom accepted, with a strained over-polite smile. Steve shrugged his shoulders. While I was taking the bottle out of the cupboard, Tom looked at my letters; that is, he examined the

77

envelopes on my desk, in the cause of not flinching from the attempt to understand human nature. I had taken the precaution of sealing them.

'I see you've written to Miss X.Y.' He paused. 'Of course, if it had been me I should have gone up to London and seen her, weeks ago.'

I poured out the glasses of sherry, and we raised them to our lips. Tom and I drank ours. Steve, instead of drinking, said:

'Tom, I've volunteered for the Merchant Navy.'

The result was devastating. Either from the sherry going down the wrong way or from pure rage, Tom's face turned purple.

'What!' he shouted, in a great splutter.

He stood up. 'You silly little fool!' He went across to Steve, and Steve looked frightened as if he thought Tom were going to beat him. Steve was the taller but Tom easily the stronger. 'Tell me exactly what you've done!'

'I've volunteered for the Merchant Navy.'

'The details! I want the details!' shouted Tom.

I say that Steve looked frightened: he did—and yet I got a distinct impression that at the same time he was enjoying himself.

'When? Where?' Tom was asking him.

And Steve was replying, in spite of his supposed fright, in an easy, provocative manner. His small eyes were lazy and bright. Suddenly I felt sorry for Tom, who was beside himself with passion. I should have felt sorrier still for Tom if I had thought there was a word of truth in what Steve was saying.

'It's got to be stopped, immediately,' Tom said.

'It can't, Tom,' said Steve.

'I'll *buy* you out!' shouted Tom.

Steve was taken aback. His signing-on had now become so real to him, from the inflating power of Tom's belief in it, that he was taking Tom as seriously as Tom was taking him.

'You're under age,' Tom repeated. 'I'll buy you out!'

'But the money?' said Steve, in a tone of anguish.

Tom looked round him. 'If we go straight away and withdraw your signature it may not be too late.'

I could see that he knew no more about the legal side of it than I did. He took hold of Steve's arm.

'Now?' said Steve incredulously.

'Of course.'

'But I don't want to.'

'Don't you see what it means, you little fool!' Tom glared at him, and explained slowly, like a corporal explaining slowly to a private. 'If there isn't a war I shall go to America. And if there is a war you'll be at sea. In either case we shall be separated for ever!'

Steve displayed a mixture of superficial discomfort and basic equanimity.

'For ever!' Tom shouted.

I thought, 'Poor old Tom.' I saw this scene going on for a long time: Steve was lying back in his chair, and Tom was tireless.

They paused, so I intervened in a reasonable tone.

'It probably could be stopped if you acted rapidly.' Tom could never resist action, and I saw it as a means of getting them out of the house and back to the town.

'Exactly,' said Tom, seizing Steve's arm, and hauling him up.

'Not now, Tom,' said Steve. 'It's too late tonight. The office will be closed. We can't go now. I don't want to.'

'Come on!'

Steve had been pulled out of his chair. 'Let me drink my sherry first,' he cried.

Tom paid no heed. Steve was torn away from his sherry. I thought 'You worthless boy, that serves you right.' Tom dragged him into the car, and pressed the self-starter.

There was a mysterious clanking noise under the car and then silence.

The car would not start.

Tom tried again and again. He got out and lifted up the bonnet. Then he got back again. There were a few more sporadic noises, and then silence of striking permanence. Steve sat, hunched up and silent, inside the car. Tom, powerful and purple, engaged in action, such as cranking the engine and stalking to and fro. I did nothing: I have occasionally felt like a professional scientist but never like a motor mechanic.

Tom muttered some kind of explanation. 'She won't start.'

And then the same thought struck both of us. 'We shall have to stay the night,' Tom said, in a masterful tone.

I was about to say there was another bus, and then remembered the wretched man had only till June 15th—I never doubted that Tom would leave for ever on June 15th. 'Who am I,' I asked myself, 'to stop him getting the most out of his last month, however singular that most may be?' I was not expecting Myrtle till the following afternoon.

'All right,' I said. 'I was going over to the pub later on.'

Tom nodded. 'We'll go for a stroll in the meantime.' He turned to the car: 'Now, Steve, you'd better get your coat.'

Reluctantly Steve got out of the car, went into the cottage, and emerged with his coat. Tom's eyes followed him. Then Tom and he walked away up the lane. I heard Tom's voice rising in power as it moved into the distance. The scene was going on.

I went indoors, and poured myself another glass of sherry. And I noticed that Steve's glass was empty—in the few seconds he had spent fetching his coat Steve had swigged off his sherry. I could not help smiling.

CHAPTER IV

NIGHT ON THE PARK

I was invited to have supper with Bolshaw and his wife at their home. I had taken care to meet Myrtle first of all. The interlude was over. Our situation had sprung up again: this time it was worse.

Myrtle lived in a street that debouched on the park. I was just entering it—I was a little late—when I met her, apparently already on her way to wherever she was seeing fit to go.

It was a light evening, and I could see from a long way off that she was in a state of abysmal depression. She had begun to look sadder and sadder during the last days. I suppose I was unfeeling and detached: I thought of it as her 'I'll-never-smile-again' expression. Really, she overdid it. I felt genuinely upset and, such was the weakness of my nature, faintly irritated by remorse. I kissed her warmly on the cheek.

'I'm sorry I'm late, darling.' I had a perfectly satisfactory excuse.

'It's all right,' she said, in a distant tone.

'Where are you going?'

Myrtle put her hand to her forehead. 'My dressmaker's.'

'Oh,' I said helpfully, 'that's nice.'

Myrtle looked at me. I knew it was not nice at all. I put my arm round her waist—when anyone looks woebegone I cannot help trying to cheer them up.

'I'm sorry you're feeling so low, darling.'

I suppose Myrtle thought the remark became me ill when my conduct was at the root of her depression.

'Have you been sleeping badly?'

Myrtle nodded her head.

'Nightmares?'

Myrtle nodded again. She roused herself sufficiently to make a tragic revelation. 'I dream that I'm *two people*.'

Satan entered into me. 'Two?' I said. 'There's no cause for alarm till it gets to ten.'

Cheering people up may be good-natured: it appears that making jokes is sadistic. All I can say is that if somebody had said it to me I should have been amused.

We were at the top of the street. Tramcars passed between us and the park. Beyond the railings we could see couples lying under the trees, and little boys playing cricket. I observed two youths from the school approaching us on bicycles: I recognized them by their blazers. They turned out to be Benny and his younger brother. They took off their caps very politely; and rode on without staring, though they missed no detail of Myrtle's appearance.

I may say that despite Myrtle's obvious misery she was beautifully dressed. I gave her great credit for that. She was wearing a new summer frock, made of material prettily printed in a pattern of greens and bright yellow and covered all over with handwriting. Her shoes were American. Her hair was dressed in the latest style.

'That's Benny,' I said encouragingly. 'I've told you about him. Do you remember?'

'I didn't know he was so old.'

I had frequently told her he was nineteen.

'He looks quite well-behaved,' she went on, apparently remembering at least that I had told her definitely that he was not well-behaved.

'He's a menace,' I said, with conviction. 'Some day one of Benny's tricks will get him thrown out. And me too, probably. I shall heave a great sigh of relief when he leaves.'

Myrtle had ceased to listen: it made me feel as if I were babbling.

I touched the material of her dress. 'Where did this come from?'

She told me without interest.

I kept my finger inside her sleeve, so that it touched her flesh. 'Darling,' I said, looking at her face.

Myrtle looked back at me. For a moment I thought she was going to weep.

'Darling,' I said, 'I do wish I could think of something to say.'

Myrtle made a perceptible effort to smile, but failed.

I wanted to take her into my arms and comfort her. The trouble was that I could only have comforted her by taking her into a registry office.

I realised that I was now late for my next appointment. Myrtle showed no signs of moving. More trams passed with a cheerful clang: I ought to have been on one of them. At last I said: 'I must go now, darling.'

Myrtle looked down. I took hold of her hand, and held on to it tenderly. There was something else I had to say before I could go.

'Are you coming out to the cottage this week-end?'

Myrtle did not reply.

I felt embarrassed, ashamed, apprehensive and determined.

'Are you, darling?'

Myrtle looked at me, absolutely blank-faced: 'Do you want me to?'

'Of course.' There was a pause. 'Will you?' I held her fingers tighter.

Myrtle made the faintest possible gesture that could be recognised as assent.

I kissed her and we parted. I took a tram down to the station and there changed to a bus. Throughout the journey my thoughts turned round and round. Why? how? and why? again. I knew by experience that she suffered this mysterious ebb and flow of mood, but I felt slightly reassured if I could link it with some external event. I had told her that Tom was due to leave England on June 15th. No event seemed too irrelevant for me to strive fatuously to make it relevant. I had not told her about Steve's signing-on for the Merchant Navy, because he never had signed-on: Tom found that out by a dramatic visit to the recruiting office. I tried to think what precisely I had said or done.

My efforts led me nowhere, and I joined the evening's entertainment in a mildly abstracted fashion.

Just as I was about to leave Bolshaw's house there was a telephone call for me. I knew what it was going to be. Myrtle wanted me to meet her again, on my way home.

Myrtle met me at the station. It was after eleven o'clock. She was already standing there, waiting, when I arrived. She had been home for a coat to put over her summer frock.

'What is it, darling?' I said.

By the light of the street lamps I could see faint signs of animation in her face.

'I wanted to see you again.'

I stared at her anxiously. Somehow I had wanted to see her as well. It felt inevitable, as if we had been drawn together. I did not speak.

We stood on the edge of the pavement, facing each other. Myrtle said:

'I wanted to say I was sorry for being rude to you earlier this evening.'

I felt a sudden stab of pain as I recognised the words—the apology of one who is in love to one who is loved. How well I recognised it! You apologise to the one who ought to apologise to you—to such straits does love reduce dignity and common sense.

The one who is loved invariably behaves badly, and I was no exception. I thought, 'Oh God! She's in love with me.'

'That's all right, darling,' I said. Fortunately I did not utter the most cruel remark the loved one can utter in these circumstances—'Forget it!' The result was more or less the same.

Myrtle drew away from me. It was not all right.

I put my arm round her waist, and began to lead her along the road.

'I realised you weren't feeling well, darling,' I said.

'Well?'

'It's a sort of malaise you're having. Being touchy is part of it.'

'Is it?' There was a faint edge to her voice.

I said comfortably: 'I wasn't perturbed.'

'Then you ought to have been!'

I was alarmed. Purposely I pretended not to have caught on. 'It wouldn't do for us both to be touchy at the same time, or else . . .'

'Yes,' Myrtle breathed. 'Or else? . . .'

'It just wouldn't,' I said. 'Clearly.'

We were silent for a while.

Myrtle was walking slowly. I suppose she must have felt me tending to go faster: I found it hard to get along at Myrtle's pace.

'Do you want to go home?' she said.

'No. What makes you think that?'

'It's getting late.' A tram lumbered past us, dimly lit and filled with people who had been to the cinemas. 'You mustn't miss your last tram.'

I said I was going to take her home before I left her.

Myrtle said: 'I suppose they were angry when I rang you up tonight.'

'Angry,' I said, in astonishment. 'Why should they be? I think Bolshaw thought you must be slightly eccentric, that's all.'

'Were you angry?'

'Not at all. I'm glad you rang.'

'Why?'

'I don't know. I think I wanted to see you again, because . . .'

'Because of what?'

'I don't know, darling.' I felt embarrassed. 'Because of the way we parted.'

'What was wrong with that? I thought you seemed satisfied.'

'Really!'

I stopped. Myrtle stopped and we stared at each other. We were quite near the end of her street, but there was no street lamp and we could not see each other very well.

'What's the matter?' said Myrtle.

'You say I seemed satisfied. You can't have any idea, darling. How could I have been satisfied?'

'I said I would see you at the week-end.'

'I thought you didn't want to come.'

Myrtle burst out with great emotion:

'It didn't seem to matter to you if I didn't!'

'Of course it does.'

'I seem to see less and less of you!'

I did not know what to say. She had seen me at the cottage just as often.

'Oh, I don't know,' Myrtle went on, passionately. 'Here we are

85

now . . . Why is it like this, darling? You go out to see your friends and I spend the evening with my dressmaker.' She looked at me. 'I spend hours and hours with people I don't really want to be with!'

People she did not want to be with—Haxby, she must be including Haxby.

'Darling . . .' I began.

'It's true. You're always somewhere else.'

'It isn't true. I have to go and see other people sometimes.' I was on the point of saying 'You could always come with me if you would' but it seemed cruel: also it was not quite true. Even had she felt at ease with all my friends, I should have wanted to see them alone sometimes.

We then began a futile argument about how often I ought to spend evenings with different friends and acquaintances. Myrtle was facing the road, and as a tram swayed past the light crossed her face. I was relieved to see no tears.

'Since Easter I seem to have seen absolutely nothing of you.'

I enumerated meetings missed through accidents chiefly on her part. I brought up the Saturday afternoon at the games field when she had dropped me. My list was impressive—impressive as a list of facts, but not as the truth.

'And it doesn't seem to matter to you,' Myrtle said, as if she had not heard.

There was a pause. We were still standing in the same place. People were passing us. I said:

'Let's go on the park!'

I knew that it was a useless thing to say, that the scene could only go on and produce no result.

We walked through the gates, and turned off along a narrow path beside some shrubbery, disturbing a boy and girl who were locked in each other's arms against the railings. They seemed curiously remote from us, as if love-making were of no interest.

We resumed our argument about how I should dispose of my evenings.

At last we came to a seat. Arid though the argument was, we could not leave it. Anyone who has ever been involved in this kind of scene will recall the peculiar boredom of it, the peculiar boredom that ties both of you together, like twine round a parcel.

There were long periods between each remark, enormously long. For me they were often spent in reframing my next remark, trying to take off the edge of my words, trying to transmute them into something of whose hardness I should be less ashamed afterwards—I could not forget that Myrtle was a tender girl and so very young. On the other hand some of the periods were spent in thinking how late it was; and others in watching car-headlamps moving along the main road—something obscured the lower part of them, a palisading, possibly. It is hard to keep one's concentration up to concert pitch in this sort of scene.

As a minor counter-attack I put forward the propostion that I never seemed to go anywhere myself nowadays. If I was not seeing Myrtle it was not because I was seeing someone else. Naturally this did not please: second only to my offence of seeing other friends was my offence of spending evenings alone.

At last, in desperation, I gave the argument a heave which overturned it on to a deeper plane. I said gently:

'Aren't we getting into this mess because I'm going to America and we shall be separated?'

Myrtle softened a little. 'Well, it is really. . . .'

'What can we do, darling? I shall have to go.'

Myrtle's emotion broke out again. 'You don't seem to mind! You want to go!'

'I don't want to go.'

'You said you did.'

'There are some things I want to do most. To do them I shall have to get out.'

'But that needn't mean being separated. That's what I don't see. You never mention me going!'

I was astounded. After all the time I had spent persuading her to think about taking a job in America, it seemed incredible. She had never listened to me. Her going to America meant only one thing—being married to me. She was unable to listen if I talked of anything else.

Hastily I began to invent reasons why she could not go to

America in a state of dependence on me. I should have no money, no job.

'I don't see that it matters,' said Myrtle. 'If you were fond of somebody you'd want them to be there all the time.'

'But not in those circumstances!'

'Why not?' said Myrtle, inexorably, there being a good deal in what she said. 'I should have thought it meant assured happiness.'

'Assured happiness!'

'And you could *work!*'

Heaven help me! I thought. By work she must mean school-teaching. I realised what I had always suspected—that not for a moment did she take my writing seriously. Assured happiness!

'You'd be settled,' said Myrtle, in a tone that was not the tone of a tender girl or a very young one either.

'Tamed!' said I, in an anguished voice. I saw myself settled, with someone I was fond of there all the time. There all the time, mark you! How could I write books about people? How could I go out and discover what they were like? How could I support my curiosity about them? How could I watch what they were doing, have long intimate talks with them—and, if it came to that, get into bed with some of them? How indeed?

'What's wrong with being settled?' Myrtle ignored my interjection. 'Everybody else is.'

I fell straight into the trap.

'I'm not like everybody else!'

'But you could be!' Myrtle went on. 'If only you'd—if only you'd . . .' She gave the sentence up, but not the meaning. The latter was only too clear to me.

Myrtle could not utter the word 'marry'. In the whole conversation neither of us had used it. I could not bring myself to utter it, as a child will not utter the name of something it does not want to happen. And I seemed to have hypnotised Myrtle into doing the same thing.

Myrtle was not entirely wrong about me: that was the trouble. Somewhere she touched in me a vestigial romantic belief that if I were abandonedly in love I should want her to be there all the time. For a moment I sensed what her idea of permanence could mean, what it could mean to me if I were somebody else.

'We can't go on talking like this, darling.' I shook my head. 'There is something deeper than these tedious mechanical reasons. I just can't have anyone about me. Somehow I do know that I want'—I searched for a phrase— 'I want to go on alone.'

It was an unusual phrase, that must have made it sound as if I were aiming at the North Pole. Myrtle said nothing.

'I've always felt like that, darling,' I said.

'Yes,' said Myrtle. 'You were careful to tell me that at the beginning.'

'Didn't you think I meant it?'

'Yes. Then.'

'Why not now?'

'It was different. We weren't so fond of each other then.'

'That doesn't alter it. Darling,' I said, 'my personality's stuck. It can't be changed.'

Myrtle had stopped listening, and I said under my breath, 'Even under the regenerating influence of a woman!'

We were silent. I felt cold. It was a dark night, with a clouded sky—no wind, yet coldish. It must have been the first time I had ever noticed the cold before Myrtle did. I took hold of her hand, and helped her up from the seat. We began to walk. Myrtle began to walk away from the direction of her home, but I gradually steered her round.

'What are we to do?'

Myrtle's voice was soft and melancholy, and she looked at the sky. Yet there was a reasonable note in it, as if she were facing the problem realistically. Still looking away, she repeated it. We were sufficiently in tune for me to know that she was raising the question of whether we should part.

I shrank from it.

'What do you think we ought to do?' I asked.

I heard her draw in her breath sharply. She knew it was not really a question.

I said: 'Darling, do you think I ought—do you think it would be better if I started keeping out of the way?'

'We couldn't not see each other!' Her voice was louder and more passionate. I thought this affair would have to end.

'I ought not to have let this happen,' I said.

'I don't see that we *shall* have to!' said Myrtle, cutting into my maunderings.

'But what else?' I began a long speech. We were standing at a cross-roads, and a tram-repair lorry came up, with a violent clatter of loose tools and implements. We were in the middle of the night.

Myrtle said something.

'What did you say?'

'Only more protestations.'

We were both silent, worn out. Aimlessly we watched two young policemen in mackintoshes shut themselves up in their little police telephone-box: a small red light flashed on the top of it.

'I think you'll have to think of it like that,' I said.

'Well, I can't . . . And I don't suppose I ever shall!'

We moved to go home. Nothing was decided. We stopped and looked at each other. When were we to meet again? I could not bring myself to ask her.

'Do you want me to come on Sunday?' Myrtle asked gently.

'Yes. But darling, I can't ask you like that. Not now. . . .'

We were holding each other's fingers.

At last I mumbled: 'I shall be there. . . .'

'Then of course I shall come.'

We whispered good night.

I walked home by the road along which I had been used to cycle so joyously on Sunday nights. I felt utterly empty. I wondered what Myrtle thought was the outcome of our scene. I asked myself how much good it had done. I thought I saw now that an end of it all was appointed for us. I could have wept.

CHAPTER V

IN DISGRACE

At this point I began to look forward much less equivocally to my departure for the U.S.A.

For the time being I looked secure in my pedagogue's niche. Ever since our talk at the games field, Bolshaw and I had been on good terms; so I judged the headmaster was hearing less about my irresponsibility, laziness and other forms of moral delinquency. All the same, I thought with unrestrained pleasure about giving in my notice at the end of the term. It would be a real coup to walk out when I was obviously in no danger of being pushed out.

One fine Monday morning I sat in the playground, counting the accumulation of worries that rose from my enforced vocation. There was a row of ancient lime trees growing up through the asphalt, and I used to let the sixth form boys sit under them to work during the summer term. It was pleasant: the sun shone down; girls in summer frocks walked briskly past the railings; scarlet buses ran to and fro.

While waiting for Frank and the others to come from prayers I was making a list of physics questions likely to be set in the coming Higher School Certificate examination. I was very adept at what the boys called 'spotting'. My skill was widely recognised, and the boys had suggested, with the intention of helping me on my way, that instead of dispensing my information free to a whole form I should sell it to them individually.

Suddenly I stared at my divining-chart. 'Why am I working on this? Why am I not writing a masterpiece?' The answer was that I had written a masterpiece; but my letter to Miss X.Y. had procured only the information that she was touring in the Balkans. 'Why am I working on this chart?' No answer, except that it fell within the scope of duties I had to perform in order to buy myself food and lodging.

From the building came the sound of the boys at their devotions. The organ chimed out and they began to sing 'Blest are the pure in heart'. Strangely enough, in spite of all they did, many of them managed to remain pure in heart. From plain observation I decided that superficially innocent they were not: yet it was quite easy to see them as surprisingly free from contamination. Pureness of heart is an odd thing, rarely comprehended by the righteous. I could write a lot more about it.

Frank came out to me, with a firm, graceful tread.

'I wanted to see you before the others come.' I saw him looking diffidently along his nose. 'Have you heard what happened on Saturday night? Trevor was run in for dangerous driving.'

Now you see the sort of worries that rose from my enforced vocation.

Frank shook his head lugubriously. 'It's a sod, isn't it?'

'What'll happen to him?'

'He'll probably get his licence endorsed.'

'The rows there'll be!'

Frank and I stared at each other.

'Hello!' Trevor had quietly joined us. The sun lit up his golden hair. Sometimes his small pale face looked debauched, sometimes angelic. This morning, when it would have been helpful to look angelic, it looked irritatingly debauched. 'I suppose you've heard?' he said, spinning out the last words with a nasal emphasis.

'Were you drunk?' I said.

'I wish I had been. I didn't do anything wrong. I think the cop was just bored. He said I jumped the traffic-light at the corner of Park Road.'

'Were there any witnesses?'

'Yes. Another cop coming off the park. One of those officious cops that goes round preventing people from copulating on the grass.'

'For Pete's sake!' Frank seized him by the back of the neck to shake him.

'Were you alone?'

'No. I'd got a girl.' Trevor languidly pushed back the hair that had fallen when Frank shook him, but there was an unmistakable look of bravado and provocative triumph in his face.

I had always known we should have trouble with Trevor.

'I didn't even jump the traffic-light.'

Frank interrupted. 'Look out! Here comes Benny and Fred.'

With their faces shining like the bright sky, the other pair joined us. Fred was soppily singing, to the tune of 'Blest are the pure in heart', some words he was making up as he went along. 'I do not want to work . . . pom, pom . . . I'd rather sit and dream . . .' He stopped singing: 'About luv. . . .'

Benny jumped behind my chair. 'What are you doing, sir? Making us a list of questions?' He breathed heavily down the back of my neck.

'I'm goin' to make a list,' said Fred, 'of questions we *won't* get. And then I won't 'ave to learn them.'

I ought to say they had all passed the examination the previous year and pretended they were going to fail it this.

Frank and Trevor had taken out their pocket-combs and were combing their hair. Benny and Fred made some show of composing themselves, since they were on view to the public. I began to collect the written work they had done over the week-end.

Out of the corner of my eye I saw Bolshaw crossing the yard. He beckoned to me. I had to go.

I followed Bolshaw into the laboratory. His form of silent oafs looked up and then down again. Bolshaw's forms spent the whole of the summer term in silent revision for the examinations.

From Bolshaw's serious statesman-like expression I deduced that he had some project in hand. I was afraid he might be going to try and lure me into his research again. He sat down at his desk with a heavy shambling movement. It occurred to me that he was looking older; his eyes looked faintly bleary, and his false teeth a trifle greener—though why false teeth turning green should be a sign of age I did not know.

'I've been working!' Bolshaw blew through his whiskers. 'I enjoy it.'

I concealed my astonishment.

Bolshaw opened his case and pulled out the folder containing some of his research papers. 'I should like you to have a look at this.'

I realised that nothing could stop him. He repeated his earlier proposition. He held up his hand as if he were going to give me his blessing.

'I think the time has come,' he said.

The time had indeed come. Simms could not delay his retirement beyond the end of the term. In our present stable condition of amity, Bolshaw was bound to nominate me as his own successor.

My heart sank at the prospect of having to do his computations for him. Till suddenly it occurred to me that I could take away the papers, so satisfying him, and not do the computations, so satisfying myself.

My inspiration was not, of course, an original one. Miss X.Y. had had it long before me, and hosts of people before her. I could have kicked myself for not having accepted in the first instance. To give the maximum satisfaction one should always accept people's papers, whether one ever intends to read them or not.

As I assented I gave Bolshaw a look of restrained enthusiasm. He was too shrewd for me to risk anything really effusive.

Bolshaw appeared to be satisfied. 'I always admire a man,' he said, with characteristic impartiality, 'who recognises when the time has come.'

I did not feel called upon to reply.

'I wish our headmaster,' he went on, 'gave me cause for this type of admiration.' Every word echoed down the room.

'It's a pity,' said Bolshaw, 'that I'm not the headmaster. A genuine pity.' He blew through his whiskers again. 'What?'

It was more than I could do to keep any trace of glimmer out of my eye. As he noticed it an answering glimmer came into his eye as well. I would not have thought him capable of it. I suddenly saw a clever, sensitive man behind this ludicrous façade. There was a moment of *rapport*. I thought 'Bolshaw's not a bad chap,' and I thought he was thinking the same about me.

I went back to my pupils. I found Trevor calculating quietly, like an angel-child, with his slide rule; and Benny absorbed in

94

tracing out a simple wireless circuit. Perhaps I was wrong to let other people's doings oppress me. It was highly satisfactory to be secure in my job. After all, I had got to consider the eventuality of my trip to America not coming off.

A few days later I was teaching a form of junior boys in the laboratory. I had them at the end of the afternoon for two consecutive periods, in which they were supposed to do experiments. They were tired. So was I. In the last two periods of the afternoon everybody was slack, and on this occasion the weather was warm and humid and oppressive. Across the playground I could see shapeless grey clouds, apparently hanging round the tops of the lime trees: I felt as if they were hanging round the top of my head as well.

I decided to ease my state by taking a leaf out of Bolshaw's book. Instead of trying to teach them anything, I commanded the boys to open their note-books and do silent revision for the examinations. Then I slumped down into my chair.

For a while I was occupied with reflections on my private affairs. The room was silent. I thought about Myrtle and America—a cloud of claustrophobic reflections hung like a veil between me and the light of happiness. There were clouds everywhere. The boys began to whisper to each other: silent revision had begun to pall.

I walked round the room, threading my way methodically between the benches. Sweat glistened on the boys' foreheads. Their hair was slightly matted and their collars soiled. Some of those who had really been revising, and so had no cause to feel guilty, looked up at me reproachfully. With a blank expression I moved on. There were toffee-papers on the floor. I inspected a boy's note-book at random, and brought to light a drawing that must have been on its way round the class. The drawing was quite unconnected with the subject the boys were revising. I tore it up and left the bits on the bench. Then I sat down again.

I began to think about the drawing. 'Why,' I asked myself, 'were they passing that round instead of studying a diagram of the earth's magnetic field?' 'Because,' I answered myself, 'it was much, much more interesting.' The subject of the drawing had fascinated the human race since the beginning of time. The earth's magnetic field had not. The boys' heads were bent silently again over their note-books. Poor little devils!

A bell rang for the end of the first period. The boys looked up. In a mood of compassion, I suddenly said:

'Who'd like to go for a walk round the yard?'

I could not have said anything sillier in the circumstances. Any schoolmaster will tell you, even I can tell you, that you should always let sleeping boys lie. I deliberately woke mine up. The idea was reasonable enough, and certainly it was kindly: not two minutes had elapsed before I regretted it.

There were cries of delighted surprise. It was the first time such a thing had ever happened. The rest of the school was bathed in a droning silence. I specified one circuit of the playground and immediate return to the class-room.

The boys rushed out. Through the window I watched them happily make their circuit. And then they embarked on a second circuit. They did not return. And the noise they made echoed wildly back to the building.

I strode out into the playground. 'Come back!' I shouted furiously.

The boys stopped. They looked up at me. I glanced up at the windows of the school. From every classroom stared the face of a master: from the headmaster's window stared the face of the headmaster. Instantly I thought: 'There's going to be a row about this!'

The boys went back into the class-room and spent the rest of the afternoon in apprehensive, agitated silence. I did the same. They were afraid I was going to punish them. I was much too preoccupied to bother. I was expecting a visit from the headmaster. The only way I could have punished them was by keeping them in after school, and I had every intention of making myself scarce the moment the last bell sounded.

I escaped, that afternoon. I received a letter from the headmaster next morning. It began:

Dear Mr. Lunn: I really think I must ask you to reconsider your choice of vocation as a teacher. After . . .

That is enough. I was not exactly sacked; I was not exactly anything. Yet in no sense was it possible to interpret the letter as favourable to my career in pedagogy. I viewed it with alarm. 'One more letter like this,' I thought, 'and things will be serious!'

I could not blame Bolshaw for intervening, because he was away ill. It was entirely my own fault. And yet, it seemed to me that my crime was not great. In the past I had committed greater. Why had the headmaster seen fit to act on this one?

From questioning the headmaster's actions, I went on to question my own. I was soon immersed in serious philosophical doubts. Perhaps the headmaster was right. It might well be that a schoolmaster really ought to behave like a schoolmaster. If I could not behave like a schoolmaster, perhaps I ought not to be one.

This left me faced with the most alarming question of all.

'What *can* I behave like?'

PART III

PART III

CHAPTER I
FALSE ALARM

The next few times we met, Myrtle and I were chiefly concerned with talking about the headmaster's letter. I am afraid we were taking an opportunity of not talking about ourselves. A week-end at the cottage had restored us, and our night on the park was not mentioned again. Nothing had been resolved: our fate still hung over us, but in tacit agreement we were ignoring it. I asked myself why we should not go on ignoring it. I was willing to ask anyone else—except Tom.

'You're behaving like ostriches,' he said.

'And what's wrong with the ostrich?' I asked. 'It's despised very unjustly. I've a great fellow-feeling for the ostrich. An ostrich doesn't look things in the face.'

Tom made an indecent rejoinder.

'I can see that looking things in the face is a moral exercise,' I said. 'But does it do the slightest good? Sometimes it does not. Some things are much better not looked in the face. You ought to know that.' I paused. 'Anyone with a grain of tact and kindliness knows it.'

Tom was silenced. I considered that I had won a small victory. I was willing to call a small victory anything which prolonged my pleasant relations with Myrtle.

In the meantime I responded with perverse anger to the prospect of being asked to resign. Out of pride mingled with political ineptitude I refused to go and see the headmaster.

Myrtle, with commendable common sense, advised me to placate the headmaster: she did not want me to move to a job somewhere else. Tom strongly advised me to go and denounce him. Neither of them understood or sympathised with my passivity. To me it seemed the way of the world. Nobody could know as well as I, who, whatever else I might be, was not a prig, the roll of my manifold offences against society.

'Darling, you didn't do anything wrong!' Myrtle said, one evening as we sat in a public-house. Outside it was raining.

'I know,' I said obtusely, 'but that doesn't have anything to do with it. As you see, my sweet.' I shaped a small pool of beer on the table into a pattern. 'You talk,' I said, getting the argument on to a really abstract footing, 'as if there were a connection between crime and punishment. I can see practically none.'

Poor Myrtle had no idea what I was talking about. She could break social conventions without a qualm; but that did not stop her feeling they were right and pretending she had not broken them.

'Darling,' she said, 'sometimes I really don't know what to make of you.' She was reproachful and cross.

'All right,' I said, relenting. I smiled. 'I'll do something about it.'

Myrtle was right. The headmaster, out of weakness and exasperation, had allowed himself to be provoked beyond the limits other people would admit.

Myrtle took a sip of beer thoughtfully.

'What will you do, darling?' she said, looking at me. Reflection was over for her, if not for me. We were on common ground again.

I decided to consult Bolshaw.

'I thought Bolshaw wanted the headmaster to get rid of you, darling.'

I explained to Myrtle about my part in Bolshaw's research. She listened with interest. I could see that she now saw much stronger reasons why Bolshaw might want me to stay. I cannot say she looked shrewd or calculating—she was too young for that. Yet her soft pink cheeks had a brighter tinge, and her brown eyes shone with a more hopeful light.

The landlord switched on the wireless, and the din made it hard for us to converse. Outside, it was still raining. We sat quietly holding each other's hand.

Next morning I saw Bolshaw. For once I had done the right thing. It happened to be Bolshaw's first morning at school after being away ill. He did not know about the headmaster's letter to me. It was a surprise to him. Bolshaw was always surprised if anyone did anything without having previously been advised to do so by him.

'Fancy him writing you a letter!' said Bolshaw, in a grand, slow manner, as if it were scarcely credible that the headmaster's hand was strong enough to hold a pen.

I showed him the letter. Bolshaw read it carefully. He was sitting in the staff-room at the time. He lifted his head, and the light gleamed on the steel frames of his spectacles. He kept his head lifted: I thought he was not going to bring it down again.

'What is it supposed to mean?' he asked.

I shrugged my shoulders, and looked at him with the nearest I could muster to a solemn, repentant expression. I described the occasion which had provoked the letter. I have to admit that I did not describe it to Bolshaw as I have described it to you. I doubt if you would recognise the description I gave Bolshaw.

On the other hand Bolshaw was not a fool. He knew me well enough. I tried to maintain my solemn, repentant expression for the sake of keeping up the appearances to which he attached so much importance, but I did not for a moment assess them at more than a marginal value in the balance he was weighing up. How much did he want me to be sacked? How much did he need me to assist in his research? How much did he deplore indepen dent action on the part of the headmaster? I do not know. I stood waiting while he swept across some kind of balance-sheet that was beyond my comprehension. All I cared for was to know whether the total for me was printed in black or red. It came out black.

Bolshaw handed me back the letter. 'A silly letter,' he said. 'A silly letter.'

I put it in my pocket.

'Let me give you some advice, Lunn!'

I knew I was safe. I nodded meekly.

Bolshaw threw back his blond head again. His voice re-sounded like that of a mythical god.

'Keep your nose to the grindstone!'

Later in the morning I rang up Myrtle. I repeated the conver-sation verbatim.

'Then it's all right, darling?'

'Bolshaw's going to see the headmaster today.'

I went back again into the school. In a sense it was all right. At least I was going to escape being asked to resign.

Though Myrtle and I were going together again, she did not give up Haxby. He existed as a perpetual reminder to me that all was not well—and I was damnably jealous of him.

I never knew Haxby, but I can tell you what he looked like. He was tall, dark and skinny; and he had a friend who was slightly less tall, dark and skinny. They had intense black eyes and jerky movements. I thought their appearance was mildly degraded, and I called them the Crows. I could see that Myrtle was wounded. I called them the Crows in a careless, natural, confident tone, as if it would never occur to anybody to call them anything else.

You may think I was being cruel to Myrtle: I can only say that Myrtle was deliberately tormenting me.

Myrtle frequently made it clear that she preferred the Crows' company to mine. They were always available; and they were young, inexperienced, never likely to give her good advice, ready to lead her into things she really liked—such as playing inane games at parties, listening to gramophone records, showing devotion to culture by long pretentious discussions, and staying up half the night.

Myrtle knew that I disliked her preference thoroughly. It was not in my style. It went further than that. It was a powerful affront to some of my deepest feelings. At this time my deepest feelings circulated round two activities—one was writing books, the other making love to Myrtle. I thought she made it only too clear that she did not care at all for the first. I would gladly have thrashed her for it. Unfortunately, thrashing your young woman does not make her admire you more as a novelist. I felt frustrated, angry and hurt. When I thought of marrying Myrtle—yes, there were many, many moments when I did think of marrying her—this angry hurt recurred. I could not get over it. It stuck, as they say, in my craw. And my *cri-de-cœur* was one of such anguish that it must be recorded.

'She doesn't believe in me as a writer!'

And so I ask you not to be too hard on me for condemning the Crows. But a veil over *cris-de-cœur!* They are embarrassing.

'How are the Crows?' I would say lightly.

'All right,' Myrtle would reply in a distant unhappy voice, indicating that she was too far borne down to argue with me.

And then she would look at me with a soft, appealing, reproachful expression, as much as to say she would never go near them if she could be with me all the time. It was the soft, appealing, reproachful expression of blackmail.

One Sunday morning Myrtle arrived at the cottage with a hangover, after an evening with the Crows.

'Bohemianism!' I cried, in a righteous tone to which print can never do justice.

You may think I had no room to express moral indignation. No more I had. No more have you, I suspect, half the time you express moral indignation—but does that stop you any more than it stopped me?

'Bohemianism!' I repeated, as if once were not enough.

Myrtle was appropriately flabbergasted.

I took Myrtle, figuratively speaking, by the scruff of the neck. I took her to the Dog and Duck for lunch, and back again in double-quick time.

The same night I asked Myrtle if she would like to go to Oxford with me the following week-end to see Robert. Myrtle was pleased with the idea. I thought if she was in Oxford she could not be with Haxby. I was pleased with the idea myself. And then I noticed an unmistakable smile of satisfaction on Myrtle's face. I had been led into doing just what she wanted. So much for the soft, appealing, reproachful looks given you by beautiful, ill-used girls!

Yet when the next week-end came near, Myrtle's enthusiasm vanished. She was afraid of meeting Robert; and she feared more discussion of our plans for going to America.

However, Myrtle did not flinch. When we met at the railway station on Saturday afternoon she was showing a brave front. She was dressed elegantly and a trifle theatrically. She had a very pretty dress and a new hat, with which she had seen fit to wear an Edwardian veil. Anyone could see the veil was becoming, but the effect was eccentric. I smiled to myself, thinking that girls of twenty-two can never help overdoing it. I was touched, and kissed her, through the veil, with great feeling.

And as I kissed Myrtle I noticed that her breath smelt odd. I looked at her closely. Her cheeks were highly coloured, and her eyes looked bright and strained. Her breath smelt of gin.

'What's the matter?' I asked.

Myrtle looked at me. 'Darling,' she said, '*you* know.'

My knees knocked together. 'Oh!' I cried. I knew exactly what she meant.

We were standing in the station entrance. The sun was shining brightly through the glass roof. A taxi drew up beside us, and a porter pushed us out of the way. I took hold of Myrtle's arm to hold her up. What a way to begin a week-end!

I led Myrtle towards the ticket office. I questioned her, but I did not doubt that she was speaking the truth. In spite of all I might have said or thought about her, I really trusted her completely. We were passing a glass case containing a model locomotive, brilliantly illuminated. The Flying Scotsman.

As usual on such occasions, I assumed a knowing matter-of-fact expression.

Myrtle's expression was less knowing, less matter-of-fact.

I said: 'It's happened before, you know.' My voice sounded clear and firm. It was the only thing about me that was clear and firm. 'There's no need to worry.'

I bought the tickets.

'Perhaps I ought not to go,' said Myrtle, looking up at me in great anxiety. 'You go by yourself.'

I glanced at her in surprise and refused to go without her.

She took hold of my arm. 'You won't tell Robert, will you, darling?'

'Of course not.' I thought I should have to tell Robert quickly enough if it turned out not to be a false alarm. He would have to lend me money.

Myrtle sat opposite to me in the railway carriage, looking meek and distracted, inside an Edwardian veil.

At Bletchley, when we changed trains, I bought Myrtle a glass of gin.

When we reached Oxford we went straight to our hotel. Myrtle stood in the middle of the stuffy little bedroom, which smelt as if people had been sleeping in it for years.

'Could you buy me a bottle of Kuyper's, darling?'

'Of course.' I did not know why I had so much faith in the efficacy of gin. I suppose the less idea you have of what to do the more readily you take over someone else's faith.

I made off to my old wine merchant's with an energetic, resourceful stride. How can men who do not know what they are about walk with an energetic, resourceful stride? They do, shams that they are.

The weather had changed. The sun had disappeared, leaving a grey, drizzly afternoon. I stood on the street corner, waiting for a stream of bicycles to pass, and I was poignantly beset by nostalgia for my undergraduate days.

I turned into Broad Street, and ran into Tom.

I was astonished. Tom was supposed to be enjoying his turn at the cottage.

'What are you doing here?'

'I got a letter this morning from the American Institute of Chartered Accountants,' Tom said, with a bland, pompous gesture. 'I thought it wise to consult Robert immediately.'

I thought 'Liar—you knew Myrtle and I were here and didn't want to miss anything.'

'We won't interfere with any of your plans,' Tom went on, in the tone of a psychiatrist reassuring a lunatic. Then he glanced at me suspiciously: 'By the way, where is Myrtle?'

'In the hotel. She isn't well.'

I could see that Tom did not believe me. He obviously thought there was a domestic quarrel brewing. He looked more suspicious when I shook him off in order to do my shopping. He bustled away down the Broad, to report the news directly to Robert.

I felt depressed and anxious and worried. 'If only I can get out of it just this once, I kept thinking. And I kept telling myself it was a false alarm—possibly brought on, I was inspired to diagnose, by being afraid to meet Robert. One inspired diagnosis led to another: for once I found the psychology of the unconscious useful and consoling. The one diagnosis I did not face was that it might have been brought on by a desire for holy matrimony.

My consolation did not last long: if it were not a false alarm there was no need for the psychology of the unconscious at all.

On my return I found Myrtle sitting in an armchair quietly reading *Vogue.* Her apparent anxiety had entirely disappeared. I did not know whether to be pleased or alarmed. She measured out a very healthy dose of gin in the single tooth glass provided by the hotel, and proceeded to drink it with signs of enjoyment.

'You have some, darling,' she said, holding out the glass.

'I don't need it.'

Myrtle smiled. 'Have some instead of tea.' She giggled.

We sat on the edge of the bed, and passed the glass to and fro. I could not help noticing that Myrtle was becoming high-spirited.

'This can only lead to trouble,' I said.

Myrtle looked at me with a wide-eyed, furtive glance, and drank some more gin.

I too drank some more gin. I had begun to feel the situation slipping outside the bounds of my comprehension. I was, quite frankly, beginning to feel amorous.

'Will you take me to see the statue of Shelley?' Myrtle said. What she was thinking about was written all over her face.

'If you want to gaze at a man with no clothes,' I said, 'there's no need to go chasing down to Univ.'

Myrtle looked deeply shocked. 'He was a poet,' she said. 'I love poetry.' She began to finger the buttons on my shirt. I could smell the warm air near to her.

'Give me some more liquor!'

'You've had enough, darling.'

'Then you have some.' I paused. 'How about me posing as Shelley?'

'Darling!' Myrtle pushed me away.

'Then you pose as Shelley!'

'Really, darling!'

'Then,' I said, triumphantly getting the better of my shame altogether, 'we'll both pose as Shelley!'

Myrtle stopped fingering the buttons on my shirt. As if she were thinking of something quite different, she put down her glass on the bedside-table. Her eyes looked smaller with excitement. I pushed her back on to the pillows. She made a feeble resistive movement. I was deciding I might as well be hung for a sheep as a lamb—when there was a knock on the door.

It was a chambermaid telling me I was wanted on the telephone.

Robert wanted to know if he should cancel our dinner-party. With badly concealed impatience I told him not to cancel it.

In surprise he asked if Myrtle was better.

'Yes,' I said, and rang off.

When I got back to the room Myrtle's high spirits had disappeared. She was now depressed, standing beside the window and looking out over the dreary back of the hotel. The drizzle had thickened into rain.

I was suddenly overwhelmed by the seriousness of our predicament. I put my arm round her, to comfort her. Neither of us spoke for a long time.

'Would you rather not dine with Robert?' I said.

Myrtle looked at me reproachfully. 'We must.'

I felt apprehensive. I felt the dinner-party was going to be disastrous.

'I think I'll change my dress,' said Myrtle.

'You look perfect as you are.'

Myrtle was not listening.

I sat down beside the dressing-table. Myrtle had brought with her a copy of a book by a successful American humorist. She sometimes read me passages which she found exceptionally funny, presumably to show me how it ought to be done. I now picked up the book and began masochistically to read it myself.

Myrtle remained in low spirits, but the dinner-party went off well, and next day her behaviour was normal.

I watched her anxiously, more anxiously, I think, than she watched herself. I did not tell Robert what was the matter, and I felt still less inclined to tell Tom. I knew that Tom, with his down-to-earth understanding, would tell me that Myrtle was trying to force me to marry her.

We returned to the town, with no sign of relief, and I spent a sleepless night.

I spent two sleepless nights—and ought to have spent three, but I was too tired for even the deepest anxiety to keep me awake.

Then Myrtle rang me up to tell me that all was well. I ought to have felt overcome with relief. I ought to have gone out and celebrated.

I was relieved, of course; and yet I felt no desire to celebrate. Myrtle's voice came to me through the telephone as if she were speaking from a long way off.

'I'm glad,' I said.

Yet I knew that I felt as if something had been lost. These things are very strange.

CHAPTER II

BESIDE THE SWIMMING-POOL

There was a short spell of hot weather and we began to frequent the local swimming-pool when we came out of work. It was an agreeable place, with a high entrance fee imposed to keep out the lower orders. Young men with rich fathers in the boot-and-shoe trade brought their girls in M.G. sports cars: we came on our bicycles. There were half a dozen showy young divers, and at least a couple of young men who could swim more than two lengths in very fast free style. The girls wore bathing-costumes made of what they called the latest thing in two-way stretch. You could not have wished for more in the way of provincial chic.

I usually arrived first, having a greater passion than the others for swimming and lying in the sun. On the evening when the course of our lives perceptibly took a new turn I had arranged to be joined by Myrtle and Tom. While I sat waiting for them I enjoyed the scene.

The owners of the pool had clearly had in view, when choosing their design, something colourful. They had got what they wanted. The bath, through which constantly flowed heavily chlorinated water, was lined with glittering cobalt-blue tiles, which gave the water a quite unearthly look. The white surface of new concrete changing-sheds glared brilliantly in the afternoon sunlight, and against it were lined deckchairs made with orange and green striped canvas. There were two plots of grass, from the centres of which sprang fountains of pink rambler roses.

Against this background, to my surprise, appeared Steve. When he was stripped Steve looked much more bony and boyish than when he was dressed: he hunched his shoulders and walked flat-footedly. He tended to hang about on the edge of the bath, though he was a fair swimmer, with his arms crossed over his chest, apparently shivering. He saw me, and came and sat on the grass beside me.

'Where's Tom?' I asked.

'I don't know.'

There was a peculiar silence, to which my contribution was more surprise.

'I suppose you know he's coming, Steve?'

'Is he?' Steve turned quickly in agitation. 'Honestly, Joe, I didn't know. What shall I do?' Steve's face assumed an expression of frantic alarm. 'What shall I do? I've arranged to meet a *girl* here!'

'Really!' I said, not committing myself immediately to unqualified belief.

'What shall I do?'

'I don't know, Steve.' Then I said helpfully: 'Perhaps love will find a way.'

'It couldn't get past Tom!' Steve hunched his shoulders. 'Honestly, Joe, it wouldn't stand a chance.'

'Oh!'

'This is terrible, Joe. Honestly, you don't understand.'

'Are you sure you didn't know Tom was coming?' Somehow I could not help feeling that in spite of his frantic alarm Steve was looking forward to a scene with Tom.

'Of course not. He'll go mad when he finds out.'

'He'll get over it.'

Steve gave me a look that was cold and cross. 'What will happen to me in the meantime?' he asked.

That question I was unable to answer. I suggested that we should go and swim, but Steve shook his head.

'I want to think,' he said. So he thought for a while. 'I want to talk.'

'What about?'

Steve turned to look at me. 'I really did like it, Joe. . . .'

'What?' I had no idea what he meant.

'Taking this girl out, of course. I took her to the pictures last night. You may think it sounds silly Joe, but it wasn't! I liked it.

It made me feel I was doing something that was real and true. It made me feel like other boys. Other boys take their girls to the pictures.'

'What film did you see?'

Steve's air of passionate sincerity vanished: he looked nettled.

'We went to the Odeon. It was a terrible film, I know. But she wanted to see it.'

'That's nothing, in the course of love, Steve. You must be prepared for greater sacrifices than that.'

'But it really was terrible. It was excruciating. All about a *sheep-dog*.'

'As you grow older, Steve, you'll realize that love is inseparable from suffering,' I said. 'Myrtle once made me go to Stratford-on-Avon to see *A Comedy of Errors*.'

'No!'

'If girls aren't ignorant, they're cultured,' I said. 'You can't avoid suffering.'

Steve spread out his towel over the grass and lay down on his stomach.

'Tell me about your girl,' I said.

'There's not very much to tell. I met her here last week. She's only a schoolgirl. Quite pretty, though. A bit silly, but I don't mind that. It makes me feel older than her, and I like that.'

'How old is she?'

'Fifteen. Nearly sixteen.'

'That's a bit young.'

'That's what I want, Joe. It's innocent, and I want to keep it innocent.'

'If she's only fifteen you're likely to succeed for a good many years.'

'Years!' said Steve, obviously presented with a new concept. He pondered it with chagrin. 'Won't it be terribly monotonous?'

'Not exactly,' I said. 'But it won't have the ups and downs of the other state.'

Steve was silent for a while.

'I did try to kiss her on the way home,' he said. 'Actually I didn't particularly want to. But I thought she'd expect it. One has to be conventional.'

'That seemed to be the aim.'

Steve turned his head up to see how I was taking it. 'She let me kiss her on the cheek.'

I maintained a serious expression. 'And then?'

A glint came into the corners of his eyes. 'She said: "Aren't I pretty!" and touched her hair.'

'But Steve!' I burst out: 'That wouldn't do for you at all!' I knew Tom constantly told him he was Adonis and this was not a whit too much or too often.

'It made a change,' said Steve, grinning, 'but not a nice one.'

Some people who were camped a little way off turned to listen to us. We stopped talking. Steve laid his face on the ground. I looked at the crowd—and saw Tom coming, bearing down like a battleship on Steve.

I greeted Tom, who spread out his towel and sat down beside us. Steve kept his face on the turf, and Tom glared at him. Steve was deliberately behaving badly. Thinking of Myrtle I asked Tom what time it was. He looked at his watch and told me. Immediately Steve heard the time he roused himself and stood up. He must have been due for his rendezvous.

'Steve, where are you going?'

'To get a handkerchief out of my locker.'

'What for?'

'I need it.'

'I've got a spare one.'

'I want my own.'

With bulging eyes Tom was watching Steve, whose errand sounded most improbable. Steve was furtively looking round at the crowd.

Tom shrugged his shoulders, and Steve shambled away, clearly searching for his schoolgirl. I glanced at Tom. It was the signal for him to plunge immediately into intimate conversation about Steve. In a moment he was asking me questions—Where was Steve going? What was he doing? How long had he been there? Had he been with me all the time? What had we been talking about?

I answered the questions as truthfully as I could without making matters worse. My heart sank as I followed the boring routine of jealousy in someone else.

'I don't know, Tom,' I found myself saying. 'How can I know?'
I paused. 'And even if I did know, it wouldn't make you any
more satisfied if I told you.'

'I should want to know all the same,' Tom said, rebuking me.

I shrugged my shoulders. I knew he was in no mood for
seeing Steve's latest manœuvres in their true ridiculous light.

'You forget that I'm in love,' said Tom.

'At least you're jealous,' said I.

'The two things don't necessarily mean the same thing,' said
Tom, 'as you ought to know, Joe.' Tom could never resist the
satisfaction of teaching his grandmother to suck eggs.

'One can be jealous without being in love,' he went on; 'but
one can't be in love without being jealous.'

He gave me a sidelong glance, so I presumed he was referring
to me. I had been too ashamed of my own jealousy to confide in
him: consequently he found my display of that emotion suspiciously inadequate.

We were silent for a while.

Then Tom said, with great feeling: 'I'm afraid this is beginning to get me down, Joe.'

My sympathy quickened. 'Can't you begin to—I don't know—
pull out?'

'Of course not.'

I felt inclined to shrug my shoulders. However, I simply said:
'I'm sorry.'

'I've never been able to withdraw,' said Tom, with some truth.
'I have to go on.' He paused. 'I'm afraid this time it may drive me
mad.'

'That appears to be what Steve's aiming at.'

'Not at all, Joe. He can't help it,' said Tom.

'Oh.'

'That's what makes it so moving. That's why he needs me.'

Thinking of cash I said: 'He certainly needs you, Tom.'

'I don't know what he would do without me.'

'He'd lead a life of vastly restricted enterprise.'

Tom indicated that my remark showed lack of understanding.

'I think he's devoted to me.'

'He is, Tom.'

'If only I could feel sure of him.' Tom shook his head. 'That's the trouble with love, Joe. If only one could feel sure . . . If only I could be sure this was going to last even another year.'

For the moment I forgot, just as Tom did, that he was supposed to be leaving the country in another three weeks. He was speaking from his heart, and I was moved. I believed the kind of love he felt for Steve could rouse as deep feeling, could cause as sudden happiness and as sharp anguish, as any other kind. But I had no faith in its lasting: I could no more believe it would last than I could believe water would flow uphill.

'But it may last six months,' said Tom, and I swear that his tone was that of a man who is announcing a not unsatisfactory compromise.

Tom was a powerful swimmer: he had a good layer of fat which kept him afloat, and strong muscles well-suited for propulsion. We dived into the bright blue waves, and came up blinking chlorinated water out of our eyes. Tom followed his usual practice of setting out to swim many consecutive lengths at a slow, steady pace. I swam beside him for a while and then changed my mind. I climbed out of the bath and looked round.

I was not the only person who knew Tom's usual practice. Steve, confident that Tom's head would be under water for most of the next fifteen minutes, was standing in full view of everybody present conversing gaily with two schoolgirls.

I did not know what to do. Intervention of any kind seemed to me fatal. I could only stand watching, while drops of water trickled down from my hair on to my shoulders, hoping for the best.

Now hoping for the best is one of the most feeble of human activities, and I ought to have known better: especially as I knew that one of the most obvious characteristics of showy divers is entire disregard for the comfort of swimmers. I glanced back and forth, from Steve and his lively, leggy, young girls to Tom's carroty head thrusting steadfastly across the bath. And I was just in time to see two boys in a double dive enter the water a yard ahead of Tom. He was immediately brought to a standstill bouncing angrily in the wash. He spat water from his mouth, and rubbed it out of his eyes, and looked all round. The first thing he saw was Steve.

In half a dozen strokes Tom was at the side of the bath, climbing out, and marching up to Steve. I saw the startled look on Steve's face as Tom tapped him on the shoulder. There was a brief exchange of words, and then they both came away together, leaving the young girls looking at each other speechlessly. Tom strode in front with the sunlight glistening in the fuzz of red hair on his chest: Steve reluctantly brought up the rear.

I went to collect my towel, and we all fetched up simultaneously at the same spot. Tom's eyes looked startling, the irises greener with rage and the whites bloodshot with chlorine.

'You're driving me mad, Steve!' he said, hurriedly wiping his face. His passionate tone was somewhat muffled by the towel.

Steve said nothing, and began ineffectually to dry the inside of his leg, where the water was dripping from his trunks.

'Do you hear?' said Tom. 'You're driving me mad.'

'What?' said Steve. 'I can't hear because of your towel.'

'You're driving me mad!'

Steve said sulkily: 'I wasn't doing anything wrong. Don't be silly, Tom.'

I thought it was time to remove myself, although I knew that Tom had no objection to my presence during his domestic rows—in fact I suspected that he rather liked me to be there, adding to the drama.

I turned away and began to dry myself. I heard Steve say:

'Here's Myrtle.'

It was a great relief. I saw Myrtle sauntering towards us, looking fresh and bright.

'You do look funny, all standing like that, drying yourselves. Like a picture by Duncan Grant.' She smiled to herself. 'Only his young men weren't wearing . . .' Her voice faded out, suggestively.

'Myrtle, you've not changed your dress,' said Tom, peremptorily. 'Aren't you going to bathe?'

I thought he was trying to get rid of her.

'No, I don't think I will,' said Myrtle and sat down on the

grass. I sat down beside her. She did not often swim: I thought she was shy of appearing in a bathing-costume because she was so slender and small-breasted. And of course she always felt cold. 'I don't think I can.'

I glanced at her. She looked at me with round, apologetic eyes: 'I'm sorry, darling. I can't stay and go home with you. I want to go somewhere later. Do you mind?'

It was my turn to be alarmed and irritated. 'Not at all,' I said.

There was a pause. Myrtle was watching Tom and Steve. I was thinking. It reminded me of other occasions when she had behaved like this. My mind went back over many events during the past year, and suddenly I saw their pattern. Provocation, leading to an outburst, leading to reconciliation—and then the cycle all over again. We were just entering the first round once more.

'You sound cross,' she said.

'I'm not cross at all.'

Tom sat down on his towel beside her, with his back to Steve. He glanced at me, and said to Myrtle:

'Joe, saying he's not cross, has a wonderfully unconvincing sound.'

'I know.' Myrtle smoothed her dress over her knees. 'He's always cross. He's always cross with me.'

Tom's anger with Steve had faded or else he was concealing it well. He smirked warmly at Myrtle.

'These introverts,' he said to her.

Myrtle shook her head. 'I suppose I must be an extravert.'

'You are, my dear,' said Tom.

Myrtle gave him a sad-eyed, appealing look.

'You're like me.' Tom returned her look. 'That's why we understand each other so well.'

Myrtle did not reply.

'That's why you'd find me so much easier to live with.' He now turned all his attention upon her, as if neither Steve nor I were there. 'You like to feel relaxed, don't you? You like to do things when you want to do them—when you *feel* like it. When the *spirit* moves you, my dear. Not when Joe does. . . .'

Myrtle looked thoughtful. I cannot say I was pleased. I felt like saying: 'That's a bit thick', or 'Come off it, Tom'.

'We're easy persons to live with,' Tom went on. 'In fact I think we above all are the easiest. We go'—he paused, before shame-lessly introducing my own phrase for it—'by atmosphere.' And he waved his hand gracefully through the air.

Myrtle put on the expression of a young girl listening to reve-lations. I may say that there was nothing false about it. Both she and Tom were in a sense carried away by what they were saying to each other. I may say also that I was not carried away, and what is more my high resolve to be patient and forbearing had wilted disastrously. The only thing that stopped me intervening now was a feeling that Tom might make a fool of himself. I was waiting.

Myrtle nodded her head.

'Ah, Myrtle!' Tom put his hand on hers. 'There isn't anything you couldn't tell me, is there?' He looked into her eyes.

Myrtle blinked. I could have sworn Tom had gone a step too far. I think she must have moved her hand, because Tom took his away.

There was a pause. Myrtle said, in a friendly tone of observa-tion:

'You're getting fat, Tom.'

This was not at all what Tom wanted her to tell him. Tom looked down at his chest, with the tufts of red hair that I person-ally found repellent, and inflated it.

'I like getting fat,' he said.

'Joe's always exercising,' Myrtle said. 'So boring.'

'It has its rewards,' I said, in a cross, meaningful tone.

Tom shook his head at Myrtle. 'He doesn't understand us, does he?' He stroked his diaphragm. 'If you and I settled down together, Myrtle, you'd fall into my easy ways, just like that'—he snapped his finger and thumb together—'and you'd get fat as well.'

This was not at all what Myrtle wanted Tom to tell her. I was pleased.

'I couldn't, Tom,' she said, faintly despairing.

'You would, my dear. And you'd love it. You wouldn't feel so cold.'

I watched Myrtle's expression with acute interest and pleas-ure. Naturally in the past I had not failed to tell her that she always felt cold because she had too thin a layer of subcutaneous fat. This explanation she regarded as mechanical and soul-less in the highest degree. Myrtle knew that her feeling cold arose from distress of the heart. Tom had missed it. She sighed painfully.

Tom apparently did not notice. After all it must have been slightly distracting for him to have my eye fixed on him while he was making up to Myrtle, and to have Steve sulkily listening to him behind his back.

'I shall always feel cold,' Myrtle said.

'Not if I were looking after you, my dear. I should know exactly how you were feeling all the time.'

Myrtle looked distinctly worried at this prospect. I sympathised with her.

'And I should know'—Tom gave a clever, shrewd glance at me—'how to give you good advice.'

It was one of Tom's theses that I did not know how to handle Myrtle, particularly in the way of giving her good advice. He appeared not to know that Myrtle hated advice of all kinds, good, bad and indifferent.

'Would you?' she said, looking at him with a soft lack of enthusiasm.

Tom was silent. He stared at her with his confident, understanding expression. He appeared to be judging, out of love and sympathy, her present state of health.

'You're tired, my dear,' he said, presumably finding shadows round her eyes.

'I am.'

Tom glanced at me again, as much as to say: 'This is how it ought to be done.' He leaned towards her, and said:

'You should go to bed earlier.'

If there was one thing Myrtle hated it was to be told she ought to go to bed earlier: in one simple move it negated her love of life, her profundity of soul and, more important still, her determination to do as she pleased.

Myrtle did not speak. She was feeling much too sad.

There is a dazzling reward for allowing your best friend to make advances to your young woman in your presence—the dazzling reward of seeing him put his foot in it.

In my opinion Tom had put his foot in it up to the knee, up to the hip.

At the same time I was a little surprised: my faith in extraverts was very strong. It did not occur to me that it was in very bad taste for Tom to talk to Myrtle in this way: I was concerned that he had not made a better job of it. I concluded that he must really be distracted by thoughts of the impression it must be making on Steve.

I glanced at Steve: it was impossible to tell what he was thinking. His dark hair had dried in a soft mop that was falling over his eyes. He appeared to have lost interest in the schoolgirls. I think he was simply bored.

The sun was beginning to go down. Myrtle stirred uneasily, and Tom began to study the people round about.

'Joe, look over there!'

I looked. Tom was pointing towards the bathing-sheds. Myrtle and Steve roused themselves.

It was Trevor and a girl. I have already remarked that Trevor was unusually small, that he was small-boned and altogether made on miniature lines. I now have to remark that Trevor's girl was unusually big.

We were startled. They came forward together, Trevor stepping firmly and delicately, and his girl walking with powerful tread. He was talking animatedly, and smiling up at her. She was listening in a big, proprietorial way. She was wearing a perfectly plain, light green bathing-dress, and a white rubber cap concealed her hair: nothing for one instant distracted one's attention from her physical form. It was a form not to be despised— far, far from it.

'She looks like Genesis,' said Tom, laughing.

'My dear Tom, you don't know anything about Genesis,' said Myrtle; and then suddenly blushed.

'The bulges!' said Tom. 'It's stupendous.'

We watched them, fascinated, as they strolled away and ensconced themselves privately in the furthest corner of the compound.

'After that,' I said, 'I think it's time for us to go.'

Tom and Steve went indoors to dress, and I bade goodbye to

Myrtle. I thought she must be going to see Haxby but I refused to ask her. She held out her cheek and I kissed it lightly. As she walked lazily away I felt sad and irritated.

I found Steve standing in the doorway of a cubicle, rubbing himself perfunctorily with a towel. I stood in the doorway of mine, next to him. Tom was having a shower.

'Is that Trevor's regular girl-friend?' I said.

'I think so.'

'Was that the one he had in his car the night he was run in for jumping the traffic-lights?'

'I don't know.' He sounded uninterested.

There was a pause.

'Joe!' Steve called.

There was an odd tone in his voice. I stepped out into the aisle to look at him. His face had a curiously worried expression. He stopped rubbing himself.

'What's the matter, Steve?'

'Has Myrtle gone?'

'Yes.' I was puzzled by the question.

'Of course, she's gone. That's silly of me . . . Listen, Joe, you know why Tom was making those advances to her? . . .' His speech came in staccato bursts. 'I know you won't believe me, when I tell you this . . . Do you know Tom's latest idea? He's planning to marry Myrtle!'

I was astounded. I stared at Steve.

'Incredible! He can't! It's ludicrous!'

It was the most incredible story Steve had ever told me, and for the first time I had not accused him of lying.

'You're not supposed to know, Joe.'

'I should think not.'

'He talked to Robert about it last week-end. That's why he was in Oxford.'

It may seem absurd, but I was believing him.

Somebody came out of an adjacent cubicle, and we had to stop talking while he pushed past me. Looking down the aisle I saw Tom, with a towel round his waist, combing his hair in front of a mirror.

'Please don't tell him I told you, Joe.'

'Don't be ridiculous, Steve.'

'But you mustn't, Joe! Please don't let him know you even suspect until he tells you. Otherwise I shall have terrible scenes.'

'Look, Steve, you'd better—'

'He's coming! I can't tell you any more.' Steve backed into the cubicle and hastily flung his shirt over his head. His elbow stuck in the sleeve.

Tom came along.

'Now Steve, hurry up!' He glanced at Steve. 'If you put on your shirt the way I showed you, Steve, you'd find it would slip straight on.'

I retired to my cubicle.

And after we had parted I went to my house. I had something new to think about.

I was utterly astounded. Apparently nothing was too ridiculous for Tom to do. First of all he professed to be wrapped up in Steve; secondly he knew Myrtle was in love with me; thirdly he was due to leave the country in less than three weeks anyway. I could not make sense of it; but I knew only too well that a situation was not less likely to arise because I was unable to make sense of it. Few situations, especially those precipitated by Tom, made sense.

'Steve must be lying,' I said to myself that night when I went to bed.

CHAPTER III

TWO SCENES OF CRISIS

It was early in the morning, and I was sitting in the school playground, waiting for Frank and company to join me. I was not preparing a lesson: I was not preparing anything. I was thinking. It seemed to me that my affairs had become desperately complicated. In fact I said to myself that they were in a hell of a mess. It was the morning after Steve had confided Tom's latest idea. I had a headache and felt curiously tense.

The sky was clouded over, and during the night there must have been some rain. Every now and then drops of water fell from the leaves of the lime tree under which I was sitting: the ground was damp, and the atmosphere carried a warm, pervasive smell of dust. Birds fluttered to and fro between the trees. Everything seemed unusually quiet.

My morning newspaper lay folded in my lap, and I noticed part of the headline. I had already read it. The fate of Europe was rolling on, but I had begun to lose any accurate sense of what it was rolling towards. I was aware to my shame that I had become less interested.

Sometimes I tried to link the disintegration of our private lives with the disintegration of affairs in the world. I saw us all being carried along into some nameless chaos. Yet it rang false. In spite of what the headlines told me every morning, in spite of what I reasoned must happen in the world, I was really preoccupied most deeply with what was going on between me and Myrtle and between Tom and Steve. People can concentrate on their private lives, I thought, in the middle of anything.

I had written to the American Consulate in London about a visa for myself. My slackness in *Weltanschauung* had not robbed me entirely of the capacity for action.

I had made a beginning with Bolshaw's computation. I had to do something. There was no reply from Miss X.Y., and I needed to know the fate of my last book before I could begin a new one. Suppose she never came back from the Balkans, suppose I were kept waiting a lifetime! My anxiety had become completely unreasonable. Small wonder I took to computation.

The idea that my true love was being pursued by my best friend did not cause me an entirely sleepless night. It was far too ridiculous. And as it had been conveyed to me by a notable liar, I reserved my right to make a scene. However, Tom's new gambit had brought me to one important conclusion; namely, that if I did not intend to marry Myrtle myself I ought not to stop anyone else marrying her.

This conclusion was important to me, and it was only afterwards that I learnt it was incomprehensible to everyone else. I must make it clear now that I not only came to the conclusion: I stuck to it. To understand it entails harking back to a revelation I made earlier on, that, feeling myself not to have been born a good man, I often sought to try and behave like one. Alas! I accepted that all was fair in love and war as far as primary things went; but if I could show a bit of decency in secondary ones, so much the better, I thought.

That was my aim. Nobody understood it. And I might have known that the result, if it was anything like the result of my previous attempts in this direction, was likely to be farcical. With my usual optimism, determination or crassness, I did not foresee it. I sat alone under the lime trees fascinated by the general concept rather than practical results. And of course I had a headache.

The boys came out and drew up their chairs beside me. I noticed that Trevor was missing and asked Frank where he was. Frank did not know.

'I saw him last night,' I said.

I thought Frank gave me an odd look.

'With 'is girl?' said Fred, getting down immediately to his favourite topic of conversation.

I did not reply.

'Wish I'd got a girl,' said Fred. 'I've been reading Freud. It's bad not to 'ave a girl.'

Had Trevor been present he would have lured Fred into an innocent, half-baked disquisition on psychoanalysis. As it was, Fred was ignored. He sighed and began to work.

A little while later a boy came out to me with a chit from the headmaster. It forbade the holding of lessons in the playground.

I was amazed. 'Look at this,' I said to Frank and passed it to him. Fred and Benny read it over his shoulder.

'What a sod!' said Frank. 'Oo-ya bugger,' said Fred.

The messenger, who had read it himself, sniggered cheerfully. I handed back the slip of paper and sent him on his way.

'What are you going to do, sir?' said Benny. It was a trivial annoyance. The practice of holding lessons in the yard was of long standing. The senior boys regarded it as one of their privileges.

'I don't propose to move now.'

I happened to look up, and saw the face of the headmaster peeping at me through his window.

Then I made a silly mistake. I decided to go and talk to Bolshaw. I thought he would be only too ready to gossip about the latest *démarche* of the headmaster. I walked into the school, and found him sitting in his room with the door open. He came out into the corridor to talk to me.

There was no excuse for me. I knew well enough that Bolshaw was unpredictable. His having recently been my ally did not make him approve of me any the more. To imagine that he would agree with me was walking into danger in the most imbecile fashion. Into it I walked, and a moment later found myself in the midst of a violent quarrel.

'I've just come out of the yard,' I said.

'Free period?'

'No. Teaching the sixth. I got the headmaster's note.'

'Have you taken them into the small lab?'

'Not on your life.'

'What do you mean, Lunn?'

'I don't propose to do anything about it.'

'Why not?'

'It's too silly.'

Bolshaw stood peering at me in the semi-darkness of the corridor, with his heavy shoulders rounded and his hands in his pockets.

'Why have you come to me?'

I ought to have known there was something wrong. To me the incident was trivial, and I was blind to his view of it. I replied:

'To see what we can do about it.'

Bolshaw raised his voice. 'Surprising as it may seem, I agree with the head for once. It's time this unconventional behaviour stopped. Look here, my good fellow, I told you that you'd got to put your nose to the grindstone. That meant this kind of thing has got to stop.'

I was furious. It crossed my mind that he had put the headmaster up to it.

'It's becoming increasingly clear to me,' Bolshaw said, 'that there's no room on this staff for people who flout the conventions.'

'What the hell's it got to do with you?'

I had been trapped into losing my temper.

'Everything. I know what the conventions are.'

'Do you indeed? Do you know that I and other masters have been taking lessons in the playground for the last seven years? When everybody does a thing—then it is conventional!'

Bolshaw snorted.

'That's what being conventional means!' I said. 'It's got nothing to do with whether they're good, bad, moral, wicked, useful or just damned lazy!'

'Listen to me, my good fellow! I don't propose to argue with you about what it means to be conventional. I *know*! And I can tell you this. Sooner or later the members of this staff who flout the conventions are going to find themselves'—he paused—'outside!' He took a blustering breath. 'It may interest you to know that it was I who decided the chit should be circulated. The headmaster agreed with me, that more persons than one have got to put their noses to the grindstone!'

It was too much for me. I shouted angrily. 'What about yourself?'

And Bolshaw clearly had not the slightest idea what I meant.

'My function is to see that the noses, having been put to the grindstone, are kept there.' He gave a braying, self-satisfied laugh. 'The proper place for them!'

'It's the proper place for yours,' I said. 'You may appoint yourself to be keeper of the conventions, but I notice you don't appoint yourself to do any teaching.'

'I do more teaching than anyone else in this school.'

'You certainly teach fewer periods.'

'That's because I have the power of imparting knowledge more rapidly than others.'

'I don't know how you manage it from the staffroom. Do you teach by telepathy?'

Bolshaw looked away in a dignified fashion.

'It's a pity that you find it necessary to quarrel with me, Lunn. It's most unwise.'

I was alarmed. I knew that he was speaking the truth. Unfortunately he had spoken it too late. I had already done myself damage.

'I don't want,' he said, 'to have our collaboration disturbed.' He paused to allow the effect to sink in.

I could have cried out with rage. I had been thinking this quarrel would mean my labours in his research coming to an end. Now I saw that he was going to use it to force me to go on. I had played into his hands.

I was silent. Nothing could be unsaid.

Bolshaw rattled the change in his pockets, and glanced into the class-room. Then he turned back to me.

'I think it's a very good rule,' he said, 'never to quarrel with one's superior in authority.' He paused. 'I'm happy to say I've always kept to that rule. Except, of course, on rare occasions when I deemed it wiser to break it.'

There was nothing for me to say.

Immediately school was over on that afternoon I went to the café to meet Tom. I felt unusually agitated, and hardly noticed when I splashed through puddles of water lying in the cobbled market-place. I was thinking the sooner I was in America the better.

Tom was not there. I sat in our customary place, watching for him through the window. I suppose the sky was still grey and damp, but I do not recall it. There must have been delphiniums and lilies on the stalls. What I do remember, and strangely enough the recollection is vivid to this day, is that the waitresses were wearing a new uniform. They had previously worn black with white aprons: now they were in brown with aprons the colour of pale *café-au-lait*. Our waitress had blonde hair, and the new colours made her look very pretty.

Tom came in.

'You're looking worried,' he said. 'Have you had bad news from Miss X.Y.?'

I shook my head. Tom ordered tea. The ritual of ordering a meal was very important, whatever else was going on.

I described my quarrel with Bolshaw.

Tom listened with patience and sympathy. I was just coming to the end of it when the waitress brought the tea. We paused.

Tom poured out some tea and gave it to me, saying: 'It probably won't be serious.'

'It's maddening. There was no need for it whatsoever. I just took leave of my senses.'

Tom smiled. Instead of saying 'You introverts,' he said:

'I do it frequently.' He looked at me with concentrated interest. 'If you lost your temper as frequently as I do, Joe, you wouldn't be so upset by it. You don't seem to realize how often other people do lose their tempers.'

'Bolshaw didn't really lose his.'

'No. He was satisfied with you losing yours. Are you under the impression there's no emotion flying about between you and Bolshaw? The two of you aren't counters in a complicated puzzle. You're both human. At this moment Bolshaw's probably feeling a glow of satisfaction, instead of feeling frustrated irritation.' Tom called the waitress: 'I should like another meringue, please.'

I confess to being comforted by this revelation of truth. Tom was speaking precisely in the tone he copied from Robert.

The next thing he said was, 'I think you'll find it cleared the air.' It might have been Robert speaking, had the remark not been so absurd.

'Cleared the air!' I cried. 'It's probably cleared me out of my job!'

Tom shrugged his shoulders.

There was a pause, and I said: 'I think the sooner I'm in America the better.'

'Yes.'

Something made me glance at Tom—he met my glance with patent evasion.

'I've been thinking about my own plans,' he said.

'Yes?' I should hope he had.

Tom adopted his weightiest manner. 'I may possibly postpone my departure.' He spread out his hands. 'Just by a fortnight.'

I was brought up sharply. 'Why?' I said.

'Certain affairs at the office are running behind time.'

I did not believe him. 'Is it Steve or Myrtle?' I asked myself. I was just framing an oblique question, when we were interrupted. There was a stir beside us, and I looked up to see Frank.

I was startled. I had not asked him to come. Occasionally we invited him to have a drink with us in a public-house, but neither he nor any of the other boys was supposed to join us without being asked. Tom looked surprised.

'I thought I should find you here.' Frank looked very embarrassed. He had naturally pleasant manners.

'Sit down,' said Tom.

Frank drew up another chair to our table. He sat down and nervously straightened his tie, which was already tied to perfection.

'I know I'm intruding,' he said, 'but I had to come.' He addressed himself to Tom. 'I hope Joe won't mind.' He pointed his nose diffidently towards me.

I shook my head.

Frank said: 'It's about Trevor.' He glanced round. 'I suppose you know he's been having an affair with a girl? Well, he's . . . you know . . . got her into trouble.'

I exclaimed in surprise.

Tom said: 'He'll have to marry her.'

At this moment the waitress came up to ask if Frank wanted anything. 'Bring some more tea,' Tom said to her commandingly.

I was silent. I was seeing us all ruined by a scandal.

'He'll have to marry her,' Tom repeated.

'That's out of the question,' said Frank.

'Nonsense. How old is he?'

'Nineteen.'

'Then why can't he marry her?'

'*She* doesn't want to marry *him*!' Frank replied, with great seriousness.

'Good gracious!' said Tom, and added: 'I can't say that I blame her.'

'That isn't the point,' said Frank.

'Why doesn't she want to marry him?'

'She wants to be a sculptor.' It appeared that all parties concerned thought sculpture and wedlock were mutually exclusive.

Tom laughed. 'She looks as if she's sculpted herself!'

I said: 'Is it that big woman we saw him with last night?'

'That's right,' said Frank. 'She's huge.'

Tom said: 'He's proved his manhood, anyway.' He smiled flickeringly. 'I suppose he thought the bigger the woman he took on the surer the proof.'

Frank laughed ruefully. 'Poor little Trev!' Tom gave him a knowing glance.

Frank's expression changed suddenly. 'But what are we to do, Tom?'

'What's Trevor doing?'

'Nothing. He's terrified. He doesn't get on with his family. He nearly got chucked out after the trouble over the car. If they hear about this . . .'

'Is it quite certain?' I asked—a question appropriate to me.

Frank looked at me. 'It's quite certain. This is the third month.'

'The little fool!' said Tom.

I said: 'It's no use taking that attitude.'

'I feel it,' said Tom. 'I feel healthy rage, Joe.'

The waitress brought us a fresh pot of tea, and a cup and saucer for Frank. Tom poured the tea out.

Frank said to me: 'I'm sorry I came to you, Joe. We couldn't think of anyone else.'

'That's all right.'

Tom said: 'We must make some plans.' He paused. 'First of all we'd better get the situation clear.' He paused again. 'They ought to get married.'

'They can't,' said Frank.

'If she doesn't want to marry him, then she ought to have the child without.'

'There'd be a terrific scandal. It would ruin Trev's career.'

Tom pursed his lips. 'Then there's only one solution.'

'Trev says she's willing. . . .'

In alarm I pushed my chair away from the table.

'Look!' I cried. 'I can't possibly be mixed up in this!'

'There's no need!' With a grandiose gesture Tom swept me aside. 'I'll handle it.'

His voice was full and resonant. He meant what he said. It was just the generous, disinterested action of which he was capable: he would plunge in without counting the risk—and also, as a matter of fact, he would enjoy himself. I forgot his bustling absurdity and felt great affection for his good heart.

'I'm afraid in my position at the school . . .' I began, feeling ashamed.

Tom interrupted. 'You'd better keep out of this.'

I nodded my head, thinking of the trouble I was in already at the school. I said: 'I think it would be best if I'd heard nothing about it.'

Frank looked worried. 'I won't say that I've told you.'

I smiled at him. 'It isn't your fault, Frank.'

Frank smiled back, readily restored.

I prepared to leave them. First of all I took out my wallet, and counted the pound notes in it. I handed them all to Tom, thinking it was rather handsome of me.

'You'll probably need these,' I said, in a solemn tone.

Tom accepted them, clearly thinking there were not enough. I was ruffled. I felt in my pockets for small change and found insufficient to pay for my tea.

'You'll have to let me have one of them back again,' I said.

'I'll lend you half a crown,' said Tom, not intending to part.

I walked away through the market-place. I realised that I had lost my resilience. I felt as touchy and cross as Myrtle accused me of being. I was inclined to ask myself rhetorical questions, such as: 'Why do I get involved with people?' and 'Why don't I leave them all?' It seemed to be that in some distant way Trevor was responsible for my having quarrelled with Bolshaw.

America, I thought, was the place for me. Land of liberty, where my pupils would not get their girls in trouble. Or would they? Exactly what sort of liberty was it? My speculations were suddenly interrupted by recalling that Tom had postponed his setting sail for the land of liberty.

My speculations changed to suspicions. 'What,' I asked myself, in a question that was far from rhetorical, 'is Tom up to now?'

CHAPTER IV

CONCLUSION IN A PUBLIC-HOUSE

It was evening and I was waiting apprehensively for Myrtle to come. We had just had a strange conversation over the telephone. For the last few days I had seen nothing of her; things were going wrong again. She had rung up to tell me she was going to a midnight matinée.

'Midnight matinée!' I had cried, in surprise. 'What on earth of?'

'Of a film.'

'You didn't tell me, darling.'

'I didn't think you'd be interested.' Her voice sounded desolate and reproachful.

As she did not tell me the name of the film I gathered it must be 'Turksib' or 'Earth'. I said: 'Who are you going with? The Crows?'

Myrtle did not reply. I thought: 'So much for that!' and began a gossipy conversation to divert her.

'I've got an excellent story about Tom,' I said. 'He told me he'd postponed going to America so I sent a postcard to Robert, asking if it was true. And got a postcard back from Tom himself.'

'How queer,' said Myrtle.

'Not queer at all. He was in Oxford, and must have been in Robert's rooms, reading through his correspondence while he was out—saw my postcard, and just replied to it.' I thought the story was funny. 'What could be simpler?'

'How queer,' Myrtle said again, rather as if she had not been listening.

I tried another tack. I said:

'I'm feeling slightly more cheerful about school. There's a bit of intrigue going on in the staff-room against Bolshaw. I'm not taking part because it won't succeed. Shall I tell you about it? It's interesting because I could reasonably support Bolshaw for once.'

'How queer.'

It was the third time. Her voice sounded distant and lifeless, as if it were repeating the phrase from some worn-out groove.

'What is the matter, darling?' I said. 'You keep on saying "How queer" in an extraordinary way.'

'Do I?'

'You do.'

'I didn't know. . . .'

'In that case, I might just as well have been talking about the weather.'

'I suppose it's because I'm so empty-headed!'

'Myrtle, what *is* the matter?'

'I often wonder how I compare with Robert and Tom!'

I gave up. I had a sudden vision of her desperate unhappiness.

'I want to see you,' I said. 'Will you meet me, darling?'

'I'm going to a film! . . .' Her voice trailed off in pain.

'Let's have a drink before you go. Will you? Please, darling!'

At last Myrtle agreed, though her tone remained lifeless.

And so it came about that I was waiting apprehensively for her to come and join me in a public-house near my lodgings.

I sat in the public bar, which I had chosen instead of the saloon because it was always empty. The floors were made of uncovered boards, and the table-tops were not scrubbed very often. The wall-paper had been given a coat of shiny brown varnish: over the fireplace there was a dusty mirror with a knot of red Flanders poppies twisted into one corner of the frame: on the opposite wall was an oilcloth chart showing the town Association football team's fixtures of three years ago, surrounded by advertisements for hairdressing, sausages and furniture removals.

On the mantelshelf stood a fortune-telling machine shaped

like a miniature wireless set. You put in a penny and selected a button to press, whereupon a coloured light flickered, and the machine delivered a pasteboard card with your fortune inscribed upon it.

I put in a penny. The card said:

YOU ARE SUNNY AND GOOD-NATURED.
BEWARE THE INFLUENCE OF OTHERS.

'Dammit!' I said aloud. I took the card between my first and second fingers and flicked it, as I used to flick cigarette cards when I was a boy, into the empty fireplace.

The door opened and Tom's red head looked in. I was astonished.

'Ah! I thought I might find you here.' Tom came towards me. 'I've just called at your house.' The latter sentence was uttered in a vaguely apologetic tone.

'Did you know I was meeting Myrtle?'

'Are you?'

I looked at him. Tom had a remarkable talent for turning up at rendezvous I had made with someone else. His instinct for not missing anything amounted to second sight. I said:

'Yes. You can push off when she comes.'

'Of course,' said Tom, as if I had offended his taste for old-world courtesy.

'Did you want to see me about anything special?'

'No.' Tom stood on his dignity for a moment. Then he went across to the service hatch, where he bought a pint of beer for himself and another one for me.

'How is Myrtle?' he asked.

I told him. I was so worried about her that I paid no attention to my suspicions of him. I confided my fears and my self-reproaches.

Tom reassured me.

'It wouldn't make the slightest difference if you married her,' he said. 'It's the ebb and flow of her nature.' He spoke with great authority, though not necessarily with great truth. 'If you married her she'd still have those bouts of accidie. It's the ebb and flow you know.' He was pleased with the phrase and illustrated it with his hands.

It seemed to me that we had too much ebb and not enough flow. 'Poor Myrtle,' I said, with a deep stir of sympathy for her. She had a lightly balanced emotional nature—that was what made her so attractive to me—but for some reason or other, alas! it tipped over too readily in the downward direction.

'I shouldn't take it very seriously,' said Tom. 'It really is her temperament, and fundamentally, you know, she's accommodated to it.' He smiled at me. 'I understand these things, Joe.'

I knew perfectly well that when he was alone with her instead of with me he approached the problem in a very different tone.

'I'm much nearer to her in this way than you are,' he said.

This remark, on the other hand, Myrtle must have had addressed to her very frequently in their *tête-à-tête*.

'Much nearer, you know,' Tom repeated.

I did not mention any steps he might be proposing to take on the basis of this peculiar nearness—time would display them soon enough.

And then I said, honestly: 'You give me great comfort, Tom.'

'That's what one's friends are for,' said Tom.

'God knows, I'm in need of it.'

Tom shook his head. 'It's time this affair was over,' he said, in the tone of great wisdom that he used when he spoke from the depths of his soul—you remember, the very old soul. I recalled Bolshaw saying: 'The time has come.' I wondered how on earth everybody but me recognised the time with such certainty. I decided it was because they lacked the capacity for recognising anything else.

Tom drank off about a third of a pint, and sighed with satisfaction. I noticed the barman had appeared at the service-hatch: he was polishing glasses which he placed on a shelf out of sight.

Suddenly the door opened. I thought it was Myrtle and my heart jumped. It was a seedy-looking man wearing a peaked cap and a muffler. He glanced at Tom and me, apparently did not care for the look of us, and went out again. We heard him go into the saloon.

We were silent. It was a warm evening, and an invisible fly buzzed round the ceiling. 'Have some more beer?' said Tom.

'It's my round.'

Suddenly I remembered Trevor's crisis. I asked Tom what had happened.

Tom smiled blandly. 'I think everything will be . . . managed,' he said. 'Apparently we have to wait. The timing is important, you know.' He stopped. 'I think it would be wise for you to be ignorant of it.'

'Will you need more money?'

Tom shrugged his shoulders. I stood up to buy the next round of drinks. Myrtle came in.

Myrtle saw me first and made no effort to raise the light of recognition. Then she saw Tom, and smiled tremulously.

'Ah, Myrtle,' said Tom, in an effusively sympathetic tone.

'Tom was just going,' I said to Myrtle, malevolently recalling the times Tom had got rid of me or of her.

Tom shrugged his shoulders, and smiled at Myrtle. 'Joe behaving as usual.'

The remark unaccountably plunged Myrtle into despair. She made it very plain and Tom was not at all pleased.

'I think I'll go,' he said.

I watched him leave while Myrtle settled herself beside me. I was suddenly overwhelmed by apprehension. I thought, 'This is going to be the worst scene.'

Myrtle and I looked into each other's eyes. It was a light evening, but the room was dark and we were sitting with our backs to the window.

I saw written in Myrtle's face all the things I wished not to see. Fear and shame suddenly rose up in me, mingled with a deep and poignant sympathy. Myrtle did not speak. She sat there, just letting me look at her. Not a word had been passed between us, not a touch, and yet I felt as if the whole scene were already over. 'This is the end.'

'How are you feeling now, darling?' I could not help myself from speaking as if she were in the grip of an illness from which she might already be recovering.

'I don't know.'

I looked at her closely. Her eyes looked bigger, and the bright patches of colour in her cheeks had spread out more widely.

Under her eyes there were brown stains. She seemed to be breathing with a deeper movement of her heart.

'Darling.' I took hold of her hand. She let it lie in mine.

'This can't go on,' she said.

I said nothing. I felt as if I had been struck.

There was a long pause. 'Can it?' she said, and looked at me.

I did not possess the courage to say 'no'. I said, nearly inaudibly: 'I don't know. If you don't think . . .'

There was a movement and the barman appeared in the hatch to see if we wanted anything.

Myrtle asked for a double whisky.

Out of surprise I bought her one, and I thought I had better have one myself. I set the two glasses on the wooden table in front of us.

We each drank a little. Neither of us said anything. We drank some more. The minutes passed by us, like the flies buzzing across the room. The flies congregated at the mirror.

'How *can* it go on?' Myrtle spoke without looking at me now.

'I don't know.'

We were silent again. I drank some more whisky. I could not tell what I was feeling or thinking. I was overwhelmed by recollections of the past.

I noticed her gulp down her drink. The expression on her face remained exactly the same. She said:

'I think about nothing else, nowadays.'

I said: 'Nor I.'

There was a pause. And I said: 'Do you want it to end?'

'How could I?' Faint life came into her voice.

'Then how? . . .'

'I love you.' She suddenly looked at me.

'Oh God!'

Myrtle drew in her breath sharply. She was holding the glass quite close to her lips, looking into it.

'What's the matter?'

'You don't want to marry me!' No sooner had she uttered the words than she burst into tears.

I was faced with the truth, with the core of my own obstinacy. I could have stretched out my hand and whispered, 'I'll marry you.' She was so near to me. It was so little to say.

I shook my head. 'No.'

Myrtle sobbed quietly. I watched her. I finished my glass of whisky. Do not think I was not caught in the throes of self-reproach and remorse. I was. I was confronted with the core of my own obstinacy, and it was a hateful thing. Yet I neither could nor would break it. Not for a moment did I see that she had a core of obstinacy too. Everything that was causing her pain was my fault. I tortured myself—because I would not give in.

We sat for a long time thus, concerned, each of us, with our-selves: and the bonds between us were snapping. We had reached the final question and the final answer—what seemed the final question and answer to us—and there was nowhere further to go.

Myrtle took out a handkerchief and tried to wipe her eyes. She glanced at the stains on it of mascara. Quietly I went and fetched us another double whisky apiece. I dropped too much water into Myrtle's. She picked it up and absent-mindedly began to drink it as if it were lemonade. I stared at my own glass. We could not speak.

In the saloon bar someone switched on a wireless set, and I heard a voice inexorably reading out cricket scores. Myrtle appeared not to hear it. We were still entirely alone in the bar. At last she looked up.

'I must go away,' she said.

'Don't go yet, darling.'

'I must. . . .'

It seemed unbearable to let her go. I put my arm round her, as if to comfort her.

'My own darling!' I cried, hiding my face against her neck. I felt as if I possessed her completely, and it touched me so that I could have burst into tears. I felt another living creature, closer to me than I had ever felt anyone before, now, at the moment when we were going to part.

Myrtle uttered a great sigh. I picked up her glass, and held it for her to drink out of it. Then I had a drink.

'I'm late already,' Myrtle said.

'Never mind.'

'But I've got an appointment.'

'Are you going with Haxby?'

'Yes.'

'He can wait.'

Myrtle freed herself from my arm in order to turn to me. 'Don't you care about anybody?'

'I don't understand what you mean.'

'Of course, you don't.' She began to show signs of life. 'You don't care if he waits. You don't care if I go.'

'That's all you know about it.'

'How can I tell? You never say anything. Other people do, but you never do. *You* never say anything one way or the other. You talk about Haxby as if he didn't matter.' She rounded upon me with impressive force. 'Do you know he wants to shoot you?'

'Good gracious!' I exclaimed.

'He's jealous!' said Myrtle.

'I suppose he must be.'

'There you go! You just put yourself in *his* place!'

'How can I be a writer if I don't?'

'I don't know *how* you can do it. You don't care about me.'

'If you mean that I don't know what it is to be jealous, then you're . . .'

'Do you? Do you?' Myrtle faced me. 'Then why didn't you tell me?'

'Because I don't tell anybody. Because jealousy's hateful!' I cried. 'I hate being jealous of Haxby. I wish I'd never heard of him!'

'There's a way out, isn't there?' She meant by marrying her.

I stood up. 'No!' I cried. 'I won't take it.'

Myrtle watched me. 'No, I realize that now. Tom made that pretty clear to me.'

'Tom?' I said. 'You've been talking to Tom about this.'

'Of course. Who am I to talk to? I haven't got any friends. And Tom understands you.'

'Says he does.'

'He understands you better than you think.'

'There's no truer word than that!'

'How horrible you are!'

I sat down again.

We were silent for a while.

'Does Tom think he understands you?' I said.

141

Myrtle did not reply.

I said: 'I'm sorry, darling.'

Myrtle looked at me, this time gently. 'You don't understand how I have no one to turn to. Tom is being kind to me, that's all. He's wonderfully sympathetic.'

I wondered if she had any inkling of Tom's motive in being wonderfully sympathetic, and decided not. It was not for me to enlighten her—anyway I was not sure myself.

I put my arm round her again, in a friendly way. My anger was subsiding and so was hers.

'Please, don't let's quarrel, darling.'

Myrtle was suddenly silent. It must have crossed both our minds simultaneously that I meant 'Don't let's quarrel before we part.'

'Don't say that!' she cried.

There was a pause. I finished my drink. Myrtle left hers. She sat looking at it, as if she wanted never to go any further with it, so as never to move from where she was now sitting with my arm round her.

The room was in twilight, and the barman unexpectedly switched on the light. We hid our faces.

Myrtle stood up, and I did the same.

'I must go,' she said.

We looked into each other's eyes. 'What is it to be?' Neither of us could utter the question.

'I'll put you on the bus,' I said.

Myrtle nodded, and we went into the street. It was less dusky than we had imagined. The air was warm on our cheeks. The street was wide, and lined with trees. We strolled to the bus-stop and waited.

I stood beside Myrtle for a while and suddenly looked at her. I saw that her expression had changed completely. Even though I was determined not to take the lead, I could not let the moment pass again without asking her:

'What do you want me to do?'

Her voice sounded hollow and distant as she said: 'I suppose we ought to stop seeing each other?'

I made no pretence of not accepting it.

'I'm terribly sorry,' I murmured, finding words feeble and

hopeless. Myrtle appeared not to hear.

We saw a bus approaching.

'Goodbye, darling.'

Suddenly we were in each other's arm. I kissed her and she clung to me.

The bus passed us without stopping. We were at a request stop and had failed to hold up our hands.

'You'll have to wait for the next.'

Myrtle drew away from me. She was crying. 'Goodbye, darling.'

'I'll wait with you.'

'No, don't; please don't! Go now!'

'I can't leave you.'

'I beg you to go!' She spoke with force and anguish.

I took hold of her hands for a moment, and then turned away.

I walked along the road, which sloped upwards and curved away to the right. As I reached the bend, I looked back. I saw Myrtle standing alone. Tears welled up into my eyes, so that I could not see where I was going. But I went on.

I went back to my house. The landlady and her niece were out, and the place was completely empty. I switched on the light in my room, and my glance fell on the telephone. I felt unutterably lonely.

I sat down in my chair, and began to think. The break had come at last. Yet there was something strange about it. Myrtle had said: 'I suppose we ought to stop seeing each other'; but she had framed it as a question, so as to leave it open for me to say, 'No, no!' I felt very confused. Had we parted or not? It seemed like it, yet somehow I felt sure that Myrtle had not. It takes two to make even a parting.

Gradually I became calmer. My mood changed. I went over the scene again and again; and I found it beginning to strike me differently. My confusion was disappearing and something definite was being revealed to me. I received the revelation with a bitter kind of resistance, because it made me feel cold and heartless.

I knew now that whatever Myrtle did in the future, for me the affair was irrevocably over.

CHAPTER V

VERTIGINOUS DEVELOPMENTS

E ach time the telephone rang during the next few days I thought it would be Myrtle. It was not. I kept away from places where I might meet her and arranged to go and spend the week-end in Oxford. I felt uneasy and miserable, and at the same time convinced that something was going to happen.

I diverted myself with tedious business-like activities. The American Consulate in London had told me it was necessary to go to the Consulate in Birmingham to obtain my visa, so I arranged to collect it on Friday afternoon, when the school had a half-holiday. And I wrote again to Miss X.Y. about my manuscript.

On the day after my ambiguous parting with Myrtle Tom rang up, aiming to discover what had happened. I made him come round to my lodgings to find out.

I was sitting in my room, beside the open french window, eating tinned-salmon sandwiches for tea, when Tom arrived.

'I see you haven't lost your appetite,' he observed.

I thought the remark was in bad taste. 'I'll ask the landlady to make some more for you.' He was very fond of salmon sandwiches. 'I hope she hasn't run out of salmon,' I added, to frighten him.

Tom greedily ate a couple of mine, just in case. He glanced over the cake-stand. 'Very nice cakes she makes you. She's very devoted to you.'

'The niece makes them.'

'Ah! She made them for Mr Chinnock, of course.' He wagged his head sagely, at the thought of more devotion in a different guise.

I took the last sandwich, and went to order more. I met the landlady bringing them of her own accord. Tom saluted her in a flowery fashion, which clearly pleased her. She was a lean, middle-aged woman, with a pale, indrawn face and narrow, dark eyes. Tom made a gleam appear in her eyes. When she had gone out of the room Tom said:

'Now she'll be more devoted to you than ever.'

As there had been numerous quarrels over Myrtle visiting me late at night, I thought a little more devotion would do me no harm. Up to date I had seen no signs of it. Possessiveness, yes: devotion, no.

Tom said: 'I hear that Myrtle was looking dreadfully unhappy at the film show last night.'

'Who told you?'

'Steve went to it. He saw her. She was with Haxby.'

I did not say anything.

'What happened after I'd left you?' Tom asked. 'Did you break it off?'

'Break it off!' I exclaimed. 'It's not a stick of toffee. You don't break things off just like that.'

Tom's disapproval was evident. In my place he would have broken it off. However he said amiably: 'Then it's still on?'

'Not exactly,' I replied. 'That's the trouble.'

'Poor girl!'

'You told me yesterday she wasn't such a poor girl.'

'Is that how you left it?'

'Well, yes.'

Tom shook his head. 'I don't understand how you can leave it neither one way nor the other. I couldn't. I should have forced a decision.'

I was feeling in no mood to be amused. 'In a sense I did. I forced one from myself—afterwards. It's over as far as I'm concerned.'

'That's better. You'll feel much better for it.'

'I don't. I feel worse.'

'Purely transient,' said Tom.

There was a pause. Tom helped himself to the last of the fresh batch of salmon sandwiches.

I decided to tell him what had happened as honestly as I

could. I repeated most of the conversation verbatim. I described Myrtle's tears and our last embrace at the bus-stop.

'My dear Joe,' said Tom, 'how you make the poor girl suffer!'

I said: 'How she makes me suffer, if it comes to that!'

'She probably thinks you don't intend to see her again.'

'That's just what you advised me to do.'

'It's positively brutal!' said Tom, paying no attention whatsoever. 'How you make her suffer!' His voice rose with anger. 'You treat her appallingly!'

You may find Tom's behaviour mildly contradictory: that is nothing to what I found it. In my own behaviour I aimed at some sort of consistency, and until I knew Tom I was under the impression that other people did the same. Not a bit of it! Tom was a revelation to me, and through him others were revealed. Only through observing Tom, I decided, could one understand the human race.

Tom denounced me for several minutes. After counselling me to break off the affair, he now abused me passionately for doing it—and at the same time managed to convey additional contempt for my pusillanimity in not making the break sharper. His face got redder and his eyes began to glare. He was carried away by his sympathy for Myrtle.

'You've ruined her life!' he cried.

I said nothing. Tom let the torrent carry him on. He turned his attention to my failings. While he ate my cakes he denounced my self-centredness, my coldness of heart, my unawareness of the feelings of others, my lack of passion—my complete unsatisfactoriness as man, thinker and lover. A few years earlier I should have lost my temper and argued furiously.

'What are you going to do next?' Tom demanded to know.

'Nothing,' I muttered.

'That's just like you.'

I did have a faint sensation of not knowing whether I was on my head or my heels. However, I pulled myself together and said ingeniously:

'What are *you* going to do next?'

Tom was brought momentarily to a standstill.

'I shall have to consider that,' he said.

I thought: 'That's unusual.'

'Myrtle has suffered terribly,' he said, more quietly. 'I think I'm the only person who understands exactly what it must have meant to her.'

'She told me you understood.'

'She said that, did she?' Tom suddenly looked at me quite naively.

I nodded my head.

'We've both suffered,' said Tom.

I nodded again. It seemed the only appropriate gesture to such monumental nonsense.

'I've been thinking about Myrtle for some time, Joe.'

'Oh?' I pricked up my ears.

Tom looked at me with a changed, unidentifiable expression. 'I've been thinking,' he said, 'that if you don't marry her, it might be a good idea for me to.'

I received the suggestion without a tremor. I was proud of having identified his expression—it was that of a man who is confident that he has introduced a delicate topic with un-equalled tact and dexterity.

I made a non-committal murmuring noise. I think Tom had expected more. He was clearly puzzled that I showed no sur-prise, let alone passion. He said:

'What do you think?'

I said: 'I've been thinking about it, from a different point of view, of course, for some time.' I paused. 'The trouble about finding a husband for one's mistress, is that no other man seems quite good enough.'

Tom was extremely cross. He laughed, but a purple flush suddenly passed over his face, making his hair look yellower and his eyes greener.

'Witty as usual,' he said.

Whenever anyone says I am something or other 'as usual', it means he is disapproving of me.

'Perhaps,' he went on, 'we ought to talk just a little more seri-ously.'

'Would you like some more tea?' I said.

'Thank you.'

A stately air had now come over the proceedings. Tom ac-cepted a cup of tea, and then said with great politeness and consideration:

'I take it that you would have no objection?'

'To your marrying Myrtle? I'm in no position to object.' I changed my tone to one of seriousness. 'I resolved some time ago that if I wasn't going to marry her myself I ought not to stop anyone else marrying her. Of course I don't want to let anyone else—or anything like it. But I shall make myself do it.'

'I see. It seems quite incomprehensible to me, of course.'

I bowed.

Tom said: 'This makes matters a little easier than I'd expected.'

'Easier?' I exclaimed. Perhaps I ought to interpolate that, even after having been prepared for it by Steve, I still thought I had never heard such a silly idea in my life as Tom's proposition. Also I thought Myrtle would see it in exactly the same light.

Tom pursed his lips and smiled.

The telephone rang. Tom and I glanced at each other, each thinking it was Myrtle. I closed the french window and took off the receiver. Tom waited to see if I wanted him to leave the room. I heard the voice of Steve.

'Joe, is Tom there?' He sounded worried.

'Yes.' I handed the receiver to Tom.

They conversed for a few moments, making arrangements to meet in half an hour. Tom put down the receiver, and turned to me with a self-satisfied smile.

'How are you getting on with Steve?' I asked.

'Perfectly well, Joe.' There was an amused glint in his eye, as much as to say: 'If you understood us you would not be alarmed.'

I called the landlady to clear away the tea.

'How's he getting on with his schoolgirls?' I said.

'I don't know. I don't really ask him.' Tom had now taken to setting me an example.

Recalling the scene at the swimming-pool, I said: 'That's wise of you.'

Tom sat in his chair again. 'He's growing up, of course. I realise that he's bound to grow away from me. It's very natural.' Tom paused. 'I encourage him. I don't want him to feel tied.'

I could not help being interested by this crescendo of lies, which, seemingly, we were only half-way through, as he said next: 'The important thing is to avoid scenes, Joe.'

'Don't you have any?' I could hardly believe my ears.

'No, Joe.'

We were interrupted by the landlady. Tom lit a cigarette. When she had gone he leaned forward confidentially, and said:

'Of course, Steve doesn't know anything about my intentions towards Myrtle.'

'No,' I said. 'No.' I accepted this last, most glorious lie, with a recrudescence of the head-or-heels sensation.

'I hope you won't mention it to him.'

'If Steve doesn't know,' I said, 'you can rely upon me not to tell him, Tom.'

'I know you're one of the discreetest of men, Joe.'

Tom rose to go away, and on this happy, fraudulent note our conversation ended.

Tom had only left the house a minute or two when the telephone rang once more.

'It's Steve again. Has Tom gone? I wanted to speak to you, not him, when I rang before.' Steve's voice was agitated. 'I want to see you, Joe.'

'What for, Steve?'

'I can't tell you now. There isn't time. Tom will be here any moment. I want to see you, Joe.'

I had taken care to have all my time booked up until I went to Oxford. Steve was insistent, and at last I agreed that we might meet in the station refreshment room while I waited for my train. He rang off promptly.

I was mystified.

On Saturday morning I received a letter in unfamiliar handwriting. It was from Miss X.Y. and she said:

Dear Mr. Lunn: I do not know how to begin this letter, as I feel I am at a terrible disadvantage. I quite understand your anxiety about your manuscript, and of course I forgive you for writing a third time. I am afraid I have to ask *you* to forgive *me*, because the manuscript has unfortunately been mislaid. The reason I have delayed so long in writing to you is because I hoped it might turn up. Of course I was looking forward immensely to reading it. . . .

I burst into a shout of mingled laughter and rage. Miss X.Y. had wasted five months of my time at a most critical point in my career; I was exactly where I started. The letter ended with an offer to read the novel, if I would send another copy, within a week.

At first I was too annoyed to accept, but in due course common sense supervened. I remained convinced, however, that should disasters of any magnitude be possible they would certainly befall me. In this mood I went off to meet Steve.

I hurried down to the platform and into the refreshment room. Steve was nowhere to be seen. I bought a bottle of beer and a cheese roll, and began to eat, keeping my eyes fixed on the door. I finished the cheese roll and I finished the beer. Still no sign of Steve. Suddenly it occurred to me that Steve was in a refreshment room on the wrong platform. I ran across the bridge, and searched for him on the other side. I found him. He was quietly reading a volume of poems by Baudelaire.

'Come out, Steve!' I said impatiently. 'You're in the wrong refreshment room.'

Steve looked injured. 'But I'm not, Joe! This is the right platform.'

'The right platform for somebody else's train, but not mine,' I said, taking him by the elbow and dragging him out. He stuck to his argument. There were two alternative routes to Oxford: he had chosen the platform for a train that left three hours later. I realised to my horror that I was behaving rather like Tom. I decided that Tom had great provocation.

'Do you want a bottle of beer?' I said, when I had safely installed him in the right place.

'Yes, please.' Steve wore the expression of a saint on the eve of martyrdom. This expression did not prevent him putting down half a Bass in one breath. 'I got very thirsty, waiting for you,' he said.

'Now, what do you want to tell me?'

We were leaning against the marble-topped counter, looking outwards at the platform. Behind us were two glass domes, containing buns, which served as a screen between us and the waitress. Steve glanced at his glass, and restrained himself out of politeness from drinking the rest of the beer before beginning his story.

'I found out that Tom's postponed his trip to America.'

'I know that.'

'I mean *again*, Joe. He's not going till the end of July now.'

This was news to me.

Steve said nothing. With a mixture of injured dignity and triumph he now finished his beer.

I was lost for a moment in alarm.

'What's his excuse now?' I asked.

'The job we're doing in the office.'

'I don't believe it.'

'That's what he's going to tell you, anyway,' said Steve.

'What's his real reason? Do you know?'

'How should I know? He tells me so many things.'

'Repeat some of them.'

'I wasn't supposed to tell you.'

'Repeat them all the same.'

'He doesn't want to arrive ahead of you and Robert. He says you intend to send him first to do all the work.'

'But we're tied till the end of July.'

'You told him you were going to make him support you.'

'That's absurd—it was a joke,' I said. 'Robert said we were going to settle on him like Russian relations.' I smiled at the thought of it. 'And then treat him badly, as if he were a servant.'

'He took it seriously.'

'He's got some other reason, I'll be bound.'

'You mean it's part of his plan for marrying Myrtle?'

'Nonsense! He can't marry Myrtle. It's idiotic!'

'He's trying to make me believe it,' said Steve. 'And he's made himself believe it.'

'That's as may be. It does seem to me that his principal obstacle is making Myrtle believe it.'

Steve looked at me with shrewd grey eyes. 'She's seeing him a lot more than you think.'

I was slightly taken aback. 'Really,' I said.

There was a pause. I sipped a little beer. Steve eyed his empty glass, having no money to buy any more.

'And where do you come into this, Steve? Is Tom's devotion to you correspondingly weaker?'

'Weaker?' said Steve. 'Did you say weaker, Joe? It's stronger. Honestly, it's terrible! I can't get away from it for a moment. He tells me I'm growing away from him, and he doesn't want me to feel I'm tied to him—and then he refuses to let me out of his sight! Last night I wanted to stay at home. To work on my poetry. Honestly, I didn't want to go out with anyone else. I just wanted to stay at home. But he came round to the house. He stood in the middle of the room and said: "I want to know. Are you coming or aren't you?" In front of my father and mother!'

I imagined the scene well, with Tom glaring across the room. 'What did you say?'

Steve shrugged his shoulders. 'I had to go with him.'

'Extraordinary,' I said.

'He's terrified of me being unfaithful.'

I could not help laughing, though it hurt Steve's feelings. 'What about when he goes to America?'

'He expects me to join him in two or three years.'

This was more news to me. 'Indeed!'

'Yes,' said Steve. 'As far as I can see, he intends to marry Myrtle and take her to America; and me to stay here and be faithful to him. For three years!'

I was speechless from the staggering imbecility of it.

'Think of it, Joe!' Steve said, in tones of anguish.

'I'm thinking of what's supposed to happen at the end of three years, Steve, when you join the happy couple in America.'

Steve said: 'I don't think he's got as far as that.'

'It seems a very arbitrary place to draw the line.' I glanced at him, and just at that moment he happened to glance at me. We caught each other's eye, and burst into helpless laughter. All the other people in the refreshment room turned and stared at us.

I glanced at the clock, and realised that the train which was drawing in was the one I had to catch.

'You need another drink, Steve,' I said. 'Goodbye!'

I threw down some money on the counter to pay for a bottle of beer, and left him to drink it.

Vertiginous Developments

I reported Tom's latest manœuvres to Robert, who was alarmed. I could see quite clearly that he thought Tom would never go to America on his own: I think he really doubted whether Tom would ever go at all. We decided to concentrate on our own plans. I now had my visa, and Robert had applied for his. Escaping from the atmosphere of the town for a few hours enabled me to see our affairs in some sort of perspective. I became aware of how events were rolling on. It was June.

We dined in the college, and afterwards went back to Robert's rooms feeling a little more relaxed. We talked about our books, and Robert laughed somewhat unkindly over Miss X.Y.'s letter. As the evening passed I confided more freely my emotions about Myrtle.

'In ten years' time I shall wish I'd married her,' I said, bitterly.

Robert made no comment.

I had begun to feel tired and I launched a boring tirade about remorse, the gist of it being that after doing what you wanted to do it was hypocritical to express remorse.

I noticed Robert looking at the clock. It was after eleven.

The telephone rang.

Robert crossed the room to answer it. I picked up something to read. It was a trunk call for me.

I was frightened: I took over the receiver, certain that I was going to hear of some tragedy.

I heard the distant voice of Myrtle.

'Is that Joe?'

'Yes.'

'It's me, Myrtle.'

'Oh.'

'Darling, I've got a dog!'

'What!'

'I've got a dog, darling. A *dog!*' Her voice sounded excited. Either her depression had been dissipated or she had been drinking.

'Isn't it wonderful?'

'Yes.' First of all I had found it impossible to believe she was saying it was a dog she had got: now I found it impossible to understand what was going on at all.

153

'I said, "Isn't it wonderful?"'
'I said, "Yes."'
Myrtle's voice came to me with reproach. 'You don't sound very enthusiastic!'
There is only one phrase for expressing what I felt. It was a bit much.
'I'm sorry,' I muttered.
Were it possible to hear anyone's spirits fall, I should have heard Myrtle's fall with an echoing 'woomph!'
'I'm glad,' I said, with as much enthusiasm as I could summon—very little, as a matter of fact.
'It's a red setter.'
'Good,' I said.
'It answers to the name of Brian.'
'What?'
'Brian. B-r-i-a-n.'
'Good heavens!'
'I can't hear you.'
'I said, "How are you?"'
'All right. I'm feeling wonderful. Brian and I went for a walk in the park this afternoon. We had a wonderful time.'
I could think of nothing to say. I just listened to her voice, which expressed pure happiness.
'You must come and see him.' She paused. 'When do you come back?'
I was suspicious. I said:
'Tomorrow evening.'
'Will you come and see Brian and me?'
'If you'd really like me to . . .' My spirits now fell.
'I'll expect you tomorrow night. Goodbye, darling.'
'Goodbye.'
I glanced at Robert, who had been standing by the fireplace listening.
There was a short silence. Then I said:
'Are we all going off our heads?'
I really meant it.

PART IV

CHAPTER I

IN AN INTERLUDE

I sat in the open doorway of my cottage, listening to the noise of the rain on the leaves. The hedgerows and trees had come to their full summer thickness. The may was all gone, and green berries were already showing, standing up instead of hanging down; and the ash trees had put out tufts of seeds with beautiful little wings on them. It was nearly the end of June. The first date of Tom's departure had passed, and we were soon to pass the second. In spite of the rain, yellow-hammers were diving like chaser-planes from the tree immediately opposite, and magpies strutted in the field. It was Saturday morning and I was expecting Myrtle.

Yes, incredible though it may seem, Myrtle was coming to spend the afternoon, and apparently she was coming to spend it in the highest of spirits. Ever since the arrival of her dog she had shown no signs other than those of happiness. Tom spoke with enormous portentous knowledge about ebb and flow. I doubted him. Through her gaiety sounded a faintly crazed note that reminded me of hysteria. I thought this kind of happiness must be unstable—just as suddenly as it had come it would collapse and plunge her into deeper despair. Tom thought I was making too much of it.

'You take your responsibilities too heavily,' he said.

I thought it over and decided that perhaps I did. I studied Myrtle, and half-reassured myself. Our meetings were sunny and light-hearted, and apparently quite casual. Of course I asked myself what Myrtle thought she was doing. Nobody could accuse me of not asking myself innumerable, internal questions. But you are more interested in the answer? I have to confess that I expressed my answer in a most undesirable form, the form of a business phrase. Myrtle was continuing our relationship on a day-to-day basis. I presume that a man who is about to go bankrupt still continues to visit his office, use the telephone, and enjoy the creative act of composing business letters. So, Myrtle, before bankrupt love.

On a day-to-day basis, Myrtle was delightful company. Having done justice to my conscience, I began to do justice to myself as a whole again. It was Myrtle's choice. 'Remember that!' I kept saying to myself: 'It's her choice.' I got a consolation from the concept of Myrtle's choice.

The rain ceased and I went out into the lane to pick some flowers. In the hedges there were two kinds of dog-roses, white and pink, and the pink ones had deep carmine buds. Though I knew it was useless I plucked a bud, and it unfolded, like a living creature, immediately. I was looking for honeysuckle. In the ditch the campions and cow-parsley had gone. At last I found some honeysuckle that was nearly in bloom: it was growing up a big tree; the stem was old and twined like bast. In the warmth of the bedroom the flowers would open. Ah! Myrtle, I thought.

I returned slowly to the cottage, kicking a loose stone along the road.

I began to think about Tom. During the week there had been a crisis with Steve. As yet I had heard only Tom's side of it, but that was enough to trouble me.

Tom and I had met by chance in the central lending library. It was a large hall with a gallery running round it. The floor was highly polished, and the room always smelt of beeswax and turpentine. Bookshelves were built out from the walls at regular intervals dividing the space into a number of alcoves. These alcoves were used by serious-minded people for silent reading, and by the young for whispered flirtation. I found the mingled amorous cum literary tone of the place most estimable, since it encouraged the seriousminded to flirt and the flirtatious to read.

I had a suspicion that Tom was trying to avoid me. However, in the course of moving round the shelves we met face to face. Caught unawares he had an unusual expression. His features looked set, and his skin showed a greyish tinge.

'What's the matter?' I asked.

'I'm a little disturbed. That's all.'

'What about?'

Tom did not reply. I followed him as he went to have his book stamped, and we left together. In the street he paused uncertainly.

'I'll walk along with you,' I said. It was about half-past six and the streets were empty: everyone was having an evening meal. The air was luminous and cool, and our reflections flashed by in the shop-windows.

'What's Steve been doing?' I asked.

'How did you know it was Steve?'

I did not imagine it was Myrtle because I believed his feeling for her to be thoroughly bogus. 'I guessed.'

Tom said: 'He told me last night that he was going on holiday with his father and mother.'

I was puzzled. 'What does that matter to you?'

'It matters to me because I was going to take him away myself.'

'But you're going to America, Tom.'

'Before I go to America.'

I was silent for a moment, distracted by confirmation of our suspicions that he did not intend to go. I remembered what Steve had told me in the refreshment room.

'When *are* you going?'

'Later.' He waved his hand impatiently. 'Later . . . my dear Joe, don't let your anxiety run away with you.'

'I see,' I said. 'Where were you taking him?'

'To France. He wants to improve his accent.'

Often I had seen the comic side of the patron-protégé relationship. I now saw the reverse. When Tom said Steve wanted to improve his French accent he was speaking with heart-felt seriousness. A vivid picture sprang up in my mind of Steve lounging in a Parisian bistro, probably drinking Pernod and trying to get himself seduced by the woman behind the cash-desk—improving his French accent.

'I promised to take him,' said Tom. And added: 'He promised he'd go'—thus giving the show away completely.

'Poor old Tom!' I said.

Tom glanced at me, but did not understand why I was smiling. I was thinking of the lectures I had received from him, Tom, the worldly-wise, on how little importance one should attach to people's promises.

'Of course, I could insist,' said Tom. 'His parents would back me up.'

'Good gracious!'

'They're ambitious for his future,' said Tom, reprovingly.

I thought: 'As if Steve hadn't got his eye on the main chance!' I said:

'Where are they going?'

'Grimsby,' said Tom, with distaste.

I said: 'I suppose he'll have to make his own choice.'

'Exactly. It would be disastrous for him to feel tied to me.'

It must have been the tenth time I had heard this phrase, from one or the other of them. Why, I wondered, did nobody point out that Steve had never been tied to anyone but himself, nor was ever likely to be? I contented myself with saying:

'Won't he feel tied to his parents?'

'Certainly! It's very foolish of him.'

It had occurred to me, as no doubt it had to Steve, that escaping from his father and mother in Grimsby would be child's play compared with escaping from his patron in Paris.

'I'm afraid,' said Tom, 'he's going off the rails.'

'Alas! he's not the only one,' said I.

We had come to a crossing of the main streets, and we stopped. In day-time the crossing was the busiest in the town: now it was deserted. In the centre, where the policeman stood on point duty, there remained his pedestal with nobody on it. We were silent. Tom suddenly lowered his head, and I saw a look of misery on his face.

'I'm awfully sorry, Tom.'

'It's my last chance. It means more to me than anything has ever done.' He looked up at me with strained eyes. 'Do you think I ought to buy a new car?'

It was a totally unexpected question. I saw quickly enough what he meant. He had so far lost control that he could envisage trying to bribe Steve with a new car. I wanted to cry 'no'. I said:

'I doubt if it would really help.'

Tom's voice suddenly went dead. 'I didn't think it would. I'm not a fool.'

We both knew the conversation had ended, and we went away

immediately in different directions. Something made me look back, and I saw Tom walking with a changed gait. Instead of propelling himself along with his diaphragm thrust out and his shoulders swinging to and fro, he was walking with the slow, stiff movements of an automaton. I had never before realized he was capable of the change. I was shocked and touched.

This sight continued to haunt me in recollection. It came back to me while I was kicking the loose stone along the road up to the cottage. I thought of Tom's predicament, and of all the other people who had found themselves in it. 'Ought I to buy a new car?' Other people; other vehicles—such as steam yachts.

'Ought I to buy him a steam yacht?'

Bearing Steve in mind, I felt the answer was almost certainly 'yes'. Amusement led me to wonder if I was taking Tom's responsibilities too heavily. Indoors, I laid down the bunch of honeysuckle.

My reflections were cut short by the sound of a bicycle bell.

'Darling!' shouted Myrtle's voice from the roadway. 'Come and see who I've brought!'

'Who?' I cried, in mixed incredulity, disappointment and anger. I went outside to see.

'Doesn't he look beautiful!' In the basket on the front of Myrtle's bicycle sat the dog.

'Well!' I exclaimed, in unmixed relief.

Myrtle's face was alight with pleasure. I kissed her. She was wearing a new kind of scent. I kissed her again, and slid my hand warmly over her back.

She made me hold the bicycle, while she set down the animal.

'Brian! Brian!' she called, without the slightest appearance of noticing the inappositeness of its name.

The animal bounded and fussed around. It was a pretty red colour, and it had a charmingly silly, affectionate expression. It kept leaving a little watery trail behind it. I led Myrtle indoors.

Myrtle stirred beside me.

'I thought you were asleep,' I murmured.

'I thought you were!'

We were quiet. The smell of honeysuckle had begun to fill the room.

'Can you hear something?' said Myrtle.

I could. It was the animal whining downstairs.

'Brian wants to come up,' said Myrtle.

'Well, he can't,' said I.

'Oh darling, why not?'

I did not want to get out of bed to open the door. 'You don't have to have dogs in the bedroom.'

'But he's crying. He's only a puppy.'

'All the more reason,' I said. 'We should make him feel shy.'

Myrtle took hold of me gently. 'Please go and fetch him, darling.'

I did as she asked me.

With a flustering patter the animal ran upstairs. Myrtle was delighted. We persuaded it to lie down on one of the mats while I got back into bed.

Myrtle began to chatter happily. She told me about the latest events in her firm. She was doing well. One of her ideas had got the firm a valuable contract from a new client in London. Her employer had promised a rise as well as commission.

I listened with entirely unselfish pleasure, hearing the voice not of hysteria but of clear-headedness and resource.

After outlining her idea with undisguised competence, Myrtle suddenly felt it was time to retrench behind her true maidenly modesty. 'Of course, it's all luck,' she said. 'I think the people in London just wanted to be nice to me.'

I took hold of her.

Myrtle fluttered her eyelids. 'Don't be silly, darling.'

I began to feel rather more attentive. 'How's your boss getting on with his mistress?' I said, leaning over her.

Myrtle frowned. 'About the same.'

'And how are you getting on with her?'

Myrtle's frown changed to a look of sadness. 'Not very well. I don't think she likes me getting on in the firm.'

'Oh dear.'

Myrtle said with absurd innocence: 'What does it matter to her if I make an extra £5 a week? She can have another £5 any time she likes, without doing any *extra* work. . . .'

'Don't you see,' I said, 'she knows everyone says she's planted

162

there because she's the boss's mistress? She probably takes her position in the firm very seriously.'

'Do you really think so, darling?' Myrtle pondered this new idea. 'She did try to prevent him taking this contract—because it would mean too much reorganization for her! . . . He didn't give in, but he forbade me to go to London again and went himself.'

I laughed quietly.

Myrtle settled herself comfortably against me. 'Ah well,' she said, with a modest smirk, 'I'll find some way of getting round him.'

We were on the verge of beginning to make plans, but something stopped us.

And it turned out that this was her most sensible stretch of conversation. My feeling that the crazed note had disappeared from her gaiety was soon dispelled. A little while later she was talking about cars.

'. . . like the one I shall have next year.'

'Myrtle!' I said. 'Are you going to have a car?'

'Next year.' She paused. 'I'm not going to have the money and not have a car.'

'Why do you want one?'

'For getting about.'

I let her run on. The next time I listened she was saying:

'My gun's come.'

'Your what?' I was constantly finding it impossible to believe my ears.

'My gun. Didn't I tell you I was getting a gun? It came yesterday.'

I felt dizzy—a dog, and a car, and now a gun. I thought she must be going mad. A gun! I suddenly connected, with emotion not far from terror. It may seem very unsoldierly of me. When girls get guns I am convinced it is time for me to go.

'What ever do you want a gun for?'

Myrtle looked thoughtfully at the ceiling. 'To shoot with.'

'Shoot what?'

'Rabbits and things.'

'But where?'

'Oh, in the fields . . . woods. . . .'

I laughed. 'Good heavens! I didn't know you could shoot. Have you learnt?'

'Not yet.'

'Then how on earth? . . .'

Myrtle sounded dignified and reproachful. 'The husband of a girl down at the printer's is going to teach me.'

'And then?'

'Then,' said Myrtle in a reasonable tone, 'if I see a rabbit, I shall take a pot at it.'

My fear that she was suffering from hysteria came back in a single bounce. Also, I must add, a certain fear that her gun might fall into the hands of Haxby.

'I rather look forward to potting at rabbits,' she said.

No, I decided: if I had to choose between her potting at rabbits and Haxby potting at me, I should probably be safer to choose the latter.

'There's a warren, or whatever it is, just before we get to the Dog and Duck.'

I suddenly realised what she was thinking.

Myrtle went on, with a giggle: 'I've ordered some tweeds for the autumn.'

I thought: 'You won't be coming here.' It was quite simple. I had no doubt of it.

Even while she was lying beside me I did not doubt the affair was over. This afternoon, for the first time for months, we had been easy and harmonious together. I had felt simple, kind, ready to please; I had said nothing to torment her—because my mind was no longer divided. I felt no temptation to jump out of bed for fear of being tamed. There was no question of my trying to live the rest of my life with someone who did not believe in me as a writer. No *cris-de-cœur!* The struggle was over. I was in the clear.

Myrtle appeared to notice nothing. She prattled on. At last she said gaily: 'Now I'll have to leave you, darling. I'm going to a party, tonight.'

I laughed, as if it were really a joke. 'With the Crows?'

'Given by them!' said Myrtle. 'And Tom's going to be there too.'

'Tut-tut,' I said, lightly smacking her.

164

'And Brian as well,' said Myrtle. 'Can you imagine it!' She began to play with the dog. 'Come on, Brian! . . .'

In the end she persuaded the animal to sit in the basket, and prepared to leave. I noticed that in the excitement we did not arrange to meet again. We kissed and she rode off, down the lane.

As she disappeared round the corner, I could hear her talking animatedly. 'Look! Brian. Are we going to see some rabbits? Brian? . . .'

I went indoors. I began to read. I failed. I found it was impossible to concentrate. I kept thinking of Myrtle, and thinking: 'It won't do.'

My spirits switched over completely. I had not relaxed when it was time to go to bed, and I found myself unable to sleep. It was light very late, and there was one of the loveliest of sunsets. The trees were quite still and the sky was glowing. I kept getting out of bed to look. Each time the rising moon was a little brighter. The flowers began to smell in the hedgerow opposite, and the birds to be quiet. It was exquisite.

Suddenly, through the open doorway, I noticed a vague patch of moonlight on the wall. I fancied it was a girl, standing soft and naked. When I looked it was nothing like it, of course. I smiled at myself. And from the window came a gust of air, blowing over my body. My imagination stirred violently, and a new thought burst in like a shooting-star.

'I must look for someone else.'

CHAPTER II

SPORTS DAY

The school sports had been postponed because of bad weather. Nobody wanted them now. Sports day was the sort of climax you could not approach twice and the headmaster's second choice of date lighted on the coldest day of summer. After morning prayers he called attention to the temperature— as if the boys were not shivering already.

'Now don't let me see any boy this afternoon without his overcoat!'

The boys listened in a docile fashion.

'Now don't let me see any boy . . .' His particular form of injunction always sounded less like an order to obey than an invitation to deceive. He descended from the rostrum, clutching his gown tightly round him. Daily he was embarrassed by little boys who waylaid him.

'Well, what is it?' This morning he had to stop because there was a long queue of them. I sauntered by. Each little boy appeared to be asking the same question.

'Please sir, will a mackintosh do?'

I moved away. I was concerned with the part I had to play in the sports. The arrangements were in the hands of Bolshaw, and in the previous year I had found myself down on his list as telegraph-steward. This meant that I was on duty beside the cricket scoreboard, thirty yards in front of the distinguished spectators' row of chairs, for the whole of the afternoon. I thought telegraph-steward was an intolerable role, suited only to someone who felt a pathological desire to be in the public eye. I aspired to be the prize-steward, since this appeared to involve no duties at all. I told Bolshaw that I thought if I were only given a

166

chance I could make an exceptionally good prize-steward. I tried to convey that I could care for the prizes as if they were my own children.

I went to the field early in the afternoon. Bolshaw had failed to circulate his list in the morning, and I was hopeful. I decided to install myself as prize-steward before he arrived. The games master was already there. Bolshaw did the organising: the games master did the work. The weather was wretched and I was wearing an overcoat. There was a wind blowing, no blustering winter wind, but a summer one that insinuated its iciness. The games master came out of the pavilion, wearing a high-necked sweater and a pair of gym shoes.

'Come on, Joe!' he said. 'Come an' 'elp me with the prizes, before the nobs come.'

The games master was a friend of mine. He was a middle-aged family man, an ex-sergeant-major, unlettered, cheerful and fond of boys. I helped him unpack the prizes. The wind rustled the pieces of tissue paper out of our fingers.

'Brr,' said the games master, jumping springily from one foot to the other. 'The ruddy Lord Mayor'll 'ave to be set up like a brass monkey for this. 'E'll need 'is gold chain to tie 'em on with.'

We surveyed the table, and the desired objects for which, like children of my own, I was to care. There were electro-plated cups of different sizes, accompanied by a collection of teaspoons, cruets, rose-bowls with wire across the top and jam-pots with electro-plated lids.

''Ere, what's this?' said the games master. 'Not something useful?' It was a safety-razor: I read the card, on which was written:

JUNIOR 100 YARDS

'Good God!' I said, and rapidly went through the other cards. Someone had playfully exchanged them all. A handsome case of silver teaspoons was going to the winner of the junior egg-and-spoon race, while the victor ludorum was going to get a plastic serviette-ring for his efforts.

We began a hasty redistribution. The Lord Mayor arrived. He was going to give away the prizes. He was a short, vigorous, red-faced man, with a bay-window and a powerful glare. He looked as if he had high blood pressure. He also looked as if he thought the games master and I were trying to steal the prizes. He stationed himself very close to the table and glared at us. We retired to the pavilion, which was filled with boys in different stages of undress, chattering at the top of their voices.

The games master pushed his way in.

'Now then! Listen to me! You all know what a cold afternoon it is. Well, we're going to get it over at the double. I'm not going to 'ave you all standing there, doing sweet fanny adams and catching your death. Understand this, now! Any boy who isn't ready for 'is race loses 'is chance!' There was a hush. 'What's more, I'll run 'im round the gym tomorrow morning with the slipper be'ind 'im.' The hush turned to laughter. 'Who's not brought 'is overcoat or 'is mac?' The laughter turned back into a hush. 'All right!'

We were about to begin what promised to be the fastest sports meeting in the history of athletics.

Many of the boys were excellent untrained athletes, and the school games record was highly creditable. But the Greek spirit burned with the lowest possible flame in the staff. Those given official duties walked about with their collars turned up and a look of hard-boiled irritation: as prize-steward, I was sorry for them.

As I walked across the field I met Bolshaw.

'Lunn,' he said, 'Lunn!'

'Yes.'

Bolshaw stared at me, with his shoulders hunched inside an old-fashioned overcoat. His hat was pulled down to his spectacles.

'Lunn,' he said, 'I've rearranged the duties. I've got a different one for you.'

'What?'

'Telegraph-steward.'

I thought: 'It's not different at all!' I said: 'But the prizes, Bolshaw. Who's to look after the prizes?' At that moment I felt devoted to the prizes.

'I've thought of that,' said Bolshaw. 'I'll keep an eye on the prizes myself.'

'Myself.' I could not argue. I turned up the collar of my over-coat and made for the telegraph-post.

At the post I found Trevor and Benny waiting to assist me. I looked at Benny. 'What are you doing here?' I said loudly.

Benny's face took on a grossly pathetic expression.

Trevor said: 'He's a menace. Send him away!' He disliked Benny.

This made me feel inclined to let Benny stay. Like a dog Benny sensed it.

'Don't listen to him, sir.'

I hesitated. Benny's expression was poised on the edge of a ludicrous, grateful smile. There was a loud bang. The first race had begun. It occurred to me that if I sent Benny away I should have to take a hand in the work myself. That settled it.

Soon I was delighted by the way things were going. I normally found sports meetings tedious: today's performance began at the pace of a smart revue—it was perfect.

As usual, perfection did not last. Bolshaw had instructed the starter not to wait for boys who were late for the start. Naturally it was not long before a wretched little boy ran up as the gun went off. The starter shouted at him. The boy jumped like a rabbit and started to run down the track. The effect was dra-matic. The spectators immediately came to life.

'Go it, the little 'un!' they shouted. He did not catch up but they cheered him loudly as he walked off the field.

Races followed each other at a pace more suited to Americans than Greeks. And then the weather took a hand. The clouds had been lowering, the wind dropped, and now there came a shower of icy rain. Immediately the spectators made for the lines of thick leafy trees on each side of the field.

The boys in the middle ran towards the pavilion. On the way they surged past the distinguished spectators, and saw the head-master beside himself with alarm because raindrops were falling on the prizes.

'Look after the prizes!' he was crying. He stripped off his overcoat and laid it over them. 'Give me some more coats! You there, boy! Give me your overcoat. Boy! Boy!'

The Lord Mayor was struggling to undo his chain. The boys

swarmed round, and in a few seconds the table was covered with a mountain of clothes.

'That's enough!' cried the headmaster. 'Enough! Enough! Don't be silly!' He furtively cuffed a boy who was taking no notice and the Lord Mayor pretended not to see.

The rain fell.

Under the trees it was dry. Several masters sat in their cars: the remainder, together with the boys and their parents, walked up and down to keep warm. It looked like a German theatre audience on the *Bummel*.

I was walking gaily with the games master. As we came to one of the turns in our promenade I glanced idly at the cars. Somebody inside one of them waved to me. The windscreen was steamed up, so I went closer. To my astonishment I saw it was our senior science master, Simms. He beckoned to me, and opened the door of his car.

Bolshaw had led me to believe he was at death's door. Simms shook my hand with a light, firm grasp, and I found myself looking into a pair of clear, healthy, blue eyes.

'I haven't risen from the dead,' he observed.

I was too embarrassed to reply.

'I expect I shall in due course,' he went on. He spoke slowly. 'But I haven't yet passed through those preliminary formalities that cause us so much concern.'

'I'm delighted,' I stammered.

I was very fond of Simms. I liked his face. He had a broad head, bald with a fringe of grey hair, and narrow, delicate jaw. His skin was pink, and his face showed his passing shades of emotion. It was the face of a man who had always gone his own way, and had thus arrived at a state of lively self-satisfaction. He was now old and frail, but it was probable that he had always looked frail. He was gentle and unaggressive—the opposite of Bolshaw. Yet had I been asked to say which of the two had done fewer things he did not want to do, I should have said Simms. The question would have been particularly relevant at this juncture, when the subject was Simms's resignation.

'Are you quite better?' I asked.

'My asthma still distresses me frequently.'

'I mean, well enough to come back to school?'

'Had you heard to the contrary?' He glanced at me. 'I'm very curious, my dear fellow,' he said, his hand on my arm. 'People come and give me advice, good and disinterested advice. And shortly afterwards I hear, to my astonishment, that I've taken it! Can you explain that to me?'

I shook my head.

'I'm very gratified that anyone should think I have the sense to take good and disinterested advice. One is. You would be, I'm sure.'

'When are you coming back?'

'Oh, quite soon, you know. This term. There's the matter of salary during the summer vacation to be considered.' He smiled slyly to himself.

I looked out of the window, amused.

The rain had stopped. I told him I must return to my telegraph-board.

'It has been nice to see you,' he said. 'I shall be seeing you again shortly. Next Monday.'

I stared at him. He was going to give up his job to nobody; and he had every intention of teasing Bolshaw and me for as long as he could spin out his time.

The weather was now colder. The headmaster and the Lord Mayor returned to their places of honour, but several of the other distinguished spectators and parents had quietly deserted. Before the headmaster sat down he called the boys to remove their overcoats from the prize table. They cheerfully obeyed, and after jostling and fighting they went away again, leaving the array of cups and cruets to shine sullenly in the grey light.

Fred joined me to watch one of the field events. His bare arms and legs looked greyer than ever. He said:

'I saw your girl-friend, Joe.'

I was surprised, because Myrtle ought to have been at work.

'While you was talking to old Simms in 'is car. She just came in to shelter and went out again.'

'Are you sure?' I said.

'It's quite true,' put in Trevor. He laughed with nasal contempt as he said: 'She was with that awful man, Haxby.'

I said nothing, and the boys were diffidently silent. Fred was upset. ''Ave I said the wrong thing?'

I shrugged my shoulders.

Myrtle's action must have been deliberate. It could only mean the interlude was now over. More than anything else I felt irritation. If the interlude was over the whole thing had to end once and for all.

It had taken me a long time, far too long a time, to steel myself to do it. Now I was ready at last. It seemed a curious off-hand occasion on which to decide, but that is how it was.

My duties at the board came to an end. The only remaining event was the senior mile, and I decided to watch it from near the winning-post. It was one of the events in which Frank was hoping to shine, since he was in the running for victor ludorum.

While I was standing in the crowd of boys I overheard a strange remark. 'Where's the victor ludorum's prize?' I turned round but I was too late to see who had spoken. I knew the answer, because I had labelled it myself: it was the case of a dozen silver teaspoons, right at the front of the table.

Frank won the race. There was cheering, and all the boys gathered round the Lord Mayor to hear him speak before giving the prizes.

The Lord Mayor spoke for a long time. He clearly had great stamina. His was the most Greek performance of all. I thought he would never stop.

At last the boys filed up to him for their prizes. He shook hands vigorously. The boys blushed and grinned and walked away with cruets, toast-racks, jam-pots and so on. The safety-razor was very properly won by a bearded boy in the fifth form.

We come to the victor ludorum. The contest had been won by Frank. He came up, with a mackintosh thrown over his athletic rig, looking pale and handsome and unusually shy. The Lord Mayor gave Frank his warmest handshake and his most powerful glare: then he prepared to give Frank his prize. The victor ludorum's prize was not there.

A sudden hush fell on the crowd of boys.

'Where is it?' came the headmaster's nattering voice. 'Where is it?' I thought if there was one question not worth asking, that was it.

'Where is it? What is it? What was the prize, I say?'

'Some silver spoons,' came the voice of his secretary, from below the horizon.

'They're not here now!'

'It's no use blaming me.'

'I'm not blaming anybody! I only want to know where they are!' Pause. 'Who was responsible for the prizes?'

I thought of the prizes, my prizes.

'Mr. Bolshaw,' said the secretary.

I looked round. There was no sign of Bolshaw: he had gone home.

'I thought it was Mr. Lunn,' said the headmaster.

I trembled.

'No. Mr. Bolshaw.'

Truth had prevailed. I could hardly believe it.

Meanwhile, the Lord Mayor was filling in time by giving Frank's hand more jolly shakes.

Murmurs ran through the crowd. 'They can't find the victor ludorum's prize. Someone's swiped it.'

'Be quiet there! Do be quiet!' cried the headmaster.

Undismayed, the Lord Mayor shook Frank's hand again. The headmaster whispered furiously into his ear. 'Send the boy away! Tell him we will give him his prize later!'

I wondered what would happen to Bolshaw.

The house-captains filed up for their shields, but the crowd now paid the scantiest attention to the proceedings. Where were the teaspoons? Who was the lucky boy?

It was quite obvious what had happened. While the boys had been clustered round the table, struggling with their overcoats, one of them had smartly caught up the silver teaspoons. The games master and I could swear to the case's having found its way safely to the table. It was up to the headmaster to find out where it had gone next.

The headmaster did not find out, nor did any of the other masters. I can tell you now that nobody ever did find out. And was Bolshaw held responsible for it all? Was he asked to resign, for lacking sense of responsibility and discipline? Does justice prevail on this earth?

I went away from the field thinking about Bolshaw. I arrived home thinking about Myrtle.

The more I thought about Myrtle's appearance with Haxby, the more I felt venomous. My forbearance, my detachment, all those qualities to which I aspired, vanished. And I can only say that to the very depths of my soul I was fed-up with her.

CHAPTER III

SCENES OF DOMESTICITY

The newspapers were filled with international crises. They were beginning to have a mesmerising effect. But I was not completely mesmerised: I had decided to see Myrtle as little as possible until the term ended; and then, whether I was going to America or not, to quit the town without leaving an address.

It takes two to make a parting, and it takes two to avoid a meeting if they live not much more than a mile apart. Never before had I been so intensely aware of playing out time. Sometimes I felt like a powerful man in control of his own destiny: sometimes I felt I was being hunted by Hitler and Myrtle in conjunction.

One evening I was sitting peacefully outside the french windows of my lodgings, marking examination papers. At the bottom of the garden the landlady's niece and Mr Chinnock were working. It was one of what Myrtle and I had been used to call their 'off-nights', and they were spending it in weeding the vegetable plot.

Occasionally one or the other of us would stop to cough. This was because smoke was blowing over us from a bonfire of weeds in a neighbouring garden. It was always the same. There were so many gardens and the neighbours were such indefatigable incendiarists, that one could never hope to sit in one's garden for an hour or so without somebody lighting a bonfire. The breeze appeared to blow in a circular direction.

I was just completing my estimation of the mathematical powers of a junior form, when I heard the landlady showing someone into my room. I looked round, and saw Steve. He stepped out of the window.

175

'I'm sorry to bother you,' he said, and sat down on the step near my chair. He waited till I put down the last paper, and then pulled out of his pocket a poem that he had written.

'You see, Joe!' he said. 'When I can get away from Tom for a week-end I really do do some work.'

I read the poem. I have observed earlier that Steve's poems showed talent. This poem showed quite as much talent as usual and somewhat greater length. I congratulated him.

The trouble I find with a poem is that when you have read it, and congratulated the author, there is nothing else to say. It is not like a novel, where you can sit down to a really good purging burst of moral indignation at the flatness of his jokes, the shapelessness of his plot, and the immorality of his characters.

A silence fell upon Steve and me. 'Britons, never, never, ne-ever shall be slaves!' whistled Mr Chinnock.

'Tom isn't going to America,' said Steve.

'Why not? How do you know?'

Steve shrugged his shoulders. 'He says there's going to be a war.'

'Oh.'

'Don't you think there is?'

'What?'

'Going to be a war.'

'Possibly,' I paused, and said with shameful lack of conviction: 'I hope so.' The fact is that I did not want to give up the idea of going to America.

Steve glanced at me. 'By the way, you know Myrtle's going about saying that you intend to go to America if there *is* a war.'

'The devil!' I was very angry.

'That's what she's saying, anyway.'

'Who told you?'

'I heard it myself.'

Though my own conduct may not have been above reproach, I was infuriated by Myrtle's perfidy. I began to question Steve for more circumstantial evidence. He was speaking the truth, and he was in a position to know what Myrtle was saying to other people, since he was now going regularly to the parties she frequented with Haxby.

In my anger, I thought: 'That's one more thing against her!'

'Surely Tom's furious?' I said.

Steve said: 'I think he thought she was saying it to provoke you.'

'Well, it has!'

Steve laughed good-naturedly.

'What else has she been saying about me?'

'I don't think I ought to repeat this scandal, Joe,' he said with embarrassment.

'You can't put me off now, Steve.'

'She told Tom,' Steve began slowly, 'that she was never in love with you.'

'For what reason does she think she? . . .'

'I know, I know. She admits that you have a curious attractive power. You're now spoken of as if you were a sort of Svengali. It's ridiculous, of course. Anybody can see that you're not like Svengali.'

'Hell!'

'I think we ought to be a little quieter, Joe.' Steve motioned towards the landlady's niece and Mr Chinnock, who were easily within earshot.

With an effort I simmered down.

'Anything else?' I asked.

Steve did not reply.

'I bet Tom put this idea into her head.'

'If you're going to break it off, it's not a bad idea, is it, Joe?'

'That wasn't why he did it. He'll next prove that she's always been in love with him. And he with her.'

'Heavens!' said Steve, not having thought of this before.

'That's his plan, mark my words. It leads to a proposal of marriage.'

Steve looked distinctly crestfallen.

'Though what her plan is, I don't know,' I went on. 'No doubt it will do her more harm than good.'

'I'm sorry,' said Steve.

I was regaining my detachment. There was much in what Steve observed about Myrtle saying she had never been in love with me. It was a face-saving device. It was the first sign of her beginning to protect herself. I suddenly thought: 'She's pulling out.'

Steve broke into my reflections.

'I suppose you know Trevor's safe.'

I felt as much shock that he knew about it as relief that a disaster had been avoided. I said: 'Oh!' in a sharp, off-hand tone.

We relapsed into silence again. Steve stepped indoors and brought a cushion to sit on.

'It's very bad to sit on anything cold,' he said.

'Nonsense.'

Steve paused, and began to smile at me. 'I know what you haven't heard about. I've been learning First Aid.' He saw my look of disbelief. 'Honestly, I have, Joe. If there's a war and I'm conscripted and I've got my certificates perhaps I'll be able to get into the Medical Corps.'

I had no idea whether he was speaking the truth, but I could see his aim was to soothe my feelings, so I let him go on.

'I've taken an exam in it,' he said. There was a glint in his eye. 'I doubt if I've passed.'

I said: 'Was it hard?'

'It wasn't hard,' said Steve, 'but it was terribly repulsive.'

Steve recounted his incompetent performance in the practical tests, and in spite of my woes I began to smile.

Steve played up.

'The theoretical was terrifying. They asked me what I'd do with a baby in a convulsion. Fancy asking *me*, Joe! I wouldn't know what to do with a baby if it was *not* in a convulsion.'

'What was the answer?'

'Put it in a bath!' Steve paused triumphantly. Neither of us heard my landlady show in somebody else. There was a bustling noise beside us, and there stood Tom. His face was like thunder.

'I have something to say to you. Would you mind coming indoors?'

Steve picked up his cushion and I my examination papers, and we trailed into my room. Tom closed the french windows behind us.

'It's as well to keep these matters private,' he said, with an air that was both polite and reproving.

I did not reply. I had no idea what Tom had come to say. Our laughter had disappeared, as if he had made us feel ashamed of it. Steve, on the grounds that nothing Tom would say was likely to make life easier for him, was already looking apprehensive.

I sat down. Steve sat down. Tom remained standing. By great effort he was keeping his features composed. I refused to open the conversation.

'I came to tell you that I've bought a new car.'

To be quite frank, the speech for me was something of an anticlimax, and also mildly funny. In my imagination Tom's new car had become mixed up with a steam yacht.

Steve had apparently not been previously informed of the manœuvre. He was not unnaturally surprised. Foolishly he said:

'What for, Tom?'

Tom turned his attention to him. 'Aren't you interested to know what kind it is?'

'Of course,' said Steve. 'But I wondered what you'd bought it for?'

'Don't you know?' Tom was looking at him fixedly. His tone of voice was level enough; but there was a look in his eye, a bursting, concentrated look.

'No,' said Steve, trying to look at me, but finding the hypnotic effect of Tom's gaze too powerful.

'Can't you guess?' Tom smiled at him.

There was a silence; in which I thought of saying: 'Tom for Pete's sake stop it!' and rejected the idea.

Steve looked down, shaking his head.

'I should have thought you would have realized,' Tom said, with ominous silkiness, 'it was to make our trip to Paris more comfortable.'

Steve looked at him. Nothing was said.

I shifted in my chair. I was irritated that Tom had not given me a chance to get out of the room if he intended to make a scene. On the other hand I was faintly hypnotized myself.

'I said I couldn't go, Tom,' said Steve.

'Don't be silly, Steve. Of course you can.'

'I can't, Tom. You know my people want me to go away with them.'

'They want you to come with me.'

'That isn't true.'

'Yes, it is.' Tom glared at him now. 'I have it in writing!'

'Look!' said Tom, pulling out an envelope from his pocket. 'This letter's from your mother, saying she agrees to your coming with me. Now we have it in black and white!' He handed it to Steve. 'Read it!'

Steve refused to read it.

'All right,' said Tom, angrily. 'If you haven't the manners to read it . . .'

'I'm *not* coming!' Steve interrupted him.

'What's your excuse?'

'I don't need an excuse, Tom.'

Tom waved the letter in front of his face. 'What are you going to say to this!' He waved it again, with a sweep of greater amplitude. 'I've got it in writing!'

I thought he must be going slightly mad. The whole of his face, though composed, now looked somehow inflamed.

'It's in black and white.' He deliberately lowered his voice again.

Suddenly Steve leaned forward, snatched the letter from his hand, and threw it in the fireplace. There was no fire.

Tom stared at it, and pursed his lips in a smile. Then he glanced at me. I felt embarrassed.

Steve said: 'This is intolerable. Why do you make these scenes, Tom?'

'Because I want you to go with me to France.'

'But I don't want to go.' Steve was looking miserable.

'I think you do, really.'

'I've told you, I don't. I can't say more than that. I want to feel free.'

'I *want* you to feel free, Steve.'

'Then why don't you give me a chance to be it?'

'You can be perfectly free with me.' Tom moved nearer to him. 'You're perfectly free now.' He made a gesture. 'There's the door. You're free to go out through it, this very moment.'

Steve did not move.

'At least go out and have a look at the car.'

'I don't want to see it. And I don't want to go in it!'

'Do you mean to say I've wasted my money?'

At the mention of money, I thought Steve looked startled.

'Are you going to let me waste my money, without even looking at it?' Tom's voice was becoming angry again.

I thought that as he must have bought the car on the hire-purchase system the waste was not permanent.

'Heaven knows!' Tom now burst out, 'I've spent enough already. And what have I got for it? I've spent pounds and pounds!'

'I didn't ask you to.'

'Pounds and pounds!' Tom shouted.

'I don't want the car.'

'Then at least, *see* it!'

'I'm not going to see it.'

'You're *going* to see it!' Tom had been getting nearer, and now he pounced on Steve.

There had been so much argument about the car that certainly I wanted to see it. Steve was determined not to. He resisted.

'Come and see it!' shouted Tom, and dragged him off his chair. He rolled towards the fireplace, and upset the fire-irons with a deafening clatter. Outside, in the hall, the landlady's dog began to bark.

'Pipe down!' I said.

They desisted. Steve picked himself up, and Tom stood glowering. Looking sulky and furious, Steve straightened his tie.

'I've had enough of this!' said Tom, in a powerful whisper.

'I'm sorry, Tom.'

'I've had enough of this! Are you going to come and see the car or aren't you?'

No reply from Steve.

'It's the last chance.'

No reply.

Tom was now oblivious of my presence. He thrust his face close to Steve's. Steve wilted.

'Are you going to come to France or not? I must have the answer now.'

No answer.

'If you don't answer now, I shall never give you another chance. I have my plans.'

181

Steve glanced at him.

'It may interest you to know that if you don't go'—Tom paused for dramatic effect—'I shall take Myrtle!'

'Don't be ridiculous, Tom!' At last Steve spoke. He glanced at me for support.

Tom was furious. 'It's not ridiculous! Who told you it's ridiculous? Joe?' He glanced at me. 'You may think it's ridiculous, but Myrtle doesn't! I know Myrtle. You may not think I'm wonderful, but Myrtle does! She needs me. It's only my responsibility for you that's kept me from going to her. She needs me, and I need her! We need each other.' His voice, though kept low, had tremendous power. 'I want your answer now. Is it to end or isn't it? If you don't speak I shall go straight to Myrtle—she's waiting for me now—and ask her to marry me!' He choked. 'Is it to end or isn't it? I shall go straight to Myrtle!'

Steve did not speak.

Tom waited.

Steve still did not speak.

I saw nothing for it but for Tom to go.

Suddenly he let out an indistinguishable cry.

Steve and I looked at him in alarm.

Tom opened his mouth to speak again and failed. He had to go.

Steve looked down at the carpet.

Tom picked up the letter from the hearth.

I thought: 'Come on, you've got to go!'

In a last dramatic move Tom tore up the letter and threw down the pieces. Then he turned. I made to open the door for him, but he pushed me out of the way. You may think it strange that I opened the door for him to go out and propose marriage to my mistress. The fact is that I was determined to see the car. I followed Tom across the hall and prevented him from slamming the door, so that I could peep out. I saw it as Tom drove away. And I concluded that Tom was not as mad as he seemed. In my opinion it was a car that would melt the heart of any boy.

I went back to Steve, who was sitting in his chair, shivering and almost on the verge of tears.

I said: 'You'd better have a drink, my lad.'

Steve waited helplessly while I mixed some gin and vermouth in a tumbler. He drank it.

I had nothing more to say, so I picked up another bundle of examination papers and resumed my marking.

After a while, when he had drained the glass, Steve stood up. I looked at him questioningly.

In a jaded voice he said: 'I suppose I'd better go after him.'

CHAPTER IV

ROUND THE CLOCK-TOWER

To relieve my feelings I wrote a letter to Robert. It will save writing anything fresh if I quote a piece of it. Here it is:

My sympathy for Tom is quite exhausted. And so is my patience. He said that Steve caused him a lot of pain, and I took it quite seriously. Sometimes the man was obviously in a state of abject misery and it would have taken a heart of stone not to be concerned for him. But his latest efforts are the limit. At one and the same time he's trying to get Steve to go away with him and proposing marriage to Myrtle! What he thinks he's doing, I cannot imagine. But it's me who's the biggest fool for being taken in by him. I thought he was heading for a tragedy. Instead of which it's quite clear it's nothing but a harlequinade. If clowns come in with red hot pokers and policemen with strings of sausages I shan't be surprised. Anything they can do has already been eclipsed by Tom's own clowning. As for his proposing marriage to Myrtle, it's laughable. What a proposal! Goodness knows how she'll take it. Faint with surprise—unless she simply concludes that he's gone off his head. It's time he went to America—only I doubt if he'll ever go. I really think he is a lunatic.

I wrote a good deal more in the same strain. After completing it I felt a certain satisfaction at having stated my position. To state one's position is a firm, manly thing to do: it is right that it should give satisfaction.

There followed a few days of unexpected respite. I neither saw nor heard anything of Tom, Steve or Myrtle. I was very busy at school, because the end of term was near. The days passed and I counted them as eagerly as my pupils counted them for not dissimilar reasons. They were days that separated me from freedom.

184

However I was doomed not to escape so easily. Myrtle began to ring me up again, wanting to see me. I tried to put her off.

'Surely you can spare me a few moments?' she said.

I felt bitterly cruel, but I kept to my resolve. Was I doing it for her sake? I do not know. But I do know that in the end it is harder to go on loving someone you do not see than someone you do.

When I refused to meet Myrtle I had not considered the possibility of our seeing each other by chance. Though the town was large, one was always running into people one knew. In the early days of my falling in love with Myrtle, when I did not know her well enough to ask her to meet me, I had spent many hours glancing into the windows of shops where I did not intend to buy anything. I used to have a superstition that if I circulated round the clock-tower long enough she would be sure to come.

I will not describe our clock-tower in detail, because I feel that if you were able to identify our town my novel would lose some of its universal air. Fortunately I can indicate its outstanding quality, since this does not distinguish it from the clock-towers in most other provincial towns. It was wondrously ugly.

Our clock-tower really did provoke wonder. Its ugliness set fire to the imagination, but that was only the beginning of wonderment. In the first place I always used to wonder why anybody had ever put it there. For displaying the time of day it was totally unnecessary: the surrounding shop-fronts were plastered with an assortment of clocks which offered the public the widest choice in times they could possibly have wished for. Could it be, I wondered as I stared at its majestic erectness, our contribution to the psychopathology of everyday life? And who had designed it? Was such a monument designed by an architect who specialised for life on clock-towers; or was it thrown off by some greater man in his hour of ease? Surely the latter! Small wonder, then, that the citizens of our town were proud of the clock-tower. It had its place in our hearts. 'It's ugly,' we thought, 'but it's home!'

Now my desire to avoid meeting Myrtle was not so frantic that I broke the routine of my movements round the town. If I happened to be circling the clock-tower, that was that. And one morning at lunch-time I happened to be circling it, on my way to lunch. It was not Myrtle I ran into; it was Steve.

Steve was walking alone, with his shoulders hunched and his face expressing misery. I caught him by the elbow, as it looked as if he were going to pass me without seeing me. He pushed the hair out of his eyes and tried to smile at me.

'I haven't seen you for a long time,' I said.

'No, Joe.' He looked down at the ground.

For some reason or other I noticed that he was taller than he had been six months ago.

'Have you been busy?'

'No. Just jogging along.' He glanced at me furtively. 'I couldn't face you after that scene Tom made in your house.'

I said: 'You shouldn't worry about that.' I paused. 'You're looking under the weather. Is Tom still playing hell?'

'I don't know.'

'What do you mean, Steve? You must know.'

'I don't, Joe. I haven't spoken to Tom since he left your house.'

I was astounded. I drew Steve out of the stream of men and women going to their lunch, so that I could go on talking to him. We leaned against some rails of steel tubing that had been erected to prevent people stepping off the pavement underneath buses.

'Where is he?' I asked.

'He's in Oxford today, but he was here before that.'

'And you didn't see him?' I continued incredulously.

'I've seen him in the office, of course.' He stopped. 'But he won't speak to me.'

'What a change for you!'

Steve did not smile. He looked extremely glum. 'It's a change for the worse.'

I had been tactless.

'He's been spending a lot of time with Myrtle, as far as I can gather. He won't spend any with me.'

I did not know what to say. I was trying to frame some appropriate remark when Steve burst out:

'It's really over!'

186

'Surely, it can't be.'

'You never took this business with Myrtle seriously enough!'

'I should think not. It's ridiculous.'

Steve shrugged his shoulders. He was completely downcast. He said:

'I feel absolutely lost without him.'

He must have noticed a look of alarm in my face. He moved away, saying: 'We can't go on talking about this, here.'

We moved a few yards further along, and then we stopped again, frequently being wedged against the railing by the passing crowds. Traffic swept by.

'Did you see his new car?' said Steve.

'Yes.'

'He's gone to Oxford in it.'

I thought this conversation was getting us nowhere. I said: 'I'd no idea you'd take it like this, Steve. I'm awfully sorry.'

'I'd no idea, either,' said Steve. 'It's come to me as a terrible shock.' For an instant I fancied I heard a dramatic note that rang false; and then it occurred to me that people often are dramatic when deeply moved. 'I suppose I shall get used to it in time,' Steve said, rather as if his mother and father had suddenly died. 'I was a fool!' he cried, and tears came into his eyes.

'This is beyond me,' I said.

'You don't understand, Joe!' Steve spoke with force: his voice was trembling. 'I feel terrible, I feel lost, Joe. There's no point in anything! . . . You can't imagine what it's like to feel that all your plans for the future have broken down. You don't know what it's like, when you've had somebody who flatters your self-esteem all the while and makes you feel you're somebody—and then he stops, suddenly! I feel like a man in a ship that's sunk.' He was trembling with anguish. 'I feel,' he cried, 'like a banker who's lost his bank!'

At that moment a bus passed so close that I could not be expected to reply. A banker who had lost his bank—never had I imagined a remark could contain so much accuracy, penetration and truth.

Steve was waiting for me to say something.

'Poor old Steve,' I said. 'You'll find another.'

The following morning I received three letters. They were from Tom, Myrtle and Miss X.Y. I looked at the envelopes. I was sitting in my lodgings, just about to begin my breakfast. I was alone in the room.

'Dammit!' I said aloud. 'Art comes first, and I'm damned if I'll pretend it doesn't!'

And I opened Miss X.Y.'s letter first. It was short and to the point, and my spirits rose incredibly. She praised my book. I felt as if my hands were trembling. She suggested some revision and some cuts: instantly I saw how they could be done. 'I'm safe!' I cried. 'I'm safe!' I did not quite know what it meant, but I knew it was true. I was ready to begin work on the manuscript immediately: I could hardly wait. The world might be falling about my ears but something went on telling me—to be correct, I went on telling myself—I was safe.

In this mood I opened Myrtle's letter. It said:

I must see you. Please. M.

And then I opened Tom's letter. It began thus:

Dear Joe: I challenge what you say about me in the letter you have just written to Robert.

I was flabbergasted. I already knew that when Robert left his room Tom took the opportunity of reading his private letters, but this was the first time he had ever taken the opportunity of replying to them. I knew that Robert could never have shown him my letter. I remembered Tom's having read one of my postcards on a question of fact—namely, the date of his departure for America. He had replied with fact—namely, a date that subsequently turned out to be false. But this was quite different, and so was the nature of Tom's reply.

Tom's letter began with a challenge, moved on to a denunciation, passed through a reproach, and ended up with a rebuke. Was there any sign of his being ashamed of having read someone else's private correspondence? No. Was there any sign of his being aware of a weak moral position? No. Was there any sign of self-consciousness whatsoever? Not a vestige.

I glowered. 'I stand by every word of it!' I said aloud.

Had I known where he was I would have written to him on the spot. I threw down his letter, and picked up Myrtle's. My glowering died away. I realised that I must see her again. I went to the telephone.

Having made up my mind to see her I wanted to behave with some show of decency, but it was not easy. I wanted the meeting to be as short as possible. I pretended I was exceedingly busy; Myrtle said she was, too. After an awkward discussion we arranged to meet in the town immediately we came out of work that afternoon. Our routes home crossed at the clock-tower, and it was there that we fixed our rendezvous. I thought of Steve. I promised myself that after I met Myrtle at the clock-tower I would go nowhere near it for months.

It was an airless, golden evening. Early in the morning the clouds had drawn away from the sky, leaving a pale brilliant dome of pure blue, from which the sun shone all day upon the roofs and streets. I arrived at the clock-tower first. There was a big chemist's shop, and I leaned against the railings in front of it. From time to time I caught its characteristic smell, though there was no breeze. Trams halted and moved on at different points in the circle. Buses passed to and fro leaving a trail of petrol fumes. The sun went on shining. Myrtle was late.

I looked at the clocks. They all showed different times. Myrtle was late and I wanted to go away. Whatever the clocks said, I had to remain.

At last Myrtle came. It was quite a long time since I had seen her, and my first thought was that she was feverish. Her face looked heavily coloured, and her eyes seemed smaller. When closer I saw that she had been crying.

'Thank you for seeing me,' she said.

I could not answer. I meant to ask her where she would like to go, for us to talk in peace, but every thought left my head. She must have thought I intended us to go on talking at the clock-tower, for she said nothing about moving on, and so we simply remained.

Myrtle spoke in a distant voice, yet she was quite firm.

'I wanted to ask your advice,' she said. 'I expect you know Tom's asked me to marry him? Do you think I should?'

I could not speak, this time for entirely different reasons. 'It's laughable. What a proposal!' My words came back to mock me. Never had I made such a stupid mistake. 'Faint with surprise— or think he's gone off his head!' Nothing of the kind. I can laugh at myself now. I know now that no girl faints with surprise at any proposal of marriage, and never, never does she think the proposer has gone off his head. But when I turned to look at Myrtle, as we stood in the sunshine, the chemist's shop behind us and the clock-tower in front, she must have seen written on my face nothing less than mixed astonishment and chagrin.

'You look strange,' Myrtle said. 'Is there something the matter?'

'No,' I muttered. 'Just emotion, I suppose.'

'Unusual for you.'

I did not comment: she must have learnt it from Tom.

Myrtle was staring at me. In her eyes I saw the faintest shade of bitter detachment.

'I can't advise you,' I said.

Myrtle said: 'Why not?'

'I don't know. I can't.' I stumbled for words. 'I'm not in a position to. You must know why.'

At that instant Myrtle's gaze faltered, and her detachment vanished never to return. She looked down and clasped her hands together. I noticed the mole on her forearm, just where it came out of her sleeve.

'Then I suppose it was no good our meeting. . . .'

Immediately, I drew back. I could see her expression beginning to change.

She said: 'What have you been doing? I haven't seen you for ages.'

I told her about my letter from Miss X.Y. Even as I spoke to her I could not help feeling my own interest quicken—and I saw hers fade. Her silence bore me down and my explanation petered out.

She went on clasping her fingers between each other. Suddenly she looked me full in the face for a moment.

'I suppose this is the end.'

The end. I looked at her. And I knew with certainty that she was there at last. I did not know the reason. I supposed that something I had said or done during the last few days must have been the last straw. I do not even now know what it was, and if I did I should not believe in it as she did. To most of us the movements of the soul are so mysterious that we seize upon events to make them explicable. Myrtle and I had come to the end because of movements of the soul. They had ebbed and flowed—we had swayed closer together and further apart. Events and actions. What were events and actions? Something I had said or done, or, if it came to that, more probably something Tom had said or done, must have seemed to her the last straw.

I said: 'Yes.'

Myrtle burst into tears.

I cannot well remember what we said after that. Some of her phrases echo still. 'After this last year I don't know how you can do it!' And, 'I only wish you were feeling half of what I'm feeling now.' But I will not go on. A love affair cannot end without heartbreak. And as I have already told so much, I think the time has come for me to draw a veil.

At last we parted. The trams were still halting and moving on. The buses were still passing to and fro. The clock-tower was bathed in golden light. There were sounds and smells, and many people going by. Myrtle lingered. Then suddenly among the traffic she saw a taxi. I did not notice her stop it. I only saw her get into it, and unexpectedly drive off.

I remained where I was. Now that I no longer needed to stay there I felt no compulsion to move away.

I do not know how long I remained there. The next thing I noticed was the glint of bright red hair in the sunshine, and a familiar vigorous swaying walk. Tom came to me.

'Ah, there you are!' he said. 'I heard that you were going to meet Myrtle . . . I didn't expect to find you still here.'

I did not speak.

Then Tom said gently: 'Come and have some tea.'

Neither of us spoke as I let him steer me to the café. Outside the shop the smell of roasting coffee was stifling. We went upstairs, and sat down at our usual table. It was long after tea-time, and we were the only people in the room. The waitress brought our tea rapidly because she was waiting for it to be time to close.

Tom said: 'Is it all over?'

I nodded my head.

There was a pause.

Tom handled his tea-cup with a nervous gesture. 'She said she couldn't marry me, of course.'

'When?'

'Several days ago.'

It was my turn to pause. I drank some tea. I said:

'What are you going to do?'

Tom said easily: 'Oh, I've just come away from having a talk with Steve. While you were seeing Myrtle, actually. He's changed his mind, of course.' He smiled with self-satisfaction. 'He's coming to France with me next week. I think it wiser for us to go almost immediately.'

At the time I was in no state to comment, so I let it pass without comment now.

Tom went on talking, and, much as I deplore having to admit it, he restored my spirits a little. It was not the moment for bickering over his letter. He was in a pleasing, philosophical mood. His confidence had come back. He could see that he was restoring me, and could not resist the old temptation to try and impress. He was an affectionate and generous man, and he was devoting himself whole-heartedly to consolation; but he was as susceptible to human weakness as anyone else. He wanted to speak of Myrtle: he wanted to ease my heart and my conscience: and he could not resist giving me a lesson in psychological observation.

'I think the trouble arose from the grave mistake you, Joe, made about her,' he said.

'What?' I asked humourlessly.

Tom spoke with warm, enveloping authority. He moved his face a little closer to mine.

'Myrtle,' he said, in a low voice, 'didn't want marriage: she wanted passion.'

I looked at him. As an absurdity it was so colossal that it took on the air of a great truth. To it, as such, I bowed my head in silence.

CHAPTER V

PROVINCIAL LIFE-HISTORIES

That is the end of my story.

A few days later the school term ended, the holidays began, and I left the town for six weeks. When I returned the second World War had broken out.

The awkwardness about finishing a novel lies in blinking the fact that though the story is ended the characters are still alive. I have chosen to end my story at this incident, because it was the last I saw of Myrtle; because the war broke out and we were all dispersed. But we all went on living. It seems to me that if you have been sufficiently interested to read as far as this you can hardly help wondering what we did after the end of the story.

I can tell you what we did. I could call a roll, indicating the fate that befell each of us. If only print could speak, you would hear my voice ring out sonorously:

Myrtle: married,
Myrtle's dress-maker: married,
Tom: married,
Steve: married,
Robert: married,
Haxby: married,
The other Crow: married,
My landlady: married,
Frank: married,
Benny: married,
Fred: married,
Trevor: married—twice!

This is all very well. It will doubtless be of interest to the race, but not, I fear, to the individual reader. So I will stop playing and get down to business. I will push on with my story just a little way, and then sum up what happened to each of the main characters.

I completed the term at school without being asked to resign. I thought I was doing rather well. Bolshaw told me my retention was dependent on his patronage. I thought the headmaster had forgotten his threatening letter to me in his agitation over not being able to trace the teaspoons. Bolshaw ceased his practice of denigrating my character in the explosion of rage he experienced when he heard Simms was coming back.

The boys of the senior sixth form left, and in the fresh term I felt lost without them. However it was not very long before I was called up for military service, and I shook the dust of the school off my shoes for ever.

Shortly after leaving for ever I had to go back for some books, and I heard that Simms had died suddenly.

'Of course it was a happy release,' Bolshaw said, in what I thought was a very ambiguous tone. He blew through his whiskers and stared at me. Certainly it had been a happy release for Bolshaw. 'I'm glad to say the headmaster has listened to reason over the reorganisation. He asked me to take over both jobs. I'm now senior science master *and* senior physics master. It will mean I shall have less time for teaching.' He gave me a grandiose smile, in which his moustache drew back from his tusks.

I left without calling on the headmaster, and I never saw him again.

My landlady must have had enough of schoolmasters. In my place she took an insurance agent twenty years older than me. Her choice could hardly have been wiser, because he married her and was kind to her dog. On the other hand, her niece has still had nothing like enough of Mr Chinnock, who calls on her at two-thirty every Sunday, like clockwork.

The friends of mine who were killed in the war are not any of those who appear in this story. Trevor, Benny, Frank and Fred all escaped.

Trevor dabbled in what he called art until he was called up, when he got into the Intelligence Corps. He remained a sergeant till the end of the war, and then he married the big girl over whom we had had all the fuss. Tom was furious when he heard about it, and proposed that Trevor should start paying back our money. After marrying her, he divorced her and married another big girl.

Frank had a year at Oxford doing science and then he became a radio officer in the Navy. He had a creditable career, he looked very handsome in uniform, and he married a thoroughly nice girl. Somehow he feels he has missed something.

Fred got a job in the corporation electricity department, did his military service, and returned to it. If you happen to be near the clock-tower and go into the electricity department's showroom, the stocky man with brilliantined hair and a good-natured soppy voice, who is trying to interest you in an immersion heater, is Fred. He has begotten a large family.

Benny worked his way into the Royal Army Medical Corps. After congratulating himself on his apparent safety, he found to his consternation that he could not be commissioned without being a doctor. Towards the end of the war the regulations were changed and he became a 2nd Lieutenant. On the basis of this medical career, he set up in a room above one of the shops in the market-place as a radiologist. He now has three rooms, an assistant, a nurse, a lot of ponderable equipment and the minimum qualifications. He has offered to X-ray me at any time free of charge.

So much for the boys.

And now we come to Steve. It will be no surprise to you that Steve did not free himself from his patron. They continued to enjoy scenes of violent emotion both with and without motor cars. Steve's French accent was improved by a holiday in France, and Tom did not go to America.

On the other hand, in the following year, the war removed Tom from the town, and his devoted interest in his protégé seemed inexplicably to wane. Steve found his freedom returning at an embarrassing pace; and soon there was literally nothing to stop him becoming as ordinary as he pleased. When he was called up Steve finally showed his independence: he volunteered to become a pilot in the Royal Air Force.

Steve actually reached the stage of flying an aeroplane—he flew it with skill, but he was unable to land it. With all his gifts, Steve had been born without the knack of bringing an aeroplane down intact. Everybody recognized it; some of us, including Steve, with relief. The Air Force tried to make him a navigator, but Steve's arithmetic let him down. They tried to make him a wireless operator and he mysteriously developed sporadic bouts of deafness. Steve was unglamorously kept to the ground. However, one thing Steve had mastered from life with his patron was the art of bearing up. Indeed he must have had a talent for it. His gesture had failed, but he was more than content from merely having made it. He bore up remarkably well. He soon began to look round.

What Steve saw was the daughter of the junior partner in his old firm of accountants. She was an attractive, strong-minded girl, and she had fallen in love with Steve. Steve wanted to be married: he wanted to be a father. And in the end he accommodated himself to the idea of becoming an accountant. This, too, cost him some suffering, but his fortitude saved him. He was just the sort of man the firm wanted back; a young Air Force officer, clever, charming, well-bred, conventional and right-minded. He married the girl.

And there in the town Steve remains. He is unostentatiously successful as an accountant. He and his wife live in style. He is very proud of his children. As the years pass he deplores other people's divagations with decreasing self-consciousness. Steve has become respectable.

There is something peculiarly edifying about Steve's life-history. Steve is now respected by others. I should like to call him a pillar of society. Yes, I will call Steve a pillar of society: it is fitting.

I said that Tom did not go to America. That is not true. He did not go to America as a prospective political refugee in August 1939. None of us went. Tom delayed and delayed, and Robert exerted no pressure to make him leave. 'There's going to be a war,' Tom said, first of all because he did not want to go, and then because there was going to be a war.

Before he was due to be called up Tom was offered a job in the Ministry of Aircraft Production. He took it, and before long he had become successful in it. He went to work in Headquarters, in London, and was unexpectedly promoted by Lord Beaverbrook. It was reported that he was promoted because the Minister left his brief-case in the lift and Tom chased after him with it. I do not think the report is true.

With the changes of regime in his ministry Tom moved up and down the scale; till finally he quarrelled with one of his superiors and was sent on a mission to Washington. So he went to the U.S.A. after all.

Now you ought to know Tom well enough to answer in one go the simple question: 'What did Tom do in America?'

Tom became an American.

In America Tom found a limitless field for his bustling bombinations, spiritual, emotional and geographical. Suggestibly he began to speak with an American accent. Rashly he proposed marriage to an American girl, who accepted and made him marry her. He was offered an attractive job if he would take out first papers. The war ended, he stayed on, and there he is.

Some time ago I was in America, and I stayed with Tom and his family. I found his appearance had changed a little: his red hair is still as thick and curly as ever, but his physique is showing signs of portliness. He has not become as portly as he would have become in England, but the signs are there. Otherwise he had not changed.

On my second evening he sent his wife to bed early, brought out a bottle of whisky, and began to talk about old times.

He asked about Steve, who no longer writes to him, and Myrtle, who no longer writes to either of us. Talking of Myrtle threw him into his pleasing philosophical mood. In the intervening years he had learnt more of the secrets of the heart, so he informed me. The thought of Myrtle stirred him.

'Ah, Myrtle,' he said, pursing his lips and smiling.

'Ah, Myrtle,' I said, myself, and drank some whisky.

'You made a grave mistake over her, Joe.'

'What?'

'Myrtle,' he said, in a low, authoritative voice, 'didn't want passion. She wanted marriage.'

I might have been listening to him in the café.

It all came back to me. The low tone of voice was exactly the same: only the words were exactly the opposite.

Tom smiled with self-satisfaction. You see that he had not changed at all.

At last, Myrtle. Myrtle married Haxby.

During the months I lived in the town after the summer holidays, I saw her only twice by chance in the street. We did not stop to speak to each other. I supposed that she must be hearing scraps of information about me as I was about her. Her bohemian parties were still in full swing, attended by Trevor and Steve. Her rejection of Tom's proposal of marriage appeared to cause neither of them any embarrassment. I think Myrtle liked him the more for it. Tom went to her parties and told me the news about her.

The first subject of gossip was my resemblance to Svengali. This wilted as a love-match with Haxby came into view. I did not pretend to try and keep up with it. At this point I left the town for good, and they had been married for some time before I heard.

Myrtle became a success in the advertising business. She remained a success. When you see the advertisements for a well-known brand of nylon stockings, sleek, attractive advertisements that at first glance look perfectly innocent and at second perhaps not, you are looking at the work of Myrtle—and she is being paid a lot of money for it.

Myrtle is happy. She looks sad and her voice sounds melancholy. Only Tom's insight could pierce to the depths of her heart: I would say she was happy. She still looks meek, and she still smiles slyly. When hard-natured business men offer her contracts she gives a fluttering downward glance, as much as to say she knows they are only doing it to be nice to her. And often they, poor creatures, grin foolishly in return.

Myself. I knew, as soon as I started telling the life-histories of the others, that I should be left with the embarrassing prospect of telling my own. It is one thing to give away what belongs to somebody else, quite another to part with what belongs to oneself. I think of the string of delights and disasters that have come my way since 1939. And then I think of all the novels I can make out of them—ah, novels, novels, Art, Art, pounds sterling!

My own life-history. The past years suddenly spring up, delightful and disastrous, warm, painful and farcical. I reach for a clean new note-book. I pick up my pen.

Scenes From
Metropolitan Life

Thirty Years After—

This Book Is Dedicated To
My Darling Daughters

CONTENTS

PART ONE

PART TWO

Contents

Contents

PART I

CHAPTER I

IN A COMMITTEE-ROOM

The windows of the room looked over Parliament Square. I was the first to arrive for the meeting, so I went and looked through them.

It was a bright September afternoon, and the square was greener than one would have expected – also, I observed, less square. Scattered with yellow-grey leaves from St Margaret's plane trees, the stretches of turf shone a damp, lively, autumnal emerald. Round the outside of the square, traffic, like one's blood, circulated all the while in a one-way stream. Scarlet buses, black official cars, khaki official cars, navy-blue taxis, dusty vans labelled *Star* and *Evening Standard,* all reflected a flash of sunlight as they turned the corner and disappeared into Whitehall. Above them big white clouds rode across the sky and a flag floated from Westminster Hall. It was a pretty scene, I thought, in which the prettiest touch of all was that last happy flash of light with which everything disappeared into Whitehall. I was a government official.

Workmen were dismantling the concrete pill-box disguised as a book-stall, which had commanded the entrance to Whitehall. I watched them. It was 1946, the Second World War had been over more than a year: they were dismantling a piece of the past. Next thing, I thought, somebody would be wanting to dismantle our department. I had always had a friendly feeling for the pill-box, partly because I had been deceived by its appearance throughout the whole of 1940, and partly because it signified to me the great flexibility of our national culture – what other nation could so readily think of a book-stall as something from behind which to shoot people?

I heard a door open. It was Robert. Robert was my boss. He

211

was a government official: he was also a very old friend of mine. I made room for him at my window, a fair amount of room. Robert was tall and had a considerable bay-windowed bulk.

'What are *you* looking at?' His tone was authoritative, natural and lofty, the tone of a man who knows other people may stare through windows but doubts if they can get as much out of it as he would. Robert had great weight of personality.

I glanced at him with amusement and indignation. I was a very different kind of man. Robert ignored my glance. He knew what it was for, and he was far too wily to let on. He examined the scene before us and said:

'Interesting ... what?'

I waited a few moments, and then I pointed across the square. Not seeing at first what I was pointing at, he frowned as if he suspected I was not pointing at anything. I went on pointing. He did see. I watched for the expression on his face. He looked at me out of the corner of his eye, and then he shook his head with a slow grave motion. He had a big handsome head. I shook my head in the same way, copying him.

Sometimes, when two people have known each other very well for a long while, their conversation seems to shed its words, leaving behind for some pairs clearly nothing at all, for others a sustained interplay of emotion into which remarks are thrown more by way of allusion than anything else.

What I had pointed to was the entrance of St Margaret's church, where they had put out a striped awning and a red carpet. A wedding was going to take place. A wedding. I was thirty-six and Robert was forty-one, and neither of us was married. Now you see why no words were needed at that moment to sustain our interplay of emotion.

Robert shook his big handsome head slowly and gravely. He knew it was time he got married.

I shook my head, copying. I knew it was time I too got married.

CHAPTER II

BOWSERS

Another door of the committee-room opened, suddenly. Someone looked in and said:

'No sign of Old Frank?'

Before we could reply the door shut again.

It was a man named James Irskine, and he was referring to his master, Sir Francis Plumer, who was Robert's boss and the head of our division. The room in which we were waiting for the meeting to be held was Sir Francis's office. That is why it had a Turkey carpet, a clock, a large mahogany desk, a hat-stand, and a handsome view over Parliament Square. The room was dusty, yet the mahogany and the carpet gave it a glow. Sir Francis was a Deputy Secretary.

I glanced at Big Ben, and saw that it was still early. Robert, I judged by his eyes, was amused by James and Sir Francis. Robert had large brilliant blue eyes, set in heavy folds of flesh. The rest of his face did not move very much, but his eyes were constantly changing. I was not amused. I said:

'There's absolutely no need for this meeting. The outcome's perfectly obvious before we ever start.'

Robert said: 'My dear Joe, when *will* you learn?'

'Learn what?'

'The way people like to run things.'

'Isn't the outcome perfectly obvious?'

Robert looked impatient.

I said: 'Couldn't you tell this Air Commodore over the telephone exactly what he can have?'

Robert's eye brightened. '*You* could. If he doesn't turn up, would you remember to do that?'

'Why must we have this meeting?'

Robert looked through the window. 'Because it's very important to people that they should have their say.' His tone became weighty, as if he were going to formulate an essential principle of life – indeed he was. 'It's one of the most important things to learn for anyone who wants to succeed in affairs. It's very important to people to have their say. They've got to be allowed to have it.' He paused, and looked at me. 'The outcome of most meetings is obvious. But that doesn't mean meetings can be dispensed with. It holds for nearly all human activities – what people enjoy most is not the outcome, it's the way they get to it.'

'Ah,' I said, seeing an opportunity to break the solemnity of the occasion. 'Just like you-know-what.'

Robert turned away, and walked over to Sir Francis's desk. I followed him. We stood looking at the amount of Plumer's work. There were files galore. They were strewn over the desk. There was no need for them to be sorted, because Sir Francis had a stupefyingly accurate memory for where each one was. He never shirked a duty, nor did he ever shirk a file. In my opinion four-fifths of the files we were looking at ought never to have come to his desk at all. I saw one that I had been wanting to deal with for days.

At this moment Sir Francis came in, followed by James Irskine and the Air Commodore.

'I'm so sorry, Robert, if I've kept you waiting. And you, too, Joseph.' Sir Francis smiled at us courteously, speaking in a quick resonant voice. 'It couldn't be helped, of course.' Nobody challenged the 'of course' though Robert's eyes sparkled again.

Sir Francis went briskly to his chair. 'Shall we begin?'

We followed him, and sat down at a long table covered with a slice of dark-blue felt that had been used for curtains during the war. Our places had been laid, with pink blotting-pads set out like table-mats, and ink-stands and rows of new pencils in place of cutlery – all ready for a stately meal of words.

There was always an air of briskness about Sir Francis, incorrigible briskness, to our way of thinking – it reminded one of a terrier. He was a small man, thin and wiry. He was always dressed in a black coat and grey striped trousers. His movements were quick and nervous, and there was something stylised about them. He was inordinately clever. You had only to glance at his face to see that. Under long sandy eyebrows that curled out like antennae, his eyes fairly shone with cleverness. He sometimes held his head on one side with a particularly sagacious expression. Robert and I were devoted to him.

In his official life, Sir Francis Plumer had two passions, one for justice and the other for accuracy. With beautifully co-ordinated formal intelligence, he sought to instal them on this earth. Since they found no observable place among the laws of nature, he had his work cut out.

Contemplating Sir Francis's activities, Robert used to repeat lugubriously 'Not an atom of sense, not one single atom'. In our organisation Robert regarded it as his own special duty to supply the sense, and he did his task with loyalty and affection. Sir Francis had the capacity for making those who worked in personal contact with him feel like that. He was impossible to revere but easy to love.

'Shall we begin?' Sir Francis looked up alertly. His eyes were as sharp and his skin as fresh as a young man's, though he must have been fifty-five. 'I understand the Air Commodore wants to talk to us about bowsers.'

Bowsers – we were there to discuss bowsers. I do not blame you if you do not know what bowsers are: they have little technical and no spiritual significance. They are big motor-vehicles carrying tanks of petrol or oil or water used for filling aeroplanes.

Now please do not think Sir Francis or Robert or I were going to supply the Air Commodore with bowsers. Our rôle was to talk about bowsers. Should you ask, why talk about them required the presence of a Deputy Secretary, a part-time Principal Assistant Secretary (Robert), James Irskine and me and an Air Commodore, you are merely falling into the error of my ways.

At the same time I ought not to give the impression that our aim was foolish or unnecessary.

The government department we were working in had been of great importance during the war, and it was likely to be pretty important during peace-time. The bit of the department of which Sir Francis was head was called a division, but it was more like a small separate unit. Its rather unusual function was to perform what might be called operational research.

What did we do? Take bowsers as an example – though I should like to point out that to us bowsers were very small beer: we were used to talking about machines that were much more impressive, ingenious, romantic and lethal.

The Air Commodore's organisation wanted some bowsers. We had two jobs. The first was to find out how many he wanted, what he wanted to use them for, how many he could manage with if he did not get the number he proposed, whether he was asking for the most suitable type for his purpose, whether he knew if new types were being invented. Our second job was to know what kind of machines various industrial firms could make, how many of them they could make in how long, what new types were being invented in research and development establishments, and whether firms could ever be expected to make *them* or not.

Our function was to collect facts and numbers, and then, through a mixture of science and commonsense, to produce compromises between people who wanted certain things and people who made them.

All of this sounds very well. It might have actually been well if we had been given executive power. But after all our researches, we could neither tell people what they had got to have nor order the things to be made.

CHAPTER III

COMMITTEE AT WORK

The Air Commodore made a preliminary speech. He was a middle-aged man, amiable in a stiff kind of way, dressed in shabby civilian clothes – he was trying to send two sons to Winchester.

The first thing I did was to write at the top of my blotting-pad K.Y.M.S. Robert had taught me to do it at the beginning of every meeting I went to. It was a trick he had picked up from one of his successful colleagues in business before the war.

I looked across at James Irskine. Whenever I looked at James Irskine I was convinced by his bearing that he thought of himself as a perfect specimen of manhood – probably in those words. He was tall, strong and handsome. His body was tall, strong and handsome, and so was his head. He was about my own age. He had a strong intelligence, strong will, strong ambition and strong conceit. In fact he had everything a man could wish for, except a sense of humour.

'I pride myself on my sense of humour,' James would observe in a determined, manly tone.

I wrote K.Y.M.S. once more, and began to listen to what the Air Commodore was saying. His conversation was spattered with letters. He was referring to his bowsers as BW 138s, a code number by which we ourselves usually referred to them. He also had the habit of referring to people by the initial letters of their titles.

'We hope D.O.R.R.S. will agree with our contention,' I heard him saying, and wondered at first what on earth he meant. He meant Sir Francis.

Robert leaned across to see what I had written on my blotting-pad. Whenever one followed Robert's advice, he

nodded with lofty, impartial approval. Incidentally, the letters
stood for Keep Your Mouth Shut.

'Our overall figure for additional requirement of BW 138s
over the next two years,' the Air Commodore was reading
from a roneo'd memorandum, 'is 651 by 1st September 1948.'

Sir Francis received the speech without a blink. It seemed to
him perfectly reasonable. The figure had been arrived at by
calculation, of all methods the most just and accurate.

'I hope that's correct,' he said, brightly. 'Let us see now.
You say your monthly requirement averages $27\frac{1}{3}$. Now $23\frac{1}{2}$
times $27\frac{1}{3}$ is' – he paused for not more than five seconds –
'$642\frac{1}{3}$.'

The Air Commodore looked irritated.

'$642\frac{1}{3}$ is correct,' said James Irskine, having rapidly worked it
out on a slip of paper.

'The figure I have been given is 651,' said the Air
Commodore. He began turning over the pages of his
memorandum.

'As one-third of a bowser is no use to you,' said Sir Francis,
making a triumphant concession to realism, 'we must, of
course, say 643.'

'What is the necessity for the other eight?' said James
Irskine, menacingly.

The Air Commodore crossly put on a pair of spectacles to
find out. His sheets of paper rustled.

Sir Francis said: 'I beg you not to trouble yourself now. I'm
sure that in due course you will find an excellent reason for
wanting them.'

'Anyway, none of them,' said James, 'exist yet.'

'I think that is hardly the point, James,' said Sir Francis,
placing the tips of his fingers together and giving James a look
of rebuke. James's face reddened with anger. There was a
pause.

'And now, Robert,' said Sir Francis, 'we haven't heard from
you.'

Robert roused himself. His fine rectangular forehead had
been bent forward and his muscular cheeks very still. He
looked at least ten years older than his age.

'I was wondering if there was anything I could usefully say.'

He glanced round the table, and his tone carried such weight that even Sir Francis looked faintly deferential.

Sir Francis recovered from his deference promptly. 'I'm sure there is.'

Robert said: 'It happens that I decided last week that we ought to have a look at BW 138s, 139s, and 152s. Joseph is working on it' – his voice sounded a shade dramatic – 'at this moment.'

'Excellent,' said Sir Francis, all smiles. 'Most opportunely.'

Robert smiled back. When Robert smiled he showed spaces between his front teeth.

The Air Commodore's irritation disappeared.

Sir Francis said happily to him: 'In effect, if your organisation does not get all it wants of one type, it will be able to make up with another.' He turned to Robert. 'I am sure your calculation takes into account the War Office demand we were discussing last week?'

Robert made a gesture with his hand. It was too late. The Air Commodore reared up suddenly.

Sir Francis turned to him: 'Out of fairness, I must not conceal from you, that supplies will not be entirely at your disposal.'

Back came Robert's lugubrious phrase to me: 'Not an atom of sense.'

The Air Commodore was dismayed and angry. Of course Robert's computation had taken the War Office demand into account: of course the total supply would not meet what everybody said they wanted. But nobody could possibly calculate exactly what they did want – the figure 651, if it meant anything at all, meant round about 400: of the 400, any old type would do, and long before the first of September 1948 the programme would be changed.

The Air Commodore wanted to know if we were deluding him. For all his stiff amiability, he was a man of some force of character. His anger and dismay concentrated on Sir Francis.

'Sir Francis, you alarm me! You shake my confidence!'

Immediately, Robert was fully alert and participant. He remained still and even slightly gloomy, but I could tell he had come into action. He made the Air Commodore a long speech, bringing it to a mildly surprising end.

'In all these discussions,' Robert wound up, quietly and with feeling, 'the figure that really signifies is not the number of things your calculating people tell you you need. It's the number that the people who use them can manage with in reasonable contentment.'

Then everybody was silent. It was not the sort of speech D.O.R.R.S. was employed to make. Sir Francis could not possibly have made it, yet he was borne down by it. The Air Commodore, on the other hand, was restored.

'That's all very well,' he said. 'But I've got to go back with something my calculating people will accept.'

Robert said: 'If you'll come back with me to my office, I think we can manage that.'

Now Robert stirred in his chair. I followed suit. Sir Francis was caught momentarily helpless. James Irskine did nothing. The meeting was over.

We all stood up, and a minute or two later Robert and I were escorting the Air Commodore down the corridor. We glanced at each other for the first time. The glance meant one thing – how long could we go on saving Old Frank?

CHAPTER IV

FOND FAREWELL

Myrtle and I looked into each other's faces, into each other's eyes. We did not see very much, because it was an unusually dark night. We were standing on the far end of a platform at Euston station, waiting for it to be time for Myrtle's train to leave. We were beyond where the lighted roof came to an end, beyond where the locomotive stood gurgling and hissing quietly. We had chosen the shadowy lee of a high stack of boxes for our exchange of whispering. The boxes smelt of fish.

'Good night, my sweet...'

'Good night, darling...'

Myrtle looked away without moving her face, and light glimmered on the whites of her eyes. I could just see her lips, long, smooth, relaxed and gently-closed. I kissed her. She fluttered momentarily with surprise. Then she sighed.

I tightened my grip round her waist, and set about kissing her again. After a little while we paused – for breath.

'Good night, darling...'

'Good night, my sweet...'

Myrtle was leaning against me. I found myself looking past the top of her head into the distance. A fog was beginning to rise. In the hazy darkness each of the signals, the green, red, yellow little lights, had a halo, and the glow from all of them seemed to be trying to creep upwards into the sky. We heard the sound of a train entering the station at a distant platform, but it was hidden by a long line of unlighted coaches. There was nobody round about us. The station seemed curiously deserted, and our stretch of platform silent, like an island.

I heard Myrtle say: 'What's the matter, darling?' Her tone

221

was melancholy.

I shook my head, and went on looking at the signals.

A pause. 'What is it?'

'Nothing.'

Myrtle's hands moved about on my shoulders. I could smell her hair, see her eyes, feel her body – yes, indeed there was something the matter!

What was the matter was quite simple. Unhappily, disclosing it, simple though it was, will spoil my hopes of showing up as the appealing, romantic lover I should have liked to be.

Myrtle lived in a provincial town. She came up to London regularly, but on this day she had come without warning. I had had a dinner engagement which it had been impossible to break – even for love. I had only got away in time to see her off at the station, and we had not been able to go to bed together. I held her in my arms.

'Oh dear,' said Myrtle, 'there *is* something the matter.'

I drew in a breath. I said:

'I wish I'd known you were coming.'

'I couldn't let you know sooner.'

'I know, darling.'

'What difference would it have made?'

I did not reply. I felt slightly ashamed of myself. Perhaps she did not know.

'What difference would it have made?' she repeated softly. With her finger she touched the corner of my mouth.

'What are you doing that for?' I asked.

'I couldn't see it,' she said.

I burst out with the only quotation from Wordsworth I knew.

'"... and oh, The difference to me!"'

Myrtle laughed.

'It's nothing to laugh about,' I said.

Myrtle kissed my chin.

'I'll see you next week,' she said.

'But we've missed tonight!'

'It won't do you any harm,' she said. 'It won't do you any harm at all.'

'You devil!'

Myrtle leaned her head forward. She never wore a hat. She had lovely silky hair, brushed up into curls on top of her head – they touched my nose, and the scent of them filled my nostrils.

'Do you like my new dressing?' came Myrtle's voice. 'I told Rudolf my boy-friend would like it, so he put on lots.'

Rudolf was a fashionable hairdresser's assistant.

'What!' I exclaimed. 'You don't talk to him about your private life, do you?'

'Of course not, darling.'

I knew Myrtle was incapable of conversing forthrightly about her private life. On the other hand, she was very capable of conversing un-forthrightly about such matters. A few allusive sentences, a smirk, a sigh, a lewd click of the tongue.

'Myrtle!' I said.

'I have to be friendly with him, darling.'

That was true. Myrtle had to be friendly with everyone. An unfriendly atmosphere was distasteful, almost painful to her. Myrtle had to be friendly, and really I loved her for it. Even if it led her to speak of me as her boy-friend to a hairdresser's assistant, I would not have changed her. It always seemed to me that far too few people in this world felt they had to be friendly.

'Sweet,' I said.

Myrtle remained motionless.

We heard a whistle blow in the distance. She lifted her head.

'It's all right. It isn't your train, darling.'

From where we stood it was impossible to see the clock. We moved apart and went down the platform. I took out my handkerchief and wiped her lipstick off my mouth.

Myrtle sauntered along, with her fur-coat flying open. She noticed me looking at her, and suddenly smiled questioningly, with a clear flicker of diffidence. She was twenty-nine: she had attractive looks, beautiful clothes, a highly successful career as a commercial artist. Yet a young girl's uncertainty about her charm sometimes overtook her.

'You look beautiful,' I said, and slipped my arm round her waist, under her coat. She was tallish and slender, and she had a small waist. I felt her body moving with a nervous laziness.

The platform was brightly lit, and I glanced at the clock.
A propos of nothing at all, Myrtle said conversationally:
'The week after next, the old b's coming on leave.'
I must now confess that Myrtle's speech was somewhat profane.
By 'the old b' she meant her husband.

CHAPTER V

A QUESTION OF MARRIAGE

I know I was doing something I should not have been doing.
I know I was falling hopelessly below the common
standards of moral behaviour that everybody sets up for
someone else to conform with. I know all that, and I would
offer the deepest, humblest excuses – if I thought anybody
would accept them. Experience tells me, alas, they would
probably not.

My only hope lies in persuading you to wait while I tell the
rest of my story. I can assure you the worst disclosure is past.
And there is even a chance that unmitigated disfavour may not
be my lot when I come to the end.

The story of Myrtle and me had really begun some eight,
nearly nine years earlier. Myrtle and I had a love-affair before
the war. A very delightful, enjoyable love-affair it was – trust
Myrtle for that. For a year or so, actually until the war began,
we were lovers. It was one of the happiest years of my youth.

Such being the case, you may ask why Myrtle and I were not
married. A question that Myrtle, it later appeared, had not
ceased to ask herself for eight years. And a question, I have to
admit, that she did not fail to ask me at the time.

My answer is not a very good one. It throws no light on
hidden suffering: it reveals no unsuspected tragic events: really
it explains nothing. I did not want to be married. That is all
there is to it. I just did not want to be married. I cannot say
more, and obviously I cannot say less.

Myrtle was not satisfied with my answer. Few girls of
twenty-two would have been. We loved each other. She knew
that I was not interested in anyone else. My attitude seemed
inexplicable. She was inspired to provoke the result she

225

wanted by trying to make me jealous. She succeeded in making
me jealous. And I hated myself and her for it – hated her the
more of the two, as it happened. At that point the war broke
out.

Until the war I had been lodging in the provincial town
where Myrtle still lived. We parted. I left the town to go off
and do my war service and never to return. The parting caused
me sadness and pain. I could not lay claim to universal
sympathy because, when all was said and done, I had had my
own way. Everyone except Robert pointed that out to me like a
shot. I admitted it, although they never explained to my
satisfaction why life would have been all jam if I had let Myrtle
have her way.

Myrtle and I parted. I relied on Time for consolation,
Myrtle relied on promptly marrying somebody else – on
marrying the man, in fact, of whom she had made me jealous.
A local newspaper reporter, called Dennis Haxby. Myrtle had
been Mrs Haxby for several weeks before I heard about the
marriage. She had been Mrs Haxby for over five years before I
saw her again.

I met Myrtle by accident in the bar of the Savoy Hotel,
where I had persuaded Robert to meet me. Robert disliked the
Savoy, and as soon as he saw Myrtle signal across to me he
finished his drink and slipped away. He had never liked
Myrtle.

I made my way through the crowd to her. We embraced, as
they say, like long-lost friends. She had a bright look in her
eye. She had a new scent. I laughed with pleasure. Then I saw
the man who was with her.

Myrtle's companion was not her husband. He was a captain
in the American army.

I took one look at the American captain, and at the same
instant he took one look at me. It was hate at first sight.

One suffers for one's weaknesses, and I had been directly
pricked on one of mine. I had always told myself I did not give
a damn about Haxby: I admitted that I did about this man. I
ought to have bowed politely and gone away. Instead, I
stayed. I ought to have known better.

The American was about the same height as me, and about

the same weight. He had a neat, clean, vigorous, compact look. His uniform was a few degrees fresher than mine. One of his wrists bore an elegant gold identity-bracelet. The other wrist ledged on Myrtle's hip. We wished each other at the opposite ends of the earth. He asked me if I would like a dry Martini, and I said I would.

Myrtle lingered between us with a fluttering, sly, innocent smile. The scene that followed reflects credit on none of us. The American conveyed to me, by tone and gesture, that he had been sleeping with Myrtle. By tone and gesture I conveyed exactly the same to him. Not a single ungentlemanly remark was uttered: not a single ungentlemanly innuendo was left out. I ought to have gone away. He ought to have gone away. Yes, he ought to have gone away. That was just the point. Of a sudden, I passionately wanted Myrtle for myself.

And that is how our love-affair began all over again. Myrtle went on seeing the American frequently during the next few weeks and then he was drafted to Germany. And then she began to see me frequently. He dropped out of the story. It was Myrtle's opinion that we had hated each other because we were alike. I did not care about that. I had Myrtle to myself again.

There is one other thing to be said, one other person to be mentioned. Myrtle's husband. When I met her again in the bar of the Savoy, Haxby was in Naples. He was in the army.

Now Haxby was moved to Rome, and came home on leave at regular intervals. In between, Myrtle was regularly seeing me. Such a state of affairs could not last. With characteristic realism Myrtle saw that it could last until Haxby was demobilised, and he was not due to be demobilised yet.

'The week after next, the old b's coming on leave.'

I did not like the remark, and I was worried by it as I walked down the platform after Myrtle's train had gone. I was beginning to think about marrying Myrtle this time. That meant I now really had got to admit to giving a damn about Haxby.

CHAPTER VI

AN ARTIST'S DILEMMA

When I was debating whether to marry Myrtle, my friends would address me in the derogatory tone which is characteristic of those who profess to love and respect me, saying: 'That's all very well for you, but what is Myrtle supposed to be getting out of it?' My opinion of myself was not so high that the question seemed unreasonable. About Robert I would not say the same. I thought many women would recognise Robert to be a catch.

There was something on a large scale about Robert's nature, in the height, the width, the depth of his wisdom and experience and insight. For fifteen years it had commanded in me love and respect to the point of veneration. That is not why I thought many women would call him a catch. Not at all: there is not much feminine realism in that. Robert also had the capacity for earning large sums of money.

Now the war was over Robert had several offers of jobs in business again, offers so desirable that few people who did not know him could understand why he stayed where he was. Robert had a reason. He wanted to stop being either a business-man or a civil servant – he always had. His greatest desire, his only desire, was to become a writer.

It seemed to me that Robert had some of the most valuable gifts for a writer, and that the sooner he became one the better. But unlike most of his friends, I saw why Robert did not find it so easy to make a break in his career. Why, they asked, if he was chafing passionately to become a writer, did he not do like other artists – hire a garret and write? When I observed that the artists who have starved in garrets have rarely been the kind of men whom people would offer to make managing directors or Permanent Secretaries, I was regarded as an evil influence that prevented Robert solving his dilemma.

CHAPTER VII

HOW TO HELP EACH OTHER

Like Robert, I too wanted to become a writer. Our literary aspirations had grown side by side, and our friendship, to begin with, was a literary comradeship.

Before the war Robert and I had each published three novels with encouraging, if exceedingly modest success. They were the works of our youth. It happened that when the war began we were both completing the first works of our maturity, the sort of books we really put our souls into. They came out in June 1940 while the British army was being driven out of France. The reviews were civil enough. The sales were unspeakable.

We bore up. It seemed to us that life was likely to be mainly a matter of bearing up. This was fortunate, because in due course worse was to befall. We decided that if England won the war (in June 1940 by no means certain to us) and if we survived it (if anything, rather less certain) we would start all over again. The Second World War was fought by Robert and me for England, freedom, and the chance to write novels.

Under literary disaster we bore up. Worse was to befall, and it did not take long about it. It befell us simultaneously in the shape of devastatingly unhappy love-affairs.

It is easy to make light of unhappy love-affairs after they are over. To do us justice Robert and I exerted all our will to make just a shade lighter of them at the time. Just a shade – to us it was that shade which seemed to prevent us cutting our throats. Our literary comradeship changed to something deeper. The comradeship of the rejected, the scorned, the tormented. The comradeship of the hideously miserable.

I will not tell the two stories or describe how and why we fell in love. Each would take a novel – a fact we thanked God we were aware of at the time.

I hated the girl Robert fell in love with. She was very beautiful, but to me she seemed so frigid as to be scarcely human. I used to call her 'The Headlamps', because she had enormous, long-sighted, beautiful grey eyes that threw a light of their own into the distance but appeared to see nothing whatsoever. I was unjust to her, poor creature. Though she tortured Robert mercilessly, she was never happy.

With rather more self-restraint I glumly began to call my own love 'My Last One'. I had a feeling that though my spirit was not broken, my heart was. This was something that could not happen again. She was not particularly beautiful, neither was she particularly cold. She was warm-hearted, snobbish, and frankly brutal – 'I hope you're not still thinking I'll ever marry you, because I shan't.'

Our darkest days of the heart coincided with some of the darkest days of the war, when Robert was certain that we were going to lose. Yet such men were we that the anguish of hearing bad war-news was little beside the anguish of waiting for letters that did not come. We helped each other to bear up. In that I think each of us had something to be proud of. Even in the most hideous depths, we lightened our miseries with a streak of high spirits.

From my side the miseries were lightened also by a streak of devotion to good meals. Robert had a well-developed taste for food, but suffering made him mope and eat nothing. Whenever we contrived to meet in London, I exerted my will to make us go out in search of a delicious luxurious dinner. A trivial pleasure? The only pleasures left to us by our dreadful young women were trivial.

And let me say here and now, that while we were eating our delicious luxurious dinner, I got an additional satisfaction out of thinking about our dreadful young women, miles away – one was in the WRNS, the other in the WAAF – distastefully munching thick sandwiches in their N.A.A.F.I. canteens. The satisfaction of a small man? Have it your own way. Robert was lucky to have a small man about the place. Experience taught me that sexual torment is better sustained on a well-filled stomach than on an empty one.

'My dear Joe,' Robert remarked, with authoritative disdain, 'will nothing break your attachment to homely wisdom?' And then he filled his mouth with whitebait.

'By the time wisdom gets homely, there's usually something in it.'

'Unlike girls.' Robert paused sadly in his eating. 'Unlike girls...'

We survived.

When the war ended, I did not have a fine career in business behind me, and was not specially enthusiastic about trying to create one in front. And though I felt bound to exhort Robert to take to a garret for his own good, I had no enthusiasm at all for it myself. Robert, out of kindness of heart, promptly got me my present appropriate and comfortable job with him. Robert had great generosity: when he found himself in a dilemma that laid him open to criticism, he was not above generously landing me in the same.

CHAPTER VIII

AN IVORY CIGARETTE-HOLDER

In the dark days, Robert and I derived repeated minute consolation from dining in the restaurant of the Carlos Hotel. It was small, it was very sedate, and it was luxurious. There was no music, there was no bar. There was no flashy head-waiter with whom one had to be familiar in order to get a table. The servants were elderly. And the cooking was delectable.

We were still frequenting the Carlos after the war had ended.

When Myrtle paid me her next visit to London with due warning,. she decided to stay the night and suggested that we should ask Robert to dine with us.

Myrtle was making a deliberate set at Robert. I do not mean that she was trying to make Robert fall in love with her. She was intent on gaining Robert's goodwill. Since the occasion when he had slipped out of the bar at the Savoy when he saw her, Myrtle had made considerable headway. She had gained well over fifty per cent of his goodwill, in my estimation.

During my first love-affair with Myrtle, she and Robert had not got on together. She had been over-awed by him: he had been contemptuous of her. Since then, times had changed.

I had encouraged Myrtle to make Robert give her a drink before dinner. It would nicely fill in her time while I went and played squash. When I arrived at the Carlos I found them already ensconced in the far corner of the lounge, Robert sitting regally on a sofa and Myrtle deep in a big armchair facing him. From the window there slanted the soft light of a fine humid September evening.

I joined them and Myrtle looked up at me.

Myrtle had never played a game of any kind in her life; and she had no sympathy with my enjoyment of athletic activities, none whatever. In the past she had ignored it. Today she looked up at me sweetly and said in her gentle, lightly-modulated voice:

'Did you have a good game, darling?'

With a lurking smile she scrutinised my face, put out her forefinger and stroked away some beads of sweat near the roots of my hair. Times had changed. Times had changed for the better.

A waiter came up to see if I wanted anything to drink. Myrtle picked up her glass. 'Robert has given me a wonderful drink.' She sighed complacently. 'So expensive.'

When the waiter had gone, Robert said: 'Look what Myrtle has given me!'

He handed across to me a small leather case, which I opened. It contained a cigarette-holder.

'Do you like it?'

I did. It was made of ivory, with a beautiful gloss, pale-coloured, lying on a dark-blue silk background.

The waiter came up with my drink. While Robert paid for it, I laid the case down on the table and looked at Myrtle. Myrtle guiltily sipped her drink without looking at me. Robert had his eye on both of us.

'I've always rather wanted a cigarette-holder,' Robert said, in a lofty, detached tone.

I thought nothing would have been easier than to buy one. He had plenty of money.

Robert's tone changed to dolorous.

'Only nobody ever gives me these things. . .'

'Ah! . .' Myrtle made sympathetic sheep's-eyes at him.

There was a pause.

'Robert says I'm the first woman,' said Myrtle, 'who's ever realised how fastidious he is.'

I thought no wonder the atmosphere had been intimate when I arrived. I thought of any speech beginning 'You're the first woman who's ever realised. . .'

'It's true,' Robert was saying, as if his past suffering had been recalled.

That Robert was fastidious was true, though not at first sight apparent. He habitually dressed in rather worn suits, but he had them fastidiously cared for. Myrtle had been observant. Robert smoked, and always removed the nicotine stains from his fingers and his teeth.

'It takes a girl like Myrtle to notice these things,' he said, and he gave me a fine, congratulatory look.

I accepted it.

You may be thinking that when Myrtle and Robert made up to each other I made fun of it, and that when Myrtle made up to me I solemnly took it all in. You are quite right.

I led the way into the dining-room thinking about Myrtle's share of Robert's goodwill. On tonight's showing, fifty per cent was a stupid under-estimate.

CHAPTER IX

AN INTERRUPTED DINNER

The Carlos restaurant was charming. It was panelled in
rosy mahogany, and had a high, pleasantly moulded
ceiling. The tables were far apart, and there were shaded
lamps on those near the walls. There were flowers on our table,
three chrysanthemums, with curled pink and bronze petals, in
a little silver-plated vase. We sat holding large white menu-
cards folded down the middle, and glanced round at the other
diners. The room was warm, busy and quiet. We were
delighted.

A born aristocrat can have no idea of the innocent pleasure
that going up in the world gives to people. Neither Robert,
Myrtle nor I had been born to such surroundings. It might
have been argued that we were three gifted and clever persons
to whom society owed them – we would not have dreamed of
taking part in such an odious argument. We sat there, not
necessarily remembering where we had come from, but very
definitely observing where we had got to, and feeling a modest,
naif satisfaction.

In the glow of a lamp, Myrtle's oval face, her round bright
eyes and long nose, her dark curls and slender neck made her
look exactly like a portrait from the First Empire. And Robert,
with his broad forehead, his smooth grey hair and his chin
slightly thrust out, looked like a ˙modern statesman –
remarkably like Franklin D. Roosevelt, in fact.

Myrtle ate her soup with relish. She liked food. She liked
alcohol more, but she liked food enough. Suddenly I thought
of the eating habits of My Last One and The Headlamps – The
Headlamps picked a little food and left most of it: My Last
One ate a good deal far too quickly. It might have been a

familiar glow from the wall, the little silver vase, the sound of a waiter's voice – something took me straight back to the evenings when Robert and I had dined here miserably, solitarily, wishing that our loves were with us. I caught Myrtle's eye, just as she was holding her spoon to her lips. I went on eating my soup. The room was warm and busy and very pleasing.

The evening went by. Robert and I entertained Myrtle with anecdotes about Sir Francis and life in the office. Myrtle told us about goings-on in the advertising business.

Most of Myrtle's talk was aimed at Robert, and I was delighted by her easy confident way with him. When she talked about business nowadays her diffidence fell right away from her. She was still working for the provincial advertising agency in which she had been employed when she first met Robert. But the agency was now so successful that it could have set up in London any time it wanted, and Myrtle knew her work was the basis of its success.

Myrtle had a marked artistic gift, of a strength in excess of what her work called for. I had always wanted her to be a serious artist. But Myrtle had an instinct for worldly success as well. How rarely, I thought, do the two go together! With shrewd feminine simplicity Myrtle had never let her aspirations fall a hairsbreadth outside the range of her talents. How unlike me! I thought – I always doubted whether Myrtle comprehended my kind of aspirations at all. I computed that as a result of her tactics, Myrtle earned as much by provincial standards as I by metropolitan. Myrtle computed the same, and it was clear she thought that until I became the greatest English writer since Shakespeare, there was nothing to choose in our aspirations.

Robert listened to Myrtle's chatter with obvious pleasure. We had come to the end of the meal and he was airing his new cigarette-holder with slightly grandiose aplomb, while Myrtle patently admired him. His face was impassive and his eyes bright.

Myrtle described a dress-show; gilt chairs, glasses of champagne, jewellery, pomade, and the buzz of fashionable voices.

'Cockatoos,' said Robert, hollowly. 'Cockatoos.'

Myrtle smirked at him.

'You wait...' she said, and a look passed between them.

I thought, 'Oho! he's been telling her about his new young woman.'

Robert had not concealed from me that his eye had lighted on someone fresh, but all I knew was that her name was Julia and that she was young and very chic.

'You wait, yourself, my girl,' Robert said. 'She'll probably put your nose out of joint. I think you'll find' – he addressed her as if she were a committee – 'she quite comes up to your own very high standards.'

Myrtle was too happily flattered to be able to form a reply.

'Her name is Julia,' said Robert.

'What's her other name?' said I, seizing the opportunity to face him with a direct question.

'Łempicki-Czyz' said Robert in a preposterously casual tone.

'What?' echoed Myrtle and I.

Robert said it again.

'Is she Polish?' asked Myrtle.

'English,' said Robert. 'Quite English.' He paused. 'She married a Colonel in the Polish army towards the middle of the war. In 1943 actually. At the time when the Polish Third Division was being formed under General Kopanski, to go to Sicily, as you no doubt recall.'

Myrtle was quite unable to recall any such thing and had not the slightest interest in trying.

'Before her marriage I don't know what her name was. His, of course, was Łempicki-Czyz.'

Myrtle and I realised that Robert must have been practising furiously.

'I shall never learn to say it,' said Myrtle.

'It's pronounced,' said Robert, 'as, in English, Wem-peet-skee-Chi-zh.'

Myrtle and I tried laboriously to imitate him. Wem-peet-skee-Chi-zh.

'I believe,' said Robert, 'most English people find it rather easier to call her Julia.' He was teasing us thoroughly. Also he was heading us off further direct questions.

'I'm sorry for Czyz,' said Myrtle. For an instant I thought she was sorry for him because Robert's eye had lighted on his wife. In fact Myrtle was sorry for Czyz because nobody in England could pronounce his name.

'Where is he?' I asked Robert.

Robert answered with an air of mystery. 'It's thought that he's at present in Poland.'

A peculiar expression passed over Myrtle's face. She was probably feeling how much better it was for everybody's sake if a married woman knew where her husband was. 'I should like to meet Julia,' she said, with lingering sympathy.

Robert smiled at her. He removed the cigarette-end from his holder. Myrtle smiled at him. A waiter appeared at his elbow and said: 'Excuse me, sir, you're wanted on the telephone.'

We were all startled.

'Who on earth is it?' I said.

Robert shook his head as he stood up and dropped his napkin on the table.

Myrtle and I looked at each other after he had gone. She was puzzled by my expression. It was the expression of a man who has come to distrust unexpected telephone-calls.

'Oh dear!..' I did not realise I had spoken aloud.

My hand was lying on the table and Myrtle touched it.

'Sweet,' I said. I had not told her all about my past woes.

Myrtle said she thought she would like to drink a brandy.

I ordered some brandies. Robert had not returned. We began to drink them. No sign of Robert. Myrtle and I began to touch hands on the table. We liked brandy. Myrtle pretended to be studying the people round about.

'We'll go home in a taxi, darling,' I said, thinking 'so as not to waste any time.'

Myrtle did not reply. She sensed a faint affront to her natural leisurely pace. She went on looking round the room and holding my hand.

In the end I thought we should have to go and look for Robert.

He returned, hurrying.

'It was Julia,' he said, quite unable to keep a triumphant note out of his voice.

'Robert!' Myrtle was smiling at him, her eyes alight.

I said to him: 'There's some brandy waiting for you.'

Robert picked up his glass. As he raised it to his mouth he glanced at me with a bright, amused look. It clearly meant: 'I'm going to need this, old boy.'

I could scarcely contain my curiosity. A few minutes later he and I were left alone together in the foyer while Myrtle restored her make-up. He could scarcely contain his excitement.

'Out with it,' I said.

'She's going down to Brighton for a weekend. She's asked me to go.'

I whistled.

Robert was buttoning his overcoat. It was a big, handsome black ministerial overcoat.

'Will you go?' I said.

Robert did not reply. He would not have dreamed of replying.

I stared at him.

Suddenly he leaned towards me. 'As a matter of fact, old boy, she said something, and I couldn't believe my ears.'

It was a recognised allusion. Robert held the theory, to which I unreservedly subscribed, that if you thought you heard somebody say something and you could not believe your ears, they most certainly *had* said it.

It was of special significance when you thought you heard someone you hardly knew say: 'Of course we shall be going to bed together.'

Our theory was based strictly on experiment. Each of us could go back with shame and with painful regret to occasions when we had, stupidly, idiotically made the most inept rejoinder of all – '*What* did you say?'

'I just could not believe my ears,' Robert repeated, as if he were deeply shocked, 'I just couldn't.' And I leave it to you to imagine the kind of look we then exchanged.

At this moment Myrtle came up. She glanced from one to

the other of us and guessed what was going on. She took my arm.

'Come on, my lad,' she said. 'It's a taxi for you.'

CHAPTER X

GOSSIP IN A CHANGING-ROOM

A few evenings later James Irskine asked me to give him a game of squash. He had a fixed habit of leaving the office punctually, rapidly drinking a bottle of Worthington in the nearest public-house, taking the Tube to Victoria and there catching the 6.20 train to East Ewell – where his wife had ready a meal which made up in heartiness for what it lacked in succulence.

If James broke his routine, it was for something really serious – either need for exercise or desire for private talk about the office. I saw his point of view. Compared with his own existence, mine was chiefly notable for its mixture of loneliness and disorder. On the rare occasions when I judged that James's rather wooden facial expression was indicating a twinge of complacent pity for my lot, I must admit I felt quite sorry for myself. I lived in a small flat in a big tumbledown Georgian house on the Embankment. I was tended by the mean ladylike owner of the house who said she used up all my rations in providing my breakfast. James was right.

We came off the Squash court and sat exhaustedly on one of the benches that lined the walls of the dressing-room. It was a long upholstered seat with a soiled white linen cover. We leaned our backs against the cool painted walls in the spaces between where our clothes hung from pegs up above.

It was a big, low, well-heated room, with wash-basins and mirrors and cupboards. It was underground and it smelt of the sweat of generations. There was an electric fan, which mingled with the smell of sweat the peculiar scent of hair oil in a couple of bottles beside the wash-basins.

I called one of the attendants to bring us some shandies.

James was sitting idly surveying his long straight legs in their neat white naval shorts.

'Have you seen Old Frank's new typist?' he said.

'Not yet.'

'She's told him to call her Lana.'

James was not gifted with a sense of humour, but he was intelligent enough to know that such a thing existed and to work out a sort of substitute.

'She's invented it,' I said.

Sir Francis had delightful courteous manners, but they did not spring spontaneously from the heart. It was his convention to enquire the Christian name of anyone newly appointed to his personal staff and then systematically to use it. James and I took to it naturally enough; but some of the lowly little girls who had been brought up to expect their boss to call them Miss Watson, or whatever it was, even while he was trying to tickle their ears, were put off by Sir Francis's behaving oppositely to the rules – calling them Lana and never even glancing at their noses. And from human contrariness they liked him less for his efforts.

I sipped my shandy. I thought James would shortly be getting down to business. He took off his shoes and socks, put a towel round his shoulders, and said:

'I'm afraid Old Frank is not giving pleasure in certain other quarters.'

I glanced at him. He was showing me an expressionless profile. He went on.

'Robert had a personal triumph with the Air Commodore that afternoon. That sort of thing doesn't do any good in the long run.'

'It saved a row on the spot,' I said, touchily.

'It didn't do Old Frank any good.'

I thought for a moment. 'It's important to remember,' I said, 'that the mood in which a man is going to report back to his boss is not necessarily the mood in which he leaves the committee –'

'I thought I was telling you that.'

'– But that's no reason for not trying to send him away mollified,' I finished up with force.

'Is that merely an expression of loyalty to Robert?' said James. 'Or does it mean something more?' I had annoyed him, and as usual his face began to redden.

'It means that, given Old Frank, I don't see what else any of us can do.'

'You can expect the opposition to start gunning for him.'

'They mustn't get away with it!'

James looked me in the face: '*I* don't want him to go.'

I looked him in the face. We both knew that Sir Francis's fate did not affect James's promotion. James was expressing loyalty to Sir Francis.

'They'll try and use the controversy over A 15s.' As he spoke, James glanced over his shoulder to see if two men wrapped in towels were listening. The controversy over A 15s was highly secret, and we were not supposed ever to refer to them other than by the code-number.

'We're ready for that.'

James kept up his fixed absence of expression.

'We'll keep Plumer out of it,' I said.

'That means keeping *me* out!' Immediately he had spoken James must have wished he had not said it. I was delighted.

As if I had not noticed, I went on. 'Do you know what they're going to do?'

'No.' James shifted his position, as if he were getting stiff. 'I'm going to have a shower.' He stood up, and with the towel still round his shoulders, he abruptly walked off and left me.

At first I thought he had some reason for breaking the conversation. When I first knew him I had looked for hidden significance in all James's manoeuvres. But as time went on I had come to realise that usually there was none. In one sense James Irskine was an interesting man – he was pursuing his career with unusual single-mindedness. On the other hand this pursuit never took him for a moment outside conventional behaviour. It would never have occurred to him to earn promotion by a display of anything other than ambition and rage. So that in another sense James Irskine was a very dull dog.

I went to the showers thinking about Sir Francis and his

enemies. I wondered if James had heard something that he was too stuffily discreet to tell me.

CHAPTER XI

AN UNSUSPECTING MAN

Unfortunately I am not able to disclose what an A 15 was. My own view is that, even for those days, the degree of secrecy with which the controversy was surrounded was exaggeratedly high. However, what an A 15 actually was does not make any difference to the story of what happened to us. Incidentally I suppose I ought to note, since the code-letter A was used for tanks during the Second World War, that the A 15 was not a tank.

To explain the controversy in its simplest terms, I have to say that the machines had been of great importance during the Second World War, were likely to be very important to the country during peacetime, and – there is no use burking the issue – would be of very great importance again were a third world war to begin within the next ten years.

There were several kinds of machines, which had different numbers, and the A 15 was the kind remaining in use since the war – that is to say, everybody was used to it and the industries of the country could readily make it. The A 16, a machine very different in design, was just being developed, and it had to be admitted its designers were not completely certain of it. The controversy was over whether the country should go on making A 15s or not. If you think of the controversy over whether certain kinds of aeroplane should have piston-engines or jet-engines, you will get some idea of the sort of thing we were dealing with.

At the present moment our department, which was largely responsible for the making of A 15s, was inclined to think we ought to stop making them. The other department involved in the controversy was largely responsible for using A 15s, and it wanted to go on.

The function of our office, under Sir Francis Plumer, was to provide relevant factual information, and in no way to try and influence the controversy one way or other. More easily said than done, of course.

Sir Francis had his weaknesses of temperament. His optimistic striving for justice and accuracy earned a good deal of impatience and irritation in his own department, let alone the other one. The other one seized on the weakness, and tried to pretend that it was something quite different – in fact the opposite. From lack of confidence in Sir Francis's judgments it worked round to lack of confidence in his impartiality. That was both serious and dangerous, and as far as we could see, it was undertaken quite unscrupulously.

'You can expect them to start gunning for him.' James Irskine had found out what was in the wind long before Sir Francis had the slightest suspicion. Sir Francis was the last to have the slightest suspicion.

One afternoon Sir Francis's personal assistant said Sir Francis would like me to go and see him in his office at twenty-two minutes past six. Sir Francis met his duty never to shirk a file by working long hours to a minutely planned time-table. This made it impossible for him to see anyone, however important, without an appointment: his own personal staff he could only see after office-hours.

The evening was unusually dark. Outside heavy rain was blowing across Parliament Square and dashing in squalls against the windows. Sir Francis had lit only his desk-lamp: it had a dark green cylindrical shade, and threw a bright glow of light on his papers. Elsewhere the room was in dusk.

Sir Francis greeted me briskly. The down-cast light upon his face seemed to make the lines of age more noticeable. I thought he looked worn.

'I wanted to speak to you in Robert's absence, because what I have to say to you affects both Robert and you. I take it that Robert will not return from his leave in Brighton till next week.'

'I doubt it . . .'

'The matter is rather urgent. It involves an addition to our staff.'

I was surprised.

'I know that you and Robert are deeply concerned with work on the A 15.' He paused but went on rapidly before I could speak. 'I would have wished that I could take a little more of the load myself. As you see, that is impossible.'

I nodded my head. 'I think Robert and I are managing all right.'

'I don't know how.' Sir Francis looked at me sharply. 'If our volume of work suddenly increases threefold you must be over-burdened.'

It was not a bit of use telling Sir Francis, who gave all his attention to everything, that to Robert and me our work was an alternation of giving more attention to this and markedly less to that. I said:

'In a sense...'

'I perceive only one sense,' said Sir Francis. I always imagined he had a high opinion of my intelligence, but at this moment I could not help feeling he thought I was not quite as clever as he would wish me to be.

'Yes,' I said. As he was clearly proposing an increase in staff to lighten the labours of Robert and me, I decided to keep quiet.

'In the ordinary way,' Sir Francis said, 'it would be impossible to persuade our establishment division that we needed an increase of complement. On the other hand our friends who are interested in A 15s have most generously offered to lend us someone for as long as the present emergency lasts.'

Now I kept quiet out of surprise and alarm. Our friends – he ought to have said his enemies. It was an attempt to plant a new man among us to represesent the opposition in our midst.

'I wish to ask you – I wrote immediately to Robert, of course, but I wish to hear your opinion. I wish to ask you if you think there is a place for such a person.'

'Who is it?'

'Dr Chubb. Dr R. A. Chubb.'

I knew him. I did not dislike him. He had struck me as a very ordinary, dim, shrewd, middle-aged engineer.

Sir Francis went on punctiliously: 'It would not affect your own position. Dr Chubb is senior to you, and a permanent member of the service, whereas you are temporary. He would report to Robert, but you would continue to report to Robert, and not to him.'

I could see that really the matter was already settled. Personally, I did not see any need for Chubb.

'I believe we are all agreed,' said Sir Francis, 'that you will need to do a much fuller survey of industrial concerns in connection with A 15s. Robert outlined his plans to me before he went away. Now, Dr Chubb has actually had industrial experience.'

If I was correct Dr Chubb was a Civil servant who had been employed in the outskirts of industry between 1919 and 1926.

The telephone rang. Sir Francis glanced at the clock, excused himself, and answered the telephone.

While he talked I went over to the window and looked out. The rain was still blowing down. Buses and cars seemed to be circulating grimly. Round the square there were lights in odd windows. Sir Francis went on talking.

I was worried. And I was astonished that the manoeuvre was going to come off. Had it been directed against anyone but Sir Francis, I thought our Permanent Secretary would have said flatly No. The trouble was that Sir Francis really did not command the confidence of his own Permanent Secretary.

The telephone conversation came to an end. I turned back.

Sir Francis had been standing up, while answering the telephone. He glanced at the clock again, and did not sit down. I saw that my time was up.

Sir Francis said: 'I should like you to let me know your opinion tomorrow. I shall be available between 9.15 and 9.40, and again between 11.45 and 11.55.'

I turned towards the door. Sir Francis walked with me. Our official business being over, his tone suddenly became friendly, almost affectionate.

'I wrote to Robert, putting it all before him. But I told him not to worry about it. I want him to enjoy his leave in Brighton.'

'I expect he will.'

'Shall you go down to see him?'

'Oh, no! Certainly not!'

'I wish you would persuade him to stay longer than a week. I thought he looked quite tired when he left.'

I spoke with gravity. 'Robert puts an unusual amount of . . . psychic energy into everything he does.'

Sir Francis thought, and then cocked his head sagaciously.

'That's a very penetrating observation,' he said. 'Thank you, Joseph.'

With a cordial, faintly stylised gesture, we shook hands.

CHAPTER XII

REFLECTIONS IN THE RAIN

I was disturbed by the prospect of Dr Chubb's arrival, partly because it was a sign of intrigue going against us, but by no means entirely. I decided to walk home along the Embankment in spite of the rain: somehow it was a mild relief to be in motion, however uncomfortable.

The rain was not as heavy as it sounded indoors. It blew in gusts and then seemed to cease for a while. Only the pools of water in the gutters constantly showed a sprinkling of drops. Wet brown leaves were stuck to the pavement, and layers of heavy autumnal cloud moved slowly at different paces across the sky. I felt glum. The fact of the matter is that I did not like the idea of any change.

Irately I invented heavy-footed quips – 'More bosses make harder work', and so on. If Dr Chubb came he would destroy the free-and-easy tenor of our office-life. He would be an intruder. He would demand work to do. People had an idea that work, any work, was a good thing in itself. I wished that I could force everybody who held that theory to observe detachedly for a day the ant-like activity of Sir Francis. And Chubb would intrigue. That was what he would be there for. I did not know him well, but I had no reason to suppose he was different from other men – he had always struck me as rather less clever than some, but that did not mean he was any less likely to want power.

While I strode past the classical grey stone front of the Tate Gallery, my thoughts took a more generalised form – there was no connection, of course. It came to me that I found it hard to sympathise with the struggle for power in affairs. These manoeuvres in our office would produce a negligible impression on whatever decision over the A 15 was emerging. Nobody thought they would. What they would produce were small advances and regressions of prestige for the various individuals concerned. I thought of the time and attention being spent on them. Why, why must they bother to do it at all?

The answer came pat. Because it was their lives, in a way that it was not mine. My heart was in writing books: that was what I thought about, schemed about, and put all my ambition into. And writing books happened to be a solitary occupation, miles away from other people. What their hearts were in, their thoughts and schemes and ambitions, was utterly different – it was in this struggle with each other, right here.

Now all this does not mean that I did not enjoy what power came my way. Far from it. The intrigue made me rage, and I began to think of moves for confounding the people who were trying to get us down. But my rage to me seemed righteous, my moves were designed to prevent the triumph of the wicked. I supposed in that respect I differed not a jot from the men with whom I found it so difficult to identify myself. On the other hand, my moves were not specifically designed to put me forward or put anyone else back. I did not so much want to go forward as to get out.

Suddenly the wind softened and the rain came down in gouts. I was within sight of home and I ran.

To my surprise I found a letter waiting for me from Robert.

My dear Joe,

I have just had a long letter from Old F. in characteristic style. He says he is going to have a talk with you and I presume that he will have had it by now. That is if his time-table has permitted it, which I very much doubt. The gang are trying to persuade him to let them lend us one Dr R. A. Chubb (you remember him, hare-eyed and slightly toothy – incidentally what is he a Doctor of? Letters, do you suppose?) to assist me with the A 15 business. I expect it will upset you, but it's bound to happen and we might do much worse. There is much we can find for him to do that we don't want to do ourselves. I needn't say it will not affect us. I have written to Old F. telling him to accept. I have made a further statesmanlike suggestion that we make use of Dr C's invaluable experience of industry by sending him on a tour of firms immediately. Would you be preparing a list for him? I think a long list, don't you?

Private affairs. Fascinating and v. enjoyable. Julia is a very remarkable woman, even more remarkable than I thought. There is a startling development that I don't want to write about now. I'll tell you when I see you.

Life and art. You are not to worry. In the odd moments in which I've been permitted to indulge my passion for thought, I've been thinking seriously. I've had enough of Old F., Chubb and all others. It's time we abandoned them to their fate. This time next year we must be free.

    Ever,

      R.

I was comforted.

CHAPTER XIII
TWO FRIENDS

I dined with Robert at his club on the evening he returned from Brighton. I found him standing in the lobby reading a copy of *The Times* which was locked down, like the Bible in the fifteenth century, to a high lectern. He was studying a column on finance.

Two bishops strode across the black and white squared floor and disappeared behind a row of pillars.

'What are *they* doing here?' Robert whispered. It was Saturday night, when they should have been home, preparing for Sunday.

'Up on a forty-eight hour pass,' I whispered back.

Robert shook his head, with the disapproving gesture of a man who does not care to contemplate such things, and dignifiedly walked towards a small room where we could drink a glass of sherry. I followed him.

We sat down on leather-covered armchairs in a corner. The club was deserted, and the only other person in the room was a dozing whiskery old man who looked like a retired professor of zoology. The room was in a corner of the building, and had windows on two sides: through them shone bands of lemon-coloured evening sky.

I watched Robert while he was ordering the sherry.

'You look very well,' I said.

His face had a relaxed glow and his eyes were sparkling. The chocolate-coloured stains which often showed below his eyes had lightened. He did not reply. I was waiting to be told the startling development.

'Well?' I said, when the waiter had gone away.

Robert sipped his sherry. Then he said:

'Julia wants me to marry her.'

I was completely taken aback.

'When?' I asked, incredulously.

'As soon as possible.'

'Will you?' I went on, even forgetting he would certainly not reply.

Robert smiled to himself. I could see that he was very happy.

Suddenly it occurred to me that I had not felt a rush of pleasure or satisfaction on his behalf. I was ashamed of myself. I had not felt a rush of pleasure on his behalf because I was envious and jealous.

'What about her husband?' I said.

'She says she'd stopped living with him before he went back to Poland.'

'Is she divorcing him?'

'As far as I know.'

'Don't you know?'

Robert glanced at me, surprised by my tone.

'There's some mystery about it,' he said, 'which I propose to solve.' He smiled at me. I guessed that he understood what was the matter with me.

We were silent for a little while. The strain seemed to be released. I said: 'That will keep you occupied.'

'Occupied?' Robert said. He looked away, with a particular glimmer in his eye. 'I've never been so occupied in my life before. Never! . . .'

We lapsed into concupiscent imagining.

'Honestly, old boy,' he said. 'A week's about as much as I'm good for. All the time.'

'And you think of marriage!' said I.

Robert said promptly: 'That wouldn't be all the time.'

'H'm,' I said.

'She's considered that.'

'Well, well . . .'

'She wants me to give her five children, straight away.'

'All at once?'

'She thinks that will be the perfect solution.'

'It's a solution, all right,' I said. 'But it sounds

comprehensive rather than perfect. Where would you keep them all?'

'I don't know,' said Robert. 'You must help me. I'll have to buy a house somewhere.' There was just a shade of the grandiose in his tone.

'A very big one,' I said.

'I suppose it will cost rather a lot?'

'Yes, but you can afford it,' I said. During his years in business Robert had saved quite a lot of money, but he always cagily prevented me from finding out how much.

'I'm afraid she has rather expensive tastes.' He checked himself. 'No. That is not correct.' He smiled. 'Very expensive tastes.' He glanced at me, and immediately gave away that Julia's expensive tastes were sweetly flattering to him.

I remained silent for a while. I ought to have been able to say I hoped he had found great happiness at last. I said:

'It really is fantastic.'

Robert nodded.

'How long has it taken all this to happen?' I said.

'About a month.'

Our glasses were empty. Robert picked up his, and twisted it round by the stem.

His tone was deep and perfectly natural. He said: 'It really does look as if she's fallen in love.'

I took his word for it, and I had none of the sharp revulsion of feeling that such a statement seemed to evoke in other people. When Robert said: 'It really does look as if she's fallen in love,' he was being neither boastful nor patronising. You must take my word for that. Neither, I must admit, was he showing any sign of blowing his brains out.

'I'm glad,' I said. I recalled the days of The Headlamps, and I thought of now. Affection swept away my jealousy. 'Perhaps your luck's changed.'

Robert said: 'Perhaps it's changed for you too, old boy.'

My own luck. 'Myrtle?' I said, with a feeling of tenderness and relief.

Robert did not speak.

'Tell me about Julia!'

'You must meet her. I want you to meet her.' He put down

the glass again and looked at me. 'She's a remarkable woman. And she's very attractive to look at.' Suddenly he came out with one of his surprising uninnocent franknesses. 'She's got a very beautiful body...'

I, who could easily have given a complete anatomical description of one of my loves, felt slightly embarrassed.

Robert glanced at his watch. 'Are you feeling hungry?'

I had been hoping for another glass of sherry, but nothing could make me lie about not being hungry.

We stood up. The whiskery old man was still dozing. The yellow light in the windows had faded. The newspapers on the tables looked tatty and abandoned. I let Robert lead the way.

I suddenly recalled my pang of jealousy and envy. I was ashamed, although I accepted it. For I knew that friendship, however free, however undemanding, gave rise to such outbursts. This outburst had done no damage. I doubted if it was the last.

CHAPTER XIV

BY THE SERPENTINE

The following Sunday afternoon Robert and I walked across Hyde Park. It was a beautiful day. The sun shone brilliantly, without heat, from a cloudless sky of purest blue. The glare of summer had gone, leaving the serene freshness of autumn, serene freshness such as was supposed to come in the autumn of life as well – I saw little prospect of it in my own.

We met at Marble Arch and crossed over to the avenue of still leafy trees, skirting the crowds of people, chiefly men, who were listening to the weekend orators, and making our way to the wide stretches of grass. There was a light steady breeze. We passed a little boy and his father who were preparing to fly a kite, a delicately-constructed box-kite made of pink and yellow paper, which instantly took one's imagination away to China, far, far away. And we passed numerous couples lying on the grass, who had taken off their jackets and undone their blouses for an afternoon's enjoyment of the erotic kiss – which brought one's imagination swiftly home again.

My scientific curiosity was aroused. 'Some of them,' I said to Robert, 'seem to kiss each other all afternoon without stopping.' I felt that Robert, in his rôle of pundit, ought to have some explanation of how they managed to keep it up.

We were making for the Serpentine. The ground sloped down before us, giving an air of spaciousness. In the distance, a long way away on the other side of the lake, there was a high, dark, hazy mass of trees and rising above it the fantastic pinnacles of Knightsbridge and Kensington. All this space! one felt – and it is only a small part of the great city stretching beyond on all sides. London lies horizontal, open to the sky.

'When is Myrtle coming up again?' Robert asked.

'Next weekend.'

I did not go on with the conversation, because it was painful to me. Haxby was on leave. This weekend Myrtle was with him. I could not bear to think of it.

We walked steadily. The grass was thick and brownish-green. We could now see the glitter of water and the dark shapes of rowing-boats on it.

'I could get on with Myrtle very well,' said Robert. There was an amused reminiscent gleam in his eye.

'What's she been saying to you?'

'Nothing in particular.' He turned to me. 'You always think we've been saying something particularly significant to each other. That's far from the case.' He looked away again, and his tone of voice deepened a little. 'Myrtle and I understand each other. That's all. Don't ask me why.'

'Very nice, too,' I said, feeling I had been left out of something.

'Don't be absurd!' Robert laughed affectionately. He became serious again. 'You could do much worse than marry Myrtle.'

I considered the comparison.

Robert said: 'She's kind and affectionate, and she loves you. In her way she's quite a remarkable woman. She's quite clever and she's damned shrewd. She has a simple, earthy idea of what men are like and what they want – '

'Well, I'm damned!' I interrupted.

Robert looked surprised.

'As if I didn't know all that!' I said. 'As if I couldn't have told *you* that. Eight years ago! In the days when you were saying your remarks bounced off her forehead.'

Robert looked hurt. He hated to be reminded of his mistakes in human judgment, and, given half a chance, tried to pretend he had never made them.

'You talk as if she were your discovery,' I said.

Robert shook his head, as if it were useless to go on talking to anyone so unreasonable.

I said: 'The fact of the matter is, you don't credit anybody else with being able to see what Myrtle's like as well as you can yourself.'

Robert walked a few steps in silence.

'That is true,' he said.

The apologetic reply would have done no good with me, but the colossal I could never resist. I gave in.

By this time we were nearly at the water's edge. The lake was a pretty sight. The breeze was still blowing, stirring the surface into tiny waves. The bank was lined with spectators, watching the row-boats – expecting them to collide and preparing to enjoy the excitement of seeing somebody fall overboard.

As usual there were boats containing sailors, who, one would have thought, saw enough of the water while they were on duty; there were boats containing giggling, incompetent girls wearing trousers; there were boats containing guardsmen, who called oafishly all the time; there were boats containing family-parties obviously exasperated with each other; and, to our delight, there was a boat-load of Indians, looking dusky, garrulous and cold.

I assumed that Robert thought I intended to marry Myrtle, and, as far as he would permit himself, was encouraging me – we were much too chary to give each other direct advice. Everything he had said about Myrtle was true. That I could do much worse than marry her I knew very well. The time had come for me to make up my mind.

In a little while we were passing the queue of people waiting to hire boats. They sat on rows of chairs, four deep, beside the water: every time the top chairs became empty they all moved up. They appeared to sit there for hours, and were therefore the subject of disapproving comment by passers-by. It seemed to me characteristic of passers-by, that their powers of observation ranged from the meanly small to the frankly negative. Anyone with half an eye could see the queue was alight with romance. Many of its members were comely, all of them were out for a good time. The chairs set them in a perfect position for flirting with strangers right and left. No wonder they sat there for hours!

We walked on a little further and sat down to talk on chairs facing the water. We began to talk about Myrtle again. Robert must have been having one of his long allusive conversations with her on her last visit. He now had no doubt that she had always been in love with me.

I said, perfectly sincerely: 'It's extraordinary. I can't think why.'

Robert said: 'You appear to be her romantic ideal, that's all.'

'Did she actually say that?'

'Of course not!'

'It's ridiculous.'

Robert grinned. 'There it is, old boy. There's no question of it. You're her romantic ideal.'

I thought it over.

At last I said: 'It's curious she and Haxby have not had any children.'

Robert glanced at me.

'She did tell me that – not in so many words, of course.' He paused.

I stared at him.

Robert said: 'It appears that you are the only man she's ever wanted to have children by.'

I could not reply. At that moment I decided to marry Myrtle.

CHAPTER XV

AN UNUSUAL PROPOSAL

One of the things that really did surprise me, when I began to find out what people in the metropolis did, was the frequency with which they proposed marriage to each other when one or both parties already had a spouse.

I felt as if my upbringing had been peculiarly – and unnecessarily – conscribed. With juvenile desire to have everything cut-and-dried, to see everything as black or white, I had imagined that people who were already married automatically could not make or receive further proposals. How wrong I was!

Things that other people do very properly surprise and shock us. And then time flows, the wheel turns .... and we do those very things ourselves. Or perhaps I should do better to speak purely for myself and say that I did.

I had decided to marry Myrtle after all. Earlier I hinted to you that I would tell the story of a modest attempt to atone for misbehaviour. That was from your point of view. It weighed with me, but, like someone else's point of view, rather less than my own. I wanted to marry, I wanted to have children, I wanted Myrtle for my wife.

I gave some thought to my proposal.

The general convention, that a man shall propose marriage to a woman *before* going to bed with her, had never appealed to me. I know I shall give offence, but I must be frank. The general convention had to me always smacked of a rather crude bargain. How much nicer it would be, I had always thought, how much more graceful and profound a compliment to propose *after*.

I decided to propose to Myrtle after, immediately after.

An Unusual Proposal

And so I waited for Myrtle's next visit with powerfully growing emotion. I imagined the scene. I wondered what she would say. Eight years she had been in love. I imagined her lazy fluttering look in collapse when she heard me propose – in soft, happy, lingering collapse.

And so the evening came round. I met Myrtle, and took her to dine at the Carlos. I bought her the expensive drinks Robert had given her a taste for. She was often rather low-spirited; tonight she was not. Her business in London had been successful. She was wearing a new elegant black dress – goodness knows where she had acquired the coupons for it. Rudolf had expended great art on her hair. She touched the beautifully arranged curls.

'I suppose it's a complete waste of money,' she said, with a lubricious sigh.

I nodded, happily.

Over dinner she asked me about Robert and Julia.

'The sly old thing,' she said.

I observed that I had not yet been allowed to meet Julia. I said:

'He's keeping her to himself.'

'I don't blame him,' said Myrtle.

We held hands across the table.

'Darling,' I said.

Myrtle sighed.

The question of drinking brandy arose. With my eye fixed on the great moment, I said:

'I've got some whisky in the flat.' Myrtle was very fond of whisky, and as it was hard to get I hoarded it for her visits.

'Why not have whisky *and* brandy?' she said.

In the taxi I kissed her. And Myrtle kissed me.

My flat was on the second floor, and it looked over the river. We stood by the bedroom window and paused for a moment. The water was high, and although the night was very dark the surface was illumined with a mysterious patch of grey light. There was very little traffic along the road, and we could hear the trees rustling.

Myrtle, standing beside me, sighed and raised her arms to the window sash. It was simply asking me to slip my hands under her breasts.

'Wonderful hair,' I whispered, pushing my nose through her curls. She laughed and turned her head back.

I drew the curtains and switched on the lamp. It was a furnished flat, and the room had little charm. All the same the glow of the lamp looked soft and inviting. Myrtle's elegant new dress seemed to slip off very simply. I kissed her shoulder with delight.

I remembered the whisky I had promised her. When I came back from the living room, Myrtle was lying in bed. Her eyes were bright and her cheeks pink. She watched me bring some water from the wash-basin. I poured some whisky into two glasses and sat on the bed beside her.

'Fancy going to bed with a whisky-bottle,' she said, and took a healthy sip.

I saw nothing wrong with it. I was not as young as I used to be. I took a healthy sip, and ran my hand down her side. We both sipped again. Her flesh had a beautiful sheen. I put down my glass. I took Myrtle's glass away from her: she dropped her eyelids as if she did not know why. The whole room seemed to give a sudden flicker.

For a time I forgot that I intended to propose marriage.

However, in due course, I remembered the great moment again. Shall I, now? I wondered. Now, or in a little while? Now? I lifted myself up a little, so that I could look at Myrtle's face. Her eyes were closed. I felt the joy of possessing. The long smooth lips, the dark pretty eyebrows – there was a gleam of sweat on her forehead. Now.

'Darling,' I said. 'There's something I want to ask you.'

Myrtle's eyes opened, wide.

'Darling,' I said. 'Will you marry me?'

And I heard her sweet, lightly-modulated voice say: 'What, me?'

PART II

CHAPTER I

AT A PARTY FOR POLES

At last I was allowed to meet Julia.
   One evening at the beginning of October, Myrtle and I
were invited to a cocktail party, given by an Anglo-Polish
society, mainly for Polish officers. Julia was employed as its
secretary.

'Shall we meet Mr Łempicki-Czyz?' Myrtle asked.

The idea of absent husbands was constantly with us. Myrtle
had promised to become my wife, so I can tell you that to a
prospective husband the beloved's present spouse, even when
he is absent, looms in the imagination like the Rock of
Gibraltar – and if you should happen not to have seen the Rock
of Gibraltar, let me explain that it is a thoroughly
unprepossessing rock.

The party was held in a house at the lower end of South
Audley Street. Julia's society had the first floor, and for the
party a room which ran the full width of the house had been
beautifully decorated. There were three tall french windows
opening on to a narrow balcony with a wrought iron
balustrade: the room must normally have been rather dark, for
the walls were painted dark green and the houses opposite
were near. Tonight, in the centre of each wall glowed an
exquisite bas-relief medallion moulded in white cartridge
paper: the artistry was dazzling, of the pale convoluted shapes
with their light shadows and clear edges. The only flowers
were bunches of asters, in white, carmine and purple-blue.
And there were male Polish faces, some of them startingly
powerful – oval, with strong cheek-bones and cleft chins;
broad, unusually flat faces with brilliant narrow eyes – some of
them startlingly powerful, and some of them, to my mind,

267

startlingly crazy.

When Myrtle and I reached the top of the staircase of the house, we were so late that the reception committee had temporarily gone off duty. Loud and cheerful talk came from the room, and a crowd of people stood in the doorway. Myrtle and I hesitated. A young woman suddenly came to us out of the crowd.

'I'm Julia.'

'That's very clever of you.'

'I made Robert describe you.' She looked at me with a bright, furtive, amused glint in her eye. It was such a strong glint that I suddenly found myself feeling bright, furtive and amused, too.

We shook hands.

'I expect you'd like something to drink.' She cast a bright, furtive, slightly less amused glance at Myrtle, and then looked at a point somewhere in between us, as she said: 'I'm afraid I've had an awful lot already.' She shook her head, and her loose silky hair swung against her cheeks. 'Let me take you to the bar.'

Myrtle had an eager, happy expression as we plunged through the crowd. I held her hand. As a matter of fact my other hand was being held by Julia, so that we should not get separated, of course. The room had a sort of glow, the sort of glow that any room has when it is filled by a party and everyone happens already to be slightly under the influence of alcohol.

I heard Julia saying: 'There's some wonderful Polish drink and lots of lovely bits of food. Personally, I go for the drink.'

I looked her up and down and thought 'Yes, I don't suppose you're much of a one for the food.' She had a lean nervous look. To care for food you have to be able to relax a bit. On the other hand she did look as if she was one for the drink.

I glanced around the room. It was then that I noticed the white medallions shining on the walls: there were only a few lamps, placed cunningly to illuminate them. I noticed the small knots of red, white and blue flowers, and the strange Polish men's faces.

'What do you think of it?' said Julia.

Myrtle replied to her, and I did not join in the conversation. I was having my first good look at Julia.

There was no doubt that Julia was a beautiful young woman, and though I had already taken Robert's word for it, I was happy to make the judgment for myself. She was tall and lean and active. Her hips were narrow, but her breasts were remarkably full and shapely. She had fair silky hair cut above her shoulders, and big, slightly protruding grey eyes. Her forehead was broad and her chin pointed: while talking to you she bent her head down a little and the impression you got was of big eyes, bright with amusement, coming at you. She talked to Myrtle while I stared at her.

'I do drawings for advertising,' I heard Myrtle saying, in a melancholy tone.

I remembered that Robert had told me Julia was chic, and I observed this to be true. She was dressed in the height of fashion. The effect was of plain elegance, differing from Myrtle's elegance, which, in spite of an equally plain dress, was a shade theatrical.

'You need another drink.' Julia turned to me suddenly, and I could have sworn she let her bosom brush against my arm. And I for my part have to admit that I did not move my arm away.

While Julia was speaking to the barman in Polish, I reflected that it is a very rare woman who can have a lot of alcohol and a lot of men without it showing somewhere. I was looking at her throat, where I thought her skin, under the layer of powder, showed a warm reddish coarsening. It was not beautiful. Yet it was attractive, because it told one that one could let oneself go.

Julia handed me my glass.

'Who's Robert talking to?' I said. I had seen him in the corner of the room, talking with the sort of affable weightiness he always displayed to strangers at parties.

Julia did not need to look. 'The general and the minister.' She gave me a knowing grin. 'Of course.'

I shook my head. 'He would.'

'He's a darling, all the same. I expect he's telling them what a wonderful secretary the society has.' Suddenly she looked at me, and said with a deep constrained force: 'Robert is a wonderful man, isn't he?'

I was taken aback by her change in tone. She was watching me. She leaned a little closer, and said in a low voice, almost whispering:

'I want you to help me.'

For an instant she searched in my face; and then as if she were afraid to risk finding an answer, she looked away. Her eyes had suddenly taken on a heightened sheen, and her head was bent. She was in love with him. I knew that somehow she was feeling a wave of romantic hope.

I could not say anything.

Julia looked up again. The moment of revelation had passed. Her eyes were glinting again with amusement. She said:

'He doesn't want me to lose my job.'

'There's nobody better than Robert at helping one to keep one's job.'

'Are you an outcast, too?'

I said: 'Not that I know of.'

'I can't imagine why he should want me to keep the job. They pay me practically nothing, Joe, practically nothing.'

'How much?'

Julia gave me a nervous direct look. 'Five pounds a week.'

I imagined the response of Myrtle or Robert to such a direct question. As Julia replied I caught the expression on Myrtle's face, round-eyed and shrewdly innocent. Five pounds a week! Myrtle made more like twenty.

I was about to say something, when Robert beckoned across the room to Julia.

'I must leave you for a moment.' She moved away, and then turned back, looking at me and ignoring Myrtle. 'Please, don't go.' Her voice became urgent. 'There's something I simply must tell you.'

CHAPTER II

AMBUSHES AND HUSBANDS

I watched Julia, and said to Myrtle: 'What do you think of her?'

'I think she's very clever, darling.' Myrtle's tone was distinctly melancholy again. She looked at me. 'What are you laughing at?'

'Just your show of ... bogus inferiority.'

'It isn't bogus!' Myrtle looked as if she were struggling with a desperate drawback. 'Did you notice how fluently she spoke Polish?'

'Did you, darling, notice she was only earning five pounds a week?'

Myrtle could not resist a complacent smirk. 'Well, there is that,' she said, doubtfully.

I touched my glass against hers.

'You're a wonderful woman.'

Myrtle softened. With a feeble effort at composure, she said: 'So I'm a wonderful woman, eh?'

I felt a strong burst of emotion.

'The sooner you're *my* woman the better.'

I was slightly drunk, and I did not keep a pressing note out of my voice.

'Oh, darling!' Myrtle was upset.

'I'm sorry, darling.' I took hold of her hand.

Myrtle's fingers tightened in mine.

'I mean it, darling,' I said unrestrainedly. 'I want you. And as soon as possible.' I looked at my glass, because I was ashamed to look at her. 'God knows, I've take long enough about making up my mind. But now I have, I'm in a hurry.' I felt as if tears were going to come into my eyes. 'I want to make

271

up for lost time. You know that, don't you, darling?'

Myrtle nodded lovingly, without a sign of reproach.

We were silent. The room was filled with loud polyglottal talk, yet we might have been alone.

'I wish you'd write and tell him!' I said.

'Darling...' We had already discussed the topic at great length.

'I know,' I said. 'But can't you change your mind?'

'It isn't a question of changing my mind. I just couldn't do it, darling. We've got to wait until he comes home. I shall have to see him, to tell him.'

I said: 'I should have thought it would be easier to write a letter than to say it.'

'Then you don't understand,' Myrtle said bitterly. 'It's easier for you than for me.'

I said: 'I can't say I feel so wonderful about it. Making love to his wife while he's overseas. And then asking him to give us a divorce when he comes home.'

'He thinks you're a cad, anyway.'

'Well, really!' I felt cross, outraged.

Myrtle stared round the room.

'If that's so,' I said, 'at least it won't come as a surprise.'

Myrtle turned slowly back to me. 'I had a long letter from him this morning. He doesn't know there's anything the matter.'

It seemed to me incredible. Myrtle wrote to him regularly. I said nothing.

'He thinks,' she said, 'he may be sent to Palestine.'

'Further away,' said I.

Myrtle ignored my remark. She said:

'I suppose it's dangerous, isn't it?'

'Dangerous?'

'Yes,' Myrtle said, impatiently. 'I suppose there are ambushes, and all that.'

'I suppose so.'

Myrtle had a sad, thoughtful, apprehensive expression, while she considered ambushes.

I did not speak, because, watching Myrtle's face, it came to me that though she could not face without great pain the prospect of wounding Haxby by asking for a divorce, she could face with just a shade less pain the prospect of his being eliminated by the Stern Gang. Poor Haxby!

Myrtle was silent for quite a long time. Then she said: 'I suppose we ought to go home.'

'Julia asked us not to.'

Myrtle glanced at me sideways. Her eyelids flickered.

'Don't you remember, darling?' I said.

Myrtle smiled, in a sly deprecating way that was next door to accusation.

At that moment a fresh contingent of guests arrived. We were surprised. The party suddenly came to life again. Through the crowd I tried to catch Julia's eye, but it was impossible. We decided to make our way across the room to join the party surrounding the minister and the general.

Robert looked pleased to see us. The trouble about attaching oneself to the most distinguished guests at a party is that it is not very easy to leave them.

Julia drew me close to her. She said in my ear:

'I must have a moment with you. *Tête-à-tête*. I'm going to take you to the buffet.'

I was puzzled. She was in high spirits, gay, excited and drunk.

'Robert's had a wild success,' she said. 'He's been invited to visit Warsaw.'

I thought Robert's chances were remote, since I gathered all the Poles present were strongly anti-Communist.

'Fantastic idea,' I said.

'Fantastic people,' Julia whispered.

We reached the buffet and Julia held an animated discussion with a waiter.

'What are you asking him for?' I said.

'Some things like little *vol-au-vents* made with shrimps.' She put her hand on my arm. 'While you're waiting try one of those slices of cucumber with honey on it. Robert says you like food.'

'Wonderful girl!' Out of enthusiasm I patted her, below the level of the table. It seemed she was wearing nothing under her dress. She turned on me and said:

'Now we're going across to the bar.'

We went to the bar, and she asked for drinks. She had somehow communicated an extraordinary tension to me. I felt as if we were in a heady kind of dream. We were looking at each other. Her eyes bulged at me with a winking brightness.

'Well?' I said.

'I don't know how to begin.' She glanced round, furtively, with her head bent.

'All right. I'll wait. . .'

We looked at each other again, and suddenly a startling exchange of remarks took place.

Fixing me with her winking brightness of eye, Julia said in amused, penetrating and ironic, friendly detachment: 'There's something slightly feminine about you.'

And instantly I said, in just the same way: 'And there's something slightly masculine about you.'

No offence was either meant or taken, on either side. We just stared at each other, amused and surprised.

'Is that what you wanted to tell me?' I said.

Julia shook her head. 'Oh no!' Her hair swung softly.

I thought we must both be drunk. I said:

'What on earth was it?'

She glanced round urgently.

'Here come Robert and Myrtle. I shall have to tell you now.' She suddenly took hold of my hand. 'You mustn't tell anyone.' She leaned towards me, so that her lips almost touched my ear. '*I'm not really married to Wladislaw!*'

CHAPTER III

MORNING BEFORE THE OFFICE

Robert and I had adjoining offices and we always met first thing in the morning for exchange of private news. The one who arrived first went through his correspondence perfunctorily, waiting for the face of the other to come round the door. And what a face he often saw!

'What's happened *now*?'

That was the tone of the first question, and it was usually justified. Sometimes one of us would silently hand over a letter. At present I am telling you about only Robert and myself: we had numerous intimate friends, in whose lives we were bound up – so that when no blow of fate was striking us we could expect it to be striking one of them.

On the morning after the Anglo-Polish party I arrived at the office first. For some little time it had been usual for me to arrive first. Robert, in his fine sombre hat and his coat that made him look like a Minister of the Crown, was arriving later and later in the day. And when he did arrive he was showing signs of not getting home till earlier and earlier in the morning – a hot brightness of the eye, a crookedness of the parting, a greyness of the cheek.

Robert came into the office. It was about half-past ten on a late autumnal morning, the sort of dully-lit morning when it seemed as if a trace of fog had got into the room. He smoothed his hair and sat on the corner of my desk. I laid aside a secret memorandum from the Ministry of Defence, and said:

'You don't look as if you've had much sleep, old boy.'

Robert picked up the memorandum instead of meeting my eye. 'Four hours.' He put it down again. There was a pause. The pause was dramatic. He said:

'Julia's told me what she told you last night.'

This left me temporarily with nothing to say.

'What did you think of it?' he said.

'I wanted to know the rest of the story.'

'I can tell you that.' He glanced at me. 'I'll tell it you as it was told to me. Though in a rather more coherent form.'

I pushed my chair back, and put up my feet on the edge of an open drawer while I listened.

'Her story is that Wladislaw was passionately anxious to marry her and that she didn't want to. In fact, she refused to marry him. Certain other things she didn't refuse. They were living together. So she agreed to compromise by changing her name to Mrs Łempicki-Czyz by deed-poll.'

'She must be crazy.'

'You must judge that for yourself.'

'Was Czyz already married?'

'There you show more insight. Yes. He was already married, but he insisted that his wife was killed by the Germans shortly after he escaped from Poland. In his opinion it was perfectly reasonable for Julia to marry him. And if not reasonable, perfectly legal. It appears that he explained this to her very clearly, and at great length. He was very anxious to marry her. I don't blame him.'

'Didn't she believe his wife was dead?'

'She couldn't be sure. One of her friends married a Czech, whose wife turned up in England about six months later. It seems to have shaken Julia's faith in Wladislaw, though I don't see why it should.'

'Does he still want to marry her?'

'Yes. He's gone back to Poland to prove that his wife is dead. He's convinced that if he brings back suitable evidence, Julia's objections will be overcome.'

'When he comes back he'll expect her to marry him.' I suddenly wondered if Robert was going to marry her before Wladislaw appeared.

'He's always expecting her to marry him.'

'But she wants you to marry her.'

'I suspect that's why she sent him back to Poland.'

I felt slightly dizzy.

Robert was watching me, enjoying my incomprehension.

'You insist on concentrating on what happens when people come back,' he said. 'Everyone else concentrates on what happens while they're still away.'

I thought he was criticising Myrtle. Before I could reply the telephone rang. I said I was in conference with Robert.

Robert had got up and strolled across the room. He was looking at a set of German ordnance maps that I had fastened to the wall with drawing-pins. I was not interested in the topography of Germany: I kept them as souvenirs, and I liked to see the brilliant blue patches of lake and sea shining from my dirty cream-painted walls.

'They don't extend to Poland,' Robert observed. As I put down the receiver he returned and drew up a chair beside me. He lit a cigarette.

'People get themselves into fantastic situations,' he said. He had dropped his tone of bantering amusement. 'We've seen a lot, old boy. But we've still got a lot to learn.' He grinned. 'And I suspect we've still got a good many surprises coming to us.'

We were both thinking about Julia. Robert said solemnly:

'It was an extraordinary experience. To have this history interspersed with incidents of a different kind.'

'There's no nicer place to listen to a woman's life-story than in bed.'

I had overstepped the mark of Robert's taste. He thoughtfully adjusted the position of his cigarette in its holder. He said:

'I don't know the whole story of her and Wladislaw. But it's obvious that he made a deep impression on her. I'm sure that in slightly different circumstances she would have married him. She's had numerous offers since she went to live with him. Offers of marriage. And turned them down.'

'Until you.'

'Until me.'

We were silent.

'She's a very remarkable girl.'

It was the same phrase again. He made it in a tone of deep feeling, and it seemed to express all the fascination, all the drawing-together of two different souls. I glanced at him. I knew that however much he loved her he would never say it in so many words. 'Very remarkable,' he repeated.

I said: 'All this means that you can marry her. She's free.'

We were silent. Suddenly I was aware that the atmosphere had changed. I was surprised. Robert was looking at me in a way I did not understand.

'In some ways you're the most worldly of men, Joe. In others you're extraordinarily innocent.'

Instantly I knew what he was going to say. I could have blushed.

'She's free,' said Robert, 'if all this happens to be the truth.'

CHAPTER IV

A NEW COLLEAGUE

When members of our staff came into the office in the morning and found Robert and me deep in discussion, at least some of them must have presumed that we were deciding the policy of our division. In offices throughout the government service, all over the country, bosses and their assistants were conferring on policy before the day's work began.

Robert had made up his mind on our policy over the A 15 long ago. Morning before the office was reserved for other purposes. One bright October morning Dr R. A. Chubb arrived, and his ideas were entirely different from ours. He was waiting in Robert's office, ready to discuss policy, before Robert arrived.

Robert promptly came to fetch me.

'How did *he* get in?' he whispered.

I shook my head, and followed him back to his office.

Dr Chubb was standing between Robert's desk and the window.

'I was just admiring the view,' he said. 'It's a very good office you have here.' He turned to Robert with the speculative air of a man who is wondering what sort of an office is going to be assigned to him and is presuming that it will be no less good.

As Robert proposed to send Chubb away immediately on a tour of firms, he had arranged for him temporarily to share my office. From Robert's window you could look into the corner of Parliament Square; from mine you could have looked into the well of the building if anyone had seen fit to remove the material pasted over it to prevent splintering in air-raids.

I looked at Dr Chubb while Robert was breaking the news to him. I judged him to be about fifty-eight. He was comfortably built, not as tall as Robert, and neatly dressed in a blue suit.

At first sight Dr Clubb would never be mistaken for a deep and powerful thinker. His bulging wide-open blue eyes had a faint look of alarm in them, and so had his mouth, which always seemed to be nervously showing his front teeth. His expression was amiable, not particularly constrained in spite of his air of alarm, and mildly absurd. Its absurdity was enhanced by a touch of old-womanishness – he wore reading spectacles that consisted of only the lower halves of lenses and he looked over the top of them all the time.

'I've been having a look at the accommodation this morning,' Dr Chubb was saying, hare-eyedly and toothily to Robert.

I thought he had not taken long about it. I looked at him with more interest. His rosy face was that of a man whom I would have expected to be dim by ordinary standards of the government service. Physically he was middle-aged and tamed. And yet I was not surprised that he was quite capable of looking after himself. Dim, yes. And shrewd. And probably persistent, too.

Robert was treating Dr Chubb with lofty consideration. He adumbrated his plan for sending Dr Chubb on tour as if he were conferring a great privilege upon him and at the same time giving him the opportunity to win the unfading gratitude of his country.

'In view of my expectation that you'd ask me to undertake this matter,' Dr Chubb began, in a humble, nervous, unhurried style, 'I gave it a certain amount of thought, as a consequence of which I concluded that I should like to make a few suggestions myself.' He paused. 'I fully realise the urgency of what you're asking me to do, but I think you'll probably agree with me that sometimes – especially on occasions like this – it doesn't do to be too hasty.' He stopped, looking as if he were expecting congratulation.

Robert stared at him.

'In the course of thinking it over,' Dr Chubb went on, 'it

occurred to me that there were one or two proposals, certainly
one proposal, which I should like to put before you for your
consideration. Personally I think it is worth considering
myself, that we should try and take advantage' – he paused –
'of every offer of help we can get, especially from all those, if
you understand what I mean, who are in a position to help us.'

'Quite,' said Robert, with a mixture of decision and patience
that I could only hope to emulate.

Dr Chubb pursued his course in his own tempo.

I was attentive enough to realise the important phrase was
'all those who can help us'. Dr Chubb's proposal, when he
finally came to it, was that we should go for 'help' to the
federation of owners of the industries. He wound up with an
open-eyed solemn expression.

'I naturally don't want to influence whatever plans you
have in mind one way or the other, but I'm convinced that we
can't do better than put ourselves in their hands, in order to
form for ourselves a really comprehensive view of the position.'

Robert received the proposal thoughtfully.

Rules about security impose on me the disadvantage of not
being able to tell you what the industries were: they now as a
consequence enable me to tell you, with delightful freedom
from fear of libel, that I personally thought half the owners
were sharks and the federation next door to a racket.

'I think it's an excellent proposal,' said Robert, catching Dr
Chubb's solemnity. 'If this survey is to be as valuable as we all
think it's going to be, it's most important that we should carry
the industries with us.'

Dr Chubb appeared to bloom with pleasure.

'I should like to say that it so happens,' he said, 'that I know
Lord —— personally.' He named the president of the
federation. 'I knew him when he was Sir —— ——.'

'Ah!' said Robert, cutting short personal reminiscence of a
historical nature.

My own first impulse would have been to reject the
proposal. Put ourselves in *their* hands, indeed! Now I saw what
Robert was up to.

'I didn't anticipate approaching Lord —— in the first place,'
Dr Chubb went on. 'He's a very busy man – '

'I think I can do that,' Robert interrupted. 'I meet him frequently on committee.'

Dr Chubb was momentarily deflated, but he picked up. 'It's possible you may think differently, if he's a close colleague of yours, but I should doubt myself if we should need him in the initial stages.' He could not prevent the return of a faintly self-satisfied air. 'I should like to say also that the secretary of the federation is an old friend of mine.' He quietly rolled off the name of another gentleman who had been knighted for services to industry. There was a peculiar look on Dr Chubb's face whenever he said Lord or Sir, a look of mingled reverence, delight and aspiration.

'Ah,' Robert said again. He glanced at me.

'And there's Sir Harold Deemer,' Dr Chubb went on, never apparently having had enough.

'And Sir Joseph Floyd,' said Robert.

'I think,' said Dr Chubb, 'there's every indication of our being able to make a thorough job of it.' And his tone of voice gave the show away completely: he was hoping for some kind of honour for himself.

'I have great hopes,' Robert said, encouraging him. He was now waiting for Dr Chubb to go.

Dr Chubb had no thoughts of going. He said: 'Sometime before I start out, I should like to have a talk with you. About the policy you would like me to pursue.'

'Certainly,' said Robert. 'Let us talk about it now.'

'I am, of course, entirely at your disposal. It is entirely for you to lay down the manner in which you wish the survey to be conducted.'

For a moment, I was puzzled. Then I saw Dr Chubb's aim. Having shown that he was bringing inestimable connections to our division, he had to assure us that the connections were not in any way binding.

'I know that my own department has tended to make up its mind already,' Dr Chubb said. 'But I shouldn't like you to think that I have.' He looked at Robert with a kind of diffident confidence. 'I wouldn't have accepted this post if it had been otherwise.' He hesitated. 'I don't like this controversy over the A 15 and the A 16, and I feel it's a great pity that it arose as it did.'

Robert made a gesture, as much as to say that these things happen. He was looking interestedly at Dr Chubb. He must have been wondering, just as I was wondering, exactly to what extent Dr Chubb was speaking the truth. I had assumed, in a superficially cynical way, that Dr Chubb had been sent to us to further the policy of his own department. When I heard him speak I was not entirely sure.

'I don't want it to be thought,' Dr Chubb went on, 'by anyone, that I accepted this post for reasons that were in any way improper, because I know the function of D.O.R.R.S. is to be impartial, and I think I may truthfully say that I'm impartial myself, so impartial that I am coming' – he paused – 'to this post with a completely open mind.'

'I'm sure of that,' said Robert. It was a formal remark, but the tone was cordial. I did not understand it.

'I have assured Sir Francis Plumer to that effect.'

Robert nodded.

From this point they went on to discuss matters of detail at great length. I had heard it all before. I was concentrating on the conversation I have recorded. I kept asking myself a question to which I could not find the answer. Who, I wanted to know, was taking in whom?

CHAPTER V

A YELLOW SAPPHIRE

At this time Myrtle used always to pause, when we were walking down Bond Street, before the window of a jeweller's shop. She had her eye on a sapphire ring. The stone was an exquisite yellow and beautifully cut: it was like a small transparent box filled with pure limpid sunlight.

The price of the ring was seven hundred pounds, and let me say at once that I had no intention of buying it. As our marriage drew nearer I felt less and less like the greatest writer since Shakespeare and more and more like a poor government official.

'I must go and look at my ring,' Myrtle used to say, whenever we were nearby. The shop was only small, but it was in the narrowest part of the street and there was no missing it. I acquiesced. Only a woman, I thought, could call 'my' something she was never likely to possess.

Myrtle sighed as she stared at the ring. I watched her. Then Myrtle glanced at me, and I had to admit the possibility of seeing in a woman's eyes, even in the eyes of the woman one loves, a light of frank cupidity.

'It's lovely,' I said. 'How vulgar the diamonds look beside it!' The diamonds cost anything up to three thousand pounds and there were a lot of them in the window.

'I like the diamonds, too,' said Myrtle. 'A girl never says no to diamonds.'

'Sometimes the man who's got to pay for them does.'

'Darling!' Myrtle laid her hand on my arm, and looked up at me lovingly. 'I don't expect you to buy it me.'

I thought I must be heartless and crude, with even a touch of the mercenary. 'I know,' I said. 'Darling.'

On the other hand I sometimes had intimations of the boot being on the other foot. Whenever Robert was with us, we stopped just the same, but the conversation took another tone.

'There you are, old boy,' Robert would say, as we looked at the yellow sapphire. 'There you are' – in a hearty cynical voice. 'That's what you've got to work for.'

And Myrtle would look up at him with an appreciative, conspiratorial smirk.

Myrtle would have liked me to give her the ring. Of course she would. Yet she was no more heartless nor mercenary than I. The ring had somehow become a symbol to her. If I gave her the yellow sapphire it would show how much I loved her. The fact that it would show literally – that I loved her to the tune of seven hundred pounds – was secondary though highly desirable. I thought of how many women I had known who loved presents for this reason. Presents as a proof of being loved – I was touched by the simplicity of it. Would they never realise some men's pockets were more easily touched than their hearts?

Myrtle's playful covetousness persisted longer than I expected. And then one day I realised the yellow sapphire had somehow become the focus of a conflict. We were strolling along Bond Street after lunch. It was near the end of November, and the weather was cold and drizzly. I remember it very well because Myrtle had an umbrella which I was holding over her head. The umbrella was made of tartan silk, with a fair amount of red in it, and although the light was grey it cast a coloured glow on Myrtle's cheeks. The road was glossy with moisture, and the tyres of silent expensive cars made a creaking noise on it as they passed.

'I must look at my ring, darling.' Myrtle was cheerful. She had her arm linked in mine. As she stopped before the window, I swung round, keeping the umbrella over her. We looked at the ring.

Myrtle sighed. 'There it is.' She glanced at me thoughtfully. 'I suppose we shall both be too old to want it by the time we can afford it.'

'Depends on how much money we make.'

'Oh, you'll make a lot, darling.'

'So will you, sweet.' I tried to slip the remark in easily. I had not looked forward to the first time this subject appeared in our discussions.

'Me?' she said. 'I'm not going to go on working after we're married.'

'Why not?'

'You've got to keep me, my lad.'

'Oh!' I was not surprised by her firm rejection of my plan, but felt compelled not to give it up.

'You don't sound enthusiastic, darling.'

'What man's ever been enthusiastic about doubling his cost of living without doubling his income?' I said.

Myrtle glanced at me, and it was clear that she found the remark neither true nor funny, let alone both.

'I should have thought you'd have wanted to keep me,' she said.

'And lose a thousand sweet smackers per annum?' I said, trying to keep the tone of the conversation light.

Myrtle said: 'Sometimes I don't understand you at all, darling.' The conversation was not light. Her tone was of grave reproach. We both knew it was a serious moment.

Myrtle and I stared at each other, under the brightly coloured umbrella. The drizzle fell around us. The yellow sapphire glittered from the window. People jostled against us on the pavement. We stared because we were two different persons, different in temperament, different in desires, confronting each other, each impelled by self.

I drew Myrtle round, away from the window, and said:

'Let's move on, darling.'

We walked side by side, in step. Neither of us said anything till we came to a street corner, where we had to wait for the traffic before we could cross.

'I really don't understand you, darling.'

Myrtle's tone had lost its reproach, but from its determination I knew that she did not want to let the discussion drop.

'It's quite simple,' I said.

'Is it? It doesn't seem simple to me.'

'What? The concept of a thousand pounds a year?'

'I didn't mean that.'

'But I did. We won't have a lot of money when we're married. A thousand a year will make a lot of difference.' I glanced at her. 'I want us to live in style and comfort, darling.'

'But I don't want to go on working.'

'Why not?'

Myrtle looked down for a moment, and then she said: 'Most husbands keep their wives, don't they?'

For an instant I was tempted to say 'Yours doesn't'. Haxby's pre-war income was about half Myrtle's, and he had lived in her father's house. Instead I said:

'Most wives aren't talented enough to earn a thousand a year.' I spoke the last phrase as warmly as I could.

Myrtle was irritated and embarrassed. We were still standing in the same place on the street corner. The flow of traffic had ceased, but she made no attempt to cross the road. She said with great feeling:

'Why can't you be like other men?'

I too was brought to a standstill. The times I had asked myself the same question – and not, as people always imagined, in a tone of self-concerned, narcissistic moral rectitude. How many times had I asked it in alarm, in bewilderment, and even in misery. I was old enough now to think that I had a singular temperament. Ninety-nine men out of a hundred perfectly naturally wanted to keep their wives. Myrtle was right. In this part of her nature she was a very ordinary young woman. It was I who could not fit into the ordinary pattern of life.

'Because I'm not made like other men.'

Myrtle looked at me, and I could tell she found it a remark of incomprehensible peevish arrogance. She was too hurt and angry to reply.

'When we're married I want you to keep some independence,' I said, trying to get somewhere near to explaining my feelings. What could I say, when I had never understood them clearly myself? I thought it was some kind of responsibility for her that I wanted to evade. But I knew that in the end it was the abandonment of myself to the complete intimacy of marriage that I resisted: I wanted to hold Myrtle off, and making her have a career of her own seemed to me at the time a way of doing it. It was irrational, peculiar, and, I suppose crazy.

'But what if I don't want independence?' said Myrtle, just as any man but me might have expected.

'Then try to want it for my sake,' I cried.

'Why?'

'Because I want to keep some independence of my own.' I suddenly burst out: 'I don't want to feel the chains!'

'Darling?' My outbursts in metaphor always left her stupefied.

I glanced at her. I tried to smile.

'I'm not going to interfere with your independence.' Myrtle spoke as if such a thing were impossible. She paused. Drizzle fell outside the edge of the umbrella. Her face, lit by the patches of tartan glow, was suddenly gentle and kind.

'What's my salary beside yours, darling?' she asked. 'Beside what you *can* earn.'

'What I *can* earn? How?'

'By writing. You can make thousands, darling. I'm sure of it.'

I forgot the disadvantages of a singular temperament in sheer surprise. My novels up to date had been well-received but had shown no signs of bringing in more than a few hundred pounds between them. And as works of art, they had made the smallest of impressions on Myrtle anyway – even out of her great love for me she never pretended to the contrary.

'Robert thinks so, too,' Myrtle said.

'You've been talking to him about it!'

'He's sure you can make a lot of money.'

'How? If I can, why haven't I?'

'If you'll write the sort of things people like, darling.'

With this classic wifely remark, Myrtle had the effrontery to lean affectionately closer to me.

People were passing us all the while. Their umbrellas caught against mine. I was aware of nothing but the proposition Myrtle was shrewdly and lovingly putting to me, the proposition that I should sell myself.

'If you'll write things that are just funny,' Myrtle said,

'people will love it.'

I saw now why during the last few weeks Myrtle had brought me a series of books by successful humorists.

'Now I know!' I cried. 'Now I know what you want. You don't just want a sapphire ring. You don't just want me to keep you. You want everything. Literally, *everything!*'

'Oh!' The smile vanished from Myrtle's lips, and the whites of her eyes reddened and shone with tears.

'Darling,' I said. I lowered the umbrella and kissed her.

'You don't understand me,' she said. The tears went back again, and she gave me a tremulous melancholy smile. I had to be gentle with her.

'We don't understand each other, if you ask me.'

We paused. I have no doubt that you understand us only too well. It is always easy to perceive the moral defects of someone else.

Myrtle said: 'Don't you think we ought to walk on?'

I glanced at my watch. 'Good God, yes.'

The traffic was moving steadily past, so we had to wait again. I noticed two women talking under an umbrella beside us, enormously big girls with French accents, mink stoles, and very fancy shoes. They were prostitutes from Cork Street. Myrtle was silent. Suddenly she touched my hand and said:

'I'm willing to go on working for the first three years.'

'Darling!' I turned to her with relief. 'A compromise!' Nothing could be more in tune with my ideas than a compromise. I had a tiresome temperament, but I was willing to try and cope with it if Myrtle would meet me half way. I thought five years would have been more satisfactory, but I did not care to argue. Myrtle had seen sense.

The traffic suddenly paused: there was an opening before us and we crossed the road at last. I had my arm round Myrtle's waist. She leaned against me as we walked along. She appeared to be glancing in shop-windows. I did the same. I saw some handsome shirts and ties, a beautiful painting of a canal by Boudin, the posters of a theatre-ticket agency. The drizzle had ceased. I suddenly felt convinced that given time and gradualness the selfish claims of my temperament might break and our marriage be a success.

At Piccadilly we had to part. I shut the umbrella, and stood facing Myrtle, waiting to see what she would say to feed my heart with hope.

Myrtle sighed, carelessly and comfortably. Then she said: 'Ah, well ... I suppose I shall start having a baby straight away.'

CHAPTER VI

NOTE ON ART

Though I had not written anything for seven years, because of the war, my art, I should like you to understand, was very important to me. Myrtle and I argued over it regularly. In this context my art was nothing abstract: it was the novels I intended to write. Myrtle, Robert, all my friends, had strong views on what sort of novels they ought to be. Their views, I hardly need say, they propounded for my own good, so it was no wonder we nearly came to blows over them.

Just as Robert and I were different as men, so were we different as writers. What we both wanted to do was more or less the same: the way we were going to try and do it was appropriate to our temperaments. Robert proposed to achieve his end through a kind of romantic and dramatic power, I through a kind of humour and wit. Naturally I thought I had some power, and Robert flagrantly fancied his chance as a wag. I was willing, being a fair-minded man, to admit that Robert did sometimes overlap my terrain – he was definitely funny. Robert, on the other hand, yielded me not a square inch of his territory.

You may say that our arguments at this point were academic. Just so. But may I remind you that Robert and I were working for the day when we might throw off the shackles of His Majesty's service and emerge free artists at last? It was essential that we should decide what kind of books we were going to write, because free artists can only pursue their beautiful high ideals if they previously take the precaution of selling their works for some money.

Robert was a part-time civil servant, I was a temporary one – we could break the links at any moment. The moment had got to come. Soon. And what then?

'If you'll only write things that are just funny, darling, people will love it.'

Just funny! Those two words. Red rag to a bull.

I tried to explain to Myrtle that I could only imagine a novel being funny about something. To ask for a novel to be just funny was like asking for the smile off the Cheshire cat – which was of course just what Myrtle wanted. I sought a more concrete image. I said:

'It's like asking you to make a woman's hat that's purely decorative – and doesn't cover her head.'

'Women's hats don't cover their heads,' said Myrtle.

Back to the abstract. Myrtle conceded that I had got to be funny about something. I said, in my novels, the something must be the stuff of human experience; and at least half the stuff of human experience is misery, torment and disaster.

'Don't write about that half,' said Myrtle promptly.

'It wouldn't be the truth if I missed it out. I must write about it.'

I hope you follow me. Many did not. Myrtle said impatiently:

'But darling, it can't be funny if you put it in.'

'Why not?'

Myrtle gave me a look of frank astonishment.

'Why not?' I repeated.

Myrtle had ceased to follow me at all. I retired into my thoughts, where I could still have my way. I recalled the words of a greater writer than myself, Horace, who had asked in powerful entreaty, 'Why should one not speak the truth, laughing?' That was what I wanted to do – it was not a question of being funny or not being funny. *To speak the truth, laughing!* How I knew what he must have felt like, how my heart went out to him! It was the last word, the most perfect word, on his art and on mine. Inflated, inspired, I said to Myrtle:

'I want to speak the truth, laughing. I'll do it or I'll die in the attempt!'

Myrtle looked at me as if she thought I was mad.

CHAPTER VII

CALLING LATE AT NIGHT

I was reading alone in my flat when the bell rang that called me to the telephone. I was surprised. The time was nearly midnight. There was only one telephone, in the hall near the front door. As I ran downstairs I met the landlady coming up in her dressing-gown.

'You're wanted on the telephone.' Her journey upstairs was quite unnecessary. I stared at her.

'It's a woman,' she said. I realised I was wrong. Her journey had been undertaken from the over-riding necessity of expressing moral disapproval.

'Excellent,' I said, not attempting to conceal my satisfaction at observing that moral disapproval made her face look even meaner and even more ladylike than it was before. I had no idea who the woman was.

As I ran along the hall to the telephone, the landlady bustled into her flat at the end of the corridor and left the door ajar to facilitate eavesdropping on my conversation.

It was Julia.

'I want you to come and see me, Joe. Now.' She stopped, agitatedly. 'Don't think I'm mad.'

'I'll reserve my judgment on that.'

'Will you come?'

'Yes.'

I put down the receiver and ran upstairs for my overcoat. My landlady must have reached an insomniac pitch of distraction on hearing me close the front door behind me.

It happened that Julia lived in a big block of flats less than half a mile along the Embankment from my house. I had often debated with Robert the project of paying her a neighbourly call.

'She'll think you want to sleep with her,' he would reply, with unusual simplicity and directness. 'That's all.'

So I gave up the project. And I recalled Robert's words as I made my way rapidly along the Embankment and heard Big Ben chiming behind me. It was a cold windy night. I turned up the collar on my overcoat and pulled my hat over my eyes. As I passed a square with trees in it a gust of dry, frozen leaves blew round my heels.

A porter showed me the right entrance and I went up in the lift to Julia's flat. It was on the eighth floor, at the end of a stuffy internal corridor.

Julia opened the door, and I looked into rooms that were close-carpeted and all painted pale green. It was like being inside a set of inter-communicating match-boxes. One felt enclosed and remote, either very high up in the air or possibly below the sea.

'This is my end of the flat.' Julia shared it with another girl. 'There's nobody else in.' She walked ahead of me, wearing a frock of dark red silk that rustled. Through the bathroom door I saw a pink slip and some silk stockings drying on a chromium towel-rail. There was a smell of scent and something else.

In the room Julia turned and faced me. I knew what she was going to say.

'I'm drinking brandy.'

That is what the other smell was, the sweet clinging spirituous odour of brandy.

'So I see.' There was a glass and a bottle on a low table beside the sofa. I glanced round the room. It was softly lit, rather over-heated, and somewhat untidy. There was a satinwood writing-table, a grand piano with some silver-framed photographs on it, dark brocade curtains, and no flowers anywhere.

'You must drink some brandy.' Julia was looking at me with a strained nervous smile. Her chin was lowered and her bright grey eyes seemed to be bulging at me. There were some specks of powder on the front of her dress. She was slightly drunk.

I took off my overcoat and sat down. She gave me a glass. It was good brandy. After a few preliminary hiccups I began to

294

drink it steadily with pleasure. There was a lot of it.

Julia moved from one place to another in the room. Suddenly she stopped and said:

'Where's Robert?'

'I don't know.'

'I thought you wouldn't.'

I was puzzled. 'Why not?'

'He was supposed to be here tonight.'

I thought she must be drunker than she looked.

Julia said: 'He didn't come. So I settled down with the brandy bottle.' She pointed to it. 'The bottle was full at seven o'clock.'

I said: 'I'm sure he hasn't done it on purpose. Are you sure you've not got the wrong night yourself?'

Julia did not reply. She shook her hair back from her face, and came rapidly towards my chair. I must confess I thought it was me she was making for – it turned out to be the telephone, which stood on a little table beside me. Julia sat on the arm of my chair, and swiftly dialled Robert's number.

'Listen!' she said, waving the receiver in the air. There was no reply.

'I really don't know where he is,' I said. 'Keep calm.'

Julia put the receiver down, and remained where she was. She turned to look at me, and her breast was very close to my cheek.

'You shouldn't take to the bottle so easily,' I said.

I thought her voice changed, and that she leaned a little closer. 'I might do worse.'

I looked up, and saw her eyes, her breast.

She whispered: 'I could, you know.'

I did not doubt it. And if it comes to that, I was far from certain of myself.

'Yes,' I said, forcing my head not to budge.

'I've been faithful to Robert for six weeks.'

I moved my head back, in order to drink some brandy. I drank a lot. 'That's not long,' I said.

'It is for me.' She stood up. 'I'm trying!' she cried. 'Because I love him!'

The remark was wrung from her. Moved by it, I jumped to

my feet.

'I've never done it for anyone else,' she said.

We were facing each other, looking into each other's eyes.
She said to me: 'And I've had a lot of men.'

I said to her: 'You must be terribly unhappy.'

Immediately she burst into laughter. 'I liked it!'

And at this moment the effects of the brandy struck me. The
pale green walls seemed to fall back into space. She swayed
towards me. I thought 'My God!'

I tensed the whole of my body.

'Robert and I,' I heard myself saying, as if it were someone
else, 'never share a woman.'

I thought 'He's done it!' – he being I – with a burst of
emotion that was either strong approval or strong disapproval,
I did not know which.

'You've just left Myrtle,' she said.

I addressed her with deep intentness. 'We never share a
woman. Or a publisher.'

I can still remember the gleam of drunken mystification in
her eye. This did not weaken my determination to complete
what seemed like a profound statement of truth.

'I won't have jealousy,' I said. I spoke slowly but not
coherently. 'You can change your woman. You can change
your publisher. But you can't change your friends.' I, myself,
was not quite sure how publishers had got into the argument. I
ended up solemnly.

'Friends take a long time to make.'

Julia was looking at me with a bright stare.

'I've no idea what you're talking about,' she said, in a
slightly edgy tone. 'But I grasp the intention.'

'Oh,' I said, non-committally.

'I suppose some men say No.'

'I don't know about that. I can tell you that quite a few
women do.'

'I can't understand it!'

'Quite a few don't, fortunately.'

'I can't understand how any woman can say No!' Julia
spoke with force.

I laughed. Then I thought again. I said:

'You must be unhappy.'

'I'm not!' She was furious. She suddenly raised her arm as if she were going to throw the contents of her glass at me. 'You prig! You say No to me and then tell me I'm unhappy.'

I felt myself sway. 'Good God, that brandy's hit me between wind and water.'

Julia put out her hand to steady me. She grinned and furtively glanced downward.

'You'd better have some more.'

She poured out another glass. I sat down. Julia sat on the arm of my chair again. A fold of her dark red silk dress fell across my lap. Her mood changed. Suddenly she said:

'I suppose you don't think much of me.'

'I don't think much of myself.'

She glanced at me thoughtfully: 'I suppose you don't.'

'Don't imagine that I think much of anybody else either!'

Julia said: 'You ought to think more of yourself.'

I laughed. 'Thanks for the advice.' I drank some more brandy. The room was very quiet. There was no sound from the hundreds of flats around us. I could hear Julia breathing. She took hold of a tuft of my hair and began to twist it.

'I wish Robert were here,' she said.

'I'm Joe. Get it straight. I'm drunk but still Joe.'

'Where's Robert?'

'You've asked that before.'

She seized the telephone again.

'Don't do that!' I said.

'Why not?' She paused to glance at me.

'You won't do yourself any good.'

'I don't care.'

I took hold of her hand and dragged it away from the dial.

'I won't sit down under it!' she cried. Her fingers tightened on mine.

'That's no reason for promptly getting on to your back.'

'Isn't it?' She was startled. Then suddenly her laughter burst out again, high-pitched, constrained, and yet gleeful.

We looked into each other's eyes, and I am sure we were drawn together in some kind of deep emotion.

'What's wrong with me?' she said. The question sprang

right up, and I could see her anxiety to know the answer shining nakedly in her face. She waited.

I held her hand. 'You're off the rails, my dear.'

'What's the use of saying that?' she cried: 'I know. I know!'

'It's never much use saying anything, but you asked me.'

She stood up. She ran her hand through her soft silky hair: it fell beautifully back into place. 'Why am I off the rails?' She was looking away.

I was drunk and I could not help myself from saying what was in my heart. 'Because you've got no sense. Because you don't know what you want. Because you keep on doing something when you ought to do nothing.'

'I know what I want.' She turned to me.

I did not speak.

'And I suppose you call it "doing something when I ought to do nothing" when I refuse to sit down under things.'

I still did not speak.

'I know what I want.' Her voice was raised.

'What?' I asked mildly.

'I want Robert to marry me.'

'Yes.'

'Don't you see? I'm in love with him. He's the most wonderful man I ever met.' She spoke passionately and then suddenly changed her tone. 'He's the one man for me. He's older than me. He's – I don't know... He can master me. He can be a father as well as a lover!' She stopped as if the inspiration had only just come to her. 'That's what he is,' she said, and her eyes widened. 'It's what I want. It's what I need.' She looked at me. 'He can bring me back on to the rails, and keep me there. When we're married, all this' – she made a gesture with her hand – 'will come to an end. And I shall be really happy.' The last sentence lay vibrant on the warm still air. Then she turned to me. 'I suppose you think I'm a fool!'

'No. I don't think you're a fool.'

'What do you think I am?'

I could not speak. In a flash the words had run through my mind – 'You're a lost soul'. And I could not say them. I saw her standing before me, strong and active, beautiful, and wild with conflict.

'What?' she cried again.

I was deeply moved. I shook my head. I said softly: 'I don't know.'

Julia lit a cigarette. I sipped a little brandy, and began to take in details of the room mechanically. Dust on the keys of the piano, ostrich plumes in the hair of one of the women in the photographs, the heels of a pair of bronze kid shoes peeping from under the sofa. I felt a new thought stirring.

Julia said: 'Do you think Robert will marry me?'

She might have known what I was thinking. I had indeed begun to see how she might take hold of Robert's imagination, and I could momentarily feel only distress. It was in Robert's temperament to be deeply drawn to lost souls. The Headlamps, frigid and beautiful, tormenting and tormented, was another, different, lost soul. And I knew that those things which drew him on to begin with could only make him wretched in the end. Had Julia asked me, 'Do you think Robert will love me?' I should have had to answer against my will: 'He may. He may...'

'Will he marry you!' I began, not knowing what to say.

There was a noise in the corridor outside.

'It's my room-mate coming in,' said Julia. 'Go on.'

I glanced at the door, which was open, hesitating as if I did not want to be overheard.

'It's all right,' Julia said impatiently.

To my relief we heard the other girl coming towards us. Knowing there would be time for me to say nothing more, to answer no more questions, I said:

'Yes.'

CHAPTER VIII
FROZEN LEAVES

I went out into the night again, and was not surprised, being full of brandy, to find that I did not feel cold. The wind was still blowing and the sky was black. Returning, I walked on the side of the road near the river. I passed the railings of a small public garden and saw that someone had left the gate open. I felt isolated in the night: the time had passed for going to bed and I might just as well be anywhere. I walked into the garden, along a gravel path between narrow allotments: there was a smell of old cabbage stalks and dead bonfires. I could see a statue, big and heavy like those in Parliament Square. I made for the Embankment wall, and looked down at the water. I thought of Julia, and was haunted by an echo – a lost soul. A gust of wind blew some leaves round my feet again.

I stayed still. I was filled with recollections from my past. My memory stirred with pictures of the world in which Julia lived, where men and women swept from place to place in insistent promiscuity. I knew something about it. I had once spent a season there myself. I had quitted it long since, and looking back on it I usually found it strange and remote – yet sometimes, as at this moment, it felt very near, as if a life off the rails were only a single jump, a single chance, from a life on them.

It was after I had been finally rejected by My Last One that I had decided in anguish to take anyone who wanted me. Not the action of a sane man? I quite agree. If it comes to that, are you sane all of the time? In a wild fit I wanted to humiliate myself, to destroy my romantic hopes and my self-respect. The results were remarkable.

When I entered the world of insistent promiscuity I first of all got some surprises. And then I found myself observing things about human nature that I had never known before. I came, I saw, I learned. What I learned would have roused in some people hatred and disgust. I came to feel neither. I was invaded by a poignant sympathy instead.

I saw men and women searching desperately for something they never found. I did not know what it was they were looking for, nor often did they. The place where they searched was in others: they never found it. I listened to their fantastic stories – having got their main preoccupation off their chests, they were always ready for a good long talk to me. I saw that they never found what they were looking for in others – it was not there. I began to realise it could not be. What they were really looking for was something in themselves, and – here was the tragedy – it was not there either.

Like a swirl of leaves they rattled along from bed to bed, sofa to floor, taxi to telephone-box – in pursuit of the act of love. I have to say that whatever else they missed, they found plenty of copulation. But the act of love is what it was not. It was not an act of passion or sensation as often as all that. It was more like an act of domination and curiosity – and because for all but the coldest of us that is not enough, it was nearly always shot through with unformulated hope. Hope that this performance might miraculously turn into an act of love.

And so they went on. Something was missing, something was incapable, within themselves. Just a few of them seemed to me to have no hearts at all: many, many had hearts that were strained and frozen.

My recollections seemed to surround me like an atmosphere, while I leaned against the massive stone wall and gazed across the river. I imagined Julia, high up in her lighted room, trying to compose her anxious conflicting mind for sleep. A lost soul – she did not notice that the single jump between the life she led and the life she hoped for was across a chasm. In her imagination she saw herself being faithful to a loving husband, while all the time she was hurrying down the raffish by-ways of sex. The romantic hope and the reality had fallen completely apart.

The tide was high, flapping harshly against the stone just

beneath me: occasionally the wind brought up a stale earthy whiff from the water. I found myself thinking about Robert, then about myself, myself and Myrtle. The wind went on blowing, cutting between the brim of my hat and the edge of my collar. With the street lamps well behind me I could see a few stars in the sky. Lighted windows, stars, lost souls, broken hearts – somehow, in spite of everything, I was feeling uplifted. I looked round. Somebody else was leaning against the wall at the other end of the garden.

I was startled. I thought it must be a man because there was no gleam of light stockings. He was quite motionless. He must have been there all the while, brooding in the middle of the night. I wondered what on earth he could be brooding about – must be crazy, I thought. His figure turned from the wall and walked quietly away. And I, who a moment before had been imagining I knew some of the secrets of others, was confronted by the utter separateness of us all, the incredible mysteriousness of one to another.

I stayed on, still feeling warm inside my overcoat and uplifted in heart. I remember thinking what a good name *eau de vie* was. The lights across the river swayed in the wind, a lorry thundered along the Embankment, once I heard voices. I stayed because the afflatus was growing stronger. Everything that had happened to me seemed close at hand. Suffering, humiliation, heartbreak – I contemplated them with powerful emotion. I had survived them all. Instead of having died I was living. What is more, I felt certain I was growing. It seemed that even the most dreadful experiences of life could make one bigger, could make one know more and finally embrace more.

The effects of the brandy must have been powerfully resurgent. I remember most vividly that I looked up at the sky and the stars.

'The universe is expanding,' I thought, 'and so am I.'

CHAPTER IX

THE PLACE ON A LIST

Next morning Robert left London for a fortnight. He took Julia with him. I did not know what was going on, as he went away without my seeing him first.

'There isn't a great deal to do in the office,' he said on the telephone. 'Come down to Brighton if you want to see me.'

Robert always told me there was not very much to do in the office whenever he went away. It would have distressed him to think that he was over-burdening me with his work.

Robert's voice became solemn. 'I'm going to begin planning a novel.'

I exclaimed in surprise, having had fornication firmly fixed in my mind.

Robert's solemnity increased. 'It's time one of us made a start.'

I stopped laughing. For one thing his remark made our break with regular employment seem closer, for another it piqued me because I had already begun a plan of my own in secret.

'Good luck to you, old boy,' I said, and it came from my heart.

'We'll get there in the end,' said Robert.

And so I began the day's work. Our personal assistant came in, a plump young woman with an admirable desire to please and not quite enough organising power. She said Mr Froggatt wanted to see me.

Mr Froggatt was our Senior Executive Officer. People in the class of Robert and me were employed to make decisions on policy: people in Froggatt's class were employed to carry them out. Thus it will be seen that Robert and I belonged to the classiest class of the service, Froggatt to the one below it. But Froggatt was near the highest grade of his class and therefore something of a power in his way. In my own mind I thought of him as our chief henchman. I liked him because he was equable and well-disposed.

I ensconced myself at my desk to receive him, and opened the heaviest file in sight. I was not above trying to make an impression on the lower orders, just like any member of the classiest class inside the government service or outside it, although I was aware that Froggatt knew perfectly well what files must be on my bench since he had sent them to me. I assumed a grave expression.

Froggatt came in. He too assumed a grave expression – he always did when he came to see me. It seemed to me ridiculous that before exchanging a word we should both look grave, but there it was.

Froggatt spoke in a slow, melodious, submissive voice. 'I'm glad you were able to see me, Mr ——' He addressed me by my surname, which is Lunn.

'That's all right, Froggatt. What's the matter?' I saw that he was holding a sheet of paper.

'It's about Dr Chubb, sir.' Froggatt glanced over his shoulder at the second desk which had been placed at the far end of my room, against the window which looked into the well of the building.

'Oh.'

'He came back last night, and was very upset by this, I believe.' Froggatt came towards me holding out the document. 'I thought I would like to see you before Dr Chubb came in.' He handed the document over. 'You'll no doubt have seen it already.'

I glanced at it. 'No.' It was a staff-chart.

Froggatt continued in his slow melodious submissive way. 'Well, we do circulate you with all such information, sir.' He was rebuking me, if not actually applying correction.

'Well, I don't read it all,' I said. 'So you can circulate it till you're blue in the face.'

Froggatt gave me an imperturbable stately smile. 'Ah, Mr Lunn, I hardly think I am likely to change colour in such a way.'

It was one of Froggatt's characteristic habits to treat my
racy exaggerations literally. I restrained myself from uttering
an improper word. What held me back was not my having
been taught never to use such words before subordinates: it
was a conviction that Froggatt would be secretly delighted to
hear me do it.

'What am I supposed to discover from this?'

'I believe Dr Chubb is somewhat dissatisfied with the
position of his name.' Froggatt took a breath, and went on at
an even slower pace. 'Before Dr Chubb comes in, I should like
to say – '

Froggatt never said what he would like to say, because at
that moment Chubb came in. He greeted me while taking off
his fine black hat and his beautiful navy-blue overcoat –
though Chubb could never look either handsome or specially
gentlemanly, his clothes were perfect. Froggatt made a genteel
exit.

Chubb promptly made an exit as well. He took his towel and
his little soap-box. He had a preoccupation with hygiene. I
was left to survey the chart, which set forth the hierarchy of our
division.

For anyone who does not know, I ought to explain that such
charts are always being circulated in the government service.
They look like genealogical trees, and fulfil the apparently
insatiable desire of all human beings to know where they stand
– not, I may say, that such knowledge brings either peace or
satisfaction. With the object of seeing that you stand a cut
above some of your fellows, you find you stand a cut below
others.

Dr Chubb, reporting to Robert as I did, had been shown on
the same level as me. Whereas he was senior to me. His name
was printed a quarter of an inch lower down the sheet than it
should have been.

'Oh dear!' I said aloud. Accidents of this kind seemed to
happen most frequently to people whose dignity was most
susceptible to affront. To me the quarter of an inch would have
made little difference one way or the other. Had the whole
division been shown reporting to Froggatt I would not have

minded – in fact it would not have been a bad idea, since Froggatt was nothing if not sensible. To Dr Chubb, a humble ambitious man, whose life had been devoted to small advancements, whose career was an accumulation of quarter inches, I knew the mistake was grave.

Chubb came in again, put away his towel and little soap-box, and came towards me. His expression spoke for him. His rosy cheeks, instead of being fixed in his habitual nervous smile, were drawn in. His teeth were not visible, and over the half-moons of his spectacles his eyes were popping with alarm.

'I'm sorry about this,' I said.

'I don't want you to think that I wish to make heavy weather over this kind of thing, because, as you'll understand,' said Chubb, 'I'm not the sort of person who does make heavy weather over, over this kind of thing ... but I should like to say, before we go any further – you'll appreciate the position I'm in – '

'Yes,' I said, while he took a breath.

Chubb finished a very long sentence, whose syntax I cannot vouch for.

'I'll tell Froggatt to get it corrected,' I said.

Chubb was not in the least satisfied. 'I really felt this was the kind of thing which ought to be brought to the notice of Sir Francis and actually I've written him a letter to that effect. I tried to see him personally.' Chubb stared at me with his gravest and most detached expression of alarm. 'It was impossible.' He paused. 'Now, I don't want to criticise the department – I feel rather uncertain of my position here, as you may guess, for various reasons – but I do feel that it should be possible to arrange to see the head on urgent personal matters without having to wait two and a half weeks for an appointment. It was only through a fortunate coincidence that I happened to run into him, coming out of the lavatory, and was able to mention briefly what had occurred.' He paused, and his tone took a note almost of horror. 'I'm afraid he put me off.'

I suddenly had an inspiration. 'You should try getting at him through James Irskine.' It seemed to me that by all the rules Chubb and James were bound to get at loggerheads –

who was I to keep nature from taking its proper course?

'Do you think so?' said Chubb.

I nodded. At that moment there was a rap on the door. We both turned to see James come in.

'Sorry to interrupt. I've had a word with Sir Francis' – he glanced at me with a faint gleam in his glaring blue eyes – 'while he was taking off his hat and coat.' He turned to Chubb. 'About you.'

'Ah,' said Chubb, hopefully.

'About this list. It was before Lunn came in. I got on to Froggatt, and told him D.O.R.R.S. wanted the old list withdrawn and a new one circulated. Correct, this time.'

It was clear that James thought Dr Chubb would be satisfied. Not a bit of it. Chubb immediately embarked on a long speech about his apprehensions. I cannot say he touched on his points. As I listened I compared him with Froggatt. If both were given a point to make, which would take the longer, Chubb with his remarkable prolixity or Froggatt with his immoderately slow articulation?

'... I'm sure I don't want to make difficulties, but you'll understand that I feel bound in certain circumstances – although I naturally don't feel certain of myself in this organisation – to put forward my point of view ...'

I had no idea what Chubb was getting at. I had time to watch James, to admire the masculine stance of a man who is satisfied with his own intelligence, looks, virility and prospective success in affairs. I perceived that his angry glare did undergo just detectable variations as Chubb's jeremiad proceeded. His face went redder. There was not the slightest doubt that in due course Chubb and James would come into a furious head-on collision over some matter of correct Civil Service procedure. The quarrel would not affect either of their careers: it would just make a powerful addition to their daily lives.

Chubb really was leading up to something. His voice was filling out and he was getting a hunted look in the eyes.

'I agree that you have a case,' James said, with wooden impatience. 'It will be put right.'

'That's not the point,' said Chubb. 'That isn't what I'm

trying to express. What I'm trying to express is this.'
Suddenly, in the outburst of naked emotion his prolixity fell
away. 'This would never have happened,' he cried, *'if I'd had a
room of my own!'*

CHAPTER X

AN OFFICE CHAIR

'Tell Mr Froggatt I want to see him,' I said to my personal assistant, as soon as James had stalked out of the room.

Froggatt came in, looking diffident. He was a man aged about forty, narrow across the shoulders and narrow all the way down. He had a long face with big eyes a bit like a bloodhound's, and he carried his head forward a little.

'Did you want me, sir?'

As Froggatt stood in front of me, I glanced at Chubb, who was sitting at his desk, apparently composing a memorandum with his own hand. I picked up the offending chart.

I said: 'If I do read this kind of document, I expect it to be correct.'

'Yes, Mr Lunn, I quite understand your irritation. First of all I should like to explain how – '

'Please don't!' I said. 'Whenever anything goes wrong in the government service, dozens of people spend valuable time on a protracted post-mortem. It doesn't stop them making the same mistake again. No, Froggatt' – he was about to try and put a word in – 'I don't want to hear explanations, analyses or reasons. I want to hear that it won't happen again.'

'I agree that excuses – '

'It's the future I'm interested in, not the past.'

A slight pause. 'Quite.' Froggatt had given up. Instead of looking stately and slyly submissive he was injured and abashed. 'I'll do my best. I'm afraid I haven't time for everything.'

'There's something else I want you to do, Froggatt.' I had another kind of trick to play on him. 'Dr Chubb is going to be in London. Will you make arrangements for him to have an office of his own?'

Immediately Froggatt's expression changed. I must explain that Froggatt had a weakness for making our staff frequently change offices. They disliked it. Most men and women get used to their place in an office, to their bench, their chair, the position of the window, the people sitting on either side of them. It was quite a while before I tumbled to what Froggatt was doing by moving them. I did not dream of interfering, even when his manoeuvres broke up the division's most romantic, if illicit, love-affair. He was showing the staff he was their master. Froggatt's expression changed to alert interest. 'Yes?' he said in a soft low tone, which I noted with pleasure.

We were interrupted. Chubb rose from his desk and came towards us.

'I hope you don't mind my butting in like this,' he said, smiling toothily. 'I don't want to make everyone a great deal of trouble over this question of rooms. After all, I shall be out of London much of the time during the next few weeks in the continuance of my present duties.'

'I don't think it will cause us much trouble,' said Froggatt, looking at me for approval and support.

'I've been giving some thought to this matter,' said Chubb, 'and it occurred to me that in view of Your Friend' – Chubb always referred thus to Robert – 'being away from his office for considerable periods – in view of his only being here part-time – it might be thought more suitable for me to occupy his office during his absence. On the advent of his return I could move back here.'

Froggatt and I glanced at each other. I did not know him well enough to be certain that he was thinking exactly the same as me: it was probably along the same lines. Everyone in the higher ranks of the government service knows that he allows someone else to occupy his office chair at his peril. If the secret history of the Second World War had an appendix showing the names of distinguished persons who left their offices on interesting expeditions and returned to find someone else in their chairs for good, no boss would ever budge from Whitehall again.

'I should like you to have an office really of your own,' I said weightily. 'We can't risk any more mistakes like this.'

Chubb hesitated nervously. At that moment he had just insufficient push.

'I think I can do as Mr Lunn wishes, without much difficulty,' said Froggatt. He knew just the right moment for that kind of move.

'Well,' said Chubb, 'I put it forward as a suggestion.'

'Thank you,' I said, warmly. 'It's very considerate of you.'

I knew that that was the end of it.

Froggatt went out. Chubb returned to his desk, and started to write again.

At first I was occupied with trying to decide whether Chubb, even when he was writing, looked through the lenses of his spectacles. And then I fell into thoughts of a deeper and more entertaining kind. 'So he'd like to plant his not inconsiderable seat in Robert's chair,' I thought. 'Now that's interesting!'

CHAPTER XI

AN UNUSUAL OFFER

The weeks were passing and the time was getting nearer for Haxby's demobilisation. I became steadily more agitated. I had persuaded Myrtle to promise she would ask him for a divorce the moment she saw him.

There was no doubt that Myrtle did not want to ask her husband for a divorce – she wanted to so little that she made great efforts not to think about it. My agitation was not diminished by such tactics. I simply could not see how, with the best will in the world, she could marry me without previously being divorced from Haxby. To me her divorce was the *clou* of our whole situation: I could not help explaining this to her.

Myrtle gave me a look of reproach and then fell into distant melancholy silence.

I thought if only Myrtle had been trained in the Civil Service she would have understood how necessary action was before results could ensue.

Myrtle had a tender nature. She was very distressed at the thought of hurting Haxby. Her reluctance once showed signs of breaking down, while she was considering whether it was sometimes necessary to be cruel to be kind.

Unfortunately I observed that you never had to be cruel to be kind, though you often had to be cruel to get what you wanted – poor Myrtle was horrified.

There followed distant melancholy silence for at least half an hour, during which her tender sensitive nature wrapped itself up again in a warm veil of obstinacy.

I tried hard to understand Myrtle's nature during this period. The more I tried, the less able I found myself to follow it. I was humble. Robert had already established by disputation that I was the crazy unrealistic partner and Myrtle the shrewd down-to-earth one. I really ought to have been able to understand Myrtle.

In the first place I discovered that Myrtle was taking quite seriously the possibility of Haxby's not surviving the fighting in Palestine. I was sure she would mourn his sacrifice for the rest of her life, permitting herself the consolation of marrying me after a discreet interval of widowhood. The idea flitted constantly through her mind, like a perfect solution. However, widowhood, like perfection, turned out to be unattainable. When there was no sign of intervention by either Jews or Arabs, Myrtle began to have hopes of the War Office: she thought Haxby's date of demobilisation might be put back. I could see no justification for such an idea. I had been demobilised myself: you were given a number, and when in due rotation your number came up, you were out. Myrtle found in this concept merely another sign of my mechanical mind.

The weeks passed, and the Cabinet made no sudden declaration that from tomorrow all demobilisation would cease. Myrtle began to wonder if Haxby would decide to stay in the Army of his own accord. She had strong arguments in favour: Haxby had no job to come home to, and, as Myrtle said, he was good at being a soldier – he had risen from Private to Captain in the R.A.S.C. On the other hand it was clear to me that Haxby had hated Army life from the moment he was called up, had never ceased to grumble about it, and was now entirely given up to waiting for his demobilisation day.

Do you begin to see why I found it hard to understand Myrtle, and impossible to follow her? Was this a difference, I asked myself, between a crazy unrealistic person and a shrewd down-to-earth one who could believe in miracles? It was most puzzling. For, take my word for it, Myrtle reached the stage of hoping for events that could arise only from divine intervention. It was like living with someone just about to go bankrupt who was constantly awaiting an unexpected legacy of one hundred thousand pounds, free of duty.

I was sorry for Myrtle, and the further she retired into her dreams of reprieve the less I said about it. I ceased to mention either Haxby or divorce. Myrtle seemed happier.

Towards the middle of December, Myrtle and I went to the wedding of one of her professional colleagues. It was a smart wedding of milliners in Caxton Hall. The bride was wearing a hat that looked like a miniature sitting pheasant. The other women's hats were so fashionable that they did not look like hats at all, but more like objects which bore no known relation to the human head, such as pagodas and wheel-barrows. For all her sophistication, Myrtle was enchanted to be there. Her eyes glowed with a romantic light. She squeezed my arm. She introduced me to some of her acquaintances. 'This is my young man.' I could only assume that they did not know she had a husband or that she had forgotten.

Myrtle and I happened to come out a little in advance of the bride and bridegroom. One of the disconcerting features of a registry office wedding is the absence of a clearly defined beginning and end to the ceremony. In a church wedding the organ tootles so loudly that even the drunks know when they have to go in and come out. Myrtle and I found ourselves in the porch of the building while the bride and bridegroom were still doing something inside. Some of the other guests were moving along behind us, and we saw two press photographers going past in the opposite direction. At the top of the steps we paused and looked round.

It was a cold dark morning, with occasional bursts of sunshine lighting up the bombed-out church on the opposite side of the road. There was something cheerless and inhuman about the white mosaic steps and heavy metal canopy of the porch – they reminded me of the entrance to a technical college. Myrtle was delighted all the same.

Suddenly a taxi drew up and a scruffy young man in a duffel-coat jumped out, carrying a camera and flash-bulb. He spotted Myrtle and me in the centre of the group, Myrtle with her hair elegantly adorned by a length of dark green net and me with a red carnation in my buttonhole.

'Excuse me, are you the newly-weds?'

Myrtle said: 'Yes.'

And our photographs were taken.

I denied it immediately. The photographer was cross. Some of the other guests laughed. Myrtle laughed with satisfaction. At that moment the true bride and bridegroom came out and posed.

Instead of waiting for one of the cars to the reception, Myrtle and I took a taxi in Victoria Street. In the taxi I remonstrated with her.

All that Myrtle said was: 'Darling, I wished it really was us.'

I could not help feeling a little mollified, and yet I could not help feeling a little frightened. I looked at Myrtle's profile, at her soft easy smile as she snuggled against my shoulder. I did not doubt she was imagining that we were driving away from our own wedding, our own – if I may say so – bigamous wedding. In a way she was right. How much easier it would have been to forget she had a husband whom she must divorce before she could marry me, how much less painful! I sympathised with her. She was not alone either. I pictured all the host of bigamists I read about every Sunday in *The News of the World*. Now I came to think about it, I was puzzled. Myrtle and I could have come out of the Caxton Hall and faced the world with ease at last. Mr and Mrs Lunn. All we were asking was the opportunity to make an honest man and woman of ourselves. What *was* wrong with bigamy?

The taxi emerged from Buckingham Palace Road and we saw a fleeting glow of sunlight on the façade of the Palace. I kissed Myrtle. Myrtle kissed me. What were we to do? What was our solution? Divorce, with its mixture of pain and moral obloquy?

We were silent. The taxi drove on towards St James's – we were making for the Mayfair Hotel. The smile faded from Myrtle's face, and I could tell she was thinking seriously. I stroked her hand, and whispered, 'Darling'.

Beside the Ritz we were held up by traffic lights. It was dark inside the taxi because the street was narrow. Myrtle leaned away from me a little. I glanced at her and saw that she was looking at me.

'What is it?'

Myrtle spoke with difficulty. 'Darling, would you like me to .... just come and live with you.' She stopped, and her eyelids fluttered down.

'You mean, set up together without being married?'

Myrtle looked away. It was what she did mean.

Only some time later did I see how time had turned the tables on me. It was the offer that once I had made to Myrtle. Now, as I heard her making the offer to me, I could hardly keep back the emotion I felt.

'Darling!' I cried. 'That wouldn't do at all!'

Myrtle glanced at me. In the half-light I could not see whether she was giving me a look of surprise or reproach or sympathy. The taxi suddenly jerked forward to cross Piccadilly.

'I want you to marry me,' I said. 'Darling, the answer's No.'

CHAPTER XII

THROUGH A CARRIAGE-WINDOW

Haxby landed in England on Christmas Eve. Myrtle spent the day in London with me. My office closed down at mid-day, and Myrtle and I walked round, looking in the lighted shop-windows. She had a telegram saying which train from Euston Haxby hoped to catch, and she intended to join him on it.

'We don't know if he'll get there in time,' she said. I felt dreadfully tense. We did not mention the fact that she had got to tell him at last. While we were sitting in a café, waiting for the waitress to bring our tea, she looked at me with a tremulous light in her eyes, and said:

'I wish it were you instead of me.'

I squeezed her fingers. There was nothing to say.

After tea Myrtle bought herself some suede boots lined with sheepskin. It seemed to comfort her. The boots were expensive. She shook her head sadly – she was convinced that we were going to have a desperately cold winter.

I bought a diary. I did not need it. I bought it because it somehow brought nearer the date when all our troubles would be over. Tonight Haxby would know. In January the divorce proceedings would start. We should have to wait through February, March, April – it was taking four or five months to get a divorce, sometimes longer. But the summer! Opening the diary at July seemed to let out the sunny glow of a millenium.

I took Myrtle to the station. It was about half-past seven, snowy, dark and slightly foggy. Crowds of people were arriving at Euston. There were taxis and lights and bright faces. The first thing we saw just inside the colonnade was a great pile of Christmas trees, lying horizontally with their sombre green branches entwined and circles of brown timber shining where the stems had been cut off. There were parcels on trucks, in children's hands, everywhere. There was the familiar fishy smell, and an occasional whiff of oranges. I took Myrtle to her train. It was very early.

Myrtle chose a seat in a comfortable new coach: the compartments had wide windows on the platform side. Myrtle got out again and walked with me to the end of the platform, so that I could kiss her in the darkness. I was hasty. I did not want Haxby to see us, and somehow I wanted to part from her as quickly as possible so that the scene could begin.

At last Myrtle let me go. From the platform I watched her sit down beside the window. I waved and walked away.

I saw Haxby. He was standing at a bookstall, choosing a book. He was in uniform. I strode past.

Off the platform, I went to one of the refreshment rooms and bought myself a drink. I had an evening newspaper but I could not bring myself to read it. I kept looking at the clock.

A quarter of an hour went by. The train was nearly due to leave. I felt an impulse that I could not resist. I went out, bought another platform ticket, turned up the collar of my overcoat, and once more went down the length of the train. The lights inside were bright. Through the windows you could see all the people. I kept in the shadows. I felt furtive. I came to the compartment where Myrtle and Haxby were. I saw them.

They were chatting together amicably.

PART III

CHAPTER I

A QUESTION OF EMPLOYMENT

It was three weeks before I saw Myrtle again. I had spent them in Switzerland, and I prayed that Myrtle had spent them in reconciling Haxby to his fate.

We met by secret pre-arrangement at the Carlos. I went straight there from the air-terminal. It was about eight o'clock in the evening. The streets of London were patchy with snow and looked to me discouragingly dark after Zürich and Geneva. As I got out of the taxi a few damp flakes fell on my head.

The porch of the hotel was glowing. A commissionaire came out to look after my luggage, and asked me if I was going to stay. I said not.

The first person I set eyes on was Myrtle. There was a chair placed in full view of the entrance: it was high-backed and sweeping-armed, suitable for Hamlet to soliloquise in. Myrtle was sitting in it, holding a glass.

'Darling!' she cried. There was a big vase full of white and yellow chrysanthemums behind her head. Her eyes were shining and her lips were parted. We embraced.

I stood back and looked at her. She was wearing a new dress. She was looking excited and happy. She was a trifle tipsy.

'Your aeroplane was terribly late,' she said. 'They've been telephoning the airport every quarter of an hour for me.' She smiled. 'There was nothing else to do but drink.' At that she dropped her eyelids. She lifted them just in time to see my luggage being carried in. 'Darling! You're going to stay here? I am. I've got a room.'

I took off my overcoat and handed it in. Myrtle watched me.

Certainly she was a trifle tipsy. There was not the slightest trace of the over-awed look she usually wore in the Carlos. Her new dress was beautiful. I slipped my arm round her waist and led her towards an alcove in one of the lounges.

'What do you think of my hair?' she asked. 'Rudolf's latest style.' She noticed a waiter passing, and skilfully gave him her glass. 'Tell George we want two more of the same.' She turned to me. 'It's something special he mixed me. I told him I was waiting for you.'

We sat down side by side on a sofa which filled the alcove.

'Darling,' I said, because she looked so happy: 'Everything's all right?'

'Everything?' She looked at me suddenly, her eyes big and round and golden.

'You've told Dennis?' I said. 'He agrees?'

There was silence, between Myrtle and me complete silence.

The waiter came up and placed two glasses on a low table before us. I paid him and he went away. The drinks were amber-coloured – they stood untouched.

'You haven't told him yet?' I said.

'You can see I haven't.'

'Darling, why?'

Myrtle put her hand to her forehead as if she had a headache. My prayers had been in vain, as not only was Haxby not reconciled to his fate – he did not even know yet what it was. For a moment I began to wonder what it was myself. It hung on Myrtle. If it came to that, my own fate hung on Myrtle. There was a long pause.

'Aren't you going to try my drink?' Myrtle spoke as if the incident were closed. Alcohol had given her unaccustomed resilience. She picked up her glass to acquire more of it.

I tried the drink, and put it down again. The incident was not closed. I said:

'Aren't you going to tell me why you haven't told him?'

'Darling, I couldn't!'

'But you'll have to.'

'It's too soon. He's only just got back. He's so at a loss . . .'

Much as I loved Myrtle I could not help wishing her conversation had a little more edge.

I said: 'Do you mean he's at a loss trying to fit into civilian life?', thinking what a stupid remark it was.

'Yes, that's just it,' said Myrtle.

'I had to fit into it.'

'You're different.'

'I don't see why.'

'You had a job to come to, but he hasn't.'

I was dismayed. 'He'll get one,' I said comfortably, but without conviction.

'Of course he will.' Myrtle turned on me. 'You were lucky.'

'Indeed!' I said crossly.

Myrtle sipped her drink again. I swallowed the whole of mine in two gulps.

'Darling,' Myrtle said, changing her tone, 'I can't leave him until he's got a job. I couldn't bear to do it.'

'Do you really mean that?' I said at last.

'Yes.' A gentle, tremulous, entirely obstinate yes.

I now had something else to think about. My fate hung on Myrtle – it hung also on Haxby's getting a job. I for one had no idea what he could be employed as. It was comic: it was appalling.

'What sort of a job is he looking for?'

'He doesn't really know.' Myrtle paused. 'Do you think you could order another drink, darling?' She paused again. 'I want to ask your advice.'

I told you Myrtle was capable of earning a lot of money in business. Now do you see why? I did not know whether to burst into laughter or to box her ears. I did neither. Myrtle had signalled the waiter, so I ordered some more drinks. I leaned my head on the cushion of the sofa. On a ledge that ran round the alcove there was a bunch of paper-white narcissus, I just caught their clear frail scent. I thought of spring, the time for all such exquisite flowers, the time for Myrtle's divorce.

'Hadn't you better tell them you want a room for the night?' Myrtle said gently, 'You can't sleep in mine' – she gave a lubricious sigh. 'It's only a single bed.'

The drinks arrived. I sat up.

'What sort of a job?' I repeated.

'He'd like to be a journalist,' said Myrtle. She went on. 'He's edited his unit's newspaper terribly well. The CO congratulated him.'

I recalled that when she married him he was a reporter on the local newspaper. I said nothing.

'And he knows an awful lot about music,' she said. 'Especially on records. I think he could do terribly well on the BBC – you know, putting on a programme of gramophone records.'

'A disc-jockey!' I cried.

'How could he become one?' said Myrtle.

I will not record the rest of the conversation. Any man's blood might run cold at the prospect of his marriage depending on his future wife's present husband getting a job as a putter-on of gramophone records.

But Myrtle's intention was perfectly real, to me deplorably real. Her tender nature revolted from deserting her husband when he had no means of supporting himself. Quite rightly. Yet there was something else. I had led her to believe in the past, when she tried to make me jealous, that I did not think much of him, and she hated it. Even though she was going to divorce him. Her vanity was wounded. Now I had got to take him seriously. 'But as a potential disc-jockey!' I thought: 'That's the limit!'

I said gravely: 'I think we must ask Robert to help.'

'Do you!' Myrtle's face lighted instantly, naively. She put her hand on mine. 'He really will get a job,' she said, 'and then I shan't mind telling him half so much.'

I said nothing. What she read in my face satisfied her.

'I think you need some dinner, darling,' she said. There was a lurking smile round the corners of her mouth. 'I must say I do.'

We made our way to the dining-room, with its softly-lit mahogany walls, but my thoughts were elsewhere. I was recalling the number of scenes in which I had begged Myrtle to tell her husband we wanted to be married. The scenes caused her distress. What is more, they caused her patent satisfaction. I asked myself an unpleasant question. 'How many more of them are there to be?'

CHAPTER II

IN THE STALLS-BAR

R obert invited me to go to the theatre with him and Julia.
We were to see a performance of *Love For Love* at the
Haymarket theatre, and Julia was to meet us in the stalls-bar –
it was Robert's way of side-stepping her efforts to make him
put on evening dress and take her to dine at the Savoy
afterwards. I was sworn to tell Julia, when a suitable moment
arose, that I had brought Robert straight from the office. We
had been quietly enjoying sandwiches and beer in a public-
house round the corner.

I recalled earlier days when Robert had been delighted to
put on his evening dress and flaunt Julia in fashionable places.
I attached no unusual importance to this change, since I had
seen it happen with all his other young women. He loved to be
seen with them in public – remember he only chose pretty
ones. But they never knew when he had had enough of it,
chiefly, I am afraid, because they had never had enough
themselves.

The Haymarket is one of London's most beautiful theatres:
we thought it was perfect. As we went up the steps we felt the
romantic thrill of having history around us – in imagination
we were going to see a play written by Robert or me. One's
own play performed at the Haymarket – perfection indeed!

We went down the corridor towards the bar and Robert
glanced at his watch. It was not quite early enough for him to
have gone home to change, not quite late enough to prevent his
having a drink before the show. He nodded his big head with
satisfaction.

It was a spacious bar, carpeted and lit by chandeliers. The
two halves of the room were on different levels with a couple of

steps between. Standing on the steps gave us a slight feeling of grandeur, so we stood there.

The choice of play was Julia's, not Robert's nor mine.

'It doesn't follow,' he said loftily, 'that girls whose tastes are far from highbrow in certain other matters, don't have remarkably highbrow tastes in literature.' And then he reminded me of one of my young women whom I would hear reciting passages from Shakespeare as I dropped off to sleep. Long passages.

There was a stir beside us. Julia had arrived.

Her eyes were brightly transparent and the skin of her neck was flushed. 'Robert, darling, get me a drink!'

While she was waiting she glanced at me furtively. 'It's the first one I've had today.'

I offered her a cigarette. She took it. There were some particles of face-powder on the front of her dress. It was the red silk dress I had seen before.

'I've just heard from Wladislaw!'

At that moment Robert returned. Julia took the glass and drank. She said:

'Wladislaw's just rung me up.'

'Where is he?'

'In Paris.'

Suddenly there was a silence.

Robert said impatiently: 'What does he want?'

'To prevent me from marrying you.' Julia shook her head, as if she were angry. Her hair swung against her cheeks.

Robert's expression changed completely. 'Have you told him?'

'Yes.'

Robert was silent. Julia stared at him with her head down, but his face showed no emotion. I glanced round the bar: it was getting quite full.

'You knew I was going to,' Julia said.

'I knew you wanted to,' said Robert.

'You knew that for me that's the same thing,' said Julia. 'You told me so, yourself.'

I was delighted to see Robert hoist with his own petard. He pretended to be thinking about something else.

Julia's tone changed.

'We've got to get things straight, darling.'

Robert still did not reply. He was no believer in the implicit virtue of straightness in private affairs.

'I didn't tell him who you were,' Julia said. 'I told him I'd got my first chance of real happiness '

'He'll find out quickly enough when he gets back.'

'What does that matter? He's got to know, sometime.' She burst out passionately. 'He's got to let me have my chance!'

I said: 'Surely he can't prevent you?'

Julia looked startled.

Robert said: 'What is he proposing to do?'

Julia said: 'He thinks he's going to prove to you that I'm married to him.'

Robert and I caught each other's eye.

I said: 'But he can't. To prove you're married to him, he'd have to produce the marriage lines.'

'There are none!' said Julia, triumphantly.

'Good.'

'I can produce the documents about my change of name.'

'Better.'

'I won't sit down under it!'

Julia finished her drink. Robert took the glass and went down to the bar-counter.

'I've sat down under it long enough.'

'Under what?'

'Wladislaw's attempts to prevent me getting out of his clutches.'

'I don't see how he can hold you.'

Julia did not reply. She was looking away. Wladislaw had got some kind of hold on her, on her imagination, on her body – I was sure he was a man of powerful direct personality.

Julia turned to me. 'I don't think Robert's as strong as he ought to be.'

'Oh.'

'He doesn't help me.'

'I don't see what he can do.' This was not true. I thought a definite proposal of marriage would have helped.

'I do!' said Julia, with force.

I glanced down at Robert, who was having to wait at the

bar.

'Then you mustn't demand it,' I said. 'Robert *has* got a strong personality.' Julia looked at me with attention. 'But it's indirect,' I went on: 'He's subtle and tricky and evasive, but he's obstinate and determined. He'll do what *he* wants.'

Julia blinked: her expression hardened. My explanation, like most of my explanations of people to each other, appeared to convey next to no meaning while having a markedly irritant effect.

I said quietly: 'He's enquiring about buying houses.' That sort of explanation could never go wrong.

Julia's face softened as quickly as it had hardened. 'In Mayfair?'

'Yes.'

Robert rejoined us. He said, thoughtfully: 'Did you find out what were the results of Wladislaw's researches in Poland?'

'Yes. He says he now has proof that his wife was killed.'

'H'm.'

Julia said: 'He's always got proof of something.'

Robert's eye suddenly sparkled. 'I suspect he's a man for me to deal with.' He was already thinking of the wily circuits he would make round Czyz.

Julia smiled at him admiringly.

'It would have been easier,' said Robert, 'if he'd found proof that she was alive.'

'He's terribly honest,' said Julia. She paused. 'He's got no sense of humour and he's terribly honest. It's an awful combination.'

'That doesn't matter.' Robert dismissed her momentarily. His imagination was moving. I glanced at Julia, because it occurred to me that she had little idea of which way it was moving. Czyz was not the only person round whom wily circuits would be made.

'It does if you have to live with him,' Julia said.

Robert suddenly glanced at her with a kind of amused concentration. 'It didn't suit you too badly.'

'I don't know what you mean!' Julia took offence.

'A man with that kind of temperament doesn't need much encouragement to burst into passionate quarrelling.'

'So you think that's what I want?'

'It's what you got. On the whole people get what they want in that way.'

'I've never had a quarrel with you!' Julia's voice broke out. Some people who were standing nearby turned and looked at us. The men continued to look at Julia.

Robert said in a low voice: 'That's because I have a strong sense of humour and am not specially honest.'

'I shall make you quarrel when we're married!'

I thought she would not find it easy. When he was really angry Robert fell into penetratingly gloomy, white-faced silence.

The first warning-bell for the play rang inside the bar. Julia began to sip the remainder of her drink.

Robert said: 'When is Wladislaw due back in London?'

'I couldn't hear him. That was what I wanted to catch most, but the line suddenly got worse. But don't worry – he'll ring again before he leaves Paris. He'll ring every night.'

I saw a suspicious look cross Robert's face.

'Anyway, it doesn't matter,' Julia said: 'He won't be coming back to the flat.'

Immediately I pricked up my ears. It ought to have occurred to me long ago that Wladislaw paid the rent of Julia's flat.

'He'll probably demand to,' said Robert.

'I shall tell him I want my girl-friend to stay. She hasn't got anywhere else to go.'

'She could find somewhere.'

'She isn't going to.'

'If he asks her to leave, she'll have to.'

'You don't see my point of view!'

'I do, my dear.'

'Robert, if you did, you wouldn't be able to even contemplate Wladislaw's coming to live in the flat again.' She looked away. 'If he does, I won't sit down under it! I'll sleep behind bolted doors!'

Robert grinned.

For an instant Julia was poised on the brink of fury. Her grip tightened on her glass. Then suddenly she burst into laughter.

'It would be the first time since I was fifteen.' Her face warmed most attractively with a careless, detached amusement.

The second warning-bell rang. I noticed that most of the other people had left the bar. I took hold of Julia's elbow and told her to come on.

Julia looked over her shoulder at Robert, who was going down to put the empty glasses on the bar-counter.

'Perhaps we'll have somewhere to live before then. Joe says you've been to some agents.'

Robert's answer was delivered weightily. 'I've been talking to some of my friends who know about these things.'

'Dear Robert, that's not very definite,' said Julia.

When Robert came back he behaved as if the exchange were over.

Julia looked up into his face, hesitated for a moment, and then smiled at him. She took hold of Robert's hand, and twisted her fingers through his while we walked down the corridor.

We went in to see *Love For Love*.

CHAPTER III

TALK BY THE FIRESIDE

Myrtle's sad and fearful prophesy of a desperately cold winter was being borne out. By the end of January we thought the weather had reached its bitterest, the snow its thickest and our fuel its shortest. Haxby had not got a job, and Robert was in bed with influenza. Dr Chubb, wearing his winter combinations and his galoshes, was an example to us all of what comes from taking every sensible precaution. He was cold, he was alarmed because the office was not heated properly, but he was clearly blooming with health. And he was in London all the time. I was at a loss to know why he was not on the second half of his tour of industries concerned in making the A 15 and the A 16, although both Robert and I were also at something of a loss to know what he had done on the first half. We had heard one or two surprising bits of gossip about his activities.

One afternoon Chubb came into my office and proposed to my surprise that we should go out for tea at his club.

'I don't think anybody can work with cold feet,' he said, giving me a nervous toothy smile. 'I know I can't.'

We got a taxi. I found that he belonged to one of the biggest, though hardly the most gentlemanly clubs in London. We were drawn through swing-doors into what looked like an American hotel, complete with tobacconist shop, bookstall, post-office and palm lounge. Dr Chubb suggested we wash our hands.

'I didn't wash before I left the office,' he said. 'I find cold water doesn't really cleanse one's hands properly. I don't know if you agree.'

The water in the wash-basins was only tepid. Dr Chubb was

dismayed.

We went into a huge lounge, where we saw a log fire burning brightly. We sat down in front of it, Chubb rubbing his hands with satisfaction. He ordered tea.

'This was a good idea,' I said, looking round me, admiringly.

'I'm glad you were able to come, because I've been wanting to have a little talk with you for some time.'

I glanced at him. He went on.

'But we're all so busy, that is to say, you and I are very busy, and of course Your Friend being only on part-time makes everything a bit more difficult...' He waited.

I pretended to think. A waiter placed a tray before us, with a pot of tea on it and some rounds of under-buttered toast. 'I expect you'd like me to officiate,' said Chubb, looking over the top of his spectacles.

I turned my attention to the room which was so big that the massive pieces of furniture seemed ordinary-sized. From the lofty ceiling hung dusty glass chandeliers in which every third bulb only was lit. Over the mantelpiece there was a mural painting whose subject I presumed to be allegorical since the swans appeared to be on an equal footing with the human beings. What interested me most was the smell of the place – I knew it was the long-standing scent of cigars, but had my nose been presented with it in other circumstances I could easily have taken it for a whiff of the stables.

Dr Chubb was talking to me. I just came in at the point where he was saying: ' – and I said to my wife I should like to read the novels you and Your Friend wrote, so she asked her library if they could get them for her.'

'Did they?' I said, really interested. Our books were out of print.

Chubb sipped his tea.

'Yes. They managed to get hold of them for us.'

'Have you read them?'

'Yes. I thought perhaps you'd like to hear what we thought about them – I may say that my wife reads a great deal, in fact she reads a great deal more than me, especially novels. I like a good biography myself, though I've read a great many novels in the past.' He began to spread some blackberry jelly on his toast. 'We enjoyed your novels and Your Friend's.'

'Excellent,' I said.

'I don't know if you'd like some of our further comments.'

'Delighted.' Nothing pleased me more than comments on my books, provided they were favourable.

Dr Chubb took another piece of toast. 'I'm afraid the tea here isn't as good as it used to be. Before the war it was quite different.'

'And the novels?' I said.

'Yes, yes.' Dr Chubb wiped his lips with his handkerchief, and pushed it back in his left cuff, leaving a point sticking out. He said:

'First of all, I think I may say that my wife preferred Your Friend's books to yours – '

'Women's books.'

' – Whereas I haven't really made up my mind, because I like to think things over a little longer before I commit myself. All the same I can see that yours were written, I don't know how to put it exactly, but perhaps I might say – seriously.'

'That's just it!'

Chubb went on. What he said was bumblingly pedestrian. Yet it seemed to me, in the light of his opening remark, sensible and perspicacious. I forgot that he had not brought me out to tea to give me a layman's literary criticism. I was flattered.

In rounding off his views Chubb came back to his original comment.

'Of course!' I said. 'You see I'm a serious writer.'

Chubb looked at me. He said:

'And I can see that Your Friend is, too.'

'Of course. We're both serious writers. It's the only thing we really care about.'

Chubb nodded encouragingly. 'I'm told he is on part-time so as to give himself more time for writing, but I should have thought writing was a full-time job.'

'It is! As soon as he gets a chance, he'll leave the government service like a shot. And I shall follow. Please God it won't be long now – six months at most!'

Chubb was silent. I had not been looking at him while I

made my speech. I now turned and saw him smiling at me over his spectacles. His eyes were brighter – and his cheeks pinker, with the radiance of a man's face when he has found out something he wanted to know. I could have kicked myself for telling him the truth: Robert would never have done it.

'I hope your estimate turns out to be correct.' His tone was full and amiable. He stood up and warmed his seat at the fire.

I watched him. Then I went to the fire and did the same. We stared round the room, at bald members having their tea. After a while he said:

'I don't think I shall go back to the office again.'

He jingled some keys in his pocket. His face looked both alert and relaxed. He was thinking, I had not the slightest doubt, that things were going very nicely.

CHAPTER IV

THE IMPORTANCE OF A SIGNATURE

I decided, after Chubb had set off for Waterloo in a taxi, that I would go back to the office after all. It was already quite dark outside, and as I trudged through the slush I wished I had Chubb's galoshes, old woman though they made him look.

I began to recall the bits of gossip we had heard about his tour. It sounded as if, in his bumbling pedestrian way, he was going much further than Robert and I towards expressing personal opinions on the A 16 controversy. I was puzzled.

In Trafalgar Square there was a trace of fog which gave the lamps a halo and diffused the pools of light on the unmelted snow. I tried to persuade myself the weather was slightly warmer.

On my desk I found a note from my personal assistant saying that Mr Froggatt wanted to see me. I rang for her.

'I told him I thought you'd gone to a meeting with Dr Chubb,' she said.

This seemed to me highly satisfactory: it came naturally to her to conceal my movements, in particular my absences from my desk.

I enquired if she had rung Robert's flat to see if he was better. An alarmed look crossed her plump, pretty face. I was reminded once again of how rarely a strong desire to please went with a talent for office method. I telephoned for Froggatt. He came in carrying a sheaf of papers.

'I was hoping to see you before the end of the afternoon, sir.' He came slowly to the end of his first period, and began the second as if he were making a fresh start. 'It's about the little matter of the Forms 404a/45.'

I pretended not to know what they were by their number. Froggatt took it with perfect ease.

'Will it help you to recall them, sir, if I remind you that they're the forms you suggested might be printed on a roll?'

'Impossible I could have said that, Froggatt. You've invented it yourself.'

Froggatt shook his head, and a faint smile crossed his long slightly bloodhound-like face. 'Ah no, sir, I'm afraid not. Not after a lifetime in the service.'

He put his sheaf of papers on my desk and remained standing. I told him to sit down. The papers were the 404a/45 forms for special reports. Froggatt said:

'You asked me to investigate a certain delay there was in 404a/45s going out. I have investigated that delay, and incidentally confirmed the idea I had in the first instance.' He paused. 'I'm afraid the delay occurred because they were in the hands of Dr Chubb, awaiting his signature.'

I said 'Dr Chubb!' in great astonishment. 'Why didn't you sign them yourself?'

Sir Francis had authorised Froggatt to sign them in the absence of Robert and me, so we always let him sign them. We thought he liked to see his signature go out in multiplicate.

'When Dr Chubb came to help the division in the matter of the A 15 and the A 16,' said Froggatt, 'he thought it proper for the signing of 404a/45s to revert to the former practice, of being signed by someone at his own level.'

Neither Robert nor I knew Chubb had taken it out of Froggatt's hands.

'He's been signing them all for some weeks past.' Froggatt had dropped his subfusc playfulness. 'Some evenings he's been here till seven o'clock.'

Froggatt was clearly not the only one who liked seeing his signature go out in multiplicate. To save him seeing my amusement I sent him away.

I was interested as well as amused by Chubb's latest manoeuvre. I did not see how or why it could reasonably be stopped. On the other hand, I saw no reason why he should not pay for it. With Froggatt's aid we might find him many many more documents on which to write his glorious name, and have him staying at the office till eight o'clock every night of the week to do it. Perhaps it might encourage him to go away on the rest of his tour.

CHAPTER V

ANOTHER MORNING BEFORE THE OFFICE

I t was a dark morning, and I was rather late setting out for the office. When I came up the street I found Myrtle standing on the pavement outside the entrance.

'Darling, what on earth?' I began, and then saw her face more closely. She was desperately unhappy.

'I was waiting to see you.'

I put my arms round her. She looked up at me, her eyes wide and her features still.

'I've told him.'

'When?'

'Last night.'

'How did he take it?'

'Terribly.'

She turned her head away, and leaned against me as if she were exhausted.

I said: 'We can't stand here in the cold.' And I led her along. Instead of going into my office-building, I took her round the square towards a café facing the Houses of Parliament. From time to time I glanced at her, but she was silent. Her cheeks, just below the eyes, were bright and puffy from weeping.

'You'd better have some hot coffee.'

'I've had some.'

'Already?'

Myrtle turned to me with deep reproach. 'We've been up all night.'

I refrained from expostulating. We had come to the café, and I took her in. It was a bare slightly steamy room, with men sitting in their overcoats at marble-topped tables. Through the

window, we could see between trays of cakes and rolls the
shadows of vehicles moving towards Westminster Bridge.

I said: 'What decisions did you come to?'

Myrtle's shoulders relaxed and she sighed helplessly. 'We
didn't decide anything.'

'Will he agree to a divorce?'

She did not reply.

A waitress came to our table, picked up the cruet, whisked
the marble-top with a damp cloth, and set two cups of coffee
before us. The coffee smelt good. Myrtle stretched her hand
out shakily. I offered her a cigarette.

'How did it all happen?' I said.

'We've been staying in London for the last three days, while
Dennis looked for a job.'

'Has he found one?'

'Yes.' Myrtle spoke as if it were something I might have
expected had I been a bit more sensible. 'He's got a job at the
BBC.'

I said mildly: 'As a disc-jockey?'

'No. In the News Room, of course.'

One of Myrtle's friends had lent her a flat, and it was there
that the scene had taken place. On the evening of Haxby's
getting a job, they had gone out to dinner, supposedly to
celebrate. The celebration had fallen hopelessly flat.

'I tried to drink a lot, but it had no effect. He drank hardly
anything. It was terrible. We both knew.'

I stared at her.

'He said: "I suppose this is where you're going to tell me!"'

Myrtle looked at me with her head slightly lowered. 'He'd
known about us all the time.'

Immediately she said it I knew that it must be true and that
it must have been obvious. We had been moderately discreet: I
had never been near Myrtle's town or any of her friends whom
Haxby knew. Yet it was absurd to think that in London we
were isolated. The only thing that had isolated us was our own
desire not to be observed when we were doing something we
did not want people to see.

I said: 'Oh God.' The man had borne up well.

Myrtle said: 'I ought to have told him before.'

I did not say anything.

She burst out: 'I wish I hadn't told him now!'

I said: 'It had to be done, darling.' Across the table I took hold of her hand: it lay limply in mine.

To attain our own selfish desires we usually had to make someone else suffer, yet if we ourselves were not completely selfish the other person's suffering was bound to hurt us in return – I refrained from explaining this idea to Myrtle.

'I wish he weren't so helpless about it,' Myrtle said. 'If only he'd been angry and violent!'

I did not think this was very reasonable if she wanted him to give her a divorce.

She said: 'He started to weep.'

'What did you do?'

'I wept too.' She added: 'We made tea about six times.'

There was a pause. I signalled the waitress and ordered some more coffee. The number of people at the other tables had diminished. I noticed that the walls of the room were covered with a mosaic of dreary grey little stones. The coffee came, steaming.

I watched Myrtle. I wanted to know exactly how far she had got towards persuading Haxby to divorce her. I said:

'I suppose he realised what it would all lead to. I mean, that you wanted a divorce?'

'It took hours before I could get round to that. I don't know... There was so much emotion, I couldn't have believed it.' Myrtle glanced away. 'I suppose when you have been married to someone for years, it's like that. He knew all about it, and yet that didn't seem to make any difference. I had to tell him that we wanted to be married – he didn't seem to have grasped the fact.' She dropped her head, as if she were going to burst into tears. 'He told me I could come and live with you, if I wanted.'

I glanced at her, wondering if she was speaking the truth. I thought she was. I said:

'Does that mean he doesn't want to divorce you?'

'I don't think he believes it's possible.'

'But, darling – '

'He's been completely faithful to me all the time.'

Suddenly I realised there must still be a hope in Myrtle's mind that he would let her divorce him. It seemed to me incredible. Then it dawned on me that her alarm and distaste at being publicly pronounced the guilty party might well be the strongest emotion of all. The first miracle, of Haxby's not returning, had failed to happen. There was now a second miracle in view. I said:

'Darling, you can't hope that he'll let you divorce him. Anyway, I wouldn't ask him. Dammit, it wouldn't be fair.'

Myrtle said: 'You don't appear to care about me!'

'Of course I do.'

'If you did you couldn't accept it so easily.'

I was silent.

Myrtle's bitterness ebbed away. She looked at me affectionately. 'It's awfully hard for me, darling. I can't bear to think of people saying...' She did not finish the sentence. Her eyes filled with tears. 'I don't know how I could ever tell my father. The poor old man, it would break his heart.'

I was at a loss before an entirely new line. This was the first time her father had come into it. Myrtle and Haxby lived in his house, and he was quite fond of Haxby. He was a kindly, affectionate and, I thought, rather sly old man.

I said tritely: 'But he wants you to be happy.' I did not really believe it would break his heart.

'Yes,' said Myrtle, in a non-committal tone.

'I'm sure he does.'

'He's so dependent on me.' It was Myrtle's belief that her father loved her more than he loved her brother and her sister.

I felt that we were getting too far away from the point.

'One can't just leave people so easily,' Myrtle said.

Nevertheless her tone made me think she was recovering a little of her strength of purpose.

'You won't be seeing any less of your father,' I said. 'It's Dennis that you'll have to leave.' I took hold of her hand. 'I want you, too, darling, and you can't have both of us.'

Her fingers tightened in mine. Suddenly she burst out: 'Oh God!' I could see she had collapsed into great unhappiness again.

'What is it?'

'You don't realise what you're asking.' She paused in such a way that I was bound to say 'What?'

With great emotion Myrtle replied:

'*He says he can't live without me.*'

I looked down at my empty cup. By instinct I recognised something really menacing. It was something I could not say myself. It would have weighed with most women. It had weighed with Myrtle.

Myrtle was looking at me.

I shook my head and was silent.

At that moment we heard the clanging of a bell outside. It was a fire-engine going past. Everyone in the café sat up. We saw a dim flash of red through the window, and a waitress near the door ran out into the street to watch. I allowed the diversion to distract us altogether. I did not want to go on with the scene. I could see only danger in discussing who could live without whom. I shifted in my chair and said:

'I really must go to the office, darling.'

Myrtle quietly put on her gloves. I called the waitress and paid the bill. We walked out into the street. The grey sky was lit by a faint sunny gleam. We passed men shovelling snow from the gutters. Big Ben began to chime quarter to eleven. At the bottom of Whitehall we paused and arranged to meet again at lunchtime. I found Myrtle a taxi and she went away.

CHAPTER VI

CONFRONTATION AT NIGHT

On the following day Myrtle went home, leaving Haxby in lodgings in London. Nothing was settled about the divorce. At the weekend she returned to stay with me.

Saturday was Julia's birthday and we were invited to dine at her flat. Myrtle decided to try and cheer herself up with a tot of whisky before we set out. She had some success, and when she met my landlady on the stairs she gave her an absurdly over-cordial, smirking 'Good evening, Mrs Burdup.'

Mrs Burdup addressed me. She had me on the hip. And she said: 'I was just coming up to tell you the boiler's broken down.' She looked me in the eye. 'So there won't be any hot water for baths tonight.'

It was quite false. She knew that I knew it was false. I did not say anything because I had been given a glimpse into the depths of her nature – her meanness was stronger than her ladylikeness.

When we were outside Myrtle said: 'Where's her husband? She doesn't look like a widow to me.'

'Left her on the wedding-night, I should think.'

'I wonder if he'll turn up again.'

I felt for Burdup. I thought he would only turn up again if he were insane. While I was thinking, Myrtle stopped a taxi. 'It's so cold,' she explained. And as she leaned her head on my shoulder inside the taxi, she said: 'If the snow doesn't go soon, I think I shall die.'

Myrtle's spirits rose when she found Julia's flat was warm. The set of pale green rooms were the warmest we had been in for weeks. Myrtle walked through them with delight. Julia followed her.

'It's very important to have a flat that's got really good

central-heating,' Julia said. Behind Myrtle's back she gave me a bright-eyed, knowing grin: 'It couldn't be more important.'

We went into the room where Julia had first entertained me. It looked different. I glanced round at the glossy paint, the satinwood writing-desk, the elegant small tables. There were flowers everywhere: I distinctly remembered that on the previous occasion there had been none. Robert was not the kind of man who gave women flowers. There were daffodils, roses, lilac. The girls were admiring each other's dresses – Julia's was black and she had two brilliant clips at the neck.

'Robert's given me these,' she was saying. She took the clips off, for Myrtle to see. I thought of the yellow sapphire.

'Robert has decided we're going to drink champagne in place of cocktails. He's going to start a new fashion.'

'Lovely,' said Myrtle, breathlessly.

More of Robert, I thought. Julia looked carefree and gay. It suddenly crossed my mind that they had chosen this evening to tell us they were going to get married.

Just then Robert arrived. He came into the room with a proprietorial air. He was wearing a beautiful new suit and a lustrous grey tie. Julia put her arm round his neck and led him to the ice-bucket. He opened one of the bottles of champagne and the party began.

I doubt if Julia was outstanding as a cook, but under the influence of champagne we thought she had made an excellent dinner. We ate with pleasure and gusto. The candle-light glowed on Julia's face and Myrtle's. The walls seemed further away and less green. The radiators poured out their warmth. We began to feel intimate, easy, united. Outside, there was cold and snow and hurrying disinterested people in the streets. Inside, everything was transformed. I thought we must all get married and go on having dinner-parties like this.

While Julia had gone out to make the coffee Myrtle put her hand softly in my lap. We looked into each other's eyes. Left to himself Robert poured the remainder of the champagne into his own glass and drank it. Julia brought in a tray with coffee-cups – as she leaned forward the candle-light glowed down her bosom. The smell of coffee wafted across to me.

'Isn't this wonderful!' I said.

And Julia, seeing me engaged with Myrtle, stood beside Robert and ran her fingers through his hair. We were all alight with amorousness.

At this moment we heard the click of a door. It was the front-door of the flat. Someone was coming in. We turned.

The dining-room door opened, a man looked in, as if by accident, and disappeared again.

We knew at once that it was Wladislaw.'

Neither Robert, Myrtle nor I could say anything. Julia called after him and ran out of the room. We stood up. From down the corridor came voices, Julia's harsh, the man's strong and nasal.

Julia was saying: 'I told you not to come back.'

'I didn't know you were here.'

'That's no excuse.'

'It's not supposed to be an excuse.'

'What have you come for?'

'To get some things from my room.'

We stopped listening for a moment. Robert said something, but I forget what it was. I no doubt replied. Our conversation was a formality.

We heard Wladislaw saying more loudly: 'I wish to speak with him.' Julia replied in a low voice that we could not catch. We heard them coming towards us. Julia appeared in the doorway, and said: 'Wladislaw wants to meet you. I'm going to introduce him.'

We saw Wladislaw standing behind her. Julia did not move. He stretched out his hand towards us but it was impossible for him to pass her in the doorway. He was not quite as tall as Julia but he was unusually broad.

'I beg your pardon,' he said politely, and stepped forward, so that he and Julia were wedged.

'Fool!' Julia whispered.

'I must apologise,' said Wladislaw to us, as if he were apologising for Julia. He turned to Julia to present him: 'Please.'

Julia introduced us in turn, and he shook hands. He was a very powerfully-built man, with a big torso and rather short legs. His neck was as wide as his face, and his muscles seemed to fill out his clothes. He looked about forty-five years old. He had close-cropped dark hair and small piercing grey eyes. By his face we knew immediately what Julia had not seen fit to tell us – that he was a highly intelligent man.

'I'm glad of this opportunity to meet you,' he said to Robert as he shook hands. He spoke English easily with a good accent. Then he turned to Julia. 'I should like coffee, please.'

There were only four chairs. We all filed along the corridor to the living-room, Wladislaw firmly and politely waiting till the last. Myrtle took hold of my hand and sat down beside me on the sofa. Robert and Wladislaw sat in armchairs facing each other, Robert in the armchair beside the telephone, Wladislaw near the piano – behind his head I noticed the photograph of the woman with ostrich plumes in her hair.

Julia gave us our coffee. Her face was tense and her eyes glittered. Provocatively she sat down on the arm of Robert's chair.

Wladislaw offered her his chair. She refused.

'Perhaps Mrs Haxby would like a cigarette,' he said. With a nervous irritated gesture, Julia handed Myrtle a box.

'I don't smoke, myself,' Wladislaw said to Myrtle. 'You know?'

Suddenly Julia turned to Robert and took hold of his arm. She said:

'Wladislaw hasn't been living here!'

There was silence.

'That is correct,' said Wladislaw.

'Robert will believe it without your corroboration.'

'Such a statement is better when corroborated.'

'If it's true it doesn't need corroboration.'

'No. People don't necessarily believe such a statement because it's true. They believe because it's corroborated.' He paused. 'Corroboration is the decisive factor.'

'Damn corroboration!' Julia was having difficulty in controlling herself. 'And don't stare at me like Svengali!'

Wladislaw jumped up from his chair.

'You're not tall enough!' Julia said.

Wladislaw sat down again.

Julia sipped her coffee triumphantly.

'I didn't know Svengali was tall,' said Myrtle. She laughed. 'I know he had a big black beard.'

I squeezed her hand to make her be quiet.

Robert said authoritatively: 'I should have thought it was a matter of presence, rather than of height or of beard.'

'Thank you,' said Wladislaw. 'That's what I thowt.' It was the first word I had heard him seriously mispronounce.

'Would you like a glass of champagne?' Myrtle said to him. I had a strong suspicion she found him attractive.

Wladislaw glanced at Julia. 'I would like some brandy.' He had noticed four balloon glasses standing on the writing-desk.

Julia had to go and fetch another glass. She poured out brandies for all of us, and handed them round. While she was doing it, Wladislaw addressed himself to Robert.

'I wish to explain why I came here tonight.'

Julia stopped to look at him. 'You didn't come to collect something?'

'Yes. That was true. I came also because I was hoping to find *him* here.' He drank a little brandy, put down the glass, and sat with his fists resting on his massive thighs. Julia, instead of sitting down, stood by the fireplace, which was glowing with an electric imitation coal-fire.

'I wanted to meet you,' Wladislaw said to Robert. 'I told Julia it's very important.' He paused. 'I asked her to arrange, but she refused.'

'Of course I refused!' Julia's eyes suddenly flashed with amusement. 'As I knew he was proposing to tell you I'm either a dipsomaniac or a nymphomaniac.'

'That's not true!' Wladislaw turned to her with startling violence.

'Of course it is!' Julia laughed at him openly. She sipped her brandy and her hair fell forward over her cheeks.

'That's not true!' His voice was louder.

Robert intervened. 'What did you want to say to me?'

Wladislaw turned back to Robert. 'I will tell you.' He was startlingly polite again. I wondered if he had been drinking before he came in. For several moments he looked at Robert with a fixed expression. He said: 'I believe you wish to make Julia happy.'

347

Robert nodded his head gravely and did not speak. He gave the impression that the occasion was too grave for speech.

Wladislaw said: 'It's very difficult. You know?'

Robert watched him with bright eyes.

'She is very difficult woman to understand,' Wladislaw said. 'You know?'

'I do know.'

Wladislaw paused. He was perfectly sober. He gave Robert a particularly piercing look:

'It's only one who understands her who can make her happy.'

I could tell it was his great point. He must have made it many times before. Instantly Julia cried:

'I deny that!'

Robert and Wladislaw glanced at each other. Robert said with enormous weight:

'I agree with you.'

Wladislaw was deeply impressed.

'I don't know,' said Robert, 'if anyone can make her permanently happy.' He shook his head, as God might while thinking of the human race.

'I have tried to understand her,' Wladislaw said.

'I try to use such insight as I have,' said Robert.

'I can tell you have insight,' said Wladislaw, looking into his eyes unwaveringly. 'I can judge a man's face.'

There was an impressive pause. Julia said with sudden amusement: 'I can't see where you two go from there.'

Wladislaw said to Robert with powerful logic:

'Can you make her happy temporarily?

Robert of course did not reply.

'I am a simple man, as you see. And so I ask you, can you offer the things she needs?' Wladislaw made a sweeping gesture with his hand. 'I bowt this flat, these flowers, these beautiful things.' He paused. 'But that's not all, to make her happy. You know?'

Julia said: 'He does know,' and drained her glass.

Wladislaw looked at her. 'You see,' he said. 'She drinks too much.'

'What did I tell you?' said Julia to Robert.

'When I am not here,' Wladislaw said, 'she drinks too much. When I am not here she sees too many men.' He was watching her all the time.

'Dipso *and* nympho!' Julia laughed gleefully. She poured herself some more brandy.

'Too many men are bad for her,' Wladislaw said loudly. He stood up.

Julia said: 'Dear Wladislaw, when will you understand I'm not the Penelope type?' She appealed to Robert: 'Can't you explain to him?'

Wladislaw said: 'No, she is not the Penelope type.'

We all turned to Julia. I cannot say that she looked like Penelope. Wladislaw said:

'She needs a man who will look after her all the time. She needs a man who will be always vigilant.' He spoke with great emotion, his eyes fixed on her fascinatedly. 'She needs a nurse. I am that man.'

'You, a nurse?' said Julia. 'You'd be dismissed the first day.'

Wladislaw was angered. 'Don't say that!'

'I won't listen to you saying you want to nurse me. I know what you want.'

'Don't provoke me! I am trying to be fair to you.'

'Fair to me!' A reddish colour rose up in Julia's neck. 'You call that fair?'

Wladislaw suddenly faced her. When he stood close to her his eyes looked hotter. 'For three years I have tried to understand your weakness and your foolishness. You know what I have to bear. You know how many times I have to forgive you – '

'I didn't ask you to forgive me!'

'You know how many lovers – '

'Stop!' Julia shouted.

'I will go on.'

'Go on, then!'

'He should know what you are like!'

'I've told him everything!'

'You are lying!'

Julia flung her brandy into his face.

For a moment Wladislaw was blinded. Then as if he had not

noticed it he went nearer to Julia. His face was close to hers. His voice trumpeted violently.

'You know what you will become if I am not here to look after you? You will be in a home for drunkards! You will be on the streets!'

Julia moved her face closer to his. 'But not *yet*!' She suddenly broke into high-pitched laughter. 'You talk as if it were all going to happen *tomorrow*!'

Wladislaw seized her. Passionate rage seemed to have brought to them the pitch of incandescence. Myrtle cried out with alarm.

Julia heard Myrtle. She tried to wrench herself free from Wladislaw. 'Stop him!'

Instantly we all jumped to our feet. There was a moment's silence. And there was another strange noise – from Robert. He was standing motionless.

'Sorry,' he said. 'Pins and needles in my leg.'

Wladislaw let go Julia. He went to Robert to support him. The rest of us watched. Even months afterwards I found it impossible to convince Myrtle and Julia that Robert was not shamming. Robert stamped his foot a few times. Wladislaw solicitously offered him brandy.

'Thank you,' said Robert. 'I'm all right.' He limped into the middle of the group. He paused. 'I think it's time we went home.'

Wladislaw was looking at Julia. He wiped the back of his hand across his face.

'I'm not staying here,' Julia said. 'Robert, take me with you!'

'Do you mean that?' Wladislaw was staring at her with desire. He could not conceal it.

'I'm not staying here!' Julia was watching him, her eyes brilliant.

We were all silent.

'Robert!' Julia put her hand on Robert's arm. 'Please, take me away from here now!'

Wladislaw was watching him. Gravely Robert nodded.

That night Julia stayed in Robert's flat.

CHAPTER VII

'SHALL I MARRY HER?'

Julia stayed only one night in Robert's flat. In the early
hours of the morning Wladislaw rang her up to apologise
for making a scene and to say that he was moving out of her
flat never to return. Although Julia did not believe a word of it,
Robert persuaded her to go home again.

Myrtle said to me: 'Darling, why doesn't Robert let Julia
stay in his flat?'

It was a difficult question to answer. Robert was not
troubled by the interventions of a Mrs Burdup, which Myrtle
could understand; nor was he short of money, as I was. I told
Myrtle I did not know, this being simpler than trying to
explain Robert's over-riding dislike of being given no option.

Myrtle said nothing more. She seemed altogether subdued
since the party, chastened and discouraged. I fancied she
recollected it as an unpleasing revelation for which I was
responsible.

Robert seemed unperturbed. From instinct I assumed that
he must really have made up his mind what he was going to
do. He watched the events that followed with lively absorbed
interest.

The first thing was a long letter from Wladislaw to Julia,
withdrawing his love and offering in its place his friendship.

'What does Julia think of that?' I asked.

'I'm afraid she regards it quite simply as another way of
trying to get into bed with her.'

'It is,' I said.

'It is,' said Robert.

Out of friendship Wladislaw proposed to go on paying the
rent of Julia's flat till the end of the month. It was at this point

that Robert discovered a fact which Julia, for all her worldliness and determination, had never got clear. Wladislaw was quite rich. He was not a White refugee. His family had since long before the war had business connections in England. Wladislaw had been to an English public-school — that was why he spoke the language so well. And he now made a substantial income in the City.

The letter ended with an expression of Wladislaw's great respect for Robert and desire to meet him again.

Robert met him one lunch-time and came back to report on it. Wladislaw was most anxious to prove that his feeling for Julia was no more than friendship. To that end he wanted to do something to help Julia, in particular to get her away from her present circle of friends whom he felt were responsible for her moral decline. He proposed to finance her going up to Cambridge to read for a degree.

I was staggered by the idea of planting Julia among seven thousand young men.

'Hasn't he thought of that?' I said.

Robert shook his head. 'He's thinking of her education.'

'And Julia?'

'She's thought of the fact to which you refer.' He smiled: 'She wouldn't go, anyway.'

Wladislaw continued to press the claims of his friendship in other different forms. Unhappily it appeared that also he was employing private detectives to watch Julia's flat. Somehow it did not remind either Robert or me of the jealousy we had felt over The Headlamps and My Last One. Wladislaw gave us a glimpse of a passion more sustained, more obsessive and more active than anything we had ever felt.

One morning Robert came into my office shortly after I had arrived. His face was pale, and his eyes were sparkling with what I thought was suppressed amusement.

To my surprise he began asking me if I had heard from Myrtle. I had received a short unsatisfactory note. Robert stood in his overcoat by the window, as if he were interested in looking through the opaque windows into the empty well of the building. I could not tell if he was listening.

Suddenly he came and sat on the corner of my desk. He took

out Myrtle's ivory cigarette-holder and lit a cigarette. Then he glanced at me.

'Look here,' he said. 'Reticent man though I am, I can't help telling you what happened last night. It was an incident simply made for you.'

I pulled out a drawer and put my feet up.

'I was at Julia's,' Robert said. 'We'd been drinking after dinner. It was about half past eleven and we'd just got to bed. In fact I'd just' – he found it impossible to say what he had just, and went on – 'when the telephone beside the bed rang. Julia picked it up, and Wladislaw's voice said resonantly: "Don't do it, Julia! Don't do it!"'

Robert took off his overcoat, and pulled up a chair beside mine. His amusement died away. After a few minutes I realised that his mood had changed to completely serious. He smoked in silence, with his head bent. I waited for him to speak to me.

At last he said: 'Ought I to marry this girl?'

I stared at him and could find no reply.

'I expect you realise I've been pretty near to it,' he said.

I nodded.

'She's closer than you think to my line.'

'I know that.'

I saw him look at me with interest. His line was The Headlamps – a lost soul, who made him suffer for loving her. I saw Julia in the same rôle. It made no difference that The Headlamps slept with nobody and Julia with everybody. The line, as he called it, could be the same. It could be the same in his loving her, and the same in his having to suffer for it.

He said: 'It's clear that she needs me.' He paused. 'She needs me more than I need her.'

I moved my feet and the drawer creaked just as he said something else. It sounded like 'That's the trouble' but I did not catch it.

CHAPTER VIII

A TOOTHY MACHIAVELLI

D r Chubb had still not left London for the second half of his
industrial tour. I grew steadily more puzzled.

We had tried to check the stories about his indiscreet
expressions of opinion on his first tour. They were absurdly
conflicting – some people said he had told them they could go
on making A 15s indefinitely; others, equally trustworthy, that
he had hinted at something new coming along which would
oust the A 15 within a year.

'Do you think he's trying to prove his impartiality?' said
Robert.

I took the rumours more seriously. Chubb might
conceivably have suspected his task was designed by Robert
for the dual purpose of getting him out of the way and putting
him in a position to make a blunder. But there was no reason
why he should go in for fantastic behaviour.

From time to time I passed Chubb going down the corridor
to wash his hands. He invariably complained that office-work
was preventing him from travelling.

One evening Froggatt had been consulting me just before it
was time to go home. I was sitting tiredly at my desk, and I
tried to cheer Froggatt and myself by saying the day's work
was over.

'It may be for you,' said Froggatt: 'I've no doubt it is.
Unfortunately I am not in that happy position.' The
bloodhound-like lines below his eyes sagged. He waited for me
to ask why, and then said: 'I now have to look forward to
another hour's consultation with Dr Chubb.' He saw my
astonishment. 'Yes, sir. It's becoming quite a regular feature.'

I straightened up. 'Don't go, for a moment.'

Froggatt waited respectfully. He said: 'I hope you don't think I'm offering a complaint. These consultations are necessary, I can assure you. And Dr Chubb is busy throughout the day.' He gave me a peculiar half-smile. 'He knows that he can always send for me when I'm just about to go home.'

It was not difficult to find out what was happening. Dr Chubb felt it was only proper that all the duties as well as document-signing, which Robert and I had delegated to Froggatt – for want of time, of course – should go to him, Chubb.

'I'm sure it's a great relief to me that they should.' Froggatt paused. 'However, at the moment Dr Chubb does not feel confident to carry them out independentli. He discusses them all with me before he makes his decisions. I'm afraid it takes up more time than ever, that way.'

Robert was extremely adept at delegation, I was practising it assiduously, and we both had great confidence in Froggatt. Chubb had been quick in the uptake.

'In addition to this,' Froggatt continued, 'Dr Chubb has undertaken various other responsibilities. For example, he suggested to D.O.R.R.S. that he should attend the fortnightly conferences with Mr Irskine on staff matters.'

'Staff?' It was too much. 'Good God!'

'Certainly,' said Froggatt. 'I'm busy preparing a detailed report on the present staffing position for Dr Chubb at this moment.'

As soon as Froggatt left me, I went to Robert's office.

Robert was sitting at his desk, writing a memorandum to Sir Francis.

I sat down and waited till he had finished. He stood up. 'Ready?' He thought we were going home.

I shook my head. He sat on the edge of the table while I told him about Chubb's latest gambit. He listened, and then went to his telephone and rang up Chubb.

'Lunn tells me you'd like to see me,' he said. 'Would you come in now?'

A few moments later Chubb came in looking a trifle flustered. 'I did want to see you about certain matters.' He cast a hare-eyed look in my direction. 'But I don't recall mentioning it to Lunn.'

Robert smiled at him genially.

After a long preamble, Chubb settled down to work on something that was of no great importance and on which Froggatt could perfectly well have advised him. Robert listened patiently. When it was ending, Robert began to lead him round to the new and onerous activities that kept him from his travels.

Chubb looked worried. Comparing our division with the department from which he had come, Chubb felt that our administration and execution left much for him at least to desire.

'There's a certain lack of integration, if you know what I mean,' he said. 'Largely, I think, because it lacks a person whose responsibility it is to be responsible for that integration.'

I thought, somewhat irrelevantly: 'There's a lack of integration about what you say to the firms about the A 15 and the A 16, not to mention your efforts to get a better job.'

'That's most interesting,' said Robert, considerately. 'Perhaps we might discuss it some evening at greater length. Perhaps you'd put down a few points on paper.'

Chubb was encouraged. He went on to discuss staff. His worried look returned. We heard about the long hours he was forced to work, about the vast amount of detail in which a highly detailed report on the A 16 position had involved him, and above all about the responsibility. His cheeks grew ruddier and his eyes more anxious-looking.

'And I don't care to think of the position in due course,' he ended up.

'In due course?' Robert said, mildly.

Chubb could not resist saying, with nervous hesitation, 'I hear from Lunn that the department will not be able to count on your services for an indefinite period.' He stammered slightly. 'I don't know if I've understood the position correctly.' And he looked at Robert. 'I heard you were going to leave this place.'

The longer he went on looking at Robert, the more hare-eyed he became, because Robert said nothing at all.

CHAPTER IX

THE JAPANESE EMPEROR

A couple of days later James Irskine asked me to give him a game of squash. I wondered what was in the wind this time, and felt bored by the prospect of discussing it with him. The conversation began as soon as the game was over. The changing-room was quite empty, and I thought if he wanted to talk about A 15s he could. I sat down on a bench against the wall and began putting my racquet in its press. James did not sit down. He stripped, picked up a towel, and to my surprise appeared to be making for the showers. It was only a feint – he sat down beside me and said:

'How are you getting on with Chubb?' He bent his tall handsome head as if he were studying his toes.

I wondered if James could have been hearing the gossip we had heard. I said I had not seen much of Chubb.

'More than you expected.' He got a note of irony into his tone.

I said: 'He's got to go on tour soon. He's behind.'

'He's made a damned nuisance of himself here.'

I hesitated, and then realised James could not be referring to the rumours. The fact was that Chubb had been attempting to cultivate James's favour. It was an impossible task. James had no favour. On the other hand James was capable of making an alliance, and I had suspected Chubb was not doing badly. Somehow they had avoided a head-on collision over correct procedure.

I beckoned one of the attendants to bring us drinks.

'On the other hand,' James said, 'he's not a fool.' He glanced at me. 'He's just going to put in a report on staffing for Old Frank's reorganisation committee. It's not bad.'

357

As Chubb had discussed his report daily with James before putting it in, the opinion came to me as no surprise.

'I've got the draft, if you'd like to have a look at it.' James stood up and took down his jacket from the hook. 'Here it is.' He gave me two folded sheets of foolscap, tied his towel round his waist and went to the showers.

I read Chubb's report. It was not bad.

I cannot pretend that the methods of Robert and me were not a trifle rough-and-ready. Nobody could have done our job better than Robert: the Permanent Secretary knew it, Sir Francis knew it, everybody knew it. But it could have been done more properly. There is not the slightest doubt that had Robert and I been giving it our entire attention, we might have done it slightly differently. This was what Chubb knew.

So when I say Chubb's report was not bad, I mean that it made some just points. Chubb, with his own particular brand of departmental illiteracy, talked about the need for greater integration. What he meant was that it would have been proper for a man in Robert's position to busy himself continually with rather more things than Robert found time for, and that his instinct for propriety told him this was a serious defect in the organisation.

You may ask – 'If the job was being done as well as it could be done, what does it matter about its being done properly?' I can see that you are not a professional civil servant like Dr Chubb or James Irskine.

Chubb had a remedy for the defect. It was to create a post for a full-time senior person, whom Robert, as long as he remained, could advise, and who, when Robert left, would take over all responsibility. And if you think Chubb gave the faintest hint of who would be the most suitable man for this post, you have not begun to understand men of affairs.

James came back from the showers after an unusually short lapse of time.

'What do you think of it?'

'I'm interested.'

James put his foot on the bench beside me and dried his calf. It was clear to me that he would support Chubb's proposal, not because he thought anything of Chubb, not because he thought he would get the job – his next promotion would be to another department altogether. James would support it because it appealed to his clear machine-like concept of how things ought to be run.

I wondered whether the moment had come to tell James that Chubb was improperly committing himself to public, though contradictory, opinions on the A 16. I decided not.

I handed the papers back to James. Then I went to the showers thinking that Robert, if he did not want to find himself being placed on a handsome stately shelf, had got to turn his mind to office intrigue.

When the situation was presented to him Robert was of the same opinion. There was a meeting about staff a couple of days later, and Robert saw fit to attend. He came back with sparkling eyes. The office was going to run on its present lines till Robert left. Sir Francis, hypnotised by Robert's warnings of all sorts of contingencies, had put down Chubb's plan for the time being. There was nothing, as Robert knew, more liable to hypnotise Sir Francis than contingencies. I felt almost sorry for Chubb, a moderately sensible man being made to look stupid.

This scene was taking place in Robert's office. He took down his overcoat from the hat-stand, and bundled it on with great determination. I had recently seen him roused to activity by his private affairs: it was a long time since I had seen him roused over his career in the government service. I sensed that under his mischievous sparkle there was real anger.

'I'm damned if I'll be relegated,' Robert said, 'like a mediaeval Japanese emperor. I refuse to be the Late-Emperor to the Present-Emperor of Chubb.'

I reflected that there was no respite for a man of affairs.

'I told Old Frank I don't intend to go until I've seen the division though its main post-war problems. That gave them something to think about.' Robert paused. 'After that I hope there won't be a job for anybody. Chubb's only got five years to go.'

I picked up my hat from the table and put it on. We went down the corridor together. Chubb's office was in darkness. Robert cocked his thumb at the door.

'You can take it he'll be setting off on the second half of his tour next week at the latest.'

Robert sometimes observed to me that like women and elephants he never forgot. I knew that he would not forget Chubb. What was he going to do? Like most men of action Robert acted not by plan but by instinct. Chubb's downfall was at the back of his mind. Something would happen by chance. Instinct would tell him this was the moment. Then he would act.

CHAPTER X

IN A PUBLIC-HOUSE

There was a long silence from Myrtle. I thought it was time I asked Robert's advice.

'I'm getting nowhere.'

Robert said: 'I'm afraid you lack the touch for this kind of situation.'

I could see that as usual my asking for advice was merely going to produce discouraging home-truths about myself. Robert surveyed me with detachment.

'You don't give the air of suffering,' he said.

'I hope I don't,' I said, huffily. 'It's repellent.'

'It's very useful sometimes.'

'Hypocrite!'

Robert's lips tightened. 'Perfectly genuine.'

'There's no need to parade about in sackcloth and ashes.'

'It's not a bad thing. It makes people realise you're serious. People are very simple.'

He was talking sense – I disliked it.

'I believe in a stiff upper lip,' I said. You may think it a remarkable statement: it was true none the less.

Robert shrugged his shoulders. I could not help being somewhat borne down by logic. At last I said:

'What do you propose I should do?'

'Give an air of suffering.'

'How?'

'Don't ask me.'

I thought it over. It was an intolerable prospect. I said:

'I simply can't say I can't live without her.'

Robert said impatiently: 'Why not?'

'If moral weakness didn't blind you, you'd see it was

because it isn't the truth.' I looked at him. 'My Last One taught me that finally. I can't die for love.'

Robert put on a grave hollow tone. 'There are deeper truths than mere verbal statements.'

'Well,' I said, after thinking it over, 'if I do say it, I won't stay up all night to do it.'

'Please yourself,' said Robert.

'None of it pleases me at all!'

Robert shrugged his shoulders again. The conversation lapsed, but he was worried on my behalf. His apprehensions were more reliable than mine. I began to feel much more worried myself.

Next time Myrtle came up to London she said she had only time for a drink with me. Though all night was too long for showing an air of suffering, I was afraid a couple of hours might be too short. We arranged to meet in Piccadilly Circus and I arrived first. There was some sign of the weather changing, a new rawness and a faint humid warmth that made one dream of a thaw. All the same it was cold, and I began to stamp my feet and pace briskly to and fro. I realised I was making a mistake right at the start. A man who is suffering does not stamp his feet and flap his arms. He just lets himself freeze. I stopped immediately, and was feeling miserably cold when a taxi drew up and Myrtle got out.

I kissed her half-heartedly.

'Where are we going, darling?' she said.

I shook my head. 'I don't know.'

This was quite new to Myrtle. I always tried to have some convenient or attractive plan. She looked at me with surprise and interest. I was distinctly encouraged.

We began to walk along Piccadilly. It was evening, and the lights were just being switched off in the shop-windows.

'Any pub will do,' I said, taking care not to notice those we were passing though they were all familiar to me.

'Yes, darling,' said Myrtle in a subdued and puzzled tone.

I decided I was probably on the right lines. I had thought it over very carefully.

When I gave Myrtle the impression that I did not care which public-house we went to and did not even notice those we were passing, she knew at once that I had something on my mind. A horrifying corollary struck me – had she throughout all my years of observation, reflection and comment on this and that, thought I had nothing on my mind? I nearly stepped under a taxi.

'Darling!' Myrtle pulled me back.

I looked at her mutely.

'I think there's a pub up there,' she said. I signified that I might be led to it.

The public-house had not been open long, and it was almost empty. It was cold and rather cheerless. We were faced with a narrow alley and a line of tall uncomfortable wooden stools. We sat down. The floor was made of plain boards. I realised that Myrtle had brought me into the public bar.

In the ordinary way I should have moved her over to the saloon in fifteen seconds. That would have been fatal. I sat quite still and asked her distantly what she would like to drink. I looked down at the brown polished deal of the bar-top.

The drinks were put before us, and I realised that I had now got to begin. What was I to say? Something told me that I had got a chance of impressing her in a different way. The atmosphere was right. Now was the time when I must fight for her, and fight for her after a fashion she understood – that is to say not my own fashion but hers. What must I say?

'I can't live without you.'

My heart sank.

What then?

I drew in my breath slowly and then gave a long loud sigh.

'I'm terribly unhappy,' I said.

Myrtle looked at me. I think she saw that I was. Tears came up into her eyes.

If only I could have said 'I can't live without you!' I let my chin rest on my neck-tie and was silent.

We were quite alone on our side of the bar. There were people on the saloon side, but it was difficult to see them, because above the counter there was a structure consisting of a set of small windows, like ventilators, at head-height. You addressed the barman obliquely through the windows: below them you had a view, across the bar, of the chests and diaphragms of people in the saloon, just as presumably they had a view of yours. It was not the sort of view one would choose. I felt slightly sick with emotion. After a long time I said: 'This waiting is getting me down.'

Myrtle made some consoling remark.

I had an idea – I was certain I must state my case in familiar language. I simply must say things she could recognise. I let several minutes elapse and then made myself say: 'I want to be certain of you.'

Myrtle took hold of my hand, warmly. 'I know, darling,' she said.

The conversation was satisfactorily started. The remarkable thing was the length of time between the individual remarks. It seemed to be taking hours. But then how can one take an impressive length of time to say 'I am suffering'? I thought of saying it in other languages. 'Que je souffre!' – or would it be more French to say 'Qu'on souffre!'? Recollecting scenes from Dostoievsky, I thought that if only I knew the language, Russian would be just the ticket for me.

In the meantime, though I imagined I was being successful, I could not help feeling ashamed of myself. All my remarks were true, but they sounded deplorably pedestrian. Anybody could have said what I was saying. That was the point of it, but it made it no more appealing. To my way of thinking what made conversation worth having, what made any human activity worth doing, was the streak in it of originality, of creative art. But what of a streak in it of originality, of creative art, when conveying to a woman that you love her and want her to marry you? Ruinous! Pedestrian though my speeches were, pedestrian they had got to stay.

'I can't sleep.'

That was quite a good speech as well as true. 'Nor can I,' said Myrtle, but I knew I had gained through getting it in first.

It took me a long time to find the next one, and at the last minute I rejected it. 'I can't think of writing anything.' For me this meant great anguish, but I had a dreadful fear that Myrtle might feel it really to be all to the good. So I kept mum for another forty-five seconds – and if you try forty-five seconds by your watch you will find it a surprisingly long time.

I began to speculate on how many seconds had elapsed to ease the strain of preventing myself from saying something.

Suddenly I realised that Myrtle had spoken, had asked me something of transcending importance. She was looking at me with naif, shrewd, penetrating enquiry. She had said:

'Why do you want to marry me, darling?'

I had a choking sensation. I did not reply. More seconds passed, and a stream of reflections fled through my mind. Why did most men marry? Why had most of my friends married? Because they wanted a home, children, somebody to look after them, a regular mate – even the last was not the most important to a lot of them. They married so as to fit easily into society. Oh dear! I looked at Myrtle. Her round hazel eyes were fixed on me, with a serious, intent, trembling look.

It was the moment everything we had been saying had led up to: it was the moment I had come for. She was waiting to hear me say I could not live without her, waiting determinedly with deep emotion. I could not say it. With unexpected insight I knew it was not truthfulness that prevented me – I could have lied to her as most men would. It was pride. I would not bend my will an inch to hers, even to get something I wanted.

I muttered something incoherent. I felt I had the rest of my life in my hands. I really was suffering. And I could not help noticing how farcical it was.

I managed to say clearly what I had been muttering.

'Life seems utterly useless...'

It was as far as I could go. Was it far enough? I wondered. Oh, would it do?

There was a long pause. Myrtle put her hand on mine. She sighed. The critical moment had passed. Her fingers tightened. I looked up at her face. I was so uncertain of myself that I could not read anything in it.

'Darling,' she said.

That night, when I was at home in my flat, Robert rang me up.

'It's all right, old boy.'

'Is it? Are you really sure?'

'Myrtle rang me up immediately after she'd left you. She was genuinely alarmed. And upset.' Robert paused. 'She

wanted to know what she could do to restore you.'
  'What did you say?'
  'Marry you as soon as possible.'
  For a moment I could not speak.
  Robert's tone changed. 'What *did* you say to her?'

CHAPTER XI

LOVE AND RENT

The following Saturday afternoon I met Julia by chance walking along the Chelsea embankment. We were both alone.

It was a charming afternoon. The thaw had come at last. It seemed as if there was water rushing in all directions – the river was flooding, gutters and spouts were gurgling, and rivulets were everywhere trickling down tree-trunks, railings, lamp-posts and walls. The sky was low and opalescent, and in its milky fawn light the last remnants of snow on the roof-tops shone like newly-cut lead.

I was standing beside the railings, idly watching the sights of the river. It was very quiet. On the opposite bank all the cranes and derricks were motionless. There was a single string of lighters coming up from the Pool, with only one of the crew to be seen, sitting on a hatch peeling potatoes over a bucket. Sounds of voices made me notice a group of Sea-scouts, standing on a flight of stone steps, waiting to embark for the weekend. Then a police launch went by, with a small red lamp flashing on top of the cabin. I was just contemplating my present affairs and wondering if I might not have done better in a sea-faring career, when I heard light vigorous footsteps.

It was Julia. She was looking very pretty, swinging along in a smart grey flannel suit, a little dachshund running at her heels.

'I'm in tremendously high spirits,' she said. 'Today's my day of liberation!'

'Please translate that into my language, Julia dear.'

'Today the occupation comes to an end.' She grinned at me furtively: 'Wladislaw moves out of my life for good.'

'I'm delighted. Are you sure of it?'

'Certain.' She glanced at me. 'I suppose you know he gave up offering me his love – I refused to accept it, anyway. So he consoles himself with the offer of his friendship. It doesn't appear to need requiting in the same way.'

'Oh, doesn't it!' I cried.

'He says definitely not.' Julia's mouth curled ironically. 'As a friend he stops paying the rent of my flat. So you see...'

'Distinctly unfriendly, I call that.'

'He offered to, but I'm not going to put myself under any more obligations to him.'

'What does that mean?'

'I'm not going to let him pay my rent.'

'Then who is going to pay it?' The ungentlemanly, if sensible, question slipped out.

At that moment the little dog ran a few yards away from her, and Julia was able to ignore my question by calling to it. We began to stroll along together.

I computed that Julia, as secretary of her Anglo-Polish society, could pay about a quarter of her upkeep.

Suddenly Julia said: 'I'm going to tell you, Joe, I simply can't keep it to myself.' She paused, and her voice, though it sounded softer, was undisguisedly triumphant. 'Robert's going to pay it.'

I said warmly: 'I'm glad.'

Julia was watching me out of the corner of her eye. 'Are you really?' Suddenly she took hold of my hand. 'You know I've always felt you were my only ally, Joe.'

'The only one?'

'Everybody else has tried to prevent me marrying Robert.'

I was silent, because I knew there was a good deal of truth in what she said. All the women in Robert's acquaintance thought it would be utterly, unmitigatedly wrong for him to marry Julia, and most of the men were doubtful. I squeezed her hand.

'You've been sweet to me, Joe,' said Julia.

'At least,' I said, 'I haven't expressed moral disapproval of you.'

'You can't imagine how happy it's made me – that Robert's

going to do it.' She turned to look at me. 'You don't know what a relief it is to a woman, to feel she's being kept.'

'Really?' I said, thinking ruefully of Myrtle.

Julia went on, her voice becoming warmer and deeper with hope: 'I think Robert's bound to marry me now.'

I forgot my own preoccupations in surprise. Could she really think that?

Julia loosed my hand. 'I can't decide whether it's the best idea for us to live together – I mean, before we get married . . .'

'I simply couldn't tell you.'

Julia said, as if she were coming to the conclusion at the moment: 'I think I'll persuade him to move in straight away.' Her tone gave away that she had reached this conclusion long ago. 'Will you help me to persuade him?'

'I've never persuaded Robert to do anything, in my life.'

Julia looked at me disbelievingly.

I suddenly thought of Myrtle. I had never persuaded her to do much either. Robert and Myrtle were alike, in that what they were deciding to do always seemed mysterious and out-of-range. The activities of Julia's will and mine were somehow near the surface, of Robert's and Myrtle's deeply subterranean. No wonder Julia and I were the ones who got the worst of it.

'It's only possible to persuade Robert to do what he wants to do,' I said.

As usual, when I enunciated a truth about Robert's temperament, I was promptly denounced for it. Julia rounded on me.

'That's a confession of weakness!'

'Well!' I said, nonplussed.

'I can see now why you don't force Myrtle to marry you.'

'She can't bring herself to tell her father, because it will upset him,' I said. 'He's just had some kind of minor seizure . . .' I paused. 'All I can tell you,' I said, pulling myself together again, 'is that being strong doesn't happen to make the slightest difference.'

Julia checked herself, and became thoughtful. We walked along slowly. 'There must be something in what you say.' She glanced at me. 'I find it hard to understand. But you're never as wrong as all that.'

I bowed. 'Never let it be said I don't know how to accept a compliment.'

Julia's eyes sparkled with amusement. We had reached a bridge, and had to wait for the traffic. As we stood on the edge of the pavement, Julia said:

'I believe that at bottom Robert does want to marry me.' She paused. 'So you can go to work on persuading him.'

I looked at her. The soft opal light made her skin look clear and unlined. Her hair was brightly silky, and her eyes were shining. I should have liked to kiss her. She was happy.

'All right.' I held out my hand, and Julia took it.

'He's coming to dinner with me tonight, and I know he's having a drink with you first. Be my ally, Joe.' She squeezed my hand.

I looked into her eyes. 'Women are devil-bitches,' I said. And I swear that as I spoke she moved her face closer to mine. I kissed her on the mouth.

'H'm,' I said.

'Yes,' said Julia.

We parted, and I went back towards my flat. On the way I tried to piece out what was happening. I looked forward to my drink with Robert, and arrived punctually at his club.

Robert took me into the small room with windows along two sides, where we usually went. There was a whiskery old man dozing in one of the chairs, the same old man – immediately it took me back to an evening when the windows were filled with lemon-coloured bands of light and Robert first told me Julia wanted him to marry her. The tatty newspapers on the centre table, the absence of servants, and a feeling of nervous excitement. While Robert rang for the waiter and ordered sherry, I glanced into Pall Mall. It was dark and, in contrast to the light walls beside the window, the damp haze outside had a bluish tinge.

Robert and I sat side by side with a dim little table-lamp between us. We talked first of all about some of our friends in Oxford who had suffered an absurd defeat in College politics, then about Myrtle and Haxby, and finally about Julia. Robert ordered some more sherry. I told him that I had seen Julia in the afternoon.

'She looked very happy.'

Robert did not speak, but I could see that he was quietly delighted.

After a pause, he said:

'I was going to tell you – I suppose you must have deduced it, as Wladislaw's gone – that today I begin to pay the rent of the flat.'

'Yes,' I said: 'How does it feel?'

'It feels,' said Robert, 'like taking on a responsibility that ought to be reserved for very rich men only.'

'But you are very rich,' I said.

Robert drank a little sherry.

'Keeping two establishments going is very expensive indeed,' he said.

'Happily I don't have to worry about that,' I said, thinking of Myrtle's income. And then I recalled, unhappily, that Myrtle aimed, when we were married, at our keeping only one establishment. I drank a little of my sherry.

We paused. The old man was dozing very erratically.

'Is he here every Saturday night?' I whispered.

'He comes up to London every weekend.'

'Does his wife let him, or is she too old to care?'

'They're never too old to care, never...' Robert paused. 'He's a widower.'

In the dim light the sherry looked a deep golden colour. I said:

'I suppose it would cost less if you moved into Julia's flat.'

Robert hesitated. 'I don't think I could do that.'

I said: 'If you're dining with her tonight, it will seem an awful bore to go home afterwards.'

Robert said: 'Do you know, I've never stayed the whole night with her? Even if it's been 5 am, I've still gone home.'

I was not surprised, because I always did the same thing myself. 'If you stay till the morning, you're trapped,' I said.

Robert was silent. We became serious.

I said: 'I thought Julia was very much less racketty and tense.' I glanced at him slowly. 'You have a wonderfully good effect on her.'

'Yes,' Robert said. 'But am I to devote myself to having a good effect on her?' He looked at me. 'The poor dear needs me. And I think – I *think* if I were certain I could save her from her fate, I might take it on..' He paused. 'I don't know. I wish to God I did. What do you think?'

I was silent. It was the first time recently that Robert had spoken so directly, and I recognised with pain a note that had run through his disastrous love affair with The Headlamps – the desire to save someone from her fate.

'I don't know,' I said, because he knew that at the bottom of my heart I did not believe in such miracles.

'I don't know if I ought to marry her,' Robert said. 'It would mean being prepared to devote myself to her pretty completely.'

I thought he was exaggerating – he had a romantic temperament.

'And,' he went on, 'there are so many other things I want to do.' His voice livened. 'We must throw off these jobs we have, and get down to what we really want to do. It's intolerable!'

'I agree.' I said gently: 'If I thought it was going to occupy you completely, looking after her, I should have to say I didn't think you ought to take it on.'

We finished our glasses of sherry. The old man had stopped breathing heavily through his whiskers and the room was silent. Robert looked thoughtful; his eyes were sparkling oddly in his impassive face, and he appeared to be speaking to himself rather than to me.

'If I did marry her, it would mean I should never know when I was going to come home and find her drunk or in bed with another man.'

I thought: 'He isn't going to marry her.'

PART IV

CHAPTER I

THE RIVALS

Myrtle unexpectedly rang me up and asked me if I would see Haxby.

I said No.

Myrtle then demanded that I should see Haxby.

I had always suspected her of wanting to arrange a scene between her two men – what woman can resist it? – but by pretending to be so stupid as not to catch on to her hints I had managed to evade it up to now. Frankly, I did not want to meet Haxby. I had nothing to say to him, and I could not help seeing that he probably did have something to say to me.

'Darling, you've got to see him. It's important.'

At that I should have had to pretend to be so stupid as not to catch on to the English language.

'What does he want?' I asked, thinking the matter might possibly be settled on the telephone.

'He'll tell you when he sees you,' said Myrtle, determined that it might not.

I gave in, and we began to arrange a rendezvous.

'I suppose it had better be on neutral territory,' I said.

'What for?' said Myrtle: 'I thought you'd want him to come round to your office.'

'Will he come?'

'If I tell him to.' Having sounded unseemly brisk her tone suddenly dropped into melancholy. 'I don't see that it matters where you meet . . .'

We fixed on my office at ten o'clock the following morning.

While waiting for Haxby to come I went into Robert's office. I had the unpleasant sensation I used to experience before taking an examination.

'You ought to have seen him before,' Robert said, with muffled certainty.

It was the first I had heard about it. Robert was looking at me with distaste, as if he thought me deficient in common respect for the feelings of my fellow human-beings.

'I don't like scenes,' I said.

Robert shrugged his shoulders. 'To most people they seem essential.'

I did not reply. I particularly disliked scenes in which I started at a moral disadvantage. One of the reasons why most people welcomed scenes was because they were always so convinced of their own moral rectitude.

It was ten o'clock and there was no sign of Haxby. I had no doubt that he would come. Fate never allowed me to escape so easily. I sat glum and silent on Robert's table. I wondered if Haxby would burst into tears, or, worse still, pull out a revolver. I felt angry with Myrtle for letting me in for a scene with him, and with Haxby for not turning up punctually for it.

I went to my own office to see if he was there, and then returned. It was getting on for a quarter past ten.

I said fretfully: 'What can he possibly want to say to me that Myrtle couldn't?'

There was a pause. 'He may want to tell you,' said Robert, 'that he's going to sue you for damages. He'd get them.'

I was astonished. It was something I had never thought of. For a moment I completely forgot my approaching encounter. It was obvious from Robert's expression that he had thought of it all along. I was as staggered by the extent of my own stupidity as dazed by the prospect of having to find some thousands of pounds ready money.

'You don't mean it,' I said feebly.

At that moment there was a tap on the door and a messenger came in.

'I beg your pardon, sir, but you do know there's a gentleman waiting to see you? In the waiting room?'

'Didn't he tell you he'd got an appointment at ten?' I could scarcely believe it.

'He never told me, sir. Never said a word.'

I stamped into my office and sat down at my desk. Haxby

was shown in. Did we shake hands or not? I made a sweeping gesture with my right arm. 'Will you sit down?'

Haxby sat down.

'I was here all the time,' I said, excusing myself with some irritation. I sat down opposite him.

'I thought you must be busy,' he replied in a manner that was, I suppose, polite. He had a slight Midland accent.

'I was waiting for you,' I said.

We sat and looked at each other. In the days before the war, when Myrtle first knew him, I had slightingly described him as tall, dark and skinny. He was still tall and dark, but in the course of Army life he had clearly 'filled-out'. He was a good deal bigger and stronger than me. As for the over-intense light in his eyes, black eyes, that had been a further subject for my jealous strictures, I could only think now that I had never looked at him properly. His eyes were not even black, they were brown; and at the present moment the light in them was no more intense than his wretched circumstances warranted. His face looked haggard but it was not unpresentable. In fact, if he had not been Myrtle's husband, who was probably just about to break the news that he wanted five thousand pounds in damages, I should have thought he looked a decent, intelligent fellow.

He was wearing an Army great-coat converted to civilian style.

'Are you warm enough?' I said.

'Thanks.' He began to take off the coat.

My unpleasant pre-examination feeling seemed to have disappeared.

'It's good of you to see me,' he said.

I did not reply. There was a note of respect in his voice. I suppose I must have looked like a successful civil servant to him. I felt like saying 'Oh dear!' I was no longer irritated with him.

'We've got to talk about Myrtle,' he said, with a show of spirit.

'Yes.'

'We can't go on like this.'

'No.' I looked at him. 'Are you going to divorce her?'

'I haven't made up my mind.'

'I wish you would.'

'I'm sure you do.' Apparently he was not as supine or respectful as I had imagined.

My telephone began to ring. I did not answer it. When it stopped he said:

'I don't propose to tell you what I think about your conduct.'

I received this information with relief.

He then embarked on a somewhat protracted tirade. There was nothing original about it, but then there was nothing very original in our situation – didn't it even come into the Bible somewhere? I had tried to evade having to hear it: the longer it went on the more right I knew I had been. My moral disadvantage was total. It is all very well to feel ashamed of oneself in one's own terms, at one's own choice. In Haxby's terms and at Haxby's choice it was an odious experience.

'I don't see the point of all this,' I said. 'What's it leading up to?'

Haxby stopped. There was a moment's silence.

'You and Myrtle seemed to have worked it all out between you,' he said. 'But I'm not going to give in without a struggle.' His tone was serious and suddenly devoid of rancour. 'If Myrtle leaves me,' he said, 'I shall resign my job.'

It was the last thing I had expected. I was greatly alarmed. It seemed incredible that he should have thought of it, but that was no consolation. If he resigned his job we were back, assuming that Myrtle had not changed her mind, where we started. I saw now why she had sent him to tell me himself.

'How could you possibly live?' I asked.

Haxby did not answer me. He looked at me directly, with a steady gaze – it was intense.

'What does Myrtle say about it?' I asked.

'Nothing.'

'Wasn't it rather a stroke of luck to get the job?'

'That means nothing to me.' His gaze dropped, and we were both silent. I stared at him. I seemed to hear Myrtle's voice echoing 'He says he can't live without me.' If he had told me he was going to sue me for damages and live on the proceeds, it

378

would have been a situation with a definite outcome. But proving that he could not live without her by being permanently out of work – I saw no end to that.

'I know she's always been in love with you,' he said. He paused. 'I've always been in love with her.'

And he looked up. His eyes were bright black with emotion. 'Oh God.'

The telephone rang again. I did not answer it.

'Are you determined to make three people unhappy?' I said. 'Have you thought of that?'

'I have.'

'You've admitted that Myrtle's in love with me.'

'*That doesn't mean she'd be unhappy if she went on being married to me.*'

I stopped in a burst of surprise. He did not repeat his remark, yet I felt as though he did. I felt as if I had suddenly heard a prophetic revelation, that expressed the truth for all of us.

The telephone rang again – I could not think why on earth my p.a. was letting the calls get through.

I stood up.

At that, Haxby stood up. He glanced finally round the office. 'Busy, aren't you?' he said.

CHAPTER II

AN IMPARTIAL REPORT

D r Chubb returned from his second tour exhausted, but apparently satisfied. What he had said and done this time, we did not know. Robert refused to confront him with the rumours about his first tour because they were so contradictory: I suspected Robert of letting Chubb have his head to make a serious blunder.

Nothing happened. A week passed and there were no reports from our personal friends in the firms on Chubb's itinerary. Perhaps Chubb had heard the rumours himself: perhaps none of them had been true. Perhaps – I have to admit that the possibility did occur to us – Chubb had become a loyal and discreet member of D.O.R.R.S.

The information had been collected. With nothing else to distract us for the time being, we were able to concentrate on preparing a report. Sir Francis decided to write the report himself, and no tactful offers of assistance could head him off. We were alarmed because he had to present the report to an inter-departmental committee at their next meeting. At the end of a week he was three days behind schedule.

'Why can't he let me write it?' said Robert.

By staying up all through one night, Sir Francis completed his task. The draft appeared on Robert's desk, and he spent a couple of hours reading it. Nobody could deny that Sir Francis had presented all the facts. It must have been one of the most comprehensive reports ever written. The order was logical, the structure was perfect. Sir Francis had displayed the grasp that was appropriate to his inordinately high degree of intelligence. The only trouble with his report was that it was impossible to gather the gist of it.

You will recall that the function of D.O.R.R.S. was to present facts impartially. No man could have been more devastatingly equipped by temperament to carry it out – Sir Francis could judge impartiality to perfection: he could raise it to the level of sheer meaninglessness.

'I think we may reasonably expect the committee to say,' he announced proudly, 'that we have not been guilty of giving them a lead of any description!'

Robert rang for me to come to his office and read the document as soon as he had finished with it. I gave up at the fifth page.

Robert was standing abstractedly by the window, watching the traffic in Parliament Square.

'The report ought not to have been more than three pages long,' he said. 'And then an enormous twenty-page appendix with all his figures in it.'

'Why don't you write one yourself and then persuade him to scrap this?'

Robert shook his head. 'He'd never agree.' He turned to me. 'How could he possibly see what was wrong with his own?'

Up to this moment we had been looking forward to the resolution of the controversy with growing excitement. We were far from impartial ourselves, and we expected the satisfaction of seeing our side win.

We had put our money – in the purely metaphorical sense, I am bound to point out in view of what certain other persons did – on the A 16. No doubt it looks easy for me to be right after the event, but it seems to me still that Robert's way of arriving at a conclusion was the most sensible. Anybody could see that the A 16, as it then stood, was not a workable proposition: the question was whether it could ever be made one, and if so, by whom.

It was our conviction that in all scientific discoveries and inventions, a major creative active act, on the part of one man only, happened in the first place. It was difficult to predict when such a man would turn up: he was born, not made, and in the world's history did not seem to be born very often. But once a major step forward had been taken, the rest could perfectly well be carried out by men of moderate originality, provided they were equipped with the necessary technique – the thing for which modern civilisation really had fitted itself was the production of such persons in fair quantity.

As far as the A 16 was concerned, the major creative act had been performed, the revolutionary step was manifest. Somehow or other, instinct told us, the rest of the work would get done. Time, money and men – we could scarcely believe the Americans were not already ahead of us. Had Dr Chubb been let loose in America they probably would have been.

Such considerations had no appeal whatsoever to the mind of Sir Francis. 'Somehow or other' was neither just nor accurate, so it was meaningless to him. 'We must look into it much more deeply than that, my dear Robert,' he said, with his head sagaciously cocked on one side. More questionnaires to industrial firms, more contingency tables, more reports.

On the other hand I must not give the impression that Sir Francis was impartial in his own personal opinions. He was quite certain that his report, properly construed – and it never occurred to him that other people would have the greatest difficulty in construing it at all – proved that we ought to go ahead with the A 16 without delay, and indicated to the department which firms should be given development contracts. 'It's all there,' he said, with triumphant cunning. It was. Among us all, the only person who obtusely insisted that the case was not proven was James.

Suddenly Robert came across to his desk and took the draft from me.

'I don't see why I shouldn't tell him what I think,' he said. 'I'm not going to be here for ever.' He took out his fountain-pen. He framed his comment, and then handed it to me to read with a subdued grin. It was formally addressed to D.O.R.R.S.

I am afraid this makes it very difficult to see the wood for the trees.

Signed with Robert's initials and dated.

I rang for his personal assistant to take the document away.

When she had gone his grin disappeared. He shook his head.
    'If Old Frank doesn't see sense in time, he'll really get into
hot water over this.'

CHAPTER III

SOMEONE NEW ON THE SCENE

The following day we went to a cocktail party at Sir Francis's house. During the afternoon the snow came back again. People watched the falling curtain of flakes with claustrophobic annoyance. It was intolerable.

The party was on the occasion of Sir Francis's only son Jocelyn's return from military service in the Far East, and Robert and I were invited to bring our young women. Sir Francis was aware that our private lives were what he was accustomed to consider bohemian, in fact we knew that was why he so enthusiastically asked us to bring Julia and Myrtle. No detail eluded Sir Francis in his energetic pursuit of fair-mindedness: he regarded our bohemianism as a satisfactory corrective to his own stiffly conventional behaviour.

The invitations had been given several weeks earlier, and Myrtle had promised to come up to London specially for the party. Consequently our meeting for the first time since my scene with Haxby was to come about automatically. I waited for her to pick me up after the office feeling distinctly apprehensive. It was clear that Robert, waiting for Julia, was feeling apprehensive too: I strongly suspected that he and Julia had been quarrelling recently. We stood at the window, watching Parliament Square under a leaden sky gradually lose its sharp outlines in a veil of thin greyish snow. Lights flashed miserably from windows and moving headlamps.

Quite apart from our general apprehensions about the future of our disordered lives, Robert and I were feeling a specific apprehension about what was likely to happen in the next few hours, when it seemed quite likely, in view of the circumstances, that our girls would get drunk.

'Damn the snow,' I said.

Robert ignored me. He was holding a handkerchief to his nose: he had a cold.

Myrtle and Julia came in together. They were chattering gaily, and expressed their surprise at finding us not radiant with pleasurable excitement. They were obviously out for alcohol, and looked as if they had had some already. I wondered what Julia had been saying to Myrtle – advising her not to sit down under something or other, I presumed.

We hired a taxi to Sir Francis's house, which was in Chester Street. The party was held on the first floor, in a handsome parqueted salon made by knocking two rooms together. At the end of the smaller part, beside a service hatch in which a little lift kept rumbling up and down, there was a bar-table set up by a professional firm of caterers. Sir Francis was a widower and had no women-folk to entertain for him. There were two fires glowing brilliantly in marble fireplaces, and the light sparkled from two small chandeliers.

Sir Francis received us formally and introduced Jocelyn, an elegant handsome youth in the Brigade of Guards. Sir Francis was a devoted father and his bright intelligent eyes were shining, his antennae-like eyebrows almost sparking with innocent pleasure in showing off his son – and, it has to be admitted, with innocent hope that one of the guests might offer the boy a job when he resigned his commission.

People were arriving in crowds, so we went immediately to the bar. I held Myrtle's hand to prevent us from getting separated, and then led her to the opposite end of the room. There were two long windows overlooking Chester Street, and the opulent dark blue curtains had been left undrawn – the white-painted lines of the window frames gleamed in rectangles across the darkness outside. We stood by a small mahogany table on which there was a vase containing leafless sprays, over three feet long, of beautiful, heavy, mauve lilac.

Myrtle unconcernedly sipped her drink and then sniffed the flowers. 'They don't smell.'

'They're hot-house. They never do.'

'They look lovely, all the same,' she murmured. I noticed with surprise that she was wearing a hat.

'Do you like it?' she asked.

While I was trying to find an answer, she ran her finger over the surface of the table. She said:

'He has some lovely furniture. I bet this is Sheraton.'

'He's quite a wealthy man.'

'Then why is he a civil servant?'

We stared at each other. I ignored the question. I could bear idle conversation no longer.

'What did Dennis say after I'd seen him?'

Myrtle's eyes looked round and light brown and innocent. 'Nothing that he hadn't said before, darling.'

'What's he going to do?'

'Give up his job if I leave him.'

'Then what are you going to do?'

'What am I going to do, darling? I honestly don't know. I can't think any more.' She looked at me. 'I wish you would tell me.'

'I?' I cried. 'I've done nothing but tell you. Leave him! Marry me!'

Myrtle shook her head sadly. 'That's too easy, darling.'

'Why should its being easy be a reason for not doing it? Do you prefer to do something difficult?'

Myrtle did not smile. 'Suppose I did leave him, what would he do?' she said, looking into her glass.

'He'd find himself another woman,' I said promptly. 'That sort of man always does.'

Myrtle glanced at me with naif interest. 'Would you, if I didn't marry you?'

'No.'

Myrtle was thoughtful. Having come out with the truth, I also was thoughtful – well I might be, as I had given two wrong answers in succession.

Before I could think of a remedy, our conversation was interrupted by James Irskine and his wife. James took me aside while the women were speaking to each other. 'I saw Robert's minute to Old Frank,' he said: 'I couldn't agree more.'

'What did the old boy say?'

'He took it rather well.'

James glared at me, and I did my best to glare back. Then we both turned to look in Sir Francis's direction. Sir Francis was talking animatedly to Robert, and at that moment Robert broke into laughter.

I wondered where Julia was, and found her in a little group surrounding Jocelyn Plumer. I went across to her, and took her away from them. She had been drinking rapidly. Her eyes were bright and bulging and furtive, and the skin at the base of her throat was reddening.

'Tell me who all these people are?' she said, to forestall any serious remark from me. 'I mean the men, of course.'

I pointed out numerous distinguished civil servants, a junior minister, one or two people who were plainly aristocratic, and one or two industrial figures who included Lord —— . I thought they looked very much like successful men from any walk of life. They were mostly heavy, vigorous creatures, with bodies that must have been meaty and powerful. At first sight some of them looked not particularly clever – what characterised all their faces was a permeating confidence and will. I was interested to observe what a high proportion of them had plain wives. I did not really find it an attractive gathering of people. I explained to Julia our function in counter-balancing their respectability. She was delighted with the idea.

'Dear Old Frank,' I said. 'He must think *we* carry an awful lot of guns.'

'*Their* armament may not be as heavy as it looks,' said Julia, and laughed somewhat intoxicatedly at her own joke. Suddenly she leaned towards me.

'I'll tell you who's on our side,' she said, and fixed me with a knowing stare. 'Jocelyn.'

'Is he?' I had paid no attention to him. Suddenly I realised that Julia was no longer looking at me, but was looking back through the crowd at him.

I waited for her attention to return. She said: 'I want another drink.' A waiter was passing with a tray. She said to me: 'I suppose you know Robert and I have had another row.'

'I guessed as much. What about?'

'I'm not going to tell you.' Suddenly she burst out. 'I'm

getting very impatient.'

'That won't do you any good with Robert.'

'I can't help it!' She now looked across at Robert, and the grip on her glass tightened. Then it relaxed.

Robert was talking weightily to Lord ——. He was holding his handkerchief.

Julia said: 'He doesn't want to take me home. He says he's got a cold.' Her high spirits seemed to have gone and her tone had a sharp disharmonious edge. 'I shall stay here and drink.' She paused. 'I suppose you're taking Myrtle back?'

'I hope so.'

'If I were you, I should be impatient with her.'

'I am.'

I was sure Julia must be recalling a conversation they had held earlier in the evening. She said:

'I think we both ought to cut our losses.'

'What does that mean? And who's we?'

'Myrtle and me.'

'What do you mean about Myrtle?'

Julia said:

'I don't think Myrtle ought to marry you.'

I was angry. 'Why not?' I cried.

'I don't think she'd settle down with you.' Julia's voice was still harsh. 'I don't think she's made for you. If you want to know why – to put it simply, I think she needs a husband where she can wear the trousers.'

At first I was too angry to reply. It was the explanation of all average people, all *hommes moyens sensuels* and their female equivalents.

'I hope you didn't tell her that!'

Julia did not reply. Of course she had told her – and a great deal more besides, I did not doubt.

Julia gave a forced laugh. She said: 'In any case, she ought to leave her husband.'

At this I really was dumbfounded. There was a long pause. I stared at Julia. I thought she had a slightly crazed look or else she was drunk. I said:

'Are you trying to break up everything? And if so, in heaven's name, why?'

She stared back at me.

'You don't understand.' She spoke penetratingly. 'You don't understand that I'm feeling antagonistic. Towards everyone.'

I thought she really was slightly mad. She took hold of my wrist and did not speak again for a few moments. I felt sorry for her, even if she had been treacherously exhorting Myrtle not to sit down under my presumed dominance.

'Poor old Julia!...'

Julia said: 'If you only knew the difficulty I'm having, in not throwing this drink in your face!'

I thought it was time for me to move along to one of the other guests. I looked back and saw Julia moving towards Jocelyn Plumer.

'Joe!' It was Robert. 'I'm going home now.' While he spoke to me his eyes were fixed on Julia. 'My cold's getting worse.'

'Julia thinks Old Frank's son is not specially respectable. She says he's on our side.' I felt as if I were somehow trying to explain away Julia's conduct.

Robert said nothing while we watched her. Before I had time to say anything else, he went away. I looked at my watch. It was time I too left the party. Myrtle was not going to stay the night in London. I went to find her.

As Myrtle and I said goodbye to Sir Francis, I glanced over his shoulder. I saw Julia talking to Jocelyn: she was standing very close to him. At that moment she glanced towards us. She waved with great zest.

CHAPTER IV

ANOTHER FOND FAREWELL

From the time when we left the party Myrtle and I got on steadily better together. The snow was falling lightly and we got a taxi straight away. When Myrtle heard me give the driver the address of my house she demurred.

'Hadn't we better go straight to Euston?' she said.

'No, darling,' said I.

'But, darling...'

'Yes?'

She gave me a soulful look.

'Didn't you expect we should be going back to the flat first?' I said.

Myrtle shook her head, looked through the window of the taxi, and then looked reproachfully at me.

'You didn't warn me, darling,' she said with plaintive emphasis.

'Oh come!...'

Myrtle pretended to make a short hopeless search through the contents of her handbag.

I looked at her with astonishment, hardly able to believe her, Myrtle, a married woman of long standing. She shook her head again, to indicate that making love was unfortunately impossible. Immediately I was taken back to the days of our first affair: whenever there was anything wrong this was exactly the trick she had played on me – I could never believe it was not a trick.

And being taken back eight years, my response to the trick was exactly the same – extraordinary determination not to submit to it. What had seemed to me a purely enjoyable experience a few minutes ago, was now transformed into a

passionate necessity. I made this clear to Myrtle. She looked
as if she was quite unable to understand me. Age had not
altered us a scrap: the years had taught us absolutely nothing.
The taxi skidded round by Victoria station.

'I know where there's a little shop that will still be open,' I
said.

'How do you know?' said Myrtle, suspiciously.

'I've used it before.'

She was furiously jealous. I shouted instructions to the
driver, and sat back in the corner opposite to her. I thought she
had got what she asked for.

You may think all this was no improvement in our relations,
but somehow it was. We were back in a familiar domestic
wrangle whose outcome was always harmonious, and we both
knew it – you see, I still think Myrtle had done it on purpose.

We went rapidly upstairs to my flat. I put a match to the
gas-fire in the bedroom and it gave a feeble glow. I put a
shilling in the meter, and was rewarded by a glow that was
feebler if anything. Outside it was snowing: I expected Myrtle
to say she was cold enough to die. Instead she said with
melancholy interest: 'What have you done with the whisky,
darling?'

On my knees by the hearth, I looked up at her.

'A gas-fire doesn't really warm a girl's heart,' she said.

When I was on my feet again I embraced her. I had
forgotten that until she married me I was supposed to give an
air of passive suffering. I thought 'Dammit, I'm going to be
myself!' I was filled with a delightful inflatory mixture of
optimism and triumph. I felt that Myrtle might as well get
used to me as I was, because that was how I was going to be
after we were married. It seemed to me that this was an
evening I had been waiting for. I had put up with doubts and
hesitations long enough. Tonight was going to settle it: all was
going to be well.

I put my watch where it was easily visible, so that we should
not miss the time for Myrtle's last train.

'What are you doing that for, darling?' she said.

I explained.

Myrtle sighed and put her arms round my neck. I recalled

her provocative trick that had failed. Mixed optimism and triumph inflated me still further.

By the time we were ready to leave the flat, Myrtle seemed to be inflated too. Her eyes were luminous and the corners of her mouth twitched as if she were amused without knowing it. I humoured her with another nip of whisky and hurried her downstairs. While I was telephoning in the hall for a taxi, Mrs Burdup came past and Myrtle deliberately made her stop and discuss the weather.

It was snowing fast now. In the slit of light from the doorway behind us we saw flakes floating down, silently, mysteriously. The taxi came up and we jumped in.

It was a romantic ride. The road was thickly covered, and the glow round each street-lamp was so reduced that we seemed to be travelling from one little world of drifting spots of light to another. I put my arms round Myrtle and held her close to me. She was warm and sweet-smelling. I kissed her. Her coat fell open. I drew her much closer. She lifted her head quickly.

'Oh, darling!...'

'What?' We were whispering to each other.

'What about the driver?'

'Taxi-drivers are used to it!...'

Over her shoulder I saw the dark shadow of the driver's back, motionless. He was wearing a cap. I felt Myrtle's body relax a little. I drew her over, and she sighed loudly in my ear. The taxi went on through the night, inexorably.

Suddenly, under a street-lamp, the taxi stopped. With a muffled cry Myrtle jumped off my lap, and hit her head on the roof. We saw the driver get out. Myrtle flung herself into the corner of the cab. He began to wipe snow off the windscreen – the wiper had jammed. We laughed with relief.

Sitting in opposite corners Myrtle and I could see each other dimly. We did not say anything, but she stretched out her hand to me and I held it. We felt far away from everything in the gentle silence and darkness of the night. The snow was all round us. The driver was whistling quietly to himself – we were not lonely. Our hearts, our souls were expanding. It was like being in youthful love again, warm, tender, ineffable.

With a faint click and a whirr the wiper began to work again. The driver got back into his seat and we drove off. We were somewhere in Bloomsbury. I looked at my watch.

'What was Robert saying to you just before we left the party?'

It was the first time in the evening that Myrtle had shown any concern for my affairs. She spoke in a light conversational tone.

It seemed no time at all before we were at Euston. We were friends as well as lovers.

I gave the driver a large tip.

Myrtle was watching me, with a slyly innocent expression that could not have been more explicit if she had actually been saying 'conscience-money'.

'Come along,' I said, haughtily. The station seemed unusually deserted, though there was no reason why a snowstorm in London should discourage people from travelling to Birmingham or Glasgow. Myrtle linked her arm through mine.

We chose a compartment, and the time came for us to make our last speeches. My optimism and triumph had given place to a stable confidence and happiness. I was certain that tonight she must make up her mind to leave Haxby. I felt I must say something to mark the occasion, rather as a good civil servant feels the compulsion to put something down on paper. I looked into Myrtle's face, trying to frame all that was in my heart. I did not know how to put it.

We went out on to the platform, and I slipped my arm round Myrtle's waist. 'It's been wonderful,' I muttered.

Myrtle gave me a long tremulous look. And then she said:

'Don't worry, darling. It will come out to *us* in the end.'

Whether anybody was watching us or not, I clasped her tightly in my arms. I was thinking 'I'll love you and keep you for ever.'

CHAPTER V

SIR FRANCIS ACTS

Next morning, in spite of his cold, Robert came bustling into the office early.

'Old Frank's sent for me.'

There was no time for our usual conversation. Robert was smiling with amusement: he was certain that Sir Francis was going to ask him to re-write the report.

While Robert was in conference with Sir Francis, I cheerfully picked up the draft and began to work out my own ideas of what it should be.

Robert returned with a very unusual expression.

'Isn't he going to let you do it after all?' I asked.

'Oh yes, that's all right.' He sat down close to me on the corner of my desk. 'As a matter of fact, there's something else afoot.' He paused, glanced away and then back again. 'Old Frank has just heard that Lord ——'s firm is already well ahead with something on the lines of the A 16.'

I exclaimed.

Robert stared at me, with his eyes looking bright and sharp.

'It's pretty surprising, I agree.'

Lord —— was chairman of the biggest group of industries in the federation of which he was president. He was neither a fool nor a gambler.

'Old Frank is astounded,' Robert went on. 'He thinks there must have been a breach of security somewhere.'

'Security!'

'You forget how seriously he takes all our formal precautions. He still imagines the firms don't know exactly why we've been making our survey. As for the side we're going to come down on – he doesn't believe yet that we really have come down. Let alone that Lord —— could have guessed it.'

'Guessed it?' I said. 'Guessed it, my foot!' I stared at Robert. 'Lord —— has heard something, and I bet you we know where.'

Robert's face became more impassive and his eyes sparkled more brightly. There was a pause.

'What's Old Frank going to do?' I said. 'Ring up Lord —— and congratulate him on his good sense?'

'You ought to know better than that. Nothing of the kind. Far, far from it. He's asked Lord —— to meet him, to confront him with a supposed breach of security and to ask him to explain it.'

CHAPTER VI

SELF-SACRIFICING FRIENDSHIP

Later that morning I got a message asking me to telephone Mr Łempicki-Czyz immediately.

I rang Wladislaw at his office in the City. He wanted me to meet him as soon as possible.

'What's the matter?' I asked.

'It is not possible to tell you on the telephone.' His strong nasal voice made the diaphragm rattle. 'The exchange-girl listens.'

I always assumed our operator had too much to do: she must have heard some surprising things if she had not. I agreed to meet Wladislaw in the Berkeley Hotel at six o'clock.

I was a little late, but Wladislaw had not arrived. The irregular-shaped room with mirrors where one had drinks was almost empty, so I chose a corner table suited to a *tête-à-tête*. Wladislaw came in. He was dressed for business, in an excellently cut black pin-stripe suit and a white shirt. His tie was made of glistening sombre silk, with a pearl tie-pin planted in the middle of it. Somehow, one would have known at sight that he was a foreigner – not by his clothes, but by the shape of him: I thought he was too cubical to be English. He sat down and called for a waiter.

It was impossible to tell what was the matter. Wladislaw's massive powerful face was not made for expressing emotion, and I imagined the only thing that could alter his piercing look was a mixture of rage and sexual desire – which no doubt made it more piercing.

Wladislaw ordered two whiskies and soda, and after we had taken the ritual first sip, he said, with his head bent:

'I have some unfortunate news.' He glanced at me. 'About

Julia.'

'I saw her last night, at a party given by my boss.'

'Yes.' Wladislaw looked at me fixedly. 'I know. She met there a young man named Jocelyn Plumer' – he pronounced the J in a continental fashion – 'and after the party she took him home with her. For the night. She was drunk.' Wladislaw watched for my response.

I was not so much surprised by the information as puzzled by how he knew.

I said: 'Did she tell you?'

'No,' said Wladislaw. 'I have her watched. By private detective.' He delivered the explanation with straightforward moral rectitude.

'Really!' I have to confess that I was shocked. Had my self-restraint been only a shade weaker I could have told Waldislaw it was not playing the game. I said: 'You don't mean to say you employ someone to spy on her?'

'Why not?'

'If you don't see it for yourself, I really doubt if I can explain it you.'

'I want to know what she is doing,' Wladislaw said. 'I have her watched all the time.'

'But the money it must cost you!' I said, momentarily forgetting about playing the game.

'It is necessary.'

'That's a matter for argument.'

'Not at all. It's necessary for me to know what she's doing. It's necessary for me to have her watched, constantly.'

I said slyly: 'For your own ends...'

'No.' Wladislaw now spoke to me with great, direct force. '*It is for her good!*'

I had no reply to make to that.

Wladislaw's small bright grey eyes seemed to glance piercingly through to the back of my skull. His voice was lower. 'Everything I do is for her good. When I offer her my friendship, it is for her good. When I sacrifice my own deeper feelings, it is for her good.'

There was a long pause. 'Then that's all there is to be said.' I drank a little whisky. If only, I thought, Wladislaw had the faintest sense of humour, I might have made some impression on him. So incapable was he of looking into his own self-seeking motives, so entirely lacking in any kind of detachment when judging himself, that he genuinely did believe every word he was saying.

'I am willing to do anything to make Julia happy,' he said. 'And I am convinced she cannot be happy leading this sort of life. She has fallen back into her old ways. We must save her.'

I could not resist pretending not to cotton on. I said hollowly: 'I doubt if there's much we can do.'

'There is always much we can do.'

I shook my head. 'One can't really save anybody.' I looked at him. 'People can't really be seriously changed.'

'If you think people can't really be changed,' Wladislaw said quickly, with his eyes flashing, 'then it follows that they cannot be saved! I think people can be saved... That is because I believe people can be changed! I disagree with your premise. When you say Julia cannot be saved, it is because your premise is false. How' – he wound up with incisiveness that would not have done discredit to Sir Francis – 'can you expect to reach correct conclusions from false premises?'

I felt as if the breath had been knocked out of me. Second only to his passion for Julia was Wladislaw's passion for abstract argument. And abstract argument of this kind was entirely outside my range. How could I expect to reach correct conclusions from false premises? I had no idea.

Wladislaw was still giving me a formidably flashing stare. He awaited a logical reply.

'I doubt if we can alter Julia very much,' I said doggedly.

Wladislaw must have been feeling a mixture of disappointment and plain contempt. He sat back in his chair and drank some more whisky He clearly did not think I was very clever. He said:

'I think we can save her from these self-destructive acts.'

Neither of us had the wit to remember that Julia got a good deal of enjoyment out of what we portentously called her self-destructive acts.

I said: 'I doubt if this was as serious as all that. She was piqued because Robert wouldn't take her home, so she took someone else.' I warmed up to my thesis. 'A lot of Julia's acts are devised for their effect on a third person.'

'I am sorry the acts are all of the same kind!'

I could not escape the feeling that I had lost another argument.

Wladislaw put down his glass and felt to see if his pearl tie-pin was in place.

'I want to know if you are willing to help me, to try to save her.'

It crossed my mind that he was a madman.

'How?'

'I want your advice about it.'

'Yes?'

'Do you think,' said Wladislaw uncunningly, 'you should tell Robert immediately?'

'Why? Do you want him to quarrel with her?'

Wladislaw paused. I wondered – did a flicker of comprehension suddenly illuminate him?

'He has great influence on Julia.' He began weightily to develop the idea.

I tried to head him off by saying: 'She'll probably tell Robert herself.'

There was a short pause.

'Then do you think,' said Wladislaw, with apparent diffidence, 'you should tell Jocelyn Plumer about me?'

I was unable to conceal my astonishment and respect. This really was a cunning manoeuvre. It took a very strong-minded youth not to be put off when he heard his mistress was being shadowed by another lover's detective, that lover being a rich Polish businessman.

'I don't know him,' I said.

Wladislaw said methodically: 'Robert knows him.'

'Well, really!' I banged my glass down on the table.

Wladislaw turned to look at me. I judged him to be surprised.

'Do you not wish to help me?' he asked. And there was strong appealing emotion in his voice.

The only thing to do was to answer in his own terms. 'I should like to,' I said, with equal fervour. I had got my next remark ready.

'Then perhaps you will speak to Robert tomorrow.'

'I will if I decide it's compatible with my friendship for Julia.'

Wladislaw understood that.

I had not the slightest intention of telling anybody anything. There was a long silence.

'I do everything for Julia's own good. I want no reward.' Wladislaw looked at me for a long time. 'Like you, I do only what is compatible with friendship.'

I did not know whether to laugh, shout at him with rage, or just stay silent. I stayed silent. There he sat, with his neck as wide as his face and his narrow eyes alight with power and sincerity. Of course he was not mad. He was only different from me.

CHAPTER VII

'WILL IT END PUNCTUALLY?'

Sir Francis had arranged his meeting for a quarter past four on the following day. He told us that he had impressed Lord —— with the importance of the occasion. At this Robert shook his head gloomily. It happened that Chubb had taken two days' leave: he was summoned to return. That cheered us up.

When Robert and I arrived at Sir Francis's room, he was busy in his personal assistant's office, so we had the place to ourselves. On the polished mahogany table there was a tray holding white earthenware cups and saucers. While we stood looking through the window a messenger brought in a plate of fancy cakes which Sir Francis had punctiliously sent him out to buy at an A.B.C.

In Parliament Square the snow was melting for the second time, and we could not help feeling a quite disproportionate relief.

'It gives one some idea of how people in the Middle Ages must have felt at the first signs of spring,' said Robert, in a tone which indicated that his imagination was ranging far beyond the scope of mine.

The messenger came in again carrying a big brown enamel tea-pot. I meditated on spring and summer – something made me recall the afternoon when Robert and I had contemplated the striped awning outside St Margaret's. I meditated on summer and divorce and fate.

Chubb came in. I thought he looked more hare-eyed than usual, and also ruddier of cheek.

'I hope this meeting is going to end punctually,' he said, giving Robert a toothy, and, I thought, frightened smile. 'I mean, it was rather inconvenient for me to come to this meeting at all. I've arranged to take my wife to the theatre tonight – it isn't often she gets a chance to go, with it being so difficult about servants in these days – so I don't want to be late. As it is, she'll have to wait for me in my club. Fortunately there's a ladies' room . . .'

He was very nervous.

'I think it rather depends on Plumer,' Robert said, as if he were taking the conversation seriously.

I reflected upon the unusual frequency with which people happened to be ill or on leave at the moment when they were about to find themselves in trouble.

'I suppose we'd better wait for our tea.' Chubb stood by the table and eyed the cakes. Big Ben chimed a quarter past.

The door opened and in came Sir Francis and Lord ——, followed by James Irskine. Sir Francis looked pink and bright-eyed; his antennae-like eyebrows were curling. Lord —— glanced at the table as he came over to shake hands with Robert.

'Tea and cakes!' he said, in the booming, important voice in which one might say 'War and peace!' or 'Love and death!'

I had never been able to prevent myself from thinking Lord —— was an ass. I was quite wrong. He was a big heavy man with a very slight stoop, and he had a completely bald egg-shaped head. It always seemed to me that his voice boomed so much because it was resounding inside his egg-shaped head. He was a very clever, able man. Nobody but a clever and able man could have reached the presidency of his particular federation, where his competitors for the honour were in my opinion so clever and able that they might have been thought dishonest.

Lord —— then turned to Chubb, who returned the false affable smile fading from Lord ——'s face, with a nervous sycophantic laugh.

'I didn't reckon on our meeting again so soon,' said Chubb.

'Very interesting. Very interesting,' said Lord ——, with a particularly disinterested boom, and turned away from him.

We sat down at the table, and James poured out the tea in a grumpy efficient manner, as if he thought the messenger ought to have been called in, even though he could do it so much more competently himself. Chubb refused a cake. Robert took one and chewed it abstractedly. Lord —— chose the best.

While we made polite preliminary conversation, I recalled the first time I had seen Lord ——, sitting at the next table in a restaurant. Gifted with a voice that would have carried to the gallery of the Albert Hall, Lord —— had cultivated the knack of commanding by sideways glances the attention of everyone sitting round about him. He had a big nose, and large, round grey eyes in deep sockets. Seeing from his sideways glances that everyone was being forced to listen to him, his eyes glowed with pleasure and satisfaction. He was not unamiable. He merely liked to be addressing the whole room rather than the person he was speaking to, and had found a happy way of doing both.

Lord —— put the last piece of his cake into his mouth. Sir Francis instantly glanced at the clock and said:

'Shall we begin?'

'Any time you like,' said Lord ——, not in the least put out. I suddenly felt Sir Francis was going to get the worst of the exchange. And then I glanced at Dr Chubb. He was smiling his characteristic fixed hare-eyed smile. I could not believe he did not know what he was going to get.

CHAPTER VIII

HOW THE MEETING ENDED

'I think you know, Lord ——, why I've asked you to come here today.' Sir Francis put his head slightly on one side, and spoke in a most courteous manner. Yet to my mind there was something arrogant about the way he said 'I'. He clearly thought Lord —— was in a weak moral position.

'I thought it wisest to ask you to meet us, so that I could ask one or two questions quite directly.' Sir Francis gave him an even more courteous smile. 'And receive equally direct answers.'

Lord —— looked at him fixedly without speaking. Had Lord ——'s head really been an egg it could not have displayed more beautiful unresponsive poise. Sir Francis was not discouraged by it. He went on briskly.

'Two days ago it came to my ears that the firm of which you are chairman is engaged on work closely connected with the A 16. It would be both indiscreet and improper to disclose the source of my information – I am sure you will understand that – '

Sir Francis paused for Lord —— to assent. Lord —— gave no sign whatever.

'As a matter of fact,' Sir Francis said, foolishly, 'I gave my word that I would not disclose it.'

'You surprise me,' Lord ——'s voice boomed.

'Indeed?' said Sir Francis.

'I am always very careful about giving my word. Especially in such circumstances as those you mention.' He nodded his egg-head gravely while managing to glance at the rest of us to make sure we were impressed.

'I'm sure I was right to do so,' said Sir Francis, nettled.

'As you will.' The boom was the boom of an ass, and yet he contrived to make Sir Francis look childish. He was helped by the fact that he was big and Sir Francis small.

Sir Francis was about to speak, when Lord —— smiling now, interrupted him. 'I should say that gossip, by definition, is something a man promises to keep secret while not intending to do so.'

'I hope you'll assure me,' Sir Francis said smartly, 'that this was idle gossip and not the truth.'

Lord —— gave him a stare for his pains.

'Is it idle gossip?' Sir Francis asked.

'The organisation of which I am chairman,' said Lord ——, 'is indeed turning its energy towards the production of A 16s at a future date.' He paused. 'I can answer your question frankly.'

The two of them stared at each other.

'I am astonished, Lord ——. I cannot understand how such a thing can possibly have happened without a break in our security arrangements.' He gave Lord —— an account of the limited number of people in the government service who were supposed to know about the A 16, ending up: 'And it's quite unthinkable that such information should find its way to the general public.'

'I think the organisation of which I am chairman can hardly be referred to as the general public.' Lord —— laughed loudly.

Sir Francis replied with some heat, and Lord —— answered him back. They wrangled together. I glanced round the table. Robert was sitting in his usual abstracted gloom, Chubb was looking worried, James Irskine was looking blank.

'Look here, Sir Francis,' said Lord ——, beginning to get angry, 'it's unrealistic, and you must know it, to suppose that we leaders of industry don't know that a new —— is coming along.' Instead of saying A 16 he actually named the machine.

'I beg your pardon!' said Sir Francis. 'We have been instructed that in no circumstances are we to refer to it as anything other than A 16.'

Lord —— gave several sideways looks round the table. I caught a glimpse of his glowing, compelling, actor's eye – it was attractive and I almost returned the smirk of a confederate. K.Y.M.S. I wrote hastily on my blotting-pad.

'I fail to see,' Lord —— said, 'how I could discuss the capacity of my firm for making the A 16, how I could discuss that capacity with a member of your staff, if I didn't know what it was.' He changed his tone. 'I will be more than frank with you. I'll tell you that I discussed the A 16 quite openly with my friend Chubb, here – no, don't interrupt me – I discussed it with him quite openly, because there was nothing he had to tell me that I didn't know already.'

'Is this true, Dr Chubb?' said Sir Francis, so horrified as apparently not to hear Lord ——'s last sentence.

'Well, yes . . .' said Chubb.

'You must take it, Sir Francis,' said Lord ——, 'that a thing of such great importance cannot be kept as secret as you appear to imagine.'

Sir Francis could not speak for a moment.

Lord —— went on. 'You can rest assured that Dr Chubb disclosed none of your secrets to me.' Suddenly he sent a booming laugh round the table that seemed to draw us all into its ambit. 'There were one or two things about the A 16 that I told *him*!'

'I take leave to be my own judge of the activities of my staff!'

There was a sudden pause. Chubb said: 'I wonder if I might say something. It's quite true, what Lord —— says, and I'm sure I was perfectly aware of the degree of secrecy surrounding A 16 and would on no account have overstepped the bounds of secrecy. But talks could only proceed usefully if there was a bit of give-and-take on both sides.' His nervousness abated a little, as commonsense took possession of him. 'It's obvious that more people knew about the A 16 than we listed. They had to know and they were bound to find out, but it doesn't mean anyone did anything wrong. We're all in this thing together – the safety of the country depends on it, as everyone knows, who finds out the smallest thing about it. When we're all in it together, like that, I don't see why the secret isn't as safe with Lord —— and his firm's research team as it is with us.'

It is fair to say that Sir Francis did not see it in that way at all. He was about to speak when Lord —— bore him down again. I was interested that Lord —— was exerting himself so far. Then suddenly I recalled that whatever the general breakdown in our security arrangements happened to be, Lord ——'s firm, and none of the others in his federation, had gone ahead with the A 16. Sir Francis had shrewdly observed it right at the beginning. Lord —— had boomed grandiloquently but his moral position was not as strong as all that.

It was clear that Sir Francis was going to deliver himself of his second accusation quite soon.

Lord —— raised his voice still more resonantly. As his bald head moved to and fro with greater amplitude the reflected light flashed from it.

'I don't deny your right to be your own judge of the activities of your staff, Sir Francis. All of us take that right. But I feel bound to say that I, and I believe you too, have reason to congratulate Dr Chubb on the part he has played in this affair. You can be assured that he definitely behaved with complete propriety regarding the restrictions of security. At the same time I found him most helpful. I found him even' – he glanced in passing first at Robert and then at me – 'statesman-like. It was as much due to his sage counsel as to anyone's, that the organisation of which I am chairman, decided to go ahead with the A 16!'

Chubb turned pale. White patches appeared below his eyes.

It was clear that Sir Francis could scarcely believe his ears. His own sense of propriety was so strong that it must really not have occurred to him before that Chubb might have advised Lord —— on the strength of what he learnt in D.O.R.R.S.

Lord —— glanced round the table with a powerful, dominating, provocatively self-satisfied look. I was certain he knew exactly what he had done.

For a moment everyone was still. Chubb was looking down at his papers, James was holding a gold pencil against his chin, Robert was watching Sir Francis.

Suddenly Chubb began to speak. I gave him great credit for it. True, it was his only chance – and not really a serious chance – but he took it with unusual spirit. He was fighting desperately, and in the strain of great emotion his face looked quite different. He seemed to be holding his head a little further back, so that he could only just see over the top of his spectacles, and his eyes looked smaller.

'I think the time has come when I must make my position clear,' he said, 'otherwise I can see the way open to grave misconstruction being put upon my actions. As I've already said, and I can't say it more strongly, at no time did I consciously overstep the bounds of security, in connection with the survey of firms I undertook for D.O.R.R.S. I agree with Lord ——, and, I'm afraid, not with Sir Francis, that the firms knew a good deal about the A 16 before I ever got there.'

Chubb paused, and to my surprise took out his handkerchief and wiped his nose: yet he appeared not to notice what he was doing and went on speaking.

'The next thing is this – I'm afraid what Lord —— has just told you may make it look to some people as if I advised him, not as a personal friend, which is what I did advise him as, but as a member of D.O.R.R.S., so making use of my official position in an improper way. I think at a time like this, the best thing – it's the only thing I can do – is to lay my cards quite frankly on the table, so that you can judge for yourselves. I may say that in my own mind my conscience is perfectly clear. And in particular I want to say that I have never felt, in anything I did, that I was being in any way disloyal to D.O.R.R.S. I know that in the first place I was sent to you by my parent department because they believed in the A 15 and they were under the impression that D.O.R.R.S. believed in the A 16 – '

He was interrupted by exclamations of passionate dissent, from Sir Francis who was still officially impartial, and James Irskine, who still obtusely believed the case for the A 16 not yet fully established.

'I came to D.O.R.R.S. with every intention of remaining completely impartial, and with every intention of being loyal to my new department. I acquired as many facts about the situation as I could. As time went on I couldn't help coming round to the D.O.R.R.S. position myself. I decided that the A 16 was what we had got to concentrate on.' He made a gesture towards Robert. 'Even if Sir Francis hadn't made up his mind, I knew that Robert was quite certain, and I agreed with him.'

Robert showed no sign that he heard.

'I decided that the A 16 was what we had to concentrate on, and that the future of the country might well depend on our getting it in hand as rapidly as possible. It was my personal opinion – D.O.R.R.S. had no official opinion. It was my personal opinion that Lord —— asked for, and I felt bound to give it.'

I could not help glancing covertly at Robert to see how he was taking it. We had surmised rightly what Chubb was aiming at in the later stages of his tour, but we had not imputed motives as entirely high-minded as this – not that we necessarily believed them when we heard them.

Chubb was roused to strong emotion. 'I believed in my personal opinion and I think it was right. I think Lord —— was right in coming to his similar decision. But I'll only say I think I was right, because we can't say yet who'll turn out in the end to be right. But I'm willing to let history be my judge.'

He was a genuinely humble man. Yet he could not help repeating it, his newly-found phrase: 'I'm willing to let history be my judge.'

'Following upon Sir Francis,' added Lord ——. It was his first cheap remark and it sheared him of some of his authority and power. There was something empty about him after all.

'I think,' said Sir Francis, with admirable gravity, 'that is all that remains to be said.'

The meeting was over. Sir Francis caught Dr Chubb's eye. 'Are you returning to your office?' It meant that he proposed to collogue further with Chubb on his own.

As I stood up I noticed the K.Y.M.S. on my blotting-pad. I grinned at Robert and at James and they looked surprised. They did not realise that they too had said barely a word.

We went out of the room, leaving Sir Francis to exchange the last civilities with Lord ——. Robert and I put on our overcoats in silence, although there was no-one to overhear our conversation. Our thoughts were in accord. We were both convinced that the upshot of Chubb's activities was laudable and reassuring. That there might have been some conspiracy between him and Lord —— did not really worry us. But we knew that it would worry Sir Francis. It would shock him to

such an extent that he would not be able to help acting upon it
    For the most sensible of his rather doubtful manoeuvres in
D.O.R.R.S., Chubb was going to be sacked.

CHAPTER IX

MEDITATIONS

In our activities there was a lull that began with days and stretched out into weeks.

Outside, everything changed. The snow suddenly disappeared from the streets and squares. The sun shone constantly and people complained of the warmth. Spring had come.

In Parliament Square the old book-stall pill-box was cleared away and workmen were slowly laying out the ground afresh with grass and arc-shaped flower-beds. Walking through the square at lunch-time we saw sunlight flashing on the glossy feathers of birds perched on the head of Abraham Lincoln's statue, and gleaming on the coloured mosaic roof of the little Victorian gothic monument that reminded me of the Albert Memorial and whose name I never knew – it has gone now.

And as Robert and I strolled in St James's Park before going back to the office we had not much new to talk about. There were odd days of interest, when Sir Francis presented his report to the inter-departmental committee, and when Dr Chubb left us.

Until the time of his departure Chubb was occupied in writing something. Through a small space where the buckram lining had been stripped from the window of his office door, we could see him as we passed. He sat very still, holding his head on one side and slightly back, so as to look through his spectacles, endlessly writing.

'What can it be?' I said.

'*The New Prince*', said Robert, without hesitation.

And then, one day, his office was empty.

'He hasn't been with us long, has he, sir?' said Froggatt, as if he knew nothing about it whereas he really knew everything. He paused and then said respectfully: 'It will, of course, give us a little more accommodation. Would you object if I moved some of the staff round a bit?'

No startling decision was reached that spring about the A 16s. We knew that in due course the A 16 would be made, but such changes in affairs do not come about so much by sudden big strokes as by the accumulating pressure of a lot of little ones. Not now, was the rule: in due course.

There was no development in my relationship with Myrtle. For days and then weeks I did not hear from her. I had expected an unrestrainedly affectionate letter from her on her return home after Sir Francis's party. No letter came. I was at first surprised and then puzzled. I waited. I received a couple of notes with a week's interval between them. I did not write to her – at first I did not know why. And then, as I noticed that I was falling back into my old state of jarring anxiety, I realised the truth. Our momentary drawing-together was of no significance. The old battle of wills was on again, as fiercely and as lastingly as ever.

What was happening between Robert and Julia, I did not know. He saw her frequently, and we talked a good deal about her, but his reticence and evasiveness made me feel that he was keeping something to himself. On several points I had no doubt. Firstly, Robert had decided not to marry Julia, although I was not certain Julia did not believe that somehow or other she could still bring him to it. Secondly, Julia was sleeping with Jocelyn Plumer; and thirdly she was regularly seeing Wladislaw – for the purpose of quarrelling violently with him.

I was haunted by a phrase that had struck me in one of Robert's novels – 'the naked clash of selves.' I was tempted to see all our divided loves and hates in terms of it. What did we all want and why did we all not get it? What overthrew us when we were at last settling for a decent compromise? We were at the mercy of stirring, ravenous selves, whose power even reason and affection could barely mitigate. No wonder we suffered. With those who were dearest to us, with those to whom we most wanted to abandon ourselves – the naked clash of our demands to possess.

I observed that Robert, Julia, Myrtle and I had all fallen back into our old pattern of behaviour. The March breezes blew round St James's Park, rippling the lake and waving the bare iris leaves. The ducks with dark satiny green heads waddled, quacking, along the gravel. I was struck by a longing to escape from the pattern. I knew what I wanted to do. I wanted to start writing a novel. It was unbearable not to be able to.

One day Robert and I were standing on the suspension bridge. It was quivering as people walked across in threes and fours. We were looking towards the pale grey towers and roofs of the Horse Guards and the Home Office. Whitehall. *A propos* of nothing, Robert said:

'We've got to think about getting out of this.'

I knew exactly what he meant. If only we could! I felt a wave of excitement, and of longing to get down to it.

CHAPTER X

A TOTALLY IRRELEVANT INCIDENT

One evening I came home to find the front door of my house bolted. I rang and for a few minutes – there was no reply. My first thought was that I had been locked out for moral turpitude, though it seemed rather belated because I had not had Myrtle up in my rooms for over a month. While I stood in the porch I saw the curtains of a ground-floor window moving. A moment later I heard the bolts being drawn and Mrs Burdup opened the door.

She closed the door behind me and shot the bolts back again.

I stared at her. 'Will you come inside for a moment, Mr Lunn?' She led me through her eavesdropper's door. She said: 'I've got something to tell you.' It was quite unnecessary to say that.

She sat down on the edge of an arm-chair. Her face was normally fresh-complexioned – there was nothing unhealthy about her meanness and ladylikeness. Her complexion now looked fresher. Her eyes seemed wider open, her thin mouth was trembling. She was twisting one of her rings round and round.

'This morning I had a mysterious telephone call. It was a man's voice. He said "Is that Mrs Burdup?" and I said "Yes", and then he said "You've read about all these murders in the newspapers recently? Well, you're the next on the list." And then he rang off.'

I said promptly: 'It was somebody playing a practical joke on you.'

She said: 'I don't know anybody who would.'

I took this to be true. She seemed to have no friends or even friendly acquaintances – I had never seen anyone visiting her.

'That isn't all. This afternoon he rang again. It was the same voice. This time he said: "If you'll do what I say, I may let you off for a little while." Those were the exact words. I said "I'd like you to say that to my maid. She's standing here beside me." And he rang off again. I nearly fainted.'

I said: 'Ah, somebody's pretending they're going to blackmail you. You don't need to be afraid.'

'I rang up the police straight away. An inspector came from Scotland Yard. He asked me a lot of questions, and he said he'd come again.' She was breathless with agitation. 'He says they have ways of tracing telephone calls.' She swallowed. 'There was another call as soon as he'd gone. I thought I really would faint if I heard the voice again... I got the maid to answer it. When he heard it wasn't me he cut off.'

She was terrified. I had always thought she was a hateful person and I genuinely found it hard to feel sorry for her. For a murderer the telephonist seemed to have made an unusually sensible choice.

Mrs Burdup then gave a long list of precautions she was taking. One of the lodgers was going to sleep in a camp-bed outside her bedroom door. Locks and bolts were to be installed – no lodger was to come in after midnight, a rule which she had been trying to find a good reason for enforcing as long as I had known her. And so on.

At last I got away from her. As I walked along the darkened corridor into the hall, the telephone rang. It made me jump. I took off the receiver and said: 'This is Lunn speaking!' There was a click, and then silence.

Mrs Burdup made a choking noise. I had to go back again and stand by while she made herself some tea – much stronger than any she ever served me for breakfast.

Finally I went up to my room for the night. I did not believe anybody wanted to murder Mrs Burdup. I did believe somebody wanted to torment her. I did not believe the man was a complete stranger. I was sure it was somebody who knew her well.

Just as I was falling asleep an inspiration brought me wide awake. The man was her husband. It was Burdup.

I recalled that Mrs Burdup had never actually told me she was a widow. And next morning I had a long conversation with the maid, who fixed me with a shrewd cynical Cockney eye and said: 'I bet I know who it is. It stands to sense, don't it?..' She shook her head. 'It's 'er 'usband. Come back.'

The mystery was never solved as far as I knew. The calls came at irregular intervals and were never traced. I got the impression that Scotland Yard had not seen fit to concentrate their entire energies on the case. Mrs Burdup remained terrified, but her terror was dissipated gradually as she ventured further from the house and was not garrotted. If she knew who it was, then the fact that she never told anybody merely strengthened my belief.

I had reflected on how the phases of my life, of Robert's and Julia's and Myrtle's, fell into a recurrent pattern. Mrs Burdup's did not. This affair was totally irrelevant. Burdup had done something completely fresh.

I asked myself how I could ever hope to understand what people were like.

CHAPTER XI

THE LETTER

One morning a long letter came at last from Myrtle. It said:

Dear Joe,

I do not know how to begin this letter to you – I have delayed writing it for so long because I did not know how to break it to you, but I realise that it can't go on any longer. You must have realised already what I am trying to say. Please forgive me, darling.

I don't know if I'm doing the right thing or not, but I have decided that whatever happens I can't really leave Dennis. I know how much you need me, darling, but somehow the break with him is something I can't bring myself to do. You know how much I long to come to you, but there is something that holds me to him no matter how I tell myself I should be happier if he gave me my freedom. It is terribly hard to explain it to you, because I don't really know how to explain it to myself. I think it's really that Dennis and I have had seven years of married happiness, and seven years of married happiness is too much to sacrifice.

I have thought about it for so long now that I feel I could go on writing to you so long that you would be bound to understand, only I am so terribly tired and worn out by it all. I expect you will have guessed how unhappy I have been through all these months since Dennis came back. I hardly seem to have slept at all. One cannot go on being torn in two indefinitely, and it made it so much worse to see that I was making you and Dennis so unhappy too. You will never know how utterly wretched I have been.

However it's all over now, and I can start trying to live a normal life again. It is such a great consolation that Dennis has forgiven me. I feel I have got so much to make up for to him. Please darling don't think I've been persuaded to do this against my will. When I think of the seven years married happiness that I had almost forgotten I know that I cannot sacrifice it even for you, darling. I feel dreadful about it and I can only hope that perhaps in time you will be able to forgive me as Dennis has done. Will you?

I am sorry I have smudged this letter, but I am crying as I write it.

My father is still seriously ill.

Myrtle

I took the letter with me to the office and gave it to Robert to read.

He handed it back.

'You won't reply, of course.'

I shook my head to signify No.

CHAPTER XII

ANNOUNCEMENT IN *THE TIMES*

Robert came into the office holding a copy of *The Times* – I took a different newspaper. He opened it, folded it back and laid it before me. I read the column of forthcoming marriages.

> CAPTAIN J. PLUMER AND MISS J.C. DELANEY
> The engagement is announced between Captain Jocelyn Plumer, Coldstream Guards, only son of Sir Francis Plumer, Bt., of 34 Chester Street, S.W.1., and Julia Christina, youngest daughter of the late Dr S. Delaney and of Mrs S. Delaney of W. Kensington.

I exclaimed. Robert made no comment.
'It'll never come off,' I said.
'No.'
I said: 'She'll go back to Wladislaw in the end.'
Robert nodded.

CHAPTER XIII
THE END

There we were, all four of us, back where we started.

Myrtle's letter caused me rage and misery, although, to be honest, my predominant feeling at first was relief. It was all over. I did not expect to see her ever again.

And then I ran into Myrtle by chance in Regent Street, about three weeks after getting her letter. She was alone and I detached myself from the friends I was with. She was dressed in black and looking woebegone.

'My father's dead,' she said.

I condoled as sincerely as I could.

She looked at me as if she were going to burst into tears: 'I keep seeing you in the street, from the tops of buses ...'

I felt quite cut off from her. She might be wishing she had changed her mind, but I was determined to have no more of it. When she had gone away, phrases from her letter kept recurring to me.

'Seven years of married happiness.'

'It's such a great consolation that Dennis has forgiven me.'

Even a saint, I felt, might have been a little ruffled by such nonsense – and it really was stained with her tears, showing that people can cry as readily over the false as the true.

I thought Robert had accepted his lot rather more easily, possibly because he had never been so deeply involved and so unreservedly hopeful. He remained very fond of Julia and she of him. Wladislaw resented their friendship, while not attempting to destroy it because he thought Robert was the only man who had a good influence on Julia – which conclusion I suspected Wladislaw had reached the more easily because Robert was the only man who was not trying to get into bed with her.

The friendship of Myrtle and Julia lapsed, though Myrtle kept in touch, against Haxby's wishes, with Robert. A really extraordinary thing happened: Myrtle met The Headlamps and they struck up an intimate relationship. As far as we could gather their bond was a great romantic love they had each lost.

Jocelyn Plumer disappeared from our story as suddenly as he had entered it. His engagement to Julia was formally broken and he married the sister of one of his friends. Sir Francis, for all his courteous manners, could not disguise his relief.

The office of D.O.R.R.S. was in due course merged with another division, and Sir Francis, because he was just about to retire, they said officially, was not made its boss. It made us sad. James Irskine was promoted and so was Froggatt: to that we were neutral.

However, when the changes in the D.O.R.R.S. were made, Robert and I were elsewhere. I have observed that we were all back where we started, battered perhaps, but undaunted. Somehow Robert and I had been carried a stage nearer to our goal.

One Saturday afternoon in the middle of spring we were walking in Kew Gardens. It was impossible to believe that the winter had been so hard. On the rolling green slopes there were thousands of daffodils and narcissi in bloom. The air was still and warm. People were strolling happily beneath the trees and round the lake.

Something made me recall Myrtle, and in spite of the sunshine a heavy, sad, reflective mood fell upon me. My first feeling of relief at the break had long since disappeared, and as the weeks passed I felt a tide of loneliness and despair rising. My irritation with her had dwindled, and now I dreamed of what I had missed. Myrtle might feel she had lost the great romantic love of her life, but I knew at the bottom of my heart that I had come off worst. It was a strange reversal that time had brought about. Who would have thought, I wondered, on seeing my first affair with Myrtle, with its youthful gaiety and carelessness, its bitter-sweet ending in my coming off best, that eight years would reduce me to this wretched conclusion? It seemed to me that Myrtle would not be seriously unhappy. Really she was a rather ordinary girl: somehow she would fit into the comfortable pattern of life. While I, though I might have had my own way for a little time at the beginning, was going to have to pay for an awkward temperament before I finished. At last I glimpsed my fate. I cannot say I liked the look of it.

We paused before a magnolia tree. The flowers were perfect. It looked as if a swarm of stiff white butterflies had alighted simultaneously on the naked branches.

'The pink magnolias come out before the white,' I said.

Robert ignored the remark.

'What are you thinking about?' I asked.

He said· 'I think we ought to count on resigning from the office by the end of June at the latest '

My elegiac mood was shattered.

'We've got enough money between us,' he said. I couldn't believe my ears.

Yet suddenly the day seemed brighter, the air warmer, the daffodils yellower; and the magnolias might have been just going to fly away to the sparkling sun – my spirits going with them, no more mornings before the office! No more depending on girls! Free men at last!

Well, Robert and I got down to Art. And there we were. The only possible thing you could ask me now is what did we write? Robert chose to write under a different name, which he has asked me not to give away. And so did I – but there is no secret about that.